# THE USBORNE INTERNET-LINKED ENCYCLOPEDIA OF WORLD GEOGRAPHY
## WITH Complete World Atlas

Gillian Doherty, Anna Claybourne and Susanna Davidson

Designers: Laura Fearn, Keith Newell, Stephen Moncrieff, Katrina Fearn, Melissa Alaverdy and Linda Penny

Project editor: Gillian Doherty

Additional contributors: Nathalie Abi-Ezzi,
Kamini Khanduri, Rebecca Treays and Stephanie Turnbull
Consultant cartographic editor: Craig Asquith
Cartography by European Map Graphics Ltd
Managing editor: Felicity Brooks
Managing designer: Stephen Wright
Cover design: Stephen Moncrieff and John Russell
Digital image processing: John Russell and Mike Olley
Picture research: Ruth King

Consultants:
Dr. Roger Trend, Senior Lecturer in Earth Science
and Geography Education, University of Exeter
Professor Michael Hitchcock, University of North London
Dr. William Chambers
Dr. Uwem Ite, Department of Geography, University of Lancaster
Susan Bermingham, Senior Lecturer, Institute of Education,
Manchester Metropolitan University
Dr. Stephanie Bunn, University of Manchester
Dr. Susan Pfisterer, Menzies Centre for Australian Studies,
King's College, University of London
Dr. Vivien Miller, Senior Lecturer in American Studies, Middlesex University
Dr. Francisco Dominguez, Head of Latin American Studies, Middlesex University
Dr. Elizabeth Bomberg, Department of Politics, University of Edinburgh
David Harrison, Professor of Tourism, Culture and Development,
University of North London

# CONTENTS

# INTERNET LINKS

This book contains descriptions of over three hundred recommended websites where you can find out more about people and places around the world.

To visit the sites, go to the **Usborne Quicklinks Website** where you will find links to click on to take you to all the sites. At Usborne Quicklinks there are also pictures from this book that you can download and use in your own projects.

1. Go to **www.usborne-quicklinks.com**

2. Type the keyword for this book: **geography**

3. Type the page number of the link you want to visit.

4. Click on the links to go to the recommended sites.

> **Internet links**
>
> For links to all the websites described in this book, and for free downloadable pictures, go to **www.usborne-quicklinks.com** and enter the keyword "geography".

## What you can do

Here are some of the things you can do on the websites recommended in this book:

- Take virtual tours of countries around the world.
- Watch video clips of volcanoes erupting and build a volcano online.
- Explore an interactive map to find the hottest and coldest places on Earth.
- Look up weather forecasts around the world and try to predict the weather.
- Find amazing facts about rainforests and watch video clips about them.

*Pictures marked with a symbol like this can be downloaded free of charge from the Usborne Quicklinks Website at* **www.usborne-quicklinks.com**

## Site availability

The links at Usborne Quicklinks are regularly reviewed and updated, but occasionally you may get a message that a site is unavailable. This might be temporary, so try again later, or even the next day.

Websites do occasionally close down and when this happens, we will replace them with new links in Usborne Quicklinks. Sometimes we add extra links too, if we think they are useful. So when you visit Usborne Quicklinks, the links may be slightly different from those described in your book.

## Downloadable pictures

Some of the pictures in this book can be downloaded from the Usborne Quicklinks Website and printed out for your own personal use. For example, you could use them to illustrate homework or a project. They must not be copied or distributed for any commercial purpose. Downloadable pictures have a ★ symbol beside them. To print out these pictures, follow the instructions on the Usborne Quicklinks Website at **www.usborne-quicklinks.com**

# Internet safety

When using the Internet, please make sure you follow these simple guidelines:

• Ask your parent's or guardian's permission before you connect to the Internet.

• If you write a message in a website guest book or on a message board, do not include your email address, real name, address, telephone number or the name of your school.

• If a website asks you to log in or register by typing your name or email address, ask the permission of an adult first.

• If you do receive email from someone you don't know, tell an adult and do not reply to the email.

• Never arrange to meet anyone you have talked to on the Internet.

# What you need

To visit the websites you need a computer with an Internet connection and a web browser (the software that lets you look at information on the Internet). Some sites need extra programs (plug-ins) to play sound or show videos or animations.

If you go to a site and do not have the necessary plug-in, a message will come up on the screen. There is usually a link to click on to download the plug-in. For more information about plug-ins, go to Usborne Quicklinks and click on "Net Help".

## Computer not essential
If you don't have access to the Internet, don't worry. This book is a complete, self-contained reference book on its own.

# Notes for parents

The websites described in this book are regularly checked and reviewed by Usborne editors and the links in Usborne Quicklinks are updated. However, the content of a website may change at any time and Usborne Publishing is not responsible for the content of any website other than its own.

We recommend that children are supervised while on the Internet, that they do not use Internet chat rooms, and that you use Internet filtering software to block unsuitable material.

Please ensure that your children read and follow the safety guidelines on the left. For more information, go to the Net Help area on the Usborne Quicklinks Website at **www.usborne-quicklinks.com**

# Computer viruses

A computer virus is a program that can damage your computer. A virus can get into your computer when you download programs from the Internet, or in an attachment (an extra file) that arrives with an email.

We strongly recommend that you use anti-virus software to protect your computer and that you update the software regularly, as new viruses are being invented all the time. You can buy anti-virus software at computer stores or download it from the Internet.

Make sure too, that you keep your computer up to date by using the latest, most secure version of your web browser.

# Help

For more information about plug-ins and using the Internet safely and securely, go to Usborne Quicklinks and click on "Net Help".

*The Earth and its moon*

# PLANET EARTH

# OUR SOLAR SYSTEM

The Solar System is made up of the Sun and all the objects that travel around it, from planets and moons, to chunks of rock and ice and huge amounts of dust. At the moment, scientists know of nine planets that travel around the Sun.

*This is a picture of the planet Saturn and some of its moons. Saturn is the one with the rings around it.*

## Planets

A planet is a large spherical object that travels around, or orbits, a particular star. As each planet moves, it also spins around on its axis (an imaginary line running through the planet).

*The Sun*

## Stars

Stars are huge balls of hot gas which give off heat and light. The stars we see in the night sky only look tiny because they are far away. Our closest star is the Sun. It is about 146 million km (93 million miles) away. Light takes eight minutes to travel from the Sun to Earth.

## Moons

Most of the planets in our Solar System have moons. A moon orbits a planet in the same way that a planet orbits a star. Earth has just one moon, but some planets have several. Saturn, for example, has at least 30 moons.

*Earth*

*Venus*

*Mercury*

Uranus

Neptune

Pluto

Jupiter

Saturn

Mars

*This picture shows the nine planets in our Solar System in the order they are from the Sun, though they are not to scale.*

# Space rocks

Asteroids and comets are pieces of rock, ice, dust and grit that whizz around our Solar System. Scientists believe that they are pieces left over from when the Solar System formed. The Solar System is also full of much smaller pieces of space debris called meteoroids. These may be grains of dust from comets, large chunks of rock or even shattered asteroids.

# Galaxies

A galaxy is a group of many millions of stars. Galaxies are so big that it can take light thousands of years to travel across one. There are 6,000 million known galaxies in the universe, all of different shapes and sizes, but there could be many, many more. Galaxies are separated from each other by vast, empty spaces. Our Solar System is part of the Milky Way galaxy.

*This picture shows stars in the southern part of the Milky Way galaxy.*

# THE EARTH

Earth is the third planet from the Sun. It is the only planet in our Solar System with the right conditions to support living things. The closest natural object to the Earth is the Moon, which is about 384,400km (240,250 miles) away.

*Factories like this one release harmful chemicals into the air, polluting the Earth's environment.*

## Life on Earth

The Earth's distance from the Sun means that it has just the right amount of heat and light for life to flourish. Its combination of gases enables plants, animals and people to breathe, and it is warm enough for water to exist as a liquid. All of these things are essential for life on Earth.

*This is a satellite photograph of the Earth taken from space. You can see the shapes of North America and the north of South America.*

## Earth in danger

As the number of people on Earth grows, we use more land, and our motor vehicles and industries release an increasing amount of waste, or pollution. This damages the environment: the land, oceans and the air we breathe. It is essential that we start taking more care of the Earth, before it is too late.

# The Moon

Earth has only one moon. Most moons are very small compared with the planets they orbit, but our Moon is unusually large. It is about a quarter of the Earth's size.

The Moon does not make its own light, but it reflects the Sun's rays, so it can look very bright in the night sky.

## Pulling power

Between objects in the Solar System there is an invisible force called gravity, which attracts, or pulls, things together. It is the Earth's gravity that holds the Moon in orbit around it.

The Moon's gravity affects the Earth too. It pulls on the water in Earth's oceans and seas, making the sea level rise and fall. These changing sea levels are called tides.

## Satellites

Today, scientists are able to monitor vast areas of Earth from space. Devices called satellites orbit the Earth and send back information about our planet. The first satellite ever to go into space was launched by the U.S.S.R.* on October 4, 1957, to study the gases surrounding our planet. It was officially named

*The Moon's surface is covered in craters. On a clear night, you can see the larger craters with your naked eye.*

*This is RADARSAT, Canada's first Earth observation satellite. It was launched in November 1995.*

*RADARSAT can produce high quality images of Earth's surface. It is used to monitor Earth's natural resources and the environment.*

"Satellite 1957 Alpha 2", but became better known by its nickname "Sputnik", which is a Russian word meaning "little voyager".

### Internet links

**Website 1** The Earth, satellites and problems facing the Earth.

**Website 2** Discover lots of fascinating facts about the Earth.

For links to these websites, go to **www.usborne-quicklinks.com**

*U.S.S.R., 204

# THE SEASONS

The Earth takes just over a year to orbit the Sun. As it makes its journey, different parts of the world receive different amounts of heat and light. This causes the seasons (spring, summer, autumn and winter).

## Tilting Earth

The Earth is tilted at an angle as it travels around the Sun. This means that one half, or hemisphere, is usually closer to the Sun than the other. The hemisphere that is closer receives more heat and light energy than the one that is tilted away. So in this half it is summer, while in the other it is winter.

As the Earth orbits the Sun, the half that was closer to the Sun gradually moves farther away, so that eventually it becomes winter in this hemisphere and summer in the other. In June the Sun's rays are most concentrated at the Tropic of Cancer and in December they are most concentrated at the Tropic of Capricorn.

*In June, it is summer in the Arctic. The warmer weather only lasts for six to eight weeks.*

*The diagram below shows how the seasons change as the Earth orbits the Sun.*

*In autumn in Maine, northeast U.S.A., the leaves on the trees turn red and golden.*

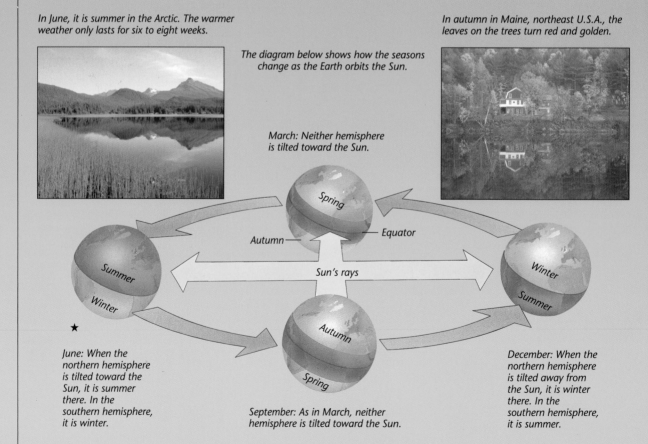

*March: Neither hemisphere is tilted toward the Sun.*

Spring

Autumn — — Equator

Summer

Winter

Sun's rays

Winter

Summer

Autumn

Spring

*June: When the northern hemisphere is tilted toward the Sun, it is summer there. In the southern hemisphere, it is winter.*

*September: As in March, neither hemisphere is tilted toward the Sun.*

*December: When the northern hemisphere is tilted away from the Sun, it is winter there. In the southern hemisphere, it is summer.*

_The heat and light that the Sun gives out are essential for life on Earth._

## Leap years

The time it takes for the Earth to orbit the Sun is called a solar year. A solar year is 365.26 days, but as it is more convenient to measure our calendar year in whole days, we round the number down to 365. In order to make up the difference, every four years we have to add an extra day to our calendar year, making it 366 days. These years are called leap years*. The additional day is February 29th. However, this does not make up the difference exactly, so very occasionally the extra day is not added.

## Equatorial seasons

_This picture shows how the Sun's rays spread out as they reach the Earth's surface._

The Earth is hottest where the Sun's rays hit its surface full on. But because the Earth's surface is curved, in most places rays hit the ground at an angle. This causes them to spread out over a larger area, which makes their effect less intense.

Temperatures are also affected by the distance the Sun's rays have to travel through the Earth's atmosphere. Over greater distances, the Sun's rays lose more heat energy to the atmosphere, which makes temperatures cooler.

Tropic of Cancer

Equator

_The Sun's rays are most concentrated near the Equator._

Tropic of Capricorn

_The Sun's rays spread out at the poles and have farther to travel through the Earth's atmosphere._

### Internet links

**Website 1** Online activities about how the sun moves and what causes the seasons.

**Website 2** See an animation showing how the seasons change as the Earth travels around the Sun.

For links to these websites, go to **www.usborne-quicklinks.com**

_At the poles, the midday Sun is low on the horizon even in summer, making it cool._

_At the Equator, the midday Sun is high in the sky all year round, so it is very hot._

15

*Leap years, 340

# DAY AND NIGHT

When it's daytime in Australia, it's night-time in South America. This is because the Earth spins around on its axis as it orbits the Sun, so the part of the Earth that faces the Sun is constantly changing.

## Rotating Earth

It takes 24 hours, or one day, for the Earth to spin around once on its axis. As it rotates, different parts of the world turn to face the Sun. The part of the Earth that is turned toward the Sun is in the light (daytime), but as it turns away from the Sun it becomes dark (night-time).

## Sunrise and sunset

In the morning, you see the Sun "rise" in the sky. This is only an illusion. What is actually happening is that as your part of the Earth is turning to face the Sun, the movement of the Earth makes it seem as though the Sun is rising. When your part of the Earth turns away from the Sun at night, it looks as if the Sun is sinking in the sky until eventually it disappears over the horizon. This is called a sunset.

*This diagram follows the change from day to night in one place (marked by the flag) as the Earth spins.*

*Path of orbit around the Sun*

*In the morning, the Sun looks as though it's rising, as your part of the Earth gradually turns to face it.*

*In the evening, the Sun seems to sink down in the sky, as your part of the Earth turns away from it.*

## Daylight hours

Everywhere in the world, apart from places that are on the Equator, days are longer in the summer than in the winter. This is because the hemisphere where it is summer receives more sunlight than the hemisphere where it is winter.

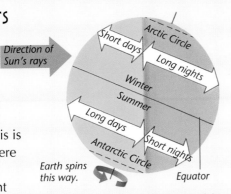

*This diagram shows how the length of day and night varies depending on the time of year and where you are on the Earth.*

## Midnight Sun

In summer, when the northern hemisphere tilts toward the Sun, the regions north of the Arctic Circle don't turn away from the Sun, even at night. For this reason it is known as the Land of the Midnight Sun.

*This shows the Sun in the Arctic Circle in the middle of the night.*

### Internet links

**Website 1** Look at a map of the Earth to see the regions where it is day and where it is night at this moment.

**Website 2** Read about the phases of the Moon then see if you can put them in the correct order.

For links to these websites, go to
**www.usborne-quicklinks.com**

## Moon shapes

The Moon doesn't give out any light of its own. It looks bright to us because we see the Sun's rays reflected off its surface. During the day, we can't usually see the Moon because the Sun is brighter.

*As the Moon orbits the Sun and we see different amounts of its sunlit side, its shape seems to change as shown in these diagrams.*

Direction of sunlight

Moon

*The pictures below show what the Moon looks like from Earth when it is in each of the positions numbered above.*

1. New moon
2. Crescent
3. Half moon
4. Waxing
5. Full moon
6. Waning
7. Half moon
8. Crescent

The Earth is mainly solid. It has a rocky surface, but inside it has different layers, some of which are partly molten (melted). If you sliced through the Earth, you would see four main layers: the crust, the mantle, the outer core and the inner core.

## Internet links

For links to websites where you can find out how compasses work using the Earth's magnetism, learn how to make a compass of your own and explore the structure of the Earth, go to www.usborne-quicklinks.com

## Earth's layers

The crust is the thinnest layer. It is between 5km (3 miles) and 70km (43 miles) thick. Beneath the crust is the upper part of the mantle, and together these make up the lithosphere.

The mantle is made of silicon and magnesium. The region in the mantle at the bottom of the lithosphere, about 100km (62 miles) down, is partly molten. This layer flows very slowly.

The core is probably made of iron and nickel. The outer core, which is about 2,200km (1,400 miles) thick, is molten, whereas the inner core is solid. The inner core, which is about 1,300km (800 miles) thick, is extremely hot (about 6,000°C, or 10,800°F).

*This diagram shows the Earth's structure, though the layers are not drawn to scale.*

Crust

Mantle

Outer core

Inner core

# The Earth's crust

There are two different types of crust. Thick continental crust forms land, and much thinner oceanic crust makes up the ocean floors. Continental crust is made of granite and similar light rocks. Oceanic crust is made of a heavier rock called basalt.

*The Earth's crust is made up of oceanic and continental crust.*

Oceanic crust is 5–10km (3–6 miles) thick.

Continental crust is 20–70km (12–43 miles) thick.

Ocean

## Investigating the Earth

It's difficult to find out about the inside of the Earth. Geologists, who study rocks, find out about areas near the surface by drilling holes into the crust and collecting rock samples. But they can only drill a short distance below the surface.

Volcanic eruptions provide some information about material deep inside the Earth. But the main way that geologists find out about the Earth's structure is by studying earthquakes. During an earthquake, vibrations called seismic waves travel through the Earth. As they pass through different materials, they change speed and direction. By studying records of earthquakes, called seismograms, geologists try to determine what rocks are found at different depths.

Earthquake

Paths of waves

*This diagram shows how seismic waves change direction as they pass through the Earth.*

## Magnetic Earth

The Earth is magnetic, as if it had a huge magnetic bar inside. This may be caused by molten iron circulating in its core. The ends of this "magnet" are called the magnetic poles. These are not in exactly the same place as the geographic North and South Poles.

*This diagram shows the Earth's magnetic field: the field of force surrounding it. The lines show the direction of the magnetic field.*

Magnetic North Pole

Magnetic South Pole

You can see the Earth's magnetism at work when you use a compass. The compass needle, which is magnetic, always points north. This is because it is pulled, or attracted, by the magnetic North Pole.

*A compass's magnetic needle always points north.*

# THE EARTH'S CRUST

The solid surface of the Earth is broken up into large pieces called lithospheric plates, which are made up of the Earth's crust and upper mantle. Many of the Earth's most spectacular features have been formed by the movement of these plates.

North American plate

Cocos plate

Caribbean plate

Plate boundaries

Nazca plate

Mantle

## A moving surface

There are seven large plates and several smaller plates. The edges of the plates are called plate boundaries. The plates move on the partly molten layer of the mantle at a rate of about 5cm (2in) a year. As all the plates fit together, movement of one plate affects the others. The study of these plates and the way they move around is called plate tectonics.

### Internet links

For links to websites where you can explore a map of the world and see how the movement of the Earth's plates builds mountains and causes earthquakes and volcanoes, go to **www.usborne-quicklinks.com**

## Ocean features

As plates on the ocean floor move apart, magma from the mantle rises and fills the gap. Boundaries where this happens are called constructive boundaries. As the magma reaches the surface, it hardens to make new oceanic crust. The new crust sometimes forms islands or underwater mountain ranges, called ridges.

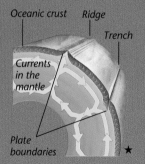

Oceanic crust    Ridge
Trench
Currents in the mantle
Plate boundaries ★

When plates push together, underwater trenches form as one plate is forced below another. These boundaries are called destructive boundaries. The deepest trench, the Mariana Trench in the Pacific Ocean, is deeper than Mount Everest is tall.

*This diagram shows how ridges and trenches form.*

## Shifting continents

As plates shift, the position of the oceans and continents on the Earth's surface changes. The maps on the right show how geologists think the continents may have shifted. ★

*Geologists think that there was once a single supercontinent, which we call "Pangaea".*

*As new rock formed at plate boundaries, the floor of the Atlantic Ocean probably widened.*

*Today, South America and Africa are drifting apart at a rate of 3.5cm (1.5in) each year.*

Atlantic Ocean

Africa

South America

## Faults

As plates move, the strain of the movement sometimes causes brittle rock to crack. These cracks are called faults. When two faults are close together, the chunk of crust between them can sometimes collapse, to form rift valleys. The raised parts on either side form mountains called block mountains.

South American plate

Eurasian plate

Ocean floor

African plate

This shows how the Earth's plates fit together. One plate has been removed to show the mantle inside the Earth.

Block mountains

Rift

★ Fault          Fault

This picture shows a fault in the Great Rift Valley in Africa.

## Fold mountains

Where two plates push together, the crust buckles and folds upward to form high mountain ranges, called fold mountains. The Himalayas, the Alps and the Andes are all fold mountains. The Earth's crust is thickest where fold mountains form.

This is part of the Himalayas mountain range in Asia, which is the highest in the world.

# ROCKS, MINERALS AND FOSSILS

The Earth's crust is made up of rock. There are three kinds of rocks: igneous, sedimentary and metamorphic. Over many years, rocks are sometimes transformed from one kind to another.

## Igneous rock

Igneous rock gets its name from the Latin word for "fire", because it is formed from magma from inside the Earth. When the magma cools, it forms solid igneous rock. The way that the magma cools determines the kind of igneous rock that is formed.

*Tuff is an igneous rock made from pieces of volcanic rock and crystals compressed together.*

*Obsidian is a shiny igneous rock formed when magma cools quickly.*

## Sedimentary rock

Sedimentary rock is made from tiny pieces of rocks and the decayed remains of plants and animals. These fragments, called sediment, are usually blown by winds, or carried by rivers, glaciers or landslides, to the sea, where they sink. The water and upper layers of sediment press down on the lower layers until, eventually, they form solid rock.

*Chalk is a sedimentary rock made from tiny sea creatures.*

*Sandstone is a sedimentary rock made up of sand grains.*

*The Grand Canyon, in the U.S.A., is a gorge formed by the Colorado River. You can see the layers of sandstone. Layers of rock like these are called strata.*

# Metamorphic rock

Metamorphic rock is rock that has been changed – for example, by heat from magma, or pressure caused by plate movements or very deep burial. It can be formed from igneous, sedimentary or other metamorphic rocks.

*Marble is a metamorphic rock formed from limestone.*

*Mica schist is a metamorphic rock that tends to split into layers.*

# Minerals

Rocks are made from substances called minerals, which in turn are made up of simple chemical substances called elements. Some minerals are cut and polished to be used as gemstones.

*These pictures show minerals in rocks and as gemstones.*

*Opal can be milky white, green, red, blue, black or brown.*

*Turquoise runs through rock in the form of veins.*

*Carnelian is a dark red stone.*

### Internet links

For links to websites where you can find out what rocks can tell us about the history of the Earth, learn more about fossils and how they form, and take a virtual tour of the Grand Canyon, go to **www.usborne-quicklinks.com**

## Fossils

The shapes or remains of plants and animals that died long ago are sometimes preserved in rocks. They are called fossils. Fossils are formed when a dead plant or animal is buried by sediment which then turns to sedimentary rock. Usually the remains decay, although hard parts such as teeth, shells and bones can sometimes survive. The space left by the plant or animal fills up with sediment or minerals which preserve its shape.

*The fossil of an ammonite (an extinct sea creature)*

# THE EARTH'S RESOURCES

*Iron is extracted from its ore in a blast furnace.*

The Earth provides all sorts of useful rocks, minerals and other materials. We quarry stone and sand for building and glassmaking, extract over 60 types of metals, and mine hundreds of useful chemicals and compounds such as salt, talc and silicon.

*Iron ore, coke (a type of coal) and limestone go in here.*

## Metals and minerals

Metals are among the most important materials we get from the Earth. They are strong, yet they can be beaten out into flat sheets or drawn out to make wire. They also conduct electricity and heat well. Some metals even have medical uses.

*The furnace is over 30m (100ft) tall.*

Most metals are found in ores, types of rocks that contain a metal in the form of a chemical compound. Metals are extracted from ores by mixing them with other chemicals to cause a reaction or by heating them strongly.

*Iron ore, coke and limestone react with each other in a blast furnace to make new chemicals, leaving the iron free.*

*Molten iron flows out here.*

As well as metals and stone, the Earth also provides many other chemicals and elements. Their uses often depend on how hard they are.

*Hot air is blasted into the furnace.*

*Waste called slag comes out here.*

★

*People have used precious metals for centuries as settings for precious stones.*

## Internet links

**Website 1** Mineral games, facts and a recipe for growing crystals.

**Website 2** Process metals and minerals to make everyday items.

**Website 3** Guess which minerals are used to make glasses, coins and other common objects.

For links to these websites, go to **www.usborne-quicklinks.com**

## The Mohs scale

The hardness or softness of minerals is measured on a scale of 1 to 10, called the Mohs scale. Soft minerals, such as talc, crumble easily into powder. At the other end of the scale are the hardest minerals, such as diamonds, which are used in cutting tools.

*Talc 1*

*Gypsum 2*

*Calcite 3*

*Fluorite 4*

*Each number on the Mohs scale is accompanied by an example mineral.*

*Apatite 5*

*Orthoclase 6*

*Quartz 7*

*Topaz 8*

*Corundum 9*

*Diamond 10*

## Silicon chips

Silicon comes from a mineral called quartz. It has become very important in modern society, because it is used to make the electronic chips that run computers, digital watches, mobile phones and millions of other everyday appliances.

*A silicon chip*

## Building materials

Rocks and minerals from the Earth are used to make bricks, cement, glass and other building materials. Stone for building is usually extracted from the ground in quarries. It's often so hard and heavy that explosives have to be used to blast it apart.

Sand is made of rocks, minerals and sometimes seashells, ground down to fragments by the action of water (which is why it is usually found near the sea). Concrete and glass are both made using sand.

*The Taj Mahal is a huge Indian tomb. Its exterior is white marble.*

# ENERGY FROM THE EARTH

T he Earth's rocks, minerals and fossils
   contain energy which we can extract
   and use. Oil, gas and coal, which can
be converted into heat and electricity, all
come from the Earth. So do other forms of
energy, such as nuclear energy.

*This huge structure is the top part of an oil platform, which sticks out above the sea's surface. It contains equipment for processing the oil, and living quarters for the workers.*

NORTH
CORMORANT

## Fossil fuels

Coal, oil and natural gas are
fossil fuels. They are called this
because, like fossils*, they form
in the ground over a very long
period of time from the bodies
of dead plants and animals.

Coal is formed from trees and
other plants. Layers of sand and
clay gradually settled on top of
them, and compressed them
slowly into thick, underground
layers, or seams, of coal.

Oil is formed from the
bodies of tiny sea
creatures. It is usually
found in rocks under the
seabed but may be
found under land.
Under certain
conditions, natural
gas is formed from
dead plants and
animals. Gas and oil are
often found close together.

## Extracting fuels

The coal we use comes
from underground mines
or opencast mines, which
are huge, open holes dug
in the ground. To extract oil
and gas, a drill, supported
by a structure called a rig,
bores a hole into the ground
or seabed. Sometimes the
fuel flows out naturally, but
usually water is pumped
into the hole to force
the oil or gas out.

*Coal being extracted from a mine at the surface of the ground, called an opencast mine.*

*Fossils, 23

# Using fossil fuels

When a fossil fuel is burned, it releases energy, which is used to heat buildings and to run vehicle engines. In power stations, heat from fossil fuels is converted into electricity.

The world depends on fossil fuels. They provide more than three-quarters of the energy we use. But we use them up more quickly than they can form, so they are running out. In around two hundred years, humans will need to get most of their energy in other ways.

As well as providing energy, oil is used to make plastic, which is made into thousands of things, from bottles to polyester clothing.

## Radiation

Some minerals found in the ground are radioactive. This means their atoms (the tiny particles they are made of) are unstable.

Instead of staying as they are, unstable minerals break up and send out particles or rays, known as radiation. As they break up, a type of energy called nuclear energy is released. Uranium, a metal, is the main radioactive mineral used to produce nuclear energy.

### Internet links

For links to websites where you can find out more about fossil fuels and other energy resources and take a virtual tour of an oil platform, go to **www.usborne-quicklinks.com**

This diagram shows how atoms of uranium produce nuclear energy.

A tiny particle called a neutron is fired at the uranium nucleus.

This is the nucleus, or middle, of a uranium atom.

The nucleus splits, giving off heat.

More neutrons fly off the nucleus and split other uranium atoms.

# SOIL

Soil covers over half of the Earth's land surface. It is vital to life on Earth, because it provides the food and conditions plants need to grow.

## Internet links

**Website 1** Go on an underground adventure and take a closer look at soil.

**Website 2** Find out how worms break down dead plants and animals.

For links to these websites, go to **www.usborne-quicklinks.com**

*As they burrow through the soil, earthworms drag dead leaves and other organic matter down to the lower levels, and break them down into humus.*

## What's in the soil?

Soil is made up of particles of rocks and minerals, dead plant and animal matter, tiny living organisms, gases and water. The particles of rocks and minerals range from big chunks of stone to tiny mineral particles which get dissolved by the water in the soil. Some minerals are taken in by plants and used as food. These are called nutrients. The dead plant and animal matter is gradually broken down into a substance called humus, by all the tiny creatures, bacteria and fungi in the soil.

Humus is what makes soil fertile (easy for plants to grow in). Living things are a vital part of the soil. If they weren't there to break down dead plants and animals, the remains of things that have died would keep piling up on the Earth's surface.

The water in the soil comes from rain, and gases come from the air and from plants and animals. Plants absorb water and gases through their roots.

*This earwig and her babies are among the thousands of insects and other small animals that live in soil.*

## Soil layers

If you looked at a slice of soil under the ground, you would see that it has several different layers, called horizons.

① *The topsoil contains a lot of humus and is full of tiny living creatures.*

② *Subsoil is made up of humus, rocks and minerals. Cracks and holes, or pores, in the subsoil help water to drain away, preventing the soil from getting too wet.*

③ *The rock that lies underneath the soil is called bedrock. Chunks of it sometimes break off into the soil.*

## Types of soil

There are thousands and thousands of different types of soil. Some are more fertile than others, but different plants prefer different soils. Farmers can choose what to grow, depending on the type of soil they have on their land.

There are three main soil textures: sand, silt and clay. Sandy soil is rough and grainy. Silt has small particles, which are hard to see, while clay soil is made of fine particles, which bind together with water to form a thick, creamy mud. Clay is used to make pottery and china.

*This picture shows parsnip roots reaching into the soil for water and minerals. Parsnips grow well in sandy and clay soils.*

*This hand contains sandy soil. Its grainy texture allows moisture to drain through it easily.*

*A handful of fertile soil contains up to six billion bacteria.*

*This hand contains loam soil. It is a very fertile soil containing a mixture of clay and sandy soils.*

# PROTECTING SOIL

Why do we need to take care of soil? The answer is that pollution, farming and cutting down trees can all damage soil and upset its natural balance. If we want to keep using the soil to grow food, we have to protect it, and replace all the chemicals that farming takes away.

This farmer in Minnesota, U.S.A., is loading up manure to spread over his land as a fertilizer.

## The soil cycle

Where there is no farming, soil is part of a continuous cycle. Minerals are gradually dissolved into the soil. Dead plants and animals fall onto the ground, begin to rot, and are broken down into humus*. The minerals and the humus provide nutrients (food) for new plants, and the cycle starts again. This means that the nutrients that are taken out of the soil eventually get put back in.

But, when soil is used for farming, the crops are taken away to be sold, instead of rotting back into the ground. This causes the soil to become gradually less fertile* as it loses its nutrients.

## Fertilizing

The best way to replace the nutrients in soil is to add a fertilizer. Fertilizers contain chemicals, such as nitrates, which plants need in order to grow. Manure (animal dung) is a natural fertilizer, but many farmers use specially made chemical fertilizers. Sometimes, if farmers use too much fertilizer, the chemicals can leak out of the soil into rivers, causing pollution.

## Crop rotation

Crop rotation means changing the crop grown on a piece of land each year. It helps to keep the soil fertile, especially if the land is sometimes left to "lie fallow". This means the farmer doesn't harvest the crop, but lets it rot back into the soil. Plants such as legumes (peas and beans) and clover make good fallow crops because they put nitrates into the soil instead of taking them out.

Bright yellow oilseed rape is used to make cooking oil and as food for animals. Oilseed rape crops are often rotated with other crops on farms in Europe.

*Fertile, 28; humus, 28

## Soil erosion

In the natural environment, plants and trees hold soil together and stop it from being washed away by the rain or blown away by the wind. But when people chop down trees for firewood and farmers dig up the land to plant crops it leaves the bare soil exposed.

However, there are some ways to protect the soil. In some places, farmers can grow crops among the trees without cutting them down. If a main crop leaves bare patches of soil, a second crop called a cover crop can be planted in the gaps to stop it from eroding. In hilly areas, farmers build steps called terraces into the hillside to hold soil in place.

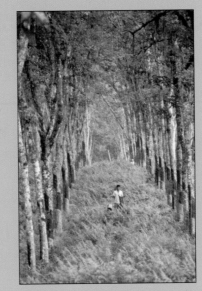

*This cover crop protects the soil between rows of rubber trees. It also lets farmers grow two crops on the same land.*

### Internet links

For links to websites about the dangers of cutting down trees and the problems of soil erosion, and fun facts, activities and word puzzles about soil, go to **www.usborne-quicklinks.com**

## Lost forever

Ancient ruins show that there were once busy towns in places that are now desert, such as parts of Egypt and Saudi Arabia.

*7,000-year-old pottery jars from an ancient civilization called Mesopotamia. The area where they were found is now desert.*

The people who lived there may not have known how to look after soil and stop it from eroding. This may be why their civilizations died out.

*With the trees cut down, the soil on this hillside could soon be washed away.*

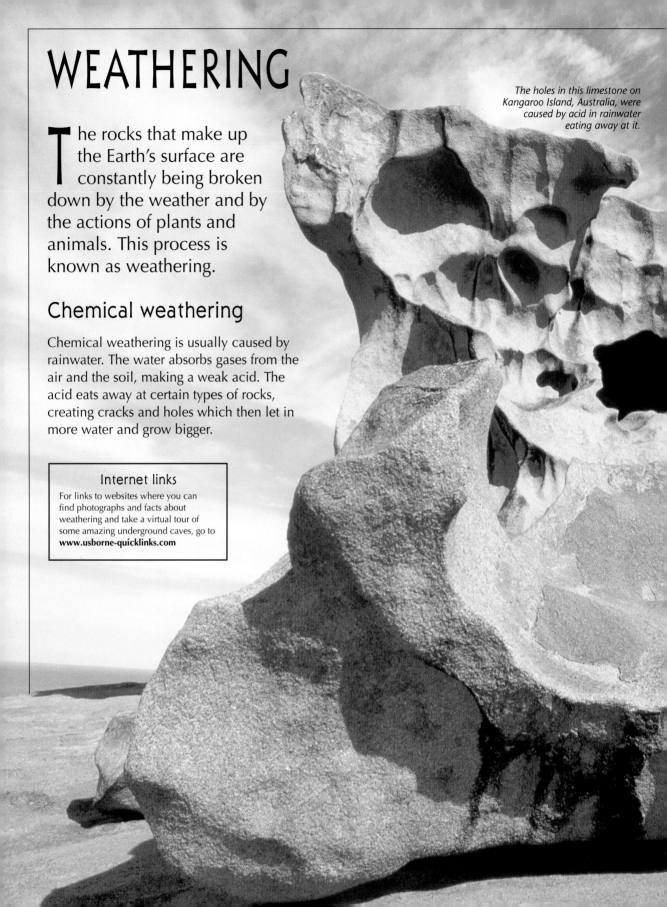

# WEATHERING

The holes in this limestone on Kangaroo Island, Australia, were caused by acid in rainwater eating away at it.

The rocks that make up the Earth's surface are constantly being broken down by the weather and by the actions of plants and animals. This process is known as weathering.

## Chemical weathering

Chemical weathering is usually caused by rainwater. The water absorbs gases from the air and the soil, making a weak acid. The acid eats away at certain types of rocks, creating cracks and holes which then let in more water and grow bigger.

### Internet links

For links to websites where you can find photographs and facts about weathering and take a virtual tour of some amazing underground caves, go to **www.usborne-quicklinks.com**

# Physical weathering

Heat makes most substances get bigger, or expand. When rocks are warmed by the Sun, they expand, and when they cool down at night they shrink, or contract. The outer layer of the rock expands more, because it is directly exposed to the Sun's heat. Eventually it separates from the rock and peels off. This is called exfoliation.

A type of weathering called freeze-thaw action occurs when water seeps into cracks in rock and then freezes and expands.

*The process of freeze-thaw action begins when rain seeps into a small crack in rock.*

*The water freezes, expands and widens the crack. When the ice thaws, more water can seep in.*

*As the temperature rises and falls, the crack gradually grows until the rock breaks apart.*

# Biological weathering

Weathering caused by plants or animals is called biological weathering. For example, lichens, which are small organisms that grow on rocks, give out acidic chemicals which eat away at the rock surface. Animals burrowing and roots growing in the ground can also contribute to rocks breaking down.

*As well as being dissolved by acidic rainwater, the Kangaroo Island rock on the left is being eaten away by lichens – the red areas on its surface.*

# Shaping the landscape

Because some rocks are harder and more resistant to weathering than others, they wear away at different rates. Harder rocks get left behind as outcrops, which stick up out of the surrounding land, or as long ridges. Over many years, weathering can produce amazing rock shapes, jutting mountain peaks and deep limestone caves*.

*This cave is still being shaped by chemical weathering, as acidic water eats away at cracks in the rock.*

*Limestone caves, 65

# EROSION

E rosion happens when wind, water, ice and gravity carry away particles of rock and soil that have been worn down by weathering*. Gradually, eroded material is carried downhill and into rivers, and most of it ends up being washed into the sea.

*You can sometimes tell old mountains from younger ones by how worn and flattened they are.*

*K2 in the Himalayas is 8,611m (28,250ft) high. It is relatively young and still has pointed peaks.*

*Mount Baker in Washington, U.S.A., is 3,285m (10,778ft) high. It has a flatter, worn shape, showing it was formed earlier in the Earth's history.*

## Wind and rain

Over hundreds of years, wind gradually blows away tiny particles from the surface of rocks. Many rocks contain different minerals, some harder than others. The wind wears them away at different rates, carving the rocks into wind sculptures.

Rain splashing onto rocks and soil washes away bigger particles and carries them into rivers. Farmers have to protect the soil* to prevent it all from eroding away in the rain.

*These pinnacles in Arizona, U.S.A., are striated, which means the wind has carved their surfaces into narrow grooves.*

## Moving mountains

On mountains, particles of rocks and soil are pulled downhill by gravity. Chunks of rock that break off near the top of a mountain fall down the slopes, knocking off other chunks as they go. Often a covering of loose stones, called scree, collects at the bottom of a slope.

Humans can add to this kind of erosion. Rock climbers sometimes dislodge scree and set off rockfalls, and walkers can slowly wear mountain paths away.

## Wearing flat

As erosion carries particles of rocks and soil away from mountains and high ground toward the sea, the Earth's land masses become lower and smoother. However, new islands and mountains are sometimes formed by volcanoes* erupting and by the plates* that make up the Earth's crust grinding together. So as old land is worn away, new land rises up to replace it.

*This photo shows the bare hillside left behind after a landslide in North Carolina, U.S.A.*

## Internet links

For links to websites where you can find examples of different types of weathering and erosion, and try an experiment to see how rain shapes the Earth, go to **www.usborne-quicklinks.com**

## Landslides

A landslide is a mass of soil and rock suddenly slipping down a steep slope. Many landslides are caused by rainwater soaking into the soil and making it heavier. Landslides are particularly likely if water soaks into a layer of shale (a type of slippery rock made from compressed clay).

## Preventing erosion

A certain amount of erosion is normal, and we could never stop it completely. In some places, though, we can try to slow it down.

On mountains that are popular with walkers, stone or wooden paths help to protect the land from being worn away by feet. In hilly areas, trees help to keep the soil in place and prevent landslides, so people have learned not to cut down hillside trees.

*A worker planting vegetation to prevent erosion near a roadside*

*Plates, 20; soil erosion, 31; volcanoes, 38; weathering, 32*

Lava flowing from the Kilauea volcano, Hawaii

# EARTHQUAKES
# AND VOLCANOES

# THE EXPLODING EARTH

A n erupting volcano is one of the most dramatic sights in the natural world. Bubbling hot lava spews out of a hole in the Earth's crust and engulfs the land. Ash, dust and poisonous gases pour into the air and chunks of rock are hurled high into the sky.

## Volcanoes

Volcanoes erupt when red-hot molten rock, called magma, from the Earth's mantle rises toward the surface. Eventually it builds up enough pressure to burst through the Earth's crust. Once magma has reached the surface of the Earth it is called lava.

## Growing

When a volcano erupts, the lava and ash it throws out eventually set as a solid layer of volcanic rock. As the layers build up, the volcano grows. Thick lava flows only a short way before setting, so it forms steep-sided cone volcanoes. Thinner lava flows farther before setting hard, so it forms shield volcanoes that have gently sloping sides.

*A cross-section through a shield volcano*

*A cross-section through a cone volcano*

Dust, ash and gases

Crater – the hole at the top of a volcano

Volcanic bomb

Layers of volcanic ash – tiny particles of lava

Vent – the main pipe up the middle of a volcano

Dyke – this leads from the vent to the surface

Magma chamber – place where magma collects below the Earth's crust

## Bombs and blocks

Volcanic bombs and blocks are thick lumps of molten lava which are blasted into the air as a volcano erupts. They start to cool and harden as they travel through the air. Blocks tend to be angular whereas bombs are more rounded.

Some blocks are the size of trucks.

As they twist through the air, some bombs form a "tail".

Tiny bombs shaped like drops form from very runny lava.

## Dead or alive?

Volcanoes that erupt regularly are known as active volcanoes. Volcanoes that won't ever erupt again are called extinct volcanoes. Sometimes, people think a volcano is extinct when actually it is only dormant (sleeping). Volcanoes can lie dormant for thousands of years.

### Internet links

For links to websites where you can watch video clips of volcanoes erupting, find out more about volcanoes and see a slide show of some of history's deadliest volcanoes, go to **www.usborne-quicklinks.com**

## Danger

Lava destroys everything it engulfs. But, because it usually flows quite slowly, it rarely kills people. There is more danger from the hot gas, bombs and ash which can sweep down a volcano's slopes at speeds of 200kph (120mph). In AD79, when Mount Vesuvius in Italy erupted, the people of Pompeii were wiped out by poisonous gas and ash.

*A plaster cast made from the hollow of a body left in the ash in Pompeii.*

# VOLCANIC VARIATIONS

**M**ost volcanoes occur at weak spots on the Earth's crust where magma bursts through. Volcanoes erupt in different ways, depending on the thickness of the lava.

## Hot spots

Some volcanoes form in the middle of plates. They may be caused by hot zones deep in the Earth's mantle. Scientists think that currents of warm rock called plumes rise slowly through the mantle and make magma which burns through the Earth's crust to make a hot spot volcano.

*A diagram showing a hot spot volcano in the middle of a plate*

## Subduction zones

Volcanoes also occur at subduction zones. These are places where two plates collide head on and one plate is pushed down beneath the other. As the plate is forced deeper and deeper underground, it begins to melt, forming magma. This newly formed magma rises up through cracks in the surface and explodes in a volcano.

*Volcanoes with runny lava, like this, erupt gently.*

## Spreading ridges

Whole mountain ranges of volcanoes can form at underwater boundaries where two plates* are moving apart. These are called spreading ridges. As the plates move apart, magma from the mantle rises to the surface. Most of it solidifies on the edge of the plates to make new crust, but some works its way up to the seabed, where it erupts as volcanoes.

*Spreading ridges form when plates move apart.*

*Rising magma*

*At subduction zones, one plate is forced underground where it starts to melt.*

*Melting plate*

*Plates, 20

# Lava

Not all volcanoes
erupt in the same way.
Some throw clouds of ash
high into the air, while
others have gentle lava
fountains. The thicker and
stickier the lava, the more
gases are trapped within it.
These gases create the
pressure which makes a
volcano erupt explosively.
When lava is thin and runny,
gases can escape more easily.
They just bubble out of the top
of the volcano.

## Internet links

For links to websites where you can
examine different types of volcanoes
around the world, build a volcano
online and find out how and where
volcanoes form, go to
**www.usborne-quicklinks.com**

*Hawaiian-type
eruptions are usually
gentle. They occur
when lava is runny,
so trapped gases
bubble out easily.*

*Plinian-type eruptions are the most
explosive. Trapped gases cause massive
explosions as they escape, and huge
amounts of volcanic ash are
thrown high into the air.*

# NATURAL HOT WATER

In areas where volcanoes are found, there are often other dramatic natural features. Hot springs, jets of hot water and underwater chimneys which belch out black water can also be caused by volcanic activity.

## Internet links

For links to websites where you can see geysers in Yellowstone Park, U.S.A. and watch a video clip of a "black smoker" (hydrothermal vent), go to
**www.usborne-quicklinks.com**

## Hot rock

In volcanic areas, when magma rises into the Earth's crust, it heats the rock around it. This rock might contain groundwater, which is rain or sea water that has seeped down into the Earth's crust through cracks in the surface. As the rock heats up, so does the groundwater around it, producing a natural supply of hot water.

Cold water

Rock heated by magma

Heated water

*Hot rock heats up groundwater.* ★

## Hot springs

Groundwater heated by hot rock sometimes bubbles to the surface as a hot, or thermal, spring. The water usually contains minerals which have been dissolved from the rock below. Minerals from the water often build up around the edge of the spring.

*This is the Morning Glory pool, one of many hot springs in Yellowstone National Park, U.S.A. The park has over 10,000 features, such as hot springs and geysers, that have been caused by hot, volcanic rock.*

## Black smokers

Around volcanic mountain ranges under the sea, hot springs sometimes emerge through holes in the seabed called hydrothermal vents.

Some vents, called black smokers, look like chimneys and puff out plumes of hot, cloudy black water. The water is cloudy because of the minerals it has dissolved from the hot rock. As minerals are deposited around the vent, the sides of the chimney build up. Some unusual creatures, such as tubeworms and blind spider crabs, live near black smokers. They feed on bacteria that live on the minerals given out by the vents.

*Black smokers form on the seabed and puff out clouds of hot, black water. Some are as tall as 6m (20ft).*

## Geysers

A geyser is a jet of hot water and steam that shoots into the air from a hole in the ground. Geysers occur when heated groundwater gets trapped in a network of cracks under the Earth's surface. Because the water is trapped, it continues to heat up until it boils and forms steam. The pressure builds up until it forces the water to find a way out of the ground. This results in occasional bursts of hot water.

*"Old Faithful" is a geyser in Yellowstone National Park, U.S.A. A fountain of hot water like this spurts out once every hour or so.*

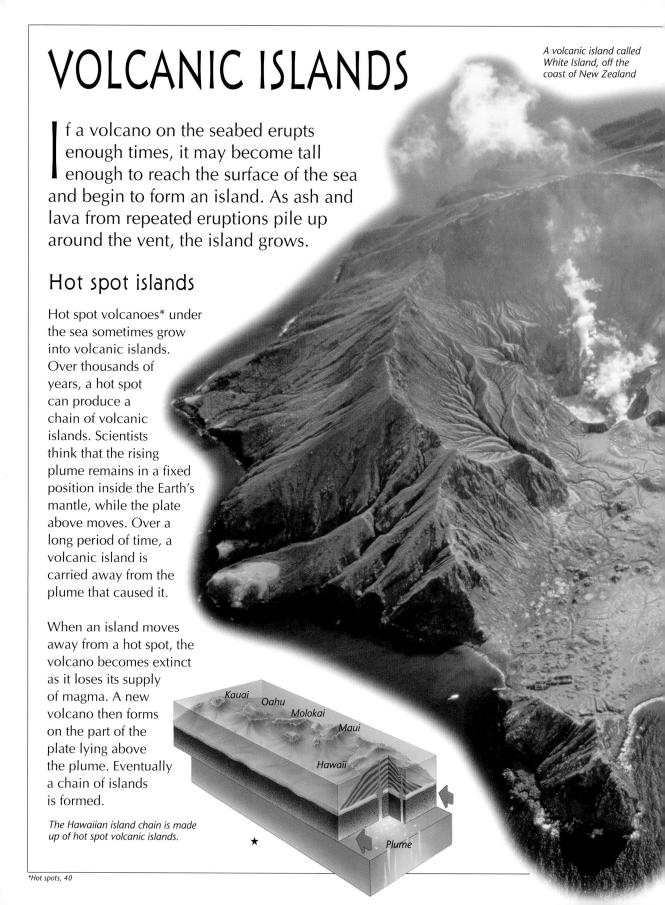

# VOLCANIC ISLANDS

*A volcanic island called White Island, off the coast of New Zealand*

I f a volcano on the seabed erupts enough times, it may become tall enough to reach the surface of the sea and begin to form an island. As ash and lava from repeated eruptions pile up around the vent, the island grows.

## Hot spot islands

Hot spot volcanoes* under the sea sometimes grow into volcanic islands. Over thousands of years, a hot spot can produce a chain of volcanic islands. Scientists think that the rising plume remains in a fixed position inside the Earth's mantle, while the plate above moves. Over a long period of time, a volcanic island is carried away from the plume that caused it.

When an island moves away from a hot spot, the volcano becomes extinct as it loses its supply of magma. A new volcano then forms on the part of the plate lying above the plume. Eventually a chain of islands is formed.

*The Hawaiian island chain is made up of hot spot volcanic islands.*

Kauai
Oahu
Molokai
Maui
Hawaii
Plume

★

*Hot spots, 40

## Internet links

For links to websites where you can watch video clips of volcanic islands and an animation of how a chain of volcanoes forms, go to
**www.usborne-quicklinks.com**

# An island is born

*This picture shows steam and ash billowing from Surtsey, a volcanic island near Iceland.*

In 1963, fishermen off the coast of Iceland saw smoke rising from the sea. They thought it must be a boat on fire. In fact, it wasn't smoke, but ash and steam from a volcano just below the water's surface.

During the next four years, the volcano erupted many times. As it emerged above the water, the eruptions became more explosive as the water pressure decreased. Lava and ash built up, until eventually they formed a volcanic island. The island was named Surtsey after Surt, the Nordic giant of fire.

## Black beaches

Some volcanic islands have black sandy beaches. This is because they are formed from basalt lava which is black. When the lava runs down to meet the sea, it cools instantly. The change in temperature makes the lava shatter into tiny pieces which form the grains of sand.

*A black sandy beach in Tahiti*

# LIVING WITH VOLCANOES

**D**espite the danger that active volcanoes present, many people choose to live on their slopes. Scientists are sometimes able to predict eruptions and warn those at risk.

### Internet links

For links to websites where you can see photographs of Mount St. Helens erupting and find out about volcanoes that threaten cities in other parts of the world, go to **www.usborne-quicklinks.com**

## Monitoring volcanoes

Before a volcano erupts, the ground may change shape. This kind of change can be measured by instruments such as tiltmeters and geodimeters. The ground may also begin to tremble. This is known as volcanic tremor. It can be detected by seismometers.

Such instruments were used to monitor the Mount St. Helens volcano, Washington, U.S.A., in early 1980. They recorded a bulge swelling by 1.5m (5ft) per day. The area around the volcano was evacuated shortly before it erupted.

*A group of experts monitoring the Mount St. Helens volcano were in a plane flying over it when the volcano began to shudder. This photograph of the eruption was taken as the pilot turned the plane to escape the blast.*

*The area around Mount St. Helens after the eruption. Despite the evacuation of the area, 61 people died.*

*A bulge on the side of Mount St. Helens swelled to 90m (295ft) before a massive eruption blasted away the side of the volcano.*

## Using volcanoes

Although volcanoes are usually a destructive force, they can also be put to productive uses. The ash from volcanoes contains minerals which make soil very fertile. As a result, the land around volcanoes is very good for farming. This is one of the reasons why people choose to live in such dangerous places.

# EARTHQUAKE EFFECTS

An earthquake is a sudden release of energy that makes the ground tremble. The effects of a large earthquake can be devastating: the ground lurches violently and buildings sway from side to side, or may even collapse. However, earthquakes only occur in certain parts of the world and most earthquakes are not felt by people at all.

*An apartment block in San Francisco, U.S.A., which has been damaged by an earthquake*

## Damaging effects

Earthquakes cause most damage when they occur in large towns and cities. During severe earthquakes, buildings and bridges collapse, and cracks called fissures may appear in the ground. There are also threats from hazards such as fire and flooding. These may be caused when underground gas pipes or water pipes crack during an earthquake.

# The power of earthquakes

Over 800,000 earthquakes occur each year, but only around a hundred of these cause very serious damage. Their power and effects are measured by seismologists, scientists who study earthquakes.

There are two scales for measuring earthquakes: the Richter scale and the Mercalli scale. The Richter scale measures the power of vibrations called seismic waves that travel through the ground when an earthquake happens. These tremors are registered using a device called a seismometer. Then a chart of the vibrations, known as a seismogram, is produced.

*This is a device called a seismometer, which is used to measure ground vibrations.*

*This shows the devastation caused by an earthquake in Maharashtra, India, in 1993.*

## Internet links

For links to websites where you can experiment online with an earthquake simulator and watch video clips to see the devastating effects of earthquakes around the world, go to
**www.usborne-quicklinks.com**

## Mercalli scale

The Mercalli scale rates earthquakes from I to XII according to the effects of the shaking, including the damage caused in different places. It is based on information from eyewitnesses.

*These pictures show how earthquakes are rated using the Mercalli scale. Ratings below IV indicate very slight vibrations.*

**IV**
People indoors may notice plates and windows start to rattle.

**V**
Small objects move and liquids in glasses and bowls splash around.

**VI**
Books and ornaments fall off shelves. Vibrations are felt indoors and outdoors.

**VII**
Walls crack and tiles and bricks fall from buildings.

**VIII**
Some weaker buildings collapse.

**IX+**
Many larger buildings collapse.

# HOW EARTHQUAKES HAPPEN

Earthquakes are most common near plate boundaries*. The movement of the plates causes stress to build up in certain areas of rock. When this stress is suddenly released, the surrounding rock vibrates, causing an earthquake.

## Fault lines

Earthquakes occur along cracks in the Earth's crust called faults. Faults can be tiny fractures or long cracks stretching over vast distances. They often occur when plates slide against each other, causing the rock to be twisted, stretched or squeezed until it splits. Boundaries where plates slide past each other in the same or in opposite directions are called conservative margins.

*An overhead view of the San Andreas fault*

San Francisco

San Andreas fault

The North American plate moves 1cm (0.4in) a year.

Los Angeles

San Diego

The Pacific plate moves 6cm (2.4in) a year.

*Earthquakes regularly occur along the San Andreas fault, on the west coast of North America. These plates slide in the same direction, but move at different speeds.*

*This diagram shows how some plates slide past each other in opposite directions.*

## Releasing energy

If the jagged edges along a fault become jammed, energy builds up as the two edges strain against one another. Eventually, the stress becomes so great that one side is suddenly forced to give way, causing a jerking movement. The energy that has built up is released, making the surrounding rock vibrate in an earthquake.

*A fault running through rock*

*Energy builds up at the point where the rocks become jammed.*

*Plate boundaries, 20

# The focus

The point where the rock gives way is called the focus. This is where the earthquake starts, usually about 5–15km (3–9 miles) underground. The point on the surface directly above the focus is called the epicentre*.

## Internet links

**Website 1** Animated diagrams that explain how earthquakes happen.

**Website 2** Take a close-up look at California's San Andreas Fault, a boundary between two of the Earth's plates.

For link to these websites, go to **www.usborne-quicklinks.com**

★

Epicentre*

Focus

Vibrations travel out from the focus.

When the rock eventually gives way, a large amount of built-up energy is released.

# Seismic waves

Seismic waves are at their strongest nearest the focus and become weaker as they travel out. There are different types of seismic waves, each of which makes the rock it travels through vibrate in a different way.

*Different types of seismic waves travel by distorting rock in different ways.*

Direction of waves

Vibrations of the rock particles as the waves pass through

Stretching and squeezing movement

**1. P-waves** ('P' stands for either primary or push and pull) travel deep below the ground. As they travel through rock, they stretch and squeeze the rock particles.

★

★

**2. S-waves** ('S' stands for secondary or shake) make rock move up and down and from side to side. They travel deep underground and can't move through liquid.

Vertical and horizontal movement

Circular movement

**3. L-waves** ('L' stands for long) only travel along the surface. Most earthquake damage is caused by this type of wave.

★

# Aftershocks

Sometimes, not all of the energy that has built up is released during an earthquake. This may mean that after the main earthquake there are smaller tremors, known as aftershocks, as the remaining energy is released. Small amounts of energy may also be released before an earthquake occurs. This produces tremors known as foreshocks.

*Epicenter (U.S.A.)

# EARTHQUAKE SAFETY

By monitoring faults, scientists can sometimes predict when and where earthquakes are likely to occur. This means that they can take steps to limit the damage caused by an earthquake or even prevent an earthquake from happening.

## Seismic gaps

Stress that builds up at fault boundaries is often released gradually by slow movement known as fault creep. Earthquakes are less likely to happen in areas where fault creep occurs, because stress is being released. They are most likely to occur at sections of a fault where there has been no movement for many years. These sections are known as seismic gaps.

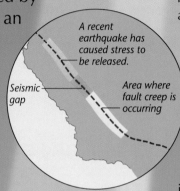

A recent earthquake has caused stress to be released.

Seismic gap

Area where fault creep is occurring

*By identifying seismic gaps, scientists can carefully monitor areas where earthquakes are most likely to occur.*

## Monitoring faults

If the surface of the Earth suddenly starts to tilt, it may be a sign that an earthquake is about to happen. Devices called tiltmeters can measure tiny changes in the level of the ground. Horizontal movement along faults can be monitored using lasers. A laser beam from one side of the fault is bounced off a reflector on the other side, which reflects it back. A computer records the time it takes the beam to travel this distance. If the time changes, it shows that movement has taken place.

*Scientists use lasers like these to detect ground movements. They can detect shifts as slight as 1mm (0.04in).*

# Preventing earthquakes

Earthquakes can be prevented by releasing jammed plates before too much stress builds up. This can be done by conducting a small explosion to shift the plates. Alternatively, drilling deep holes and injecting water into rocks reduces friction, enabling smoother movement along a fault.

# Keeping safe

During an earthquake, if you are indoors, the safest place to be is under a solid table or desk. You should cover your eyes to protect them from flying glass and hold on tightly to the leg of the table. If you are outside, it's better to be in an open space, away from buildings, trees and power lines.

## Internet links

For links to websites where you can find fascinating earthquake facts, pictures and activities, watch animations of buildings that can withstand earthquakes and learn how to stay safe in an earthquake, go to **www.usborne-quicklinks.com**

# Animal instincts

Scientists think that animals' highly developed senses may alert them to earthquakes before they happen. It is possible that they can detect slight vibrations, changes in electrical currents in rocks, or the release of gases. In San Francisco, U.S.A., zoo animals are monitored in case the way they behave gives warning of an earthquake.

*If animals become unusually agitated, it may be a clue that an earthquake is about to happen.*

# Safe buildings

In areas where there is a high risk of earthquakes happening, more buildings are being designed so that minimum damage is caused if there is an earthquake. The foundations of some buildings are constructed to absorb vibrations and reduce the effects of shaking. Steel frames can be used to strengthen buildings, so that a building may sway but will not collapse when the ground trembles.

*The Transamerica skyscraper in San Francisco, U.S.A., is designed to withstand tremors.*

# GIANT WAVES

An earthquake or a volcanic eruption under the sea or near the coast can cause giant waves called tsunami. These waves surge across the sea in all directions. Just before a tsunami crashes onto the shore, it may swell to an enormous height.

*In 1998, a tsunami caused incredible devastation in Papua New Guinea. This is a still from a video taken there. It shows steel roofing wrapped around a tree by the force of the water.*

## Tsunami

Tsunami begin when an earthquake or volcano causes the water to shift and waves to form. Out at sea, tsunami are a similar height to ordinary waves, but the distance between one tsunami and the next can be more than 100km (62 miles). What makes tsunami so dangerous is their speed. They race across the sea at speeds of up to 800kph (500mph). Normally tsunami do not break like ordinary waves. As a tsunami enters shallow water, its height increases and it surges over the land. This is what causes the devastating flooding of coastal regions.

### Internet links

For links to websites with animated diagrams, facts and photos, and an online to the cause of the 2004 tsunami, go to **www.usborne-quicklinks.com**

*Tsunami travel out rapidly in all directions from the place where they initially form.*

*An underwater earthquake or volcanic eruption displaces the seabed.*

*Tsunami swell to great heights before surging over the land.*

# Tsunami warning system

Most tsunami occur in the Pacific Ocean. For this reason, there are observation stations throughout the Pacific to monitor earthquakes. If an earthquake is large enough to generate tsunami, warnings are issued to coastal towns, so that they can prepare for it. Tide stations along the coast then monitor the arrival of the tsunami.

*Observation and tide stations in the Pacific monitor tsunami.*

North America

PACIFIC OCEAN

Central Pacific tsunami warning station

South America

Australia

Tide stations

Observation stations

*Tsunami look like a huge wall of water. They can reach heights of up to 50m (165ft).*

A group of Atlantic salmon swimming

RIVERS AND OCEANS

# RIVERS

The water in rivers comes from rainfall, from snow and ice melting, and from water inside the Earth, called groundwater. Rivers carry this water downhill to lakes and oceans.

*Hippopotamuses live in and around slow, muddy rivers in Africa. This one has an egret on its head.*

## A river's course

A river changes as it flows downhill along its path, or course. Many rivers begin in mountain areas, where rain and melting ice run into steep, clear streams. Mountain streams cut narrow, deep valleys and join together as they flow downhill. Smaller streams and rivers that flow into a bigger river are called tributaries.

*Mountain streams, like this one in Connecticut, U.S.A., form series of mini waterfalls as they tumble down over the steep, rocky slopes.*

Away from the mountains, the water flows more smoothly in broader channels and larger valleys. As the land levels out, the river starts to form large bends, or meanders.

Finally, the river widens out into a broad estuary, or sometimes splits to form a delta*, before flowing into the sea (or sometimes into a large lake). The part of a river where it meets the sea is called the river mouth.

### Internet links

For links to websites where you can find lots of river facts, follow a river from its source to the sea and see diagrams of river systems, go to **www.usborne-quicklinks.com**

*Stonefly larvae live in mountain streams. They cling to stones with their claws so they don't get swept away by the water.*

# Drainage

The area of land from which a river collects its water is called its drainage basin. When water drains into streams and rivers, it forms different patterns, depending on the shape of the land and the type of rock it is made of.

When there is only one type of rock, streams form a tree-like pattern like this. It is called a dendritic drainage pattern.

# River records

The Manu River, a tributary of the Amazon, winding its way through the rainforests of Peru

The longest river in the world is the River Nile in Africa. It travels northward for 6,671km (4,145 miles) from its source in Burundi to its delta in Egypt, where it flows into the Mediterranean Sea. However, the world's biggest river, or the one that holds the most water, is the Amazon in South America. It is about 6,440km (4,000 miles) long, and flows across South America from west to east. Every single second, it pours about 94 million litres (20 million gallons) of water into the Atlantic Ocean. At its mouth, the Amazon is 240km (150 miles) wide.

A Nile crocodile stalks its prey by swimming silently along in the river, with most of its body underwater.

# RIVERS AT WORK

Rivers can carve through solid rock and move huge boulders hundreds of miles. Over many years, rivers have eroded deep gorges and huge waterfalls, and carried vast amounts of rock, sand, soil and mud to the sea.

This satellite photo shows the Mahakam River, in Indonesia. You can see how a network of channels and islands, or a delta, is formed where the river runs into the sea.

## How rivers erode

As a river flows, the water sweeps along any loose soil, sand or rocks in its way. As they roll, slide and bounce along, the rocks and pebbles chip away at the riverbed, making it deeper and wider. They also grind against each other, which wears them down and breaks them into smaller pieces.

The river forces water and air bubbles into cracks in the riverbed, breaking off more chunks of rock. Another reason that rivers erode is that river water is slightly acidic, because it comes from rain*. It gradually wears away some types of rocks by dissolving them.

## Deposition

In its upper stages, a river is very turbulent and has lots of large boulders and pebbles on its bed. As it flows downstream the riverbed becomes smoother, so the water flows slightly faster. It starts to drop, or deposit, sand, silt and then mud. This is why the lower sections of a river have muddy beds. Near the sea, the deposited sediment may build up to form whole islands. The river splits up and forms a network of channels called a delta. The rest of the sediment flows into the sea.

*These rocks have been smoothed and rounded by the action of the water in the river.*

*Meander, 58; rainwater, 32

## Changing course

Rivers flow faster around the outside of a meander* than on the inside. The outside edge is slowly eroded, while the river deposits debris on the inside edge. Eventually the two sides of the meander meet, and the river cuts through to form a new course.

### Internet links

For links to websites where you can watch animations of river erosion and follow an online guide to rivers and how they change over time, go to **www.usborne-quicklinks.com**

★ A river erodes the outside of a meander and deposits sediment on the inside, making a loop.

The loop grows longer and narrower until the river finally breaks through.

The river flows past the ends of the loop and they slowly become silted up.

Eventually the loop gets cut off completely and forms a lake called an oxbow lake.

*This is the Horseshoe Falls, part of Niagara Falls, which is a huge waterfall on the border between Canada and the U.S.A. The waterfall moves upstream by around 3m (11ft) per year.*

## Waterfalls

Waterfalls begin when a river flows from an area of hard rock onto soft rock. The river wears away the soft rock more quickly and creates a ledge. Water falling over the ledge erodes a hollow at the bottom called a plunge pool. The action of the water and pebbles churning in the plunge pool can undercut the hard rock, creating an overhanging ledge. Chunks of the overhanging rock break off and very gradually, over hundreds of years, the waterfall moves backward, cutting a deep valley called a gorge.

*This diagram shows how a waterfall is formed.*

Waterfall cutting back

Falling water cuts away at the soft rock below.

Hard rock

Plunge pool

Softer rock

Spray undercuts here.

# USING RIVERS

Rivers are central to the way human civilization has developed. They have been used for thousands of years for drinking and washing and as transport routes. Farming and industry depend on the water they provide and we can convert their flowing force into useful energy.

*This engraving shows London, England, in 1631, with large ships plying their trade up and down the River Thames.*

*Amsterdam in the Netherlands is not on the sea, but is an important port, with over 80km (50 miles) of canals dividing it into over 80 islands.*

## River ports

A port is a city where ships can load and unload. When most international transport was by sea, many large ports, such as Montreal in Canada, Manaus in Brazil, and London in England, grew up near navigable rivers, that is rivers that can be used by ships. For example, most of the Amazon is navigable, because it is so wide and deep.

## Canals

Canals are artificial waterways built to replace or extend rivers. Irrigation canals divert water from rivers onto fields. Navigational canals are built for boats or ships to travel on. For example, the Suez Canal joins the Mediterranean Sea to the Red Sea, so that ships can take a short cut between Europe and the Indian Ocean. The beds and banks of canals are usually built of brick or concrete, so they suffer less erosion* than rivers.

### Internet links

For links to websites where you can find facts about famous canals, take a virtual tour of a hydroelectric project and learn about dams and how they affect the land and communities around them, go to **www.usborne-quicklinks.com**

*River erosion, 60

## Clean energy

Electrical energy from water power is called hydroelectric power or HEP. An HEP plant usually consists of a dam built on a river to create a large reservoir or lake. High-pressure jets of water are released from the lake through narrow channels, and used to spin turbines which produce electricity.

Water power is increasingly important as an energy source. Unlike fossil fuels, it is renewable (it won't run out). It also causes little pollution. But there can be problems when hydroelectric reservoirs take up precious land, or when dams collapse.

*Part of the Shasta Hydroelectric Dam in California, U.S.A. The spillway in the picture releases water to stop the dam from overflowing.*

## Dam disasters

*The present-day ruins of the Malpasset Dam, in France, which burst in 1959.*

In the past, several large dams have caused disaster by breaking or overflowing. One example is the Malpasset Dam in Frejus, France. It collapsed in 1959, causing a flood which killed over 500 people. The dam failed because it was built on rock called schist, which cracks easily.

*This small waterwheel generates electricity for a rural area of Washington State, U.S.A.*

## Water power

The energy in a river can be converted into electricity or other useful forms of energy. The earliest water power systems used a river or stream to turn a waterwheel. The turning force of the wheel was then used to drive machines, such as mills for grinding flour. Simple waterwheels like this are still used in many countries.

# WATER IN THE GROUND

Water doesn't just flow over the surface of the Earth; it flows under it too. As well as the rivers and lakes that we can see, there is a huge amount of water, called groundwater, stored underground in rocks and caves.

*Bottling mineral water and spring water to sell as drinking water is a major industry in some areas.*

## Groundwater

Many types of rocks are permeable, which means that water can soak through them. Water that has soaked into the ground and then been soaked up, or absorbed, into a layer of permeable rock is known as groundwater. Underground, the upper layers of rock press down on the lower layers, compressing them so that they are less permeable. So the amount of groundwater decreases farther down. The top level of the water-soaked layer is known as the water table.

Aquifers are layers of rock that can hold water. Some stretch for thousands of miles under the ground. In some places they are an important source of fresh water.

## Springs

A spring is a stream of fresh water springing out of the ground. Springs form where a layer of water-filled rock meets the surface of the Earth, especially on a hillside. The groundwater flows out of the rock and forms a small pool or stream.

Spring water is often clean and sparkling because it has been filtered through layers of rock. Sometimes the water dissolves minerals from the rocks. Some of these minerals are thought to be good for your health.

*Rain and snow seep through permeable rock.*

*Mountain rivers*

*Rivers, lakes and springs may appear where an aquifer meets the surface.*

*A spring emerges where saturated rock meets the surface.*

*Water table*

*Saturated rock*

*Aquifer*

*Lake*

*Impermeable rock*

## Rivers under the ground

Water can also be found in underground rivers, waterfalls and even large lakes in caves and tunnels. These usually form in limestone. The water eats away at the rock through chemical weathering*.

### Internet links

For links to websites where you can take an interactive look at the water cycle and follow the journey of water underground, go to
**www.usborne-quicklinks.com**

## Stalactites and stalagmites

In some caves, long columns of stone, called stalactites, hang from the ceiling, and columns called stalagmites rise up from the floor. They are formed when water full of dissolved minerals drips from the cave roof. With each drop, a tiny deposit of rock is left behind and over time this grows into a long column. As the drips hit the ground, they deposit more minerals, which build up into stalagmites.

*These stalactites are constantly growing as more water drips off them, depositing a tiny amount of dissolved rock with each drip.*

*Inside this cave in Mexico, long stalactites have grown down from the ceiling, while water has gathered to form a still underground pool.*

# RIVERS OF ICE

A glacier is a huge mass of ice that flows downhill, a little like a river. Glaciers flow much more slowly than rivers. But, because they are solid, they cut through the landscape more easily, gouging deep U-shaped valleys as they carry rocks and soil along with them.

*This is a glacier in Glacier Bay National Park, Alaska, U.S.A.*

**Internet links**

For links to websites with glacier and iceberg photo galleries and amazing examples of the powerful force of glaciers, go to **www.usborne-quicklinks.com**

## Ice force

Glaciers are very heavy and powerful. As a glacier flows along, the ice and rocks caught in it scrape soil and rock from the sides and floor of the valley, carving a deep channel. When the ice melts, it deposits thick layers of debris, called moraine, and boulders, known as erratics, on the valley floor.

## How glaciers form

Glaciers are found in cold places, such as high mountains. At the top of a glacier, known as the accumulation zone, layers of snow collect and become packed down into hard, solid ice. As more snow falls on top, the mass of ice gets heavier and heavier, until it starts to move down the mountain.

As the ice gradually flows downhill, it gets warmer, because the air is warmer lower down. At the lower end, called the ablation zone, the glacier melts and the icy-cold water, known as meltwater, flows into streams and rivers.

Fresh snow falls here.

Accumulation zone

As a glacier moves over bumps and around corners, it may develop cracks called crevasses.

Boulders carried along by the glacier scratch grooves in the rock below.

The glacier melts here.

Ablation zone

Meltwater

★

*This diagram shows the different parts of a glacier and the way it moves downhill.*

## Glacial clues

If the climate gets warmer, glaciers sometimes melt, leaving behind a glacial valley. You can recognize a glacial valley by its deep, rounded U-shape and by debris, such as boulders and moraine hills, or drumlins, left on the valley floor. Sometimes, valleys called hanging valleys, that once joined the glacier, are left high above the main valley. At the coast, some glacial valleys are filled with seawater. They form narrow inlets called fjords.

*This diagram shows some of the features that will help you to recognize a glacial valley. A glacial valley filled with seawater, like this, is called a fjord.*

*Smaller valleys that once joined the glacier are left high above the main valley. They are called hanging valleys.*

*A U-shaped glacial valley*

★

*Drumlins are low rounded hills, probably formed by deposited debris.*

*Boulders known as erratics are sometimes deposited by glaciers.*

## Ice sheets

Not all glaciers are found on mountains. They also form in very cold places near the poles, such as Greenland and Antarctica. There, ice collects in huge sheets, called continental ice sheets. The ice flows outward at the edges as more snow falls and more ice forms in the middle. Parts of the glacier can be pushed right into the sea and break off, forming icebergs.

*Icebergs float away into the ocean, gradually melting as they reach warmer areas.*

# THE EDGE OF THE SEA

The coast, where the land meets the sea, is constantly being broken down and built up by the action of waves. The ebb and flow of the tide means that the environment at the seashore is always changing. Specially adapted animals and plants make their homes there.

### Internet links

For links to websites where you can explore shorelines and learn more about coastal environments, erosion, tides and waves, go to **www.usborne-quicklinks.com**

## Waves

Waves are formed far out at sea by the wind. Although they travel through water, they do not move the water itself forward. They make water particles move in circles under the surface. When a wave reaches shallow water, these circles are interrupted at the bottom and the wave breaks.

*Out at sea, wind blows the surface of the ocean into waves.*

*The waves make particles of water move in circular patterns under the surface.*

*On a shallow, flat beach, waves break before they reach the shore.*

*On a sloping coast, waves break at the shore and crash onto the beach.*

*On a very steep slope, waves do not break, but surge against the shore.*

★

## Coastal erosion

*This archway in Dorset, England, is called Durdle Door. It was created over many years by the destructive action of waves. It started as a headland with caves on either side. The waves gradually eroded the caves until, eventually, they broke through, creating an arch.*

Waves that crash onto the shore are known as destructive waves, because they gradually wear away, or erode, the coast. When they break onto beaches, they drag sand, pebbles and other debris out to sea. When they crash onto rocky cliffs, any debris they are carrying is flung against the rock, wearing it down. Waves force water and air into cracks in cliffs, carving out caves.

Destructive waves erode the coastline at different rates. Soft rock wears down quite fast, and is worn away into curved bays. Hard rock is left behind, forming cliffs and jutting pieces of land called headlands. Sometimes two caves form on either side of a headland, and the sea breaks through, leaving an arch. The arch may collapse, leaving a tower of rock called a stack.

## Building beaches

While destructive waves wear away parts of the coast, other waves, called constructive waves, wash up debris onto the shore, forming beaches. When a wave breaks gently onto a flat coast, it slows down and loses energy. This makes it drop any debris it may be carrying, such as pebbles and grains of sand previously broken off into the sea from cliffs and rocky shores. Over time, this deposited material builds up into a beach.

*Stones and pebbles in the sea are polished and rounded by the action of the waves.*

## Tides

Tides* are caused by the gravity, or pulling force, of the Moon. The Moon pulls the sea slightly towards it. So, as the Earth spins, the part nearest the Moon has a high tide. There are roughly two high tides each day.

Animals and plants that live on the seashore have to be able to survive in the water at high tide, and in the air at low tide. They also have to find ways to avoid being smashed to pieces or swept away by crashing waves.

*Crabs, like this rock crab, can breathe in both water and air. They have hard shells to protect them from the sea, and can burrow into the sand to hide from predators.*

## Coastlines

Over many years, the action of the sea changes the shapes of countries, as it builds up the land in some places and wears it away in others. Buildings near the sea sometimes fall in or get washed away as the land is gradually eroded.

For example, the coast of Holderness in Lincolnshire, England, has worn away quickly. Over 50 coastal villages listed in a national survey of towns and villages called the Domesday Book in 1086 have since been washed into the sea.

# SEAS AND OCEANS

More than two-thirds of the Earth's surface is covered with salt water. The Earth's five oceans and its seas are all connected, so sea water flows freely among them. The seas and oceans, and the creatures that live in them, still hold many mysteries for scientists to explore.

*The ballan wrasse fish is found mainly near rocky shores in Europe.*

## Under the sea

Near the land, the seabed slopes gradually downhill, forming a wide shelf called the continental shelf. At the edge of the shelf, a cliff called the continental slope drops away to the deeper part of the ocean floor, which is called the abyssal plain.

*A 3-D map of part of the floor of the Atlantic Ocean*

Just like the land, the abyssal plain has valleys, hills, mountains and even volcanoes. It also has ridges* where new rock is pushed out from inside the Earth, and trenches* where the Earth's crust is swallowed up again.

## Exploring the sea

By studying the seabed and the creatures that live there sea scientists, called oceanographers, can find out about how the Earth was formed and how life began. Oceanographers visit the seabed in mini-submarines called submersibles, or explore it from the surface using unmanned robots called remote operated vehicles (ROVs). They also map the seabed using sonar. This sends out sounds which are bounced back as echoes, showing how deep the seabed is.

*This diver is retrieving a rock from a remote operated vehicle (ROV). The ROV has returned to shallow waters after collecting rock samples from the seabed.*

*Ridges, 20; trenches, 20

# Life in the oceans

Seas and oceans contain a huge variety of plant and animal life, from the surface all the way down to the deepest trenches.

The loggerhead turtle lives in warm, shallow seas and comes ashore to lay its eggs.

The main food source in the sea is phytoplankton, a type of microscopic plant. Billions of phytoplankton drift near the surface of the sea, making food from sunlight, water, gases and minerals.

*Part of a coral reef in the Red Sea, which lies between Egypt and Saudi Arabia*

# Coral reefs

Coral reefs are amazing undersea structures made of the skeletons of tiny animals called coral polyps. When old polyps die, new ones grow on top of their bodies, and over many years a huge reef builds up.

### Internet links

For links to websites where you can explore the world's oceans, find out about the latest submersibles and take a virtual dive to the bottom of the sea, go to **www.usborne-quicklinks.com**

# Ocean zones

The deeper down you go in the ocean, the darker and colder it is, and the fewer plants and animals are found.

**Sunlit zone**
*Sea plants and many animals live here.*

Down to 200m (650ft)

**Twilight zone**
*Many fish, such as swordfish, survive here.*

Down to 1,000m (3,300ft)

**Sunless zone**
*Animals feed on dead food that falls from above.*

Down to 4,000m (13,100ft)

**Abyssal zone**
*The water is cold and dark. Few creatures live here.*

Down to 5,000m (16,400ft)

# USING SEAS AND OCEANS

For thousands of years, the sea has provided people with food. We also carry passengers and goods by sea and go on trips to the coast. But the oceans are often used as a place to dump waste, which causes pollution and may endanger wildlife.

## Fishing

Most sea fish are still caught using nets. There are three main types of nets. Purse seine nets are drawn closed around schools of fish that swim near the surface. Otter trawl nets are dragged along the seabed to catch fish that live there, while drift or gill nets can be used near the surface or on the seabed. Fishing boats now find schools of fish by using sonar* and satellite* technology.

*Above and top right: sea bass are the most common fish caught and eaten around the world. These were caught in Tokyo Bay, Japan.*

## Overfishing

Because of advances in fishing technology, fishing boats are now able to catch more fish than ever before, and the number of fish in the sea is falling rapidly. International laws have now been passed to restrict the areas where fishing boats can fish and the numbers and types of fish that can be caught.

*A Japanese fishing boat at work in Tokyo Bay, Japan, drawing a large net behind it.*

CB3-50869

### Internet links

For links to websites with cool facts about oceans, ideas on how to conserve ocean resources and lots of information about overfishing and pollution, go to **www.usborne-quicklinks.com**

*Satellites, 252; sonar, 70

## World travel

A century ago, if you wanted to travel across the sea, you had to go by boat. Huge ocean liners carried people around the world, and travel could take months.

Today, most people go long distances by plane, but boats such as ferries, hovercrafts and hydrofoils are still used for shorter distances. The only ocean liners left are cruise ships, which take people on long, relaxing sea journeys on vacations.

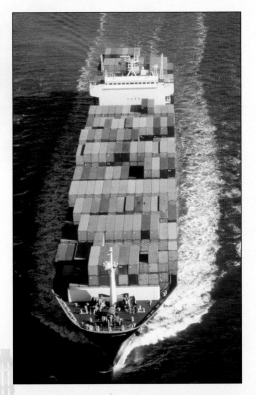

Container ships carry all kinds of goods in large metal boxes called containers. Cranes lift the containers off the ships and transfer them to trucks or trains.

## Shipping

Millions of different products, from oil and bananas to books and computers, are transported around the world on cargo ships. Ships travel more slowly than planes, but they can carry a lot more goods at once and are much cheaper to use.

## Sea pollution

The seas and oceans are huge and can absorb and break down a lot of the waste we pump into them. For example, a lot of sewage (waste from drains and toilets) goes into the sea and is broken down naturally into harmless chemicals.

However, some waste and litter doesn't break down fast enough, and ends up polluting the seas. Plastic, for example, dropped from ships or washed off beaches, can take up to 80 years to be broken down by the sea. Chemical and radioactive waste from factories, farms and nuclear power stations* can also end up in the sea and may poison plants, fish and other animals.

Oil tankers occasionally sink and spill the oil they are carrying. It can harm plants and animals, such as this seabird, by poisoning them or by coating them in oil so that they cannot breathe or move properly.

73

*Nuclear power, 27

Frost on a window

# WEATHER

# WHAT IS WEATHER?

Weather is the way the Earth's atmosphere* behaves, whether it is hot or cold, windy or still, raining, snowing or hailing. Climate* means the overall temperature and patterns of weather in a particular place.

## The importance of weather

Weather affects everyone's life. Anything from crops to summer vacations can be ruined if the weather behaves unexpectedly. Weather is also a factor in many of the world's worst disasters, such as floods, droughts and famines.

For thousands of years, people have worshipped weather gods and used rituals to try to affect the weather. But, even with modern technology, it is almost impossible to control.

*This Japanese dancer wears a special costume as part of a traditional dance which is meant to make the rain fall.*

## Internet links

**Website 1** A good introduction to weather and climate.

**Website 2** Play a weather game and try to beat the computer.

**Website 3** Weather fact files and a weather photo of the week.

**Website 4** Watch a video clip about how weather occurs.

For links to these websites, go to **www.usborne-quicklinks.com**

*Atmosphere, 94; climate, 100; cumulus clouds, 79; evaporation, 78

## What weather is

Weather is made up of three main ingredients: temperature, the movement of the air, and the amount of water in the air.

Hot weather is caused by the Sun heating up the land and the atmosphere*. If the Sun is hidden by clouds, or if a cold wind is blowing, the temperature is cooler.

Wind is also caused by the Sun. As air gets hotter, it expands, gets less dense, and rises. A mass of colder, heavier air rushes in to replace it, making wind.

Finally, the Sun's heat makes water from plants, soil, rivers and seas evaporate* into the air. High up, this condenses into water droplets which form clouds, and may then fall as rain, snow or hail.

These factors are always changing and affecting each other. They combine to make complicated patterns, known as weather systems.

Umbrellas have been used for hundreds of years to protect people from the weather. These paper umbrellas, called parasols, help to protect people from the Sun.

## Traditional signs

*Cumulus clouds usually appear when the weather is warm and sunny.*

*The way bees behave could help us predict the weather.*

Today, scientists can predict the weather using satellites and computers. But before these were invented, people predicted the weather by observing signs, such as the way the clouds look, and the way animals behave. For example, cumulus clouds* usually mean sunny weather, and bees usually go home to their hives before a storm.

## Weather facts

• The heaviest hailstones, weighing up to 1kg (2lb 2oz), fell in Gopalganj, Bangladesh, in 1986.

• The wettest place in the world is Mawssynrma, India. It gets nearly 12m (40ft) of rain a year.

• The biggest recorded snowflakes were 38cm (15in) across and fell on Montana, U.S.A., in 1887.

• The driest place in the world is the Atacama Desert, Chile. In some spots, there has been no rain for 500 years.

# WATER AND CLOUDS

The amount of water on Earth doesn't change, but water changes its state as it moves in a cycle. It exists as a liquid (water) in seas, rivers and cloud droplets, it freezes into a solid (ice) as snow and hail, and it exists as an invisible gas in the air.

*Snowflakes form when water droplets freeze into ice crystals. These snowflakes have been tinted so you can see their six-sided shapes more clearly.*

## The water cycle

When water is heated up, it changes from a liquid into an invisible gas. This process is called evaporation.

The Sun's heat causes water to evaporate from rivers, lakes and seas. Plants suck up water from the ground and it escapes from their leaves as a gas. Similarly, people and animals breathe out water as a gas.

As the gas molecules rise, they get cooler. This makes the water condense, or turn into liquid again, to form tiny droplets which can be seen as clouds. As the cloud droplets move around they collide with each other and grow bigger. When they are heavy enough, they fall as rain, and the water flows back into rivers, lakes and seas. This process is known as the water cycle.

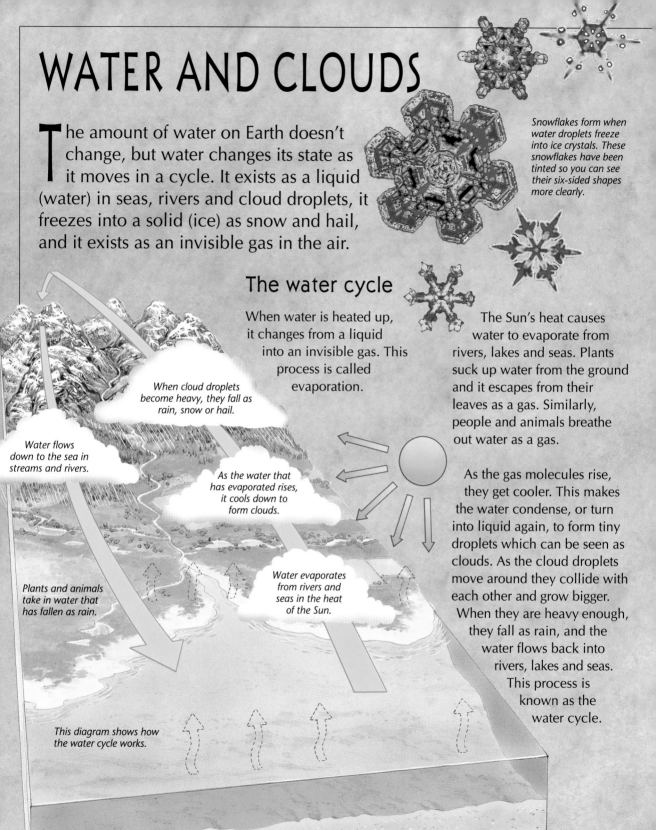

*When cloud droplets become heavy, they fall as rain, snow or hail.*

*Water flows down to the sea in streams and rivers.*

*As the water that has evaporated rises, it cools down to form clouds.*

*Plants and animals take in water that has fallen as rain.*

*Water evaporates from rivers and seas in the heat of the Sun.*

*This diagram shows how the water cycle works.*

# Clouds

The way clouds look depends on how much the air is moving up and down and how much water is in them. When clouds form in calm air, they spread out in sheets. On hot days, they puff up into heaps, following the rising air. Clouds full of big droplets look darker.

*Cumulus clouds look like white, puffy heaps. They often form high in the sky in warm sunny weather.*

*Stratus clouds form low, flat layers and often block out the sunshine.*

*Cirrus clouds are high and wispy. (The word cirrus means "like wispy hair" in Latin.)*

*These tall, piled-up cumulonimbus clouds were photographed over the Gulf of Mexico. A cumulonimbus cloud is freezing at the top, but warmer at the bottom.*

# Precipitation

Water that falls onto the Earth's surface is called precipitation. Rain is the most common kind. There are many types of rain, from light drizzle to monsoon rains*. In freezing weather, precipitation sometimes takes the form of snow or hail instead of raindrops.

*This diagram shows how hailstones are formed.*

Hail begins as ice crystals in giant cumulonimbus clouds.

Air currents push the crystals up and around inside the cloud.

As they move, the crystals bump into water droplets, which freeze around them in layers, like the layers of an onion.

The layers of ice build up until they form heavy hailstones, which fall to Earth.

### Internet links

For links to websites where you can find out about clouds and what they tell us about weather and watch an animated introduction to the water cycle, go to **www.usborne-quicklinks.com**

*Monsoons, 120

# THUNDERSTORMS

Sometimes in warm weather, huge storm clouds form very quickly. These clouds are full of water and fast-moving air currents. They can build up a store of electricity powerful enough to make lightning and thunder.

**Internet links**

For links to websites with amazing pictures of lightning, a lightning experiment to try at home and an animation that explains what happens when lightning strikes, go to **www.usborne-quicklinks.com**

## Electric clouds

In hot, damp weather, the evaporated water in the air rises very fast. When it hits the colder air above, tall, piled-up clouds called cumulonimbus clouds form.

Inside the cloud, water droplets and ice crystals rub together in the swirling air. This rubbing causes the crystals and droplets to build up a strong electric charge. Some have a negative charge (-) and some have a positive charge (+). Negative charges collect at the bottom of the cloud, making a huge energy difference between the cloud and the ground, which has a positive charge.

The difference builds up so much that it has to be equalized. A giant spark jumps between the bottom of the cloud and the ground, allowing the different charges to even out. The spark appears as a flash of lightning.

*The satellite photograph on the left shows piled-up cumulonimbus storm clouds viewed from above.*

*Lightning zigzags through the air as it finds the easiest path from the cloud to the ground.*

*Ball lightning is a very rare kind of lightning which appears as a small, floating ball of bright light. It can travel through walls and has been seen inside buildings and aircraft.*

## Lightning

When lightning strikes, it travels first downward, then upward. The first stroke, called the leader stroke, is invisible. It jumps from the cloud to the ground. This creates a path for the main stroke, which sparks from the ground back up to the cloud.

The main stroke contains so much energy that it heats up the air around it. The heat makes the air expand quickly, causing an explosion. This is the loud noise of thunder.

## Struck by lightning

Lightning always travels the shortest distance it can between a cloud and the ground. So it usually strikes high places, tall buildings or prominent objects such as trees or people.

Lightning quickly heats up whatever it strikes. When a tree is struck, the water in the tree boils instantly and turns into steam, which makes the trunk explode. But although lightning is dangerous, being struck is very rare. You can stay safe by avoiding trees and open spaces during storms.

# WINDSTORMS

**B**ecause of the way the world spins, wind doesn't flow in straight lines, but swirls into spirals. Sometimes, wind spirals grow into terrifying storms, such as hurricanes and tornadoes, which contain the fastest wind speeds on Earth.

*A satellite picture of the hurricane Typhoon Odessa*

## Coriolis effect

Winds are caused by high-pressure air rushing toward low-pressure areas, called cyclones. But instead of moving straight into the cyclone, the air circles around it in a spiral. This is called the Coriolis effect, and it happens because the spinning of the Earth always pushes winds to one side.

## Hurricanes

Hurricanes are very powerful windstorms that can be hundreds of miles wide and last up to ten days. They only form in warm, wet conditions, usually over the sea in tropical areas near the Equator. No one knows exactly what makes a hurricane start.

*The warm, wet air has a very low pressure, so cooler winds spiral toward it.*

*The damp air rises higher and condenses into thick clouds. They are blown into a spiral by the wind.*

After hurricanes form, they sometimes hit land and cause massive damage. Winds of up to 240kph (150mph) destroy buildings and rip trees out of the ground. But hurricanes die down soon after they hit land, as there is not enough moisture to keep them going.

# Tornadoes

Tornadoes are much smaller than hurricanes, but they can be even more dangerous. Tornadoes form during violent thunderstorms, when a hot, fast-moving upward air current meets a cold, downward air current. Because of the Coriolis effect, the hot and cold currents spiral around each other into a tight funnel of clouds.

The wind inside a tornado's funnel can be as fast as 480kph (300mph), the fastest wind speeds measured on Earth. Where the funnel touches the ground, it can be up to 500m (1,640ft) wide. It roars across the land, dragging people, animals and even cars into the air. Most tornadoes only last a few minutes.

### Internet links

For links to websites where you can explore the violent nature of hurricanes and tornadoes, create a tornado online and find an animated guide to how hurricanes form, go to **www.usborne-quicklinks.com**

*A tornado looks like a huge black or grey trunk, twisting from the thunderclouds down to the ground.*

## Tornado Alley

Some places have frequent thunderstorms and lots of tornadoes. Part of the U.S.A., between Texas and Illinois, has so many that it is known as Tornado Alley. The worst tornado ever recorded there hit Ellington, Missouri, on March 18, 1925. It lasted 3½ hours, destroyed four towns and killed 689 people.

## Waterspouts

When a tornado moves over the sea a narrow column of swirling water droplets reaches into the clouds above. These tornadoes are called waterspouts (though not much water is actually sucked up from the sea). Sailors used to think they were sea monsters.

*This 19th-century engraving shows monstrous waterspouts.*

# FLOODS AND DROUGHTS

Plants, animals and people need water to survive, and they rely on the weather to bring it to them. If there is too little rain, rivers dry up and crops fail. On the other hand, too much rain causes floods, which can damage crops and buildings and wash away precious soil.

## Wet and dry

Some parts of the world always have more rain than others, and many places have wet and dry seasons. Rainy and dry periods like these are not usually a problem if they are regular, but too much or too little rain can be dangerous when unexpected weather changes take people by surprise.

*This picture shows terrible flooding in Vietnam. People are forced to use boats to get around.*

## Too much rain

Normally, rainfall soaks into the ground or flows away in streams and rivers. Floods happen when there is suddenly too much water for the ground to hold, and streams, rivers and drains overflow. The extra water can come from rain, brought by heavy storms, from ice and snow on mountains melting and flowing into streams and rivers, or even from the sea spilling onto the land.

River Nile

Aswan High Dam

Lake Nasser

*The Aswan High Dam enables people to control the flooding of the River Nile. When the river floods, it waters the land, making it fertile (good for growing crops) without causing destruction.*

## Dirt and disease

Floods are very dangerous. As well as drowning people and animals and destroying homes and crops, floods can actually cause water shortages. They cover the land with dirty water, contaminating clean water supplies and helping diseases to spread.

*Lack of rain can make soil harden, crack into lumps, and eventually crumble into dry dust.*

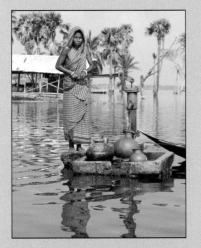

*This pump is an important source of clean water, but the dirty floodwater surrounding it could contaminate the water supply.*

## Not enough rain

A drought happens when there is less than the expected amount of rain. Droughts are often hard to predict, but they usually happen when winds change direction and no rainclouds are blown over the land. Droughts can happen in almost all climates. A bad drought may last several years and make the land completely infertile. The effects of drought can be much worse if the land has not been used carefully.

### Internet links

For links to websites with photographs, video clips and information about floods, facts about the world's wettest town and an account of the 1930s drought in the U.S.A., go to **www.usborne-quicklinks.com**

# FREEZING AND FRYING

The temperature on Earth can range from a bone-numbing -88°C (-127°F), measured at Vostok in Antarctica, to an unbearably hot 58°C (136°F), recorded at Al Aziziyah, Libya. Extreme hot and cold weather can be deadly, and often has strange effects on people and places.

*This woman is carrying frozen milk home. It is so cold in Siberia, where she lives, that there's no danger of the milk melting.*

## World of ice

Ice storms are caused by rain falling onto very cold surfaces. They happen when a mass of warm air passes through a cold area in winter, bringing rain that falls in the form of liquid raindrops, instead of as snow or hail. But when the drops of water hit cold surfaces, they immediately freeze into a coating of solid ice. Ice storms are beautiful, but lethal. If enough rain falls, outdoor surfaces can get covered in a layer of ice up to 15cm (6in) thick. It makes roads hazardous to drive on and builds up on rooftops until they cave in.

*This branch was caught in an ice storm that hit Kingston, Canada, in 1998.*

The ice also weighs down power lines until they snap. People can freeze to death in their homes.

## Blizzards

Blizzards are a combination of heavy snow, strong winds and cold temperatures. They are especially dangerous because blizzard victims are blinded by the swirling snow, as well as being caught in the freezing cold.

### Internet links

For links to websites where you can make a snowstorm online, test your knowledge of blizzards and explore an interactive map to find the hottest and coldest places on Earth, go to **www.usborne-quicklinks.com**

# Heatwaves

A heatwave is a period of extra-hot weather. Heatwaves are caused by a combination of factors. Usually, a lack of wind and cloud allows the Sun to heat up the land and the atmosphere much more than normal. The hotter the air is, the more moisture it can hold as a gas. This makes the air very humid, which makes it feel "sticky".

In some hot places, people have siestas – they sleep during the hottest part of the day to avoid the Sun.

*This Egyptian boy's white clothes reflect the Sun's heat and help to keep him cool in hot weather.*

# Heatstroke

Heatstroke is usually caused by staying out in the sun too long. Normally, if you get too hot, your body sweats. The sweat evaporating from your skin helps you cool down. But heatstroke stops your body from sweating so that you get much too hot, and may go into a coma.

Heatstroke can happen quickly, especially inside a car, where the windows act like a greenhouse and stop heat from escaping. This is why animals and babies should never be left inside cars on hot days.

# Sun and skin

Although the Sun provides warmth and energy, direct sunlight can be bad for you. It can cause wrinkles, sunburn and even skin cancer.

*A poster advising Australians to wear T-shirts, sunscreen and sunhats*

# Hot and bothered

Hot weather can affect how we behave. For example, statistics show that in New York, U.S.A., the murder rate rises as the temperature goes up, and most big riots start on hot, humid nights. No one is sure why heat makes people angry.

*This riot took place in the hot city of Los Angeles, in western U.S.A., in 1992.*

# STRANGE WEATHER

U nusual, extreme weather, often called freak weather, can take people by surprise. Sometimes it can be so odd it doesn't seem like weather at all. Strange lights in the sky, clouds that look like UFOs, and even showers of frogs, are all natural weather phenomena.

## Weather beliefs

When strange weather strikes, people often think they're seeing something magical or supernatural. Weather may lie behind many traditional beliefs in fairies and ghosts, and also behind sightings of UFOs. One type of cloud, called a lenticular cloud, looks exactly like a flying saucer.

*Lenticular clouds are shaped by waves of wind blowing around mountaintops. This one was seen at Mauna Kea, Hawaii, U.S.A.*

## Strange lights

The aurora borealis and aurora australis light up the sky around the poles with blue, red, green and white patterns. They are caused by streams of electrical particles which come from the Sun. When they interact with the gases in the Earth's atmosphere, they release energy which lights up the sky.

*A solar flare is a storm on the Sun that sends electrical particles out into space, causing auroras on Earth.*

*The aurora borealis appears in the northern skies, and is sometimes called the Northern Lights.*

# Raining frogs

"Rain" consisting of animals, fish or other objects has been reported many times through the centuries. The Roman historian Pliny reported a shower of frogs almost 2,000 years ago, and in the fourth century, fish fell on a town in Greece for three days. During a storm in England in 1939, so many frogs fell that witnesses were afraid to walk around in case they squashed them.

Showers like this, also known as "skyfalls", are probably caused by tornadoes* sucking up animals from ponds and rivers. Frogs are most often reported, but there have also been showers of snails, maggots, worms, pebbles and even sheep.

*The common frog, a species seen falling from the sky*

*This magazine from May 1958 shows a skyfall of frogs which had recently been reported.*

## Internet links

For links to websites where you can watch video clips of auroras and find out about weather folklore and superstitions, go to **www.usborne-quicklinks.com**

# Big waves

Freak waves are one of the most dangerous types of unusual weather, though not all big waves are freak waves. Freak waves can appear from nowhere, even in calm conditions. Scientists think big waves like this may form when several smaller waves merge together. These waves are especially dangerous because people are not prepared for them.

*Tornadoes, 83

# WEATHER FORECASTING

W eather often seems random but, by careful observation, meteorologists (weather scientists) can learn how weather behaves and how to predict it. Radar and satellites* help them to track clouds and watch weather patterns from space.

*This satellite image shows the temperature of the sea. Water evaporates from warm areas (shown in pink) and forms clouds. Maps like this are used to predict rain or droughts.*

## Measuring weather

Meteorologists measure different aspects of the weather, such as temperature, atmospheric pressure* and the amount of rainfall, at weather stations around the world. Weather balloons and weather planes carry instruments into the sky, where they can track the movements of clouds and high-altitude winds.

## Weather technology

Weather satellites have been used since about 1960 to record the Earth's weather from space. From their positions in orbit above the Earth, satellites can take photographs and measure the temperature of the Earth's surface.

*Geostationary satellites, like the weather satellite shown here, hover 36,000km (22,370 miles) above the Equator.*

On the ground, radar equipment is used to detect cloud patterns. Radar waves are sent out, bounce off raindrops and are collected by giant radar dishes. Computers collect the signals and create maps which show where rain clouds are heading.

*Atmospheric pressure, 96; satellites, 252

# Predicting weather

To forecast weather, readings from weather stations and satellites are stored in powerful computers. The data can then be examined to detect patterns and make predictions. At the moment, meteorologists can only predict weather a few days in advance. Weather can change so quickly that the forecasts are sometimes wrong.

## Internet links

For links to websites where you can look up weather forecasts around the world, see examples of what weather satellites do and try to predict the weather, go to **www.usborne-quicklinks.com**

**Morning**

Isobars show atmospheric pressure. Each line joins up points that have the same pressure.

*A cyclone (area of low pressure) in the middle of a storm*

*Widely-spaced isobars show a very slight change in atmospheric pressure, which means gentle winds.*

*Weather maps use lines called isobars to show differences in atmospheric pressure\*, and symbols to indicate sunshine, rain and snow.*

*A satellite photograph of a hurricane over the Pacific Ocean*

Autumn in the Cache National Forest, Idaho, U.S.A.

# CLIMATE

# THE EARTH'S ATMOSPHERE

Surrounding the Earth is a blanket of gases which makes up its atmosphere. The atmosphere contains the air we need to breathe. It also affects weather and climate and protects us from extremes of temperature and from the Sun's harmful rays.

## The atmosphere's structure

The gases surrounding the Earth are held by its gravity, a force which attracts things to Earth. The atmosphere is divided into layers according to the temperature of these gases. The diagram below shows the different layers.

*This diagram shows some of the layers in the Earth's atmosphere. The outermost layer, the exosphere, is not marked; it is around 500km (310 miles) from Earth.*

HEIGHT (km)

100
90
80
70
60
50
40
30
20
10
Sea level

**THERMOSPHERE**
*Bright lights in the sky, called auroras\*, are caused by electrical particles in this layer.*

— MESOPAUSE

**MESOSPHERE**
*Falling rocks, called meteors, burn up as they reach this layer.*

— STRATOPAUSE

**STRATOSPHERE**
*Planes usually fly in this layer because the air is very still.*

— TROPOPAUSE

**TROPOSPHERE**
*This is the layer where the weather is created.*

## The troposphere

The troposphere is the layer of the atmosphere nearest to the Earth's surface. As well as a mixture of gases, this layer contains clouds, dust and pollution. It extends to between 10km (6 miles) and 20km (12 miles) from the Earth. Temperatures are high near the Earth because the air is heated from below by the Earth's surface, which is warmed by the Sun. Higher up, the air is thinner and can't hold as much heat, so temperatures decrease.

The troposphere is the layer where the weather is produced. It gets its name from the Greek word *tropos* which means "a turn". This is because the air there is constantly circulating\*.

## The stratosphere

The upper limit of the stratosphere is around 50km (30 miles) from the Earth's surface. The stratosphere contains a concentration of ozone gas. This layer of ozone gas is very important, as it absorbs ultraviolet rays, which can cause skin cancer, from the Sun.

## The mesosphere

The mesosphere reaches to a height of around 80km (50 miles). Temperatures there are the coolest in the atmosphere because there is very little ozone, dust or clouds, which absorb energy from the Sun. It is warmer at the bottom as there is more ozone there.

## The thermosphere

Temperatures in the thermosphere can be extremely high, reaching up to 1,500°C (2,732°F). This is because there is a high proportion of a gas called atomic oxygen. This gets warmed as it absorbs energy from the Sun.

*The bright pink areas in this picture show a hole in the layer of ozone gas over Antarctica.*

## The ozone layer

The layer of ozone gas in the stratosphere is being damaged by chemicals called chlorofluorocarbons (CFCs), which are used in some spray cans and refrigerators. At certain times of year, a hole in the ozone layer appears over Antarctica, and in other areas the ozone layer becomes very thin. This damage means that more of the Sun's harmful ultraviolet rays reach the Earth's surface.

### Internet links

For links to websites where you can see the latest images of the ozone hole and find out more about the Earth's atmosphere with activities and experiments, go to **www.usborne-quicklinks.com**

*When you fly in a plane in the stratosphere you can often see the clouds in the troposphere below.*

PH-BFO

# AIR AND OCEAN CURRENTS

As the Sun heats the Earth, it causes air and water to move around in the form of currents. As particles of air and water are heated, they first expand and rise and then they cool and fall, producing patterns of circulating air and water, which are crucial in determining climate.

*The circular shapes on the satellite image in the background are called spiral eddies. They are swirls of water that have separated from the main band, or current, of water.*

## Moving air

The air around us is constantly pushing in every direction. The force that it exerts is known as atmospheric pressure.

The movement of air is affected by temperature. The Sun heats up the land and oceans, which in turn heat the air directly above in the troposphere*. As the air is heated, it rises and so leaves behind an area of low pressure. When the air cools, it sinks down on the Earth's surface in a different area, causing high pressure.

Because the Sun doesn't heat up the world evenly, there are differences of pressure. Where there is a difference, air flows from high to low pressure areas in order to even out the pressure. This moving air is wind. As the air moves, the spinning of the Earth causes it to be deflected sideways. This deflection is known as the Coriolis effect*.

## Global winds

Air is constantly circulating between the tropics and the poles as global winds. Warm air flows from the tropics and displaces the cold air at the poles, which then flows back toward the tropics. Global winds form because areas near the Equator receive more heat from the Sun than other areas. As the air is heated, it rises and spreads out. When it cools, it sinks at around 30° north and south of the Equator. This increases pressure at the Earth's surface and air at the base of the atmosphere is forced outward in the direction of both the Equator and the poles. The surface air currents moving toward the Equator are called the trade winds.

*A satellite image showing winds over the Pacific Ocean. The tiny arrows overlaying the image show the direction of the winds.*

*Coriolis effect, 82; troposphere, 94

# Moving water

*This image shows ocean currents around the world. The red areas are fast currents and the light blue areas are slow currents.*

Ocean currents are wide bands of water, like rivers that flow in the world's oceans. They sweep around the oceans, moving water between hot and cold places.

Heat from the Sun also causes the movement of water in the form of currents. However, in the oceans, the temperature difference between the poles and the Equator is greater than it is on land. Near the Equator, the Sun's rays penetrate far below the ocean's surface. At the poles, the Sun's rays hit the water at a shallow angle. This causes the water to act like a mirror, reflecting rather than absorbing the Sun's rays.

*A satellite picture of part of the Gulf Stream, a current of water that flows in the Atlantic Ocean*

## Internet links

For links to websites where you can watch animations of air and ocean currents and find out what El Niño is and how it can wreak havoc around the world, go to **www.usborne-quicklinks.com**

## Effects of currents

Currents vary in temperature and move at different speeds. If a current is much warmer or cooler than the surrounding water, it can dramatically affect the climates of the nearby coastal areas. A warm current called the Gulf Stream, which runs between the Gulf of Mexico and Europe, brings a mild climate to northwest Europe.

## El Niño

The incredible effect that the warming of the ocean can have on weather and climate is illustrated by a phenomenon known as El Niño. Every few years, a current of water in the Pacific, off the northwest coast of South America, suddenly becomes warmer. Scientists are not sure why it happens, but it causes a chain of climatic changes around the world, including floods and severe storms.

# NATURAL CYCLES

Some substances, such as nitrogen and carbon, are constantly changing form as they move around in huge cycles. This exchange of substances is essential to life on Earth. The air, land, water, plants, animals, and even your own body, all form a part of these cycles.

*This magnified part of a pea plant contains bacteria which convert nitrogen from the air into a form the plant can use.*

## Keeping a balance

Living things take in substances such as oxygen, nitrogen, carbon and water from the world around them through food, soil and air. They use them to live and grow. When a plant or animal dies and decays, its body is broken down and gases are released into the air. The cycle continues, with these substances being used again and again. This process maintains the balance of gases in the air.

## The nitrogen cycle

*This diagram shows some of the different forms that nitrogen takes.*

*Plants take in nitrogen from the air.*

*Plants are eaten by animals.*

*Bacteria convert ammonia in the soil into nitrates, which are then taken in by plants.*

*As dead plants and animals decay, nitrogen is released into the soil.*

Nitrogen (chemical symbol – N) makes up 78% of the air. Plants and animals need it for growth. Plants take in nitrogen from the air and the soil. Bacteria convert the substance into a form the plants can use. Animals obtain nitrogen by eating plants or by eating animals that have eaten plants. When plants and animals die and decay, fungi and bacteria break down their remains and nitrogen is released back into the soil.

*This dung beetle is feeding on animal dung. Insects like this help to break down plant and animal matter.*

One form that carbon can take is charcoal, as shown here. Charcoal can be burned as a fuel. When it is burned, it gives out carbon dioxide.

## Upsetting cycles

Left alone, these cycles create a natural balance of gases. However, human activities interfere with this balance by adding waste and pollution to the atmosphere. The effects of human disruption on the carbon cycle are described on pages 102 to 103.

When farmers harvest crops, they break the nitrogen cycle because the plants are not allowed to decay naturally. Farmers often use a chemical fertilizer* to replace nitrates in soil. If too much is added, it can seep through the soil into rivers, where it can affect plants and animals.

## The carbon cycle

Carbon forms part of the gases in the air, mainly as carbon dioxide (chemical symbol – $CO_2$), which is a compound of carbon and oxygen. Plants take in $CO_2$ from the air and use it to make food. At night, they give out $CO_2$.

Animals obtain carbon by eating plants. They release carbon in their waste and when they breathe out. $CO_2$ is also released when plants and animals die and decay. Carbon can be stored in the form of fossilized remains. Eventually these form fossil fuels* such as coal and oil, which release $CO_2$ when burned.

The algae in this canal are thriving because of excess nitrates running into the canal from fertilizer used on nearby farmland.

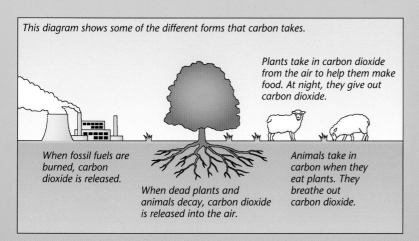

This diagram shows some of the different forms that carbon takes.

Plants take in carbon dioxide from the air to help them make food. At night, they give out carbon dioxide.

When fossil fuels are burned, carbon dioxide is released.

When dead plants and animals decay, carbon dioxide is released into the air.

Animals take in carbon when they eat plants. They breathe out carbon dioxide.

### Internet links

For links to websites where you can take a closer look at the Earth's natural cycles and explore animated scenes and try a quiz on how the carbon cycle works, go to **www.usborne-quicklinks.com**

*Fertilizer, 30; fossil fuels, 26

# WORLD CLIMATES

The long-term or typical pattern of weather in a particular area is known as its climate. Climates vary enormously in different parts of the world. They determine the character of an area, affecting the plants, animals and people that live there.

*This map of the Earth's surface contains information from several different satellites\*. It shows some of the main climate types around the world.*

*Maple trees grow in temperate regions.*

 *Temperate and tropical regions are green. They contain lots of vegetation.*

 *Tropical grasslands and deserts are yellow and brown. They are dry, with little vegetation.*

 *Snowy regions are light blue or white. The swirling white masses are clouds.*

## Climate types

Areas can be grouped into several main climate types, such as polar, temperate and tropical. These are also known as biomes\*. The most important factor in determining an area's climate is its latitude\*, because this affects the amount of heat received from the Sun. This in turn has a crucial effect on the vegetation and animals which give each climate zone its distinctive characteristics.

The map above shows how areas at the same latitude share broadly similar climates. The different climate zones are described in more detail on pages 116–131.

Other factors, such as height and distance from the ocean, are also very important in determining the climate of a particular area.

## High places

Mountain regions have a different climate from the surrounding lowland areas. It rains and snows frequently, as the mountains force clouds to rise higher. Temperatures can be extremely cold because mountain air is thinner and can't hold as much heat.

### Internet links

For links to websites where you can explore an interactive climate map, take a tour and find facts about world climates and make your own climate map, go to **www.usborne-quicklinks.com**

*Moose live in forests in cool temperate regions.*

## Land and sea

Climate is affected by the oceans. Places near the sea have a maritime climate, a milder and wetter climate than areas farther inland. Temperatures there are not usually so extreme as inland areas at the same latitude. This is because ocean temperatures change less than land temperatures and this affects the climate of areas nearby. The climates of inland areas are known as continental climates.

## Land surfaces

Different land surfaces absorb the Sun's rays differently. Light surfaces, such as snow-covered land or deserts, reflect the Sun's rays, whereas dense forests and dark soils absorb them. Where a higher proportion of the rays is reflected, clouds are less likely to form. This means that areas with lighter land surfaces will have less rainfall. Clouds also reflect the Sun's rays, affecting the amount of energy reaching the Earth's surface.

# GLOBAL WARMING

Some of the gases in the atmosphere help to keep the Earth warm. They trap heat from the Sun in the same way that a greenhouse traps heat. This process is known as the greenhouse effect. But, as these gases increase, the Earth might be getting too warm.

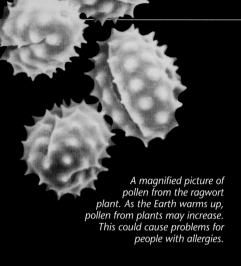

*A magnified picture of pollen from the ragwort plant. As the Earth warms up, pollen from plants may increase. This could cause problems for people with allergies.*

## Greenhouse gases

The Earth's surface absorbs much of the heat from the Sun. This is then given off as heat energy into the atmosphere. It gets trapped there by gases, such as carbon dioxide, which are known as greenhouse gases. As the amount of greenhouse gases increases, more heat is trapped.

Most greenhouse gases occur naturally, but industrial processes and other pollution are increasing the amount of greenhouse gases in the atmosphere. Scientists think that this may be causing the Earth to become warmer. This process is known as global warming.

*Plants are important for the balance of greenhouse gases because they take in carbon dioxide.*

## Balance of gases

Whenever we burn oil, coal or wood, carbon dioxide is released. For example, when forests are burned to make room for farming, they release carbon dioxide. This also reduces the number of plants available to absorb carbon dioxide, upsetting the natural balance of the carbon cycle*. Factories, power stations and cars also give out pollution which may contribute to global warming.

*Huge roads, like this one, are useful for car drivers, but the pollution from cars could be contributing to global warming.*

McArthur Blvd
n Wayne Airport
NEXT EXIT

*Venice, Italy, is a city built on over 100 tiny islands in the Lagoon of Venice. If the sea level rises, it may eventually disappear under the sea.*

## Rising sea level

As atmospheric temperatures rise, so does the sea level. This will eventually result in the flooding of low-lying areas. Scientists estimate that the sea level is rising at a rate of 1–2mm (0.04–0.08in) each year. It may rise by another 0.25–1m (0.8–3.3ft) by the year 2100. There are two main reasons for the increased volume of water. Firstly, as the oceans heat up, the water expands. The sea level rises because the water takes up more space. Secondly, the higher temperatures may cause glaciers and icecaps on land to melt. This water will then flood into the sea.

## Changing climate

Scientists predict the average atmospheric temperature will increase by around 2°C (3.6°F) this century. Extreme weather may become more common. Climate change will affect the habitats* of plants and animals. Some species may thrive, but others may struggle to survive.

### Internet links

For links to websites with the latest climate news, and games, quizzes and animations on the greenhouse effect and the causes of global warming, go to **www.usborne-quicklinks.com**

## Shifting the balance

People have already begun to take steps to reduce the emission of gases that contribute to global warming. The main ways that this can be achieved are by looking at alternative energy sources and reducing pollution levels.

*Carbon cycle, 99; habitats, 112

# CHANGING CLIMATES

**E**ver since the Earth was formed, its climate has been changing. Volcanic eruptions, collisions with asteroids, and the path of the Solar System through space may all have caused climate changes that affected the atmosphere, the landscape and living things.

*The red outline on this map shows the areas of the Earth that were covered in ice during the last Ice age. The white areas are those places that are still covered in ice today.*

*Long ago, widespread volcanic activity could have caused fires which damaged habitats, wiping out various species.*

## Ice ages

Throughout its history, the Earth has gone through several Ice ages, when the climate was colder than it is now, and glaciers* and ice sheets spread across much of the globe. Sea levels were lower as well, because so much of the water was frozen into ice on land.

Ice ages have several causes. As the galaxy spins, the Earth may enter the magnetic fields which shield it from the Sun's heat. Earth may also sometimes change its orbit, move away from the Sun and get cooler. There may be another Ice age in the future.may enter

### Internet links

**Website 1** Explore a climate timeline for the past ten billion years.

**Website 2** See an animated map of how climate zones have changed.

For links to these websites, go to **www.usborne-quicklinks.com**

## Explosions

Long-term climate patterns can be affected by sudden events, such as huge volcanic eruptions, or asteroids* hitting the Earth. Events like this in the past could have filled Earth's atmosphere with smoke and dust which blocked out the sunlight, making the climate cold and dark and killing plants and animals.

# Geological evidence

We can tell the Earth's climate has changed by looking at rocks and fossils. Many rocks form gradually in layers. These layers provide a record of what happened, called the fossil record. In warmer periods of the Earth's history, more plants and animals were alive and more fossils were preserved. Layers with fewer fossils show colder periods, when there were fewer living things.

Landscapes also hold clues about the past. For example, a U-shaped valley shows where a glacier gouged out a huge channel during an Ice age.

*Fossils found in stone, such as this well-preserved bird fossil, can reveal which types of animals lived in which places long ago.*

*As well as blocking out vital sunlight with smoke and ash, volcanic eruptions can destroy plant life by smothering the land with lava, hot molten rock that burns everything in its path.*

# Moving continents

As the plates* that make up the Earth's crust have slowly changed position, the climate of each continent has altered. For example, what is now West Africa was once at the South Pole. As it got nearer the Equator, its climate warmed up as it received more sunlight. Climates are also affected by ocean currents*. As the continents separated from each other, currents could flow between them, bringing cold or warm water from other parts of the Earth.

# WORLD ECOSYSTEMS

*A red-eyed tree frog*

# PLANT LIFE ON EARTH

The Earth is the only planet known to support living things, or organisms. There are millions of different kinds of living things on Earth. They fall into two main groups: animals and plants. To survive, nearly all of them need light and heat from the Sun, food, water and air.

*The Earth is the only planet so far discovered whose land looks green from space.*

## The green planet

Most plants are green because they contain a green substance called chlorophyll, which helps them to make their food. From space, the Earth's land looks mainly green, because of the billions of plants on its surface.

## Plant food

Plants feed themselves by turning sunlight into food chemicals. This process is called photosynthesis, which means "building with light". For this to happen, plants also need water and nutrients* from the soil, and carbon dioxide from the air. They then use all these things to make glucose, a kind of sugar, which they can feed on.

### Internet links

For links to websites where you can find out why we need plants, take a fun look at how photosynthesis works and test your knowledge with a quiz, go to **www.usborne-quicklinks.com**

*The Sun provides energy, in the form of light.*

*A plant's flowers contain parts that make seeds. These grow into new plants.*

*This part of the underside of a leaf has been magnified.*

*Leaves convert water and carbon dioxide into glucose and oxygen.*

*The stalk carries water and nutrients from roots to the leaves and flower.*

*Leaf stalk*

*Tiny holes called stomata let carbon dioxide in, and water and oxygen out.*

*Nutrients, 28

## Why we need plants

Plants are essential for life on Earth. Without them, the planet would look totally different, and there would be no people or animals. Animals – even meat-eaters – need plants, because plants form the basis of all food chains*.

Plants also give out oxygen and water, which animals and people need; and their roots hold the soil together. Without them, much of the soil would wash away into the sea. We use plants to make medicines, fabrics and perfumes, and we get wood from trees.

*The aloe is one of the thousands of plants we use to make cosmetics and natural medicines.*

## Plant babies

Like all living things, plants reproduce (make new versions of themselves). Most do this by making seeds. The seeds usually form inside the flower. They may then be carried a long way by the wind before falling to the ground and beginning to grow.

*A sunflower contains hundreds of seeds like these. Like the seeds of many plants, they are an important source of food for people and animals.*

## Types of plants

Different types of living things are called species. There are millions of species of plants, from tiny flowers to enormous trees called giant sequoias, which are the biggest living things on Earth. Different species are suited, or adapted, to living in different parts of the world. In deserts, for example, where water is scarce, cactuses grow thick stems for storing water.

*A giant sequoia tree. These are found mainly in California, U.S.A.*

*Food chains, 112

# ANIMAL LIFE ON EARTH

There are millions of types, or species, of animals living on Earth. They include insects, fish, birds, reptiles, amphibians and mammals, such as humans. Unlike plants, animals can move around to find food and water.

*The bald eagle is a carnivore. It feeds mainly on fish, swooping down and snatching its prey from lakes and rivers.*

## How animals live

All animals have to eat in order to survive. Herbivores eat plants and carnivores eat animals. There are some animals, such as giant pandas, that eat both plants and animals. These are called omnivores. Most humans are also omnivores.

*Honeyeaters are herbivores. They feed on nectar, a sweet juice found inside flowers.*

Many animals have to watch out for predators, which are other animals that want to eat them. Their bodies have to be adapted for running fast or hiding. Some animals, such as zebras, are camouflaged, which means they are patterned so that they blend in with their background and are harder for predators to see. But some predators are also camouflaged, so they can creep up on their prey.

## Tools for eating

Animals' bodies are adapted to suit the kind of food they eat. Herbivores usually have flat, broad teeth designed for munching plants, while most carnivores have sharp teeth to help them grab and grip their prey (the animals they eat) and tear raw flesh.

*You can see the long, sharp teeth in this badger's skull. They are good for gripping and slicing through flesh.*

*In this roe deer's skull, you can see the long front teeth which are suited to biting off pieces of plants and flat molar teeth which are good for chewing plants.*

## Natural selection

Why are animals and plants so well adapted to their way of life? One answer might be that they have gradually changed, or evolved, over a very long time to suit the places they live in and the food that is available to them. In the 19th century, a scientist named Charles Darwin (1809–1882) put forward a theory, which he called "natural selection", to explain how these changes might happen.

According to Darwin, individual animals and plants sometimes have qualities that help them to survive. For example, in a green forest, a green bug would probably survive longer than a brown bug, because its appearance would help it to avoid being seen and eaten.

The individuals that survive the longest are likely to have more babies, and will pass on their useful qualities to them. Over a very long time, each species will gradually develop all the most useful qualities for surviving in its own habitat.

### Internet links

For links to websites where you can watch video clips of animals, read lots of animal facts and find online games and activities, go to **www.usborne-quicklinks.com**

## Breathing

As well as eating food, animals need to breathe oxygen, a gas which is found in air and water. All animals take oxygen into their bodies, in a variety of different ways.

*Gills*

Fish have gills, which filter oxygen from the water as it flows through them.

*Spiracles*

Insects take in oxygen through tiny holes in their bodies, called spiracles.

*Lungs*

Humans and many other animals have lungs, which extract oxygen from the air.

## Useful animals

Animals are very useful to humans, providing meat, milk, eggs, wool, silk, leather and even medicines. Many animals are farmed carefully, but some species are in danger of dying out and becoming extinct, because humans have killed too many of them. You can find out about these endangered species on page 115.

*Guanacos are hunted for their long, thick wool.*

# ECOSYSTEMS

A place where a plant or animal lives is called its habitat. For example, seas, rivers, mountains, forests and deserts are all habitats. Together, a habitat and the group, or community, of plants and animals that live in it form a whole system, called an ecosystem.

*Snowy owls and lemmings are part of the ecosystem in the Arctic.*

*Meat-eaters survive by eating other animals found in their habitat. These cheetahs are chasing a Thomson's gazelle.*

## Food webs

In an ecosystem, many different food chains intertwine to make up a complicated system known as a food web. Each animal in the web may eat many different species and be hunted by several others. The diagram below shows part of a food web in a mountain forest in a northern country, such as Canada. Each blue arrow points from a species that is eaten to a species that eats it. (This is a simplified diagram. In fact, there would be many more species than this in one ecosystem, and the whole food web would be too complicated to fit on the page.)

## Food chains

The animals and plants in an ecosystem depend on each other for food. One species eats another, and is in turn eaten by another. This is called a food chain. Plants form the first link in a food chain, because they make their own food from sunlight, using a process called photosynthesis*. Plant-eating animals (herbivores) eat plants, and meat-eating animals (carnivores) eat herbivores and other carnivores.

*As in all ecosystems, plants form the basis of this food web.*

*Photosynthesis, 108; soil, 28

## Trophic levels

A food web has several layers, known as trophic levels. There are different kinds of plants or animals on each level.

*The Sun provides light and energy for plants.*

**Tertiary consumers**
*Animals that eat other meat-eating animals*

**Secondary consumers**
*Animals that eat plant-eating animals*

**Primary consumers**
*Animals that eat plants*

**Producers**
*Plants that use the Sun's energy to manufacture food*

**Decomposers**
*Organisms that feed on dead plants and animals and break them down in the soil\**

## The energy cycle

Plants and animals use food to make energy, which helps them grow, move, keep warm, make seeds and have babies. When plants or animals die, they are broken down by decomposers, such as fungi, and the energy goes back into the soil in the form of chemicals. These help plants to grow, and the cycle begins again.

### Internet links

**Website 1** Predators and prey, habitats, food webs and the cycle of life.

**Website 2** Find out more about ecosystems.

For links to these websites, go to **www.usborne-quicklinks.com**

## Competition

Each type of plant or animal has a unique place in its ecosystem, known as a niche. If two different species try to compete for the same food, the stronger one survives, and the other dies out or has to move away. Different species in an ecosystem can survive side by side by eating slightly different types of food. For example, in African grasslands, elephants reach up to eat the higher branches of trees and bushes, gerenuks eat leaves lower down and warthogs nibble grasses on the ground.

## Biomes

The Earth has several climate types, or biomes, such as rainforests and deserts. Each biome supports many ecosystems, but can also be seen as one big ecosystem. Together, all the biomes combine to form the biggest ecosystem of all, the Earth itself.

*An elephant's long trunk allows it to reach to the tops of trees to collect food, while other animals eat the leaves lower down.*

# PEOPLE AND ECOSYSTEMS

Like every other plant and animal on Earth, you are part of an ecosystem. But there are now so many humans that we need more energy and make more waste than our ecosystem can deal with.

## Using up energy

The first humans were suited to the ecosystems of the places they lived in. They ate the food that was available and used only as much energy as they needed to survive.

Now, though, we use up lots more energy than we really need to survive, because of all the things that modern humans do, such as running factories, getting around in cars and planes, and using electric lights and machines. We get most of our energy by burning fossil fuels*. This creates waste gases which can't be broken down quickly enough, so they build up around us as pollution.

## Pollution

Pollution is any waste product that nature can't easily process and recycle. Things such as exhaust from cars, smoke from factories, and plastic packaging are all pollution.

Some pollution is just ugly, but some can be dangerous. For example, exhaust fumes that build up in the air can cause asthma, and chemicals that leak from farms into rivers can kill fish and upset the local food web*.

*Smog is a kind of pollution caused when fossil fuels* are burned and give off waste gases.*

## Upsetting ecosystems

Each part of an ecosystem depends on all the other parts, making a natural balance. If one part is damaged or destroyed, it affects all the others.

*If the plants in this food chain* were destroyed, the animals farther up the chain might starve.*

## Using up space

Our farms, cities, roads and airports all need space. We use space that used to be the habitats of plants and animals. Without its habitat, an ecosystem can't work, and animals and plants die. If this happens too often, some species become extinct, which means they die out completely.

Extinction is sometimes caused by natural disasters, such as volcanic eruptions, but often it is brought about by people. Pollution, hunting and introducing animals into new areas can all cause extinctions. For example, several species of flightless birds were wiped out when humans brought dogs and cats to Australia and New Zealand.

*Wind turbines like these convert the energy of the wind into electricity. This causes less pollution than burning fuel.*

*The dodo, which lived on the island of Mauritius, died out in about 1680 after it was hunted to extinction by Dutch settlers.*

### Internet links

For links to websites where you can find out more about the delicate balance of ecosystems, play games and activities about pollution and read about conservation projects, go to **www.usborne-quicklinks.com**

## Conserving the Earth

Conservation means trying to reduce the damage done to the Earth and its species by pollution and other human activities. We can begin to conserve the Earth by using less energy, making less waste, and replacing as much as possible of the resources we use up. This is sometimes called sustainable living.

We cannot bring back plants and animals that are already extinct, but endangered species (those that are in danger of dying out) can be protected. Conservationists work to save natural habitats and protect rare wild animals from being hunted, so that they can build up their numbers.

*Snow leopards are an endangered species. They are now protected by laws and bred in zoos to try to save them.*

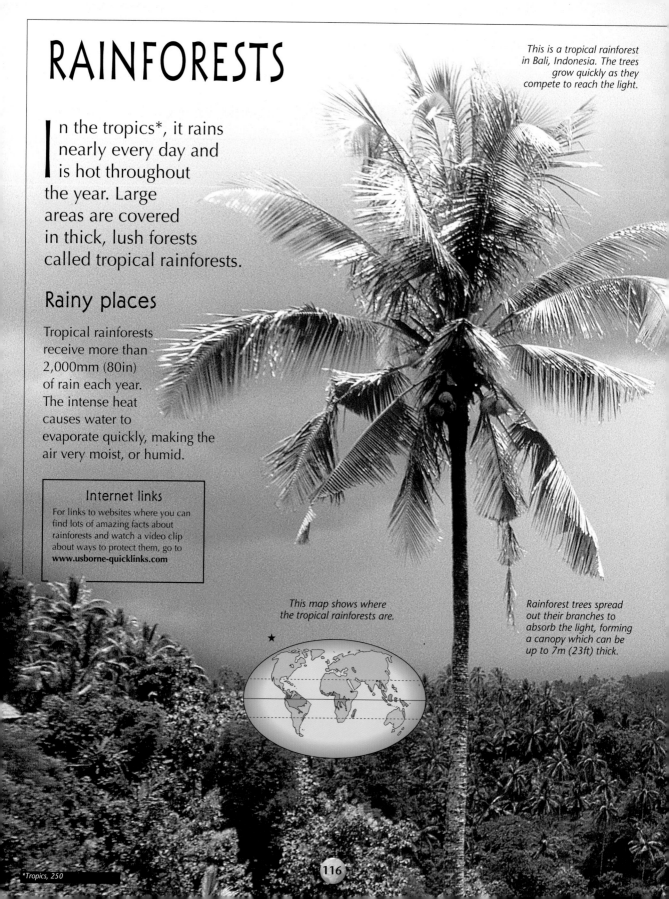

# RAINFORESTS

*This is a tropical rainforest in Bali, Indonesia. The trees grow quickly as they compete to reach the light.*

In the tropics*, it rains nearly every day and is hot throughout the year. Large areas are covered in thick, lush forests called tropical rainforests.

## Rainy places

Tropical rainforests receive more than 2,000mm (80in) of rain each year. The intense heat causes water to evaporate quickly, making the air very moist, or humid.

### Internet links

For links to websites where you can find lots of amazing facts about rainforests and watch a video clip about ways to protect them, go to **www.usborne-quicklinks.com**

*This map shows where the tropical rainforests are.*

*Rainforest trees spread out their branches to absorb the light, forming a canopy which can be up to 7m (23ft) thick.*

*Tropics, 250

## Rainforest people

Many small ethnic groups living in tropical rainforests survive by hunting animals and gathering plants, or by small-scale farming. However, their lifestyle has been threatened by people who have moved to these areas for commercial reasons. They chop down trees and burn them in order to clear land for farming and mining.

*These rainforest trees are being burned to create space for farming.*

## Animal life

Rainforests are home to over half the world's plant and animal species. Different kinds of animals have adapted to living at different levels in the rainforest. Many animals live in the branches of trees. They need to be good at climbing and able to move easily from tree to tree by swinging, jumping or gliding.

On the forest floor, it is dark and the tangled vegetation makes it difficult for some animals to move around. The larger animals tend to be sturdy so they can easily force their way through. There are also many insects.

*Colugos climb trees for food. They use the flaps of skin between their arms and legs to help them glide between trees.*

### Forests in danger

Every year, huge areas of rainforest are chopped down or burned. The disappearance of so many trees affects the balance of gases in the atmosphere. This may cause an increase in global warming*. Due to the destruction of their natural habitat, many rainforest plants and animals have died out and many others are endangered.

*Golden lion tamarins are an endangered species of monkey.*

*Global warming, 102

# TROPICAL GRASSLANDS

The tropical grasslands are flat, open plains in the central parts of continents. They occur between 5° and 15° north and south of the Equator and get their name from the grasses that make up the majority of their vegetation.

This map shows where the tropical grasslands are.

## Two seasons

The tropical grasslands have two seasons: a dry season, when the vegetation is dry and brown, and a rainy season, when the grasses become tall and green.

The rainy season occurs when the Sun is directly overhead and the trade winds* meet and cause rainfall. As the Sun moves, so does the point where the trade winds meet until the dry season begins.

## Vegetation

Only a few trees grow in the tropical grasslands, for example the acacia tree whose thick trunk is resistant to the fires that sometimes rage during the dry season. However, there are around 8,000 species of grasses, which are suited to dry conditions. They have long roots which can reach downward and sideways in search of water.

*Acacia trees in the Taragire National Park, Tanzania, Africa. Acacias are among the few trees that can survive in the dry tropical grasslands.*

### Internet links

**Website 1** Find out more about tropical grasslands.

**Website 2** Go on a photo safari in the Serengeti grasslands in Tanzania, Africa.

For links to these websites, go to **www.usborne-quicklinks.com**

*Trade winds, 96

## Grassland animals

The tropical grasslands are home to large numbers of herbivores (plant-eating animals). These attract large hunting animals, such as lions and cheetahs, that feed on them. Because the land is so exposed, many animals live in large groups, so that some animals can watch out for predators while others feed or rest.

Some of the fastest animals, such as cheetahs, gazelles and ostriches, live in grasslands. Speed is important for survival, both for the hunters and the hunted. With so few hiding places, a hunt for food often results in a chase.

*During the dry season, wildebeest move away, or migrate, to find food and water. Many thousands of wildebeest migrate together for protection.*

*Cheetahs are the fastest land mammals, reaching speeds of up to 110kph (68mph).*

## The tsetse fly

Many grassland areas are now used for farming. However, the largest grasslands, in Africa, are almost untouched. This is because of a parasite, carried by an insect called the tsetse fly, which infects humans and animals. In humans, it causes sleeping sickness, the effects of which are sluggishness, fever and sometimes death. In animals, it causes a similar disease called nagana.

*A close-up of a tsetse fly feeding on a human arm*

# MONSOONS

At certain times of year, some areas of the tropics have a period of torrential rain and another period of drier weather. This strong seasonal change is known as a monsoon. The rain can cause severe flooding, but people also rely on it for survival.

## Three seasons

Monsoons occur in certain parts of the tropics, particularly in Southeast Asia. Monsoon regions have three seasons – a long, cool dry season, a hot humid season when the land is very dry and a rainy season when there are thunderstorms on most days.

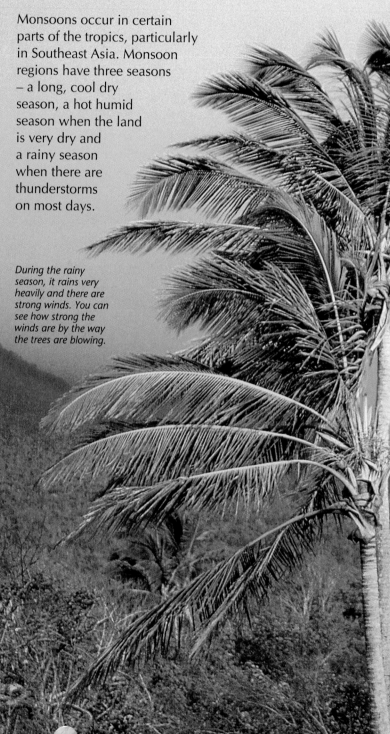

*During the rainy season, it rains very heavily and there are strong winds. You can see how strong the winds are by the way the trees are blowing.*

## Changing winds

The word *monsoon* is from an Arabic word meaning "season". It refers to the seasonal reversal of the wind direction. During the cooler season, the land is cooler than the ocean, and so winds blow from the land to the ocean, giving dry weather over the land. The warm season occurs when the midday Sun is almost directly overhead. The land is hotter than the ocean, so moist winds rush in from the ocean and shed their moisture on the land as heavy rain.

*In the dry season, winds blow from the land to the sea.*

*In the rainy season, moist winds rush in from the sea.*

# Farming

Around a quarter of the world's people live in monsoon areas. Many of them rely on growing their own food. The main crops are rice and tea, which grow well in wet conditions.

Rice in particular needs lots of water to grow. The seedlings are planted during the wet monsoon season in flooded fields called paddy fields. Rice is an important food for many poor nations, because it can be grown cheaply and in large quantities. If there is too little rain, it can be disastrous, resulting in crop failure which may in turn cause famine.

*A rice farm in China. The field has been flooded with water, as rice plants grow well in waterlogged soils.*

## Internet links

**Website 1** See dramatic pictures and find out more about monsoons.

**Website 2** Build a virtual rice paddy.

For links to these websites, go to **www.usborne-quicklinks.com**

# Diseases

*A mosquito magnified. These insects thrive in monsoon regions.*

A number of serious diseases spread easily after the wet monsoon season, because stagnant floodwater provides an ideal breeding ground for the bacteria that cause them. Typhoid and cholera are particularly common. Mosquitoes, insects which can carry diseases such as malaria and yellow fever, also thrive in the warm, wet conditions of monsoon regions.

# TROPICAL DESERTS

The tropical deserts are the hottest and driest places in the world. With so little water or shelter, only a few animals and plants are able to survive in the burning heat of the day. Very few people live in tropical deserts.

*Tropical deserts exist mainly between 15° and 30° north and south of the Equator.*

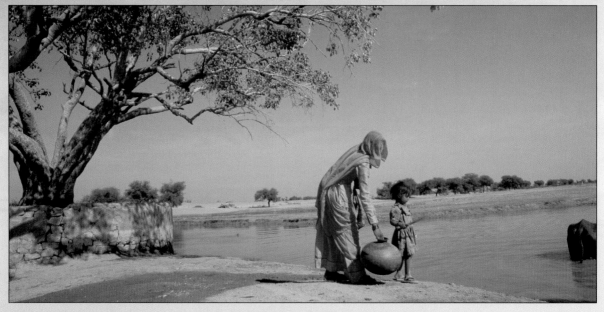

*This is a fertile area, called an oasis, in the Thar Desert, Rajasthan, India. The people are collecting water.*

## Desert climate

Most deserts are hot during the day and cold at night. During the day, the heat is intense because the Sun is high in the sky and there are few clouds to block the Sun's rays. Temperatures can reach over 52°C (126°F). At night, the lack of clouds allows heat to escape, so temperatures can drop to below freezing. Less than 250mm (10in) of rain falls on deserts each year. When it rains, it is usually in short, violent storms. If the land has been baked by the heat of the Sun, these brief rainstorms can cause floods because the rain is not absorbed quickly enough by the dry ground.

## Oases

There is water in the desert, but most of it is located underground in rocks that are porous, which means they can hold water like a sponge. In a few places, where these rocks are at the surface, moist areas called oases are formed. Birds, animals and people gather at oases to drink.

## Desert landscapes

Only 25% of the world's deserts are sandy. Most deserts consist of bare rock or stone. Some even have dramatic rocky mountains. In sandy deserts, sand often collects together to form hills called dunes, which move and change shape as the wind blows the sand across the desert.

Strong winds sometimes sweep across deserts, causing sand-storms which can wear away the rocks in their path. Over many years, this "sand-blasting" effect can produce some unusually-shaped rocks. The process of wearing away rocks in this way is a type of erosion*.

*This is a sand dune in the Sahara Desert, Africa, the biggest desert in the world. The man is one of the Tuareg, a group of people who live in the Sahara.*

### Internet links

For links to websites where you can explore the climate, landscape and geography of deserts around the world and find out how camels can survive the extreme conditions, go to **www.usborne-quicklinks.com**

## Adaptation

In order to survive in the desert, those plants and animals that live there have adapted so that they are able to cope with the heat and limited supplies of water. Some desert plants can store water in their stems or can access water deep in the ground through long roots. Many desert animals have dry droppings to help them save water.

*Camels can drink gallons of water in a few minutes and then last days without any.*

## Desert expansion

The world's deserts are increasing in size. This process, known as desertification, is caused by the destruction of the vegetation near the edges of deserts. People living in these dry areas need grass for their animals to eat and wood from trees to burn as fuel. This destruction of vegetation means that the soil is easily washed or blown away and the water cycle* is disrupted. Once this has happened, it is very difficult for vegetation to grow there.

*Erosion, 34; water cycle, 78

# MEDITERRANEAN CLIMATES

**M**editerranean climates are warm temperate* climates. They get their name from the regions bordering the Mediterranean Sea. However, other parts of the world, such as small areas around Cape Town (South Africa), Perth (Australia), San Francisco (U.S.A.) and Valparaiso (Chile) also have Mediterranean climates.

*This map shows those areas with a Mediterranean climate.*

## Warm and dry

Mediterranean climates cover only a small part of the world. They are found on the west coasts of continents between 30° and 40° north and south of the Equator.

In summer in the Mediterranean, descending air usually causes hot, cloudless weather. In winter, the westerly winds bring moist air from the Atlantic, causing wetter weather.

In the Mediterranean region itself, the Mediterranean Sea (an inland sea with a narrow link to the Atlantic Ocean) has a moderating influence on the climate of the surrounding countries, making the winters milder than they would be otherwise.

In other parts of the world that have Mediterranean climates, cold offshore currents* have a similar effect on the local climate as the Mediterranean Sea has on southern Europe.

*This town in the south of France overlooks the Cote d'Azur, a stretch of coastline by the Mediterranean Sea which is a popular spot for tourists.*

*Oranges grow well in Mediterranean climates.*

## Vegetation

There are two main types of vegetation in Mediterranean regions: trees such as cork oaks and olives, and low woody plants, or scrub. The vegetation is well adapted to the dry summer climate. Plants have thick, waxy leaves which reduce the amount of water they lose, and long roots which enable them to reach water deep underground.

## Tourism

*People sunbathing on a beach in the Cote d'Azur, southern France*

The hot, dry summers in Mediterranean countries such as Greece, Spain, Italy and southern France have made them popular destinations for tourists from cooler climates searching for summer sunshine. This has meant that tourism has become an important part of the economies of these countries. Resorts tend to be developed in strips along the coast, where closeness to the sea and pleasant beaches are also major attractions for people.

## Farming

Those places with Mediterranean climates are home to some of the world's most important wine producers. Grape vines are particularly well adapted to the climate, as they have long roots and tough bark.

*A vineyard in the Douro Valley, Portugal. The grapes are being hand-picked to make wine.*

The Mediterranean climate is also good for growing citrus fruits, such as oranges and lemons. These have thick skins which help them to retain moisture and the hot summers help the fruit to ripen quickly.

### Internet links

For links to websites where you can read more about the plants and animals that thrive in Mediterranean climates, then play a game to match plants to different biomes, go to **www.usborne-quicklinks.com**

*Ocean currents, 97; temperate climates, 126*

# TEMPERATE CLIMATES

The areas of the globe between the Arctic and Antarctic Circles and the tropics have a temperate climate. As the term temperate suggests, temperatures there are never very extreme. This vast area contains a wide range of landscapes.

*The dark blue areas of this map show the parts of the world with temperate climates.*

## Varied climates

The vegetation in temperate regions ranges from forests to dry grasslands. However, all the different areas have four seasons*: spring, summer, autumn and winter. This is because of the Earth's tilt and the way that each hemisphere faces the Sun in one season and then faces away from it in another.

## Green lands

The mid-latitudes (between 40° and 60° north and south of the Equator) have a rainy climate, which is usually described as cool temperate. The steady rain throughout the year is the result of cool air from the poles meeting warm air from the tropics. The warm air is forced upward, causing swirling patterns of clouds and rain known as depressions.

The moderate temperatures in cool temperate regions mean that vegetation has a long period of uninterrupted growth, so the landscape is very green. Most trees are deciduous, which means that they lose their leaves in winter.

This region, which includes most of Europe, contains the richest farmland areas. The fertile soil and rainfall throughout the year make it suitable for a wide variety of crops, including grains, green vegetables and deciduous fruits.

*Before the leaves on deciduous trees fall, they change from green to orange, red and yellow.*

*Seasons, 14

# Grasslands

*A view of the huge grasslands, or prairies, of North America*

The prairies of North America and the steppes of Russia are huge temperate grasslands which lie in the middle of continents. Their summers are hot and sunny, but their winters can be quite harsh because they are away from the warming effects of the ocean*.

These areas receive too little rainfall for trees to grow, so the main vegetation is grasses. In the vast, treeless prairies of North America, winter frosts break up the rich soils, but summer days are long and warm. Wheat is suited to these conditions and is grown extensively.

# Seasonal life

The lives of many animals and plants in temperate regions follow the cycle of the seasons. Annual plants complete their life's cycle in a year. They begin growing from seeds in spring and then flower in summer. In autumn, they produce their own seeds and fruit. At the end of the year the plants die.

### Internet links

For links to websites where you can find out more about temperate regions and see if you can build a healthy prairie ecosystem, go to **www.usborne-quicklinks.com**

Many animals prepare for the winter by storing up food. Some, such as the dormouse, cope with the lack of food by going into a deep sleep known as hibernation. During hibernation, an animal's breathing and heartbeat slow down and it does not need to eat. There are also animals that avoid the cold weather altogether by moving, or migrating, to warmer places.

*A dormouse hibernating in its nest during the winter months*

# POLAR REGIONS

The Arctic, the area around the North Pole, and the Antarctic, the area around the South Pole, are known as the polar regions. The temperatures there are usually below freezing and huge expanses of land and sea are covered in ice and snow.

## Antarctic

In the middle of the Antarctic Ocean is a land mass, or continent, known as Antarctica, which is covered in a thick layer of ice. Temperatures there are so low that when snow falls it doesn't melt, but builds up with each snowfall. The weight of the snow on top presses down on the lower layers to form ice.

No land mammals live permanently in Antarctica because it is so cold, but some animals, such as seals, go there to breed. A number of seabirds, including penguins, live there permanently.

*Young penguin chicks sit on their parents' feet and snuggle under a special flap of skin to keep warm. This one is a little too big for this, but it still huddles up close for warmth.*

## Arctic

The Arctic is mainly made up of the Arctic Ocean, but several countries, including Canada, jut into it. The land there, called tundra, is warm enough for animals and plants to survive.

In summer, the ice on the tundra melts and the surface of the ground thaws. The ground often becomes boggy, because deeper down it is still frozen and the water can't seep through. The frozen layer is called permafrost.

## Keeping warm

Some polar animals, such as penguins and seals, have adapted to living in the sea, away from icy winds. Other animals have different ways of coping with the cold. Polar bears have a thick layer of fat under their skin and musk oxen have thick, shaggy coats. Many polar animals have small ears, which help to reduce heat loss.

## Internet links

**Website 1** Discover the frozen wilderness of Antarctica.

**Website 2** Trek through the Arctic regions of Canada.

For links to these websites, go to **www.usborne-quicklinks.com**

# Blending in

Many polar animals have white coats, which enable them to blend in with the snowy landscape. This is called camouflage. It helps them to hide from predators or to sneak up on their prey without being seen. A few animals, such as arctic foxes and snowshoe hares have different winter and summer coats. During the summer they have brown coats which blend in easily with rocks and plants. Then as the snow falls in the winter, their coats change and become white, so they don't stand out.

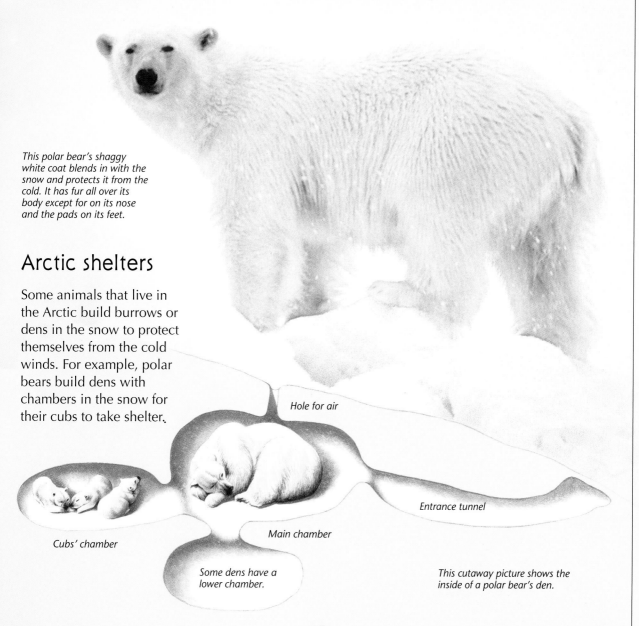

*This polar bear's shaggy white coat blends in with the snow and protects it from the cold. It has fur all over its body except for on its nose and the pads on its feet.*

# Arctic shelters

Some animals that live in the Arctic build burrows or dens in the snow to protect themselves from the cold winds. For example, polar bears build dens with chambers in the snow for their cubs to take shelter.

*Hole for air*

*Entrance tunnel*

*Cubs' chamber*

*Main chamber*

*Some dens have a lower chamber.*

*This cutaway picture shows the inside of a polar bear's den.*

# MOUNTAINS

About 5% of the world's land surface is covered by high mountains and mountain ranges. Mountain areas have more than one type of climate because, as you go up a mountain, there are fewer particles in the air and the temperature falls.

The Great Basin Desert in Nevada, U.S.A., lies on the sheltered side, or rain shadow, of the Sierra Nevada mountains.

## Mountain ranges

Most mountains are formed when the plates that make up the lithosphere* push together, forcing the land into fold mountains*. This is why mountains often occur in long lines, or ranges.

When air flows from the sea onto a mountain range, it is forced to rise. Clouds form as a result of condensation and rain or snow then falls on the mountainside. The sheltered land on the other side of the mountain, called the rain shadow, gets very little rain, and may become a desert.

*Mountain peaks in the Andes, on the border between Chile and Argentina*

## Mountain levels

The higher up a mountain you go, the colder it gets. This is because the air higher up is thinner, so it can store less heat. There are different types of weather, vegetation and animal life at different heights up the mountain. Few species live on the windy peaks, but mountain goats and sheep graze on the grassy, rocky slopes below. Farther down, below a line called the treeline, it is warm enough for trees to grow. Animals such as cougars and hares live in mountain forests.

## Internet links

For links to websites where you can find facts about the highest mountains in the world and go on a virtual climb of Mount Everest and see the panoramic view from the summit, go to **www.usborne-quicklinks.com**

*The Alpine forget-me-not flower is adapted to mountain climates. It has shorter, thicker stems and deeper roots than the common forget-me-not.*

*This shepherd from the Basque region of France is holding two baby goats. Goats are suited to the mountain climate.*

# Mountain dwellers

Both animals and people living in high mountain areas have bigger lungs to help them breathe more easily in the thin air. Animals need thick fur and people need thick coats to keep them warm. Mountain people may be cut off from other cultures. For example, the Basque people, who have lived in the Pyrenees mountains between France and Spain for thousands of years, have a very unusual language which is unlike any other on Earth. This is because, for centuries, they rarely mixed with other peoples.

*Fold mountains, 21; lithosphere, 18

These tourists riding on dromedaries in Rajasthan, India, cast huge shadows on the desert sand.

# PEOPLE AND
# THE WORLD

# FARMING

Farming means growing plants or raising animals to meet human needs. It is the biggest industry in the world and produces much of what you eat, wear and use.

This pie chart shows how the world's land is used. Livestock farming uses more space than crop farming, but produces less food.

## Types of farming

Growing plants is called crop farming or arable farming, and keeping animals is called livestock farming or pastoral farming. A mixture of both is called mixed farming. Farmers choose what to farm according to the type of land they have, the soil and the climate.

### Internet links

For links to websites where you can meet Caribbean banana farmers, visit other farms around the world and try a "You're the Farmer" game, go to **www.usborne-quicklinks.com**

*Yaks are adapted to surviving in high mountain areas. Farmers in the Himalayas keep them for milk and wool.*

## World industry

Around 45% of the world's workforce are farmers. Instead of just growing their own food, many farmers grow cash crops – crops grown specially to be sold and exported around the world. This is why, in some countries, you can buy different kinds of foods from all over the world in one supermarket.

*Wet soil and a warm climate are ideal for growing rice. In hilly areas, farmers build steps of land, or terraces, to hold the water and soil in place. This picture shows rice terraces in China.*

# Growing crops

*Combine harvesters are used to gather all kinds of crops. This one is gathering wheat. It is much quicker than harvesting crops by hand.*

Crop farming uses up around 11% of the world's land. It is the best way of producing as much food as possible from the soil, so poor countries usually grow a greater proportion of crops than rich countries do. Planting, protecting and harvesting (collecting) crops is hard work, but many farmers use machinery to do these tasks.

## Animal care

Like crops, livestock has to be looked after carefully. The animals need food, water, shelter and protection from predators and diseases. Animal products also have to be "harvested", which means collecting the animals' milk, wool or eggs, or killing them for their meat.

Farm animals often have more than one use. We may use their wool or skins as well as meat. In many countries they also work, pulling carts or farm machinery.

★

*Ostriches are farmed for meat, eggs and leather, and their feathers are used in fashion accessories.*

# FARMING METHODS

Farmers want to get as much as they can from their land. There are various ways of improving the yield, or amount of produce that comes from the land.

Helicopters like this are used by intensive farmers to spray fertilizers or pesticides onto their crops.

## Choosing the best

An important part of farming is selective breeding, which involves choosing the best plants and animals and developing them to make more useful varieties. For instance, wheat started off as a type of grass called einkorn. When replanting, early farmers chose the einkorn with the biggest seeds because these would provide more food. Gradually, einkorn developed into modern wheat, which has lots of large seeds on each stalk.

*Modern farmed wheat, developed from einkorn*

*A grass called einkorn*

### Internet links

For links to websites with virtual tours of organic farms in Uganda and Canada and an interactive map of the world's crops, go to **www.usborne-quicklinks.com**

*Modern farm pigs, such as Landrace pigs (right), are descended from wild boar (below).*

*Some of the chemical spray used by farmers may be carried by the wind and affect other areas.*

# Intensive farming

Intensive farming means using chemicals and technology to get as much as possible out of the land. Intensively farmed animals, such as pigs or hens, are kept in small stalls or cages to save space. They are fed by automatic water and food dispensers and may be given drugs to make them grow faster. Intensive farming can increase yields, but the chemicals used can also cause pollution.

*Chemical spray units attached to a helicopter*

Some people think intensive farming is cruel, because the animals are kept in unnatural conditions. "Free range" animals live in more natural conditions and are allowed to move around, or range freely.

# Organic farming

Organic farming means farming without using artificial chemicals or processes. Organic farmers use animal dung or compost instead of artificial fertilizer, and don't give animals drugs to make them grow faster. Organic food is expensive, because without drugs and artificial chemicals, diseases are harder to control and yields fall. However, there is a demand for organic products from people who are worried about their health, pollution and animal welfare.

# Bug warfare

Insects and other bugs that eat farm crops can be a big problem. Intensive farmers (see right) often spray crops to kill insects, but organic farmers do not use chemical sprays. Instead, they sometimes try biological pest control. They change the ecosystem* in their fields by introducing another species to feed on the pest species.

*These tiny aphids damage many crops. Instead of spraying, some farmers release ladybirds (ladybugs) to eat them.*

*Intensively farmed battery hens live in small cages and are usually fed by machines. The eggs they lay roll into a tray and are carried away on a conveyor belt.*

*Ecosystems, 112

# SCIENCE AND FARMING

Farming has always made use of science and technology, in the form of machinery and selective breeding. But today, more complex science is being used. Computers can make farms more efficient, while genetic engineering is being used to create new crop species.

## Big fields

Some modern farm machines, such as combine harvesters, are hard to use in small fields. So, in the last 100 years, fields in many parts of the world have been made bigger and bigger. They are more efficient than small fields because less space is taken up with walls and paths. However, large fields can also be harder to manage, as one field can contain several types of farmland and soil can be eroded more easily*.

*The picture below shows a huge wheat field on a modern farm in Sweden.*

## Precision farming

Precision farming is a new way of using science and technology to manage farms, especially those with very large fields.

For example, some combine harvesters have recording systems that measure how much yield is being collected. At the same time, the farmer uses a Global Positioning System, linked to a satellite* in space, to record where the harvester is in the field. This information is used to make a yield map.

## Computer power

Computer maps are used to compare the yield with other factors, such as the acidity or dampness of the soil. The computer then calculates how much fertilizer or water is needed. This saves time and money, and helps farmers avoid using unnecessary fertilizer or water.

*This computerized map shows which parts of a field are the most fertile. Darker areas show the highest yield, and pale areas show the lowest yield.*

Yield in tonnes per hectare

10
8
6
4
2
0

*Satellites, 252; soil erosion, 31

*The tomatoes above are covered in a type of fungus, but the plant that produced the ones on the left was genetically engineered so that its tomatoes would be resistant to the fungus.*

*Instead of being grown from seeds, the plant shoots in this tub have been "cloned" from fragments of a parent plant to make sure they have exactly the same DNA.*

# Genetic engineering

Scientists have recently learned how to make changes to DNA, the code inside cells that tells living things how to grow. This is called genetic engineering and it is very important for farming. By altering DNA, we can now change plant species to make them work better as crops.

For example, cotton plants have been genetically engineered to resist a type of weedkiller called Roundup®, which kills all other plants. When the farmer applies the weedkiller, all the weeds die, but the crop stays alive.

## Genetically modified foods

Many food crops are being genetically changed, or modified, to make them grow faster or resist pests. GM (genetically modified) foods are tested before they can be sold, but some people worry that they may be bad for us. Nobody yet knows what long-term problems they may cause. GM crops may also damage the environment, for example, by encouraging farmers to use more weedkiller which could harm animals. On the other hand, GM crops could be good news for farmers and consumers in places where crops often fail.

### Internet links

For links to websites where you can read the latest debates and try a quiz about GM foods, go to
**www.usborne-quicklinks.com**

# POPULATION

Population is the number of people who live in a particular area. The population of the world has been rising for thousands of years, and is now going up faster than ever. In very crowded areas, it can sometimes be hard for people to get enough work, food or housing.

## Counting people

With thousands of people being born and dying every day, it can be hard to measure population. Many countries hold a census, or population count, every ten years. Each household fills in a questionnaire, saying how many people live there. Experts use the results to estimate the population of a country at any one time, and to calculate the total population of the world.

## Rising numbers

The world's population began to rise quickly in the 17th century, when there were about 500 million people on Earth. There are now over six billion. Population is shooting up because the birth rate (the number of people being born in every 1,000) is higher than the death rate (the number of people dying in every 1,000). The death rate has dropped dramatically with advances in medicine and technology.

*This graph shows how population is predicted to rise and then start falling.*

## Predicting a fall

Population scientists, called demographers, predict that attempts to control population will soon have an effect. They suggest the world's population total will peak at around ten billion people in the 21st century and then begin to fall.

# Over and under

The world's population is not spread out evenly. Some areas are overpopulated, with not enough food, water or work for everyone. Other areas, such as the French countryside, are underpopulated, as young people leave the towns and villages for the big cities.

# Population density

Population density is the number of people living in a given amount of space. It is measured in people per sq km or sq mile. For example, Mongolia (a big country with a small population) has a low population density of less than two people per sq km (five people per sq mile).

## Internet links

**Website 1** Find out about population growth with animations, games and a world population atlas.

**Website 2** See how population growth affects the world's resources, with interactive maps and activities.

**Website 3** Predictions for world population growth by the year 2050.

For links to these websites, go to **www.usborne-quicklinks.com**

*This map shows the average population density by country.*

*The shading indicates the number of people per sq km (0.386 sq miles).*

- Over 500 people
- 200–500 people
- 100–200 people
- 50–100 people
- 10–50 people
- Fewer than 10 people

*Makeshift towns like this one near Cape Town, South Africa, are called shanty towns. They spring up in overpopulated areas where there is not enough housing to go around.*

# MOVING AROUND

People have been moving from one part of the world to another for thousands of years. We travel for relaxation, to find food or better jobs, to escape from danger and poverty, and to transport goods around the globe.

This picture shows Haitian refugees sailing on a rickety boat to the U.S.A. They are fleeing Haiti for economic and political reasons, and hope that the U.S.A. will let them in.

## Migration

A large number of people moving from one place to another is called a migration. The word migration is usually used to describe a permanent change of home, but it can also refer to seasonal and daily journeys. People may move within a city or country, or between countries. Many people migrate to places that have better jobs and opportunities, better schools for their children, or a better climate. Advantages like these are known as pull factors.

## Forced to move

Sometimes people leave their homes because of negative factors, or push factors, such as war or low wages. People may be forced out because they are being attacked for their ethnic origin or political views. People who have been forced to find a new place to live are often called refugees (because they are seeking refuge, or safety).

## Nomads

Some groups of people have a lifestyle which involves constantly moving around. This is called a nomadic lifestyle. Traditional nomads make their living from hunting and gathering or herding. For example, the !Kung San* people of southern Africa move around to find food and water, while the Sami* people of Lapland follow the seasonal migrations of the reindeer. There are also commercial nomads who make a living from trade and entertainment.

*A family of Bella nomads from Burkina Faso using donkeys to transport themselves and their belongings*

## Right to enter

Most people have an identity card or passport showing which country they belong to. A passport allows you to travel out of and back into your country. Some countries will only let you cross their border if you also have a visa, which shows you have been given permission to be there for a certain period of time.

*These children are descendents of American soldiers in Vietnam. They are waiting for visas so that they can travel to the U.S.A.*

### Internet links

**Website 1** View a graphic slide show of refugees displaced by war, with useful maps.

**Website 2** Find facts, personal stories and photographs about refugee lives and a world map of refugee hotspots.

**Website 3** Read the history of immigration to the US and UK.

For links to these websites go to **www.usborne-quicklinks.com**

*!Kung San, 243; Sami, 225

# SETTLEMENTS

Most people in the world live in groups of houses, apartments, huts or tents. These groups are known as settlements. There are two main kinds of settlements: rural settlements, such as farms, hamlets and villages, and urban settlements, which are towns and cities.

A satellite view of Washington D.C., capital of the U.S.A., which began as a small settlement by the Potomac River

## Choosing a site

When people first looked for permanent places to settle, it was very important to choose a site that had nearby water and fuel supplies, fertile land and shelter from strong winds. Today, people also choose sites for political, social or economic reasons.

## Good situations

Whether or not a settlement grows can depend on its situation in the surrounding area. Good situations for growth have tended to be near river mouths, in gaps in ranges of hills and at crossroads. In these areas it is easy for people to meet and trade with one another, so settlements in such places usually do well.

## Fulfilling functions

Every settlement fulfils certain functions for the people who live there, and for those who live in the surrounding area. A settlement's functions can include providing housing, employment and services such as hospitals, schools and public transportation.

The site of this village in Sudan, East Africa, may have been chosen because it has nearby wood supplies for cooking and building.

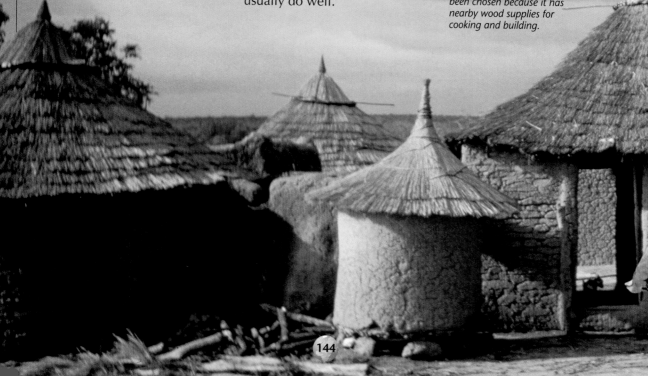

## Rural and urban

Rural settlements usually have smaller populations than urban settlements and cover smaller areas. Most of the people who live in rural settlements are employed in rural activities, such as farming or forestry, whereas people in urban settlements have a wider variety of jobs. Urban settlements are also more likely to be on good transportation routes.

## Services

Urban settlements usually provide more goods and services than rural settlements. A village is likely to have only very basic services and will probably only serve the few hundred people living there. Geographers call small settlements with few services low-order settlements.

A town usually has many stores, businesses and special services such as banks and hospitals. As well as serving the thousands of people living there, it may serve people in surrounding rural areas. Large settlements with lots of services are known as high-order settlements.

*Many urban settlements have shops and markets which offer a wide range of goods. This food market is in Hong Kong.*

### Internet links

For links to websites where you can explore the history of settlements and find key facts and information about settlement patterns, go to **www.usborne-quicklinks.com**

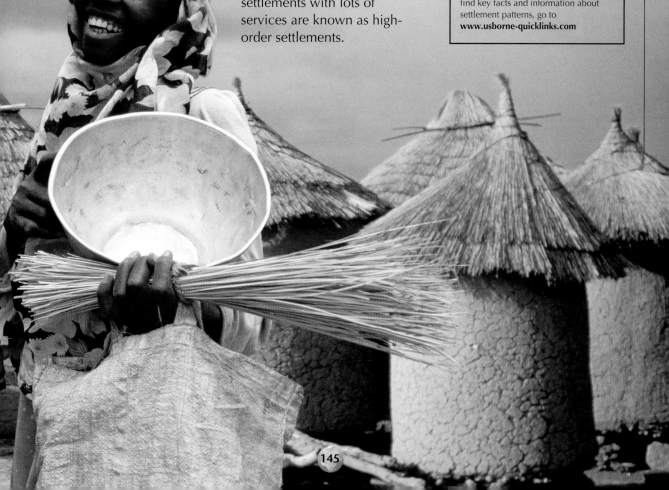

# TOWNS AND CITIES

Today, more people live in towns and cities than in the countryside and the numbers are increasing all the time as people move in search of jobs. This process of city growth is called urbanization.

A model of a typical city structure in a well-developed country

| | |
|---|---|
| 1 | Central business district |
| 2 | Light manufacturing |
| 3 | Medium-class residential |
| 4 | High-class residential |

## Megacities

Some cities have so many people living in them that they are known as megacities. Megacities have populations of more than ten million people. They are formed when people from rural areas move to one or two urban areas in their country.

Geographers predict that these megacities will continue to grow. Mexico City, for example, has an estimated population of around 18 million people, although it's difficult to get accurate figures and the population changes rapidly. Most of the world's biggest cities are in less developed countries*.

## Growing cities

As the population of a city grows, so does the size of the city itself. Eventually, towns and cities may merge and become one huge urban area, called a conurbation.

*Less developed countries, 152

## City structure

Different parts of towns and cities usually have different functions. For example, in one part of a town you may find shopping areas, offices and banks. This is called the central business district (CBD), and is generally found in the middle of a city.

Another part of town may be mainly made up of housing, and yet another may be industrial. Many cities have industrial areas lining the major roads that lead out of the city.

*This view of Atlanta, U.S.A., shows the busy roads leading in and out of the city.*

## Problems in cities

As urban populations continue to grow, towns and cities are faced with problems such as overcrowding, homelessness and pollution from industry and traffic. Housing shortages are a particular problem in poorer countries. Many people who move from the countryside to cities cannot find anywhere to live. They build huts from whatever they can find, usually on the outskirts of cities. Whole makeshift towns, called shanty towns, have grown up in this way. Some governments have tried to improve shanty towns by adding electricity, running water and sewage systems.

*This shanty town in the Philippines has been improved by building a children's playground.*

### Internet links

**Website 1** Find out about the inhabitants, histories and customs of five of the world's most famous megacities.

**Website 2** Read about how three cities (Alexandria, Cordoba and New York) developed in different periods of history.

For links to these websites, go to **www.usborne-quicklinks.com**

# EARNING A LIVING

**M**ost of the people in the world have to work to survive and support their families. As well as providing an income for their own families, the jobs most people do create wealth for their countries through taxes.

## Working the land

Billions of people live by growing crops or raising animals. Some have small farms, while others move around with their herds of animals. They usually keep some of their produce for themselves, and sell the rest to make money to buy other things.

## Working for wages

As the world becomes more industrialized and modern technology develops, more and more people are employed in paid jobs on big farms, in factories and mines, or in service industries* such as banking. Others are self-employed, which means they have their own businesses selling goods or services to other people.

*A worker in a steel factory in Germany. Steel is important in industry because it is used to make tools, machinery and vehicles. Jobs like this that involve processing steel or other materials are called secondary jobs.*

### Internet links

For links to websites where you can find out more about children working in different countries around the world and read key facts about earning a living, go to **www.usborne-quicklinks.com**

*Service industries, 151

*In small factories, like this glass factory in Bangladesh, people still do many tasks by hand that would be done by machines in larger factories. This woman is inspecting glass containers.*

# Working conditions

Most countries have laws to protect workers. For example, they make sure workplaces are safe and make it illegal for young children to work. Some places have a minimum wage and maximum working hours. However, millions of people are very poor because they are paid too little for their work. In some parts of the world, children still work in factories and down mines to make enough money for their families to survive.

*This mechanic is checking the engine of a jet plane to ensure that it is in good working order. Jobs like this that involve servicing products, transporting them or helping other people are called tertiary jobs.*

# Types of jobs

Geographers divide jobs into four main types:

**Primary** jobs involve obtaining raw materials from the Earth, e.g. mining, farming, fishing.

**Secondary** jobs involve making things out of raw materials, e.g. building, making cloth in a factory.

**Tertiary** jobs provide services for people, business and industry, e.g. hotel management, transporting goods.

**Quaternary** jobs provide information resources, e.g. accountancy, computing, property-development.

# MANUFACTURING AND SERVICES

Making new products is called manufacturing. There are many different kinds of manufacturing industries, such as making clothes and making cars. People who work in service industries are doing or supplying something for other people, such as teaching and providing banking services.

*Energy production is an example of a manufacturing industry. This power plant produces energy for homes and factories.*

## Heavy and light industries

The materials that are used to make new products are called raw materials. If an industry uses a large amount of heavy raw materials, such as coal and iron ore, it is known as a heavy industry. For example, ship-building is a heavy industry. Light industries use fewer raw materials and make products that are easy to transport.

*This machine is being used to mine lignite, which will be used as fuel by industries close to the mining site.*

## Choosing a location

Today, most manufacturing companies make goods in factories. When a company builds a new factory, it has to choose its location carefully. Most factories are built near transportation links, so that they are accessible for workers and goods, and raw materials can be moved easily. Heavy industries tend to have factories near ports, as it is cheaper to transport heavy goods by ship. Heavy industries also need to be close to the source of their bulky raw materials, to reduce transport costs.

## Footloose industries

Light industries, such as electronics companies, are often located near airports or major roads, so that they can transport their goods easily.

However, unlike heavy industries, they do not have to be close to their raw materials. Because light industries are more flexible about where they locate, they are also sometimes known as footloose industries.

## Services

There are many different kinds of services, such as healthcare, transportation, tourism and retail. Many of these services are located in the central zones of towns and cities, where they are easily accessible to their customers and workers. However, if the land in a town becomes too expensive, people may build out-of-town shopping areas.

*This is the sign for a motel in the U.S.A. Many of the people who work in the service industry have jobs in hotels, motels and restaurants.*

## Service jobs

In richer countries, many more people work in services than in manufacturing. This is because most of the work in manufacturing is now done by machines. However, service industries still need huge numbers of people. In poorer countries there are often only a few basic services available, so people have to do most things for themselves.

## Computers at work

Many service jobs are now being done with the help of computers. For example, more and more train tickets are sold by computerized machines instead of by people. Computers speed things up and make people's jobs easier to do.

### Internet links

**Website 1** Find key facts about industrial activity.

**Website 2** Look up the industries of different countries.

**Website 3** Explore the world of manufacturing and read about the different methods used to make everyday products.

For links to these websites go to
**www.usborne-quicklinks.com**

# RICH AND POOR

Standards of living vary greatly around the world. Over 80% of the world's wealth is owned by less than 20% of its people. Most of this wealth is concentrated in Europe and North America. By contrast, many people in southern African countries live in total poverty.

*There is poverty in wealthy countries as well as poorer ones. These people are homeless. They are sheltering under a bridge in Hamburg, Germany.*

*A Vietnamese businessman talking on a mobile phone and standing beside an expensive car. Ownership of cars and phones is often used as a measure of wealth.*

## Development

Development is about improving the conditions in a country or region. Poorer countries are known as less developed countries and richer countries as more developed countries. The less developed countries are mostly in the tropics and southern hemisphere.

Some poorer countries, such as Brazil, Mexico and Argentina, have recently increased wealth and improved standards of living through the development of modern industries. These are called newly industrialized countries.

## Living in poverty

Poverty isn't just about having little money. In some countries many people lack basic resources such as food and safe drinking water. They may not be able to get a job or an education and may only have access to the most basic healthcare, so life expectancy is low. Many richer countries have some people living in poverty too.

# Measuring development

Development can be measured in different ways. Sometimes a country's GNP, or Gross National Product, is used. This is the value of goods and services produced by a country. However, this only gives an indication of a country's wealth. An organization called the United Nations has studied the standard of living in different countries and has devised a system called the Human Development Index which considers other factors, such as life expectancy and education. These give us an idea of people's quality of life.

## Internet links

**Website 1** Find out about the United Nations (U.N.), an international organization working for peace and development around the world.

**Website 2** Read more about development and the Millennium Development Goals - targets to help most people fulfil their basic needs.

For links to these websites, go to **www.usborne-quicklinks.com**

# Causes of poverty

Regions can be poor for many reasons. One main cause of poverty is the exploitation of certain countries by more powerful countries. Wars can also increase poverty. As well as killing and injuring people, they lead to the destruction of buildings and resources and interrupt food production and distribution.

Some countries have problems transporting people, food and goods, because of the long distances to remote places. Others suffer from natural hazards like floods and droughts. All these things can increase poverty.

*This porter, in India, is carrying a tourist up a mountain. In some countries, jobs in tourism pay better than other jobs, but many people are still not paid fair wages or fees for their work.*

# A SMALL WORLD

With the invention of new, fast forms of transportation and communication, people often say that the world is getting smaller. This is because getting from place to place and sending messages is quicker and easier than ever before.

*Satellites in space have greatly improved communication speed. This is the DIRECTV 1-R satellite. It picks up radio, TV and telephone signals from one part of the Earth and relays them to other parts of the globe.*

*Like many forms of transportation, trains are becoming faster. This is a magnetic suspension train developed in Germany. It uses magnetic forces to travel at high speeds.*

## Transportation and trade

Moving people and things from place to place is now one of the world's biggest industries. Millions of people have jobs building cars, planes, trains, trucks and ships, and transporting goods from one country to another.

If people want to transport things over long distances, the quickest way is usually by plane. However, heavy or bulky goods are generally carried by truck, train or boat. This takes longer but is much cheaper.

## Globalization

People are now able to organize industry on a worldwide scale. This is called globalization. It means that companies in one part of the world can get materials or employ workers in another part of the world, often because they are cheaper or there are specialist skills or facilities there.

This may enable poorer countries to attract investment. But it can lead to exploitation, with companies profiting from the workforces and resources of poorer countries without paying a fair price.

## Communication

With satellite communication and the Internet, information can be relayed quickly to a huge number of people. People can work from home via online computers and have video conferences with people on the other side of the world. Some people argue that a negative effect of this is that certain cultures become dominant and that local traditions are lost as people follow similar lifestyles.

## Global tourism

Tourism is one of the world's fastest-growing industries. Over 600 million trips abroad are made by tourists each year. The sudden growth of tourism can damage the environment and culture of an area, and benefits may not be spread evenly. However, in some places people are developing sustainable tourism which addresses these problems.

## Isolated areas

People around the world are not affected equally by improvements in transportation and communication. Africa has less than 1% of the world's online computers, while North America has over 40%. In poorer countries, the roads are often in bad repair and few people have cars. Physical isolation often causes poverty because it makes trade and development difficult.

### Internet links

**Website 1**  See a history of technology and find out how it has changed the way we communicate.

**Website 2**  A guide to globalization, with case studies on clothing and sugar.

**Website 3**  Learn more about tourism, the world's largest industry.

For links to these websites go to
**www.usborne-quicklinks.com**

*Hong Kong's port, shown here with the Central Island district in the background, is very important to the city's success in international trade.*

*In many parts of the world people use animals to transport heavy loads. This is a bullock cart in Thailand.*

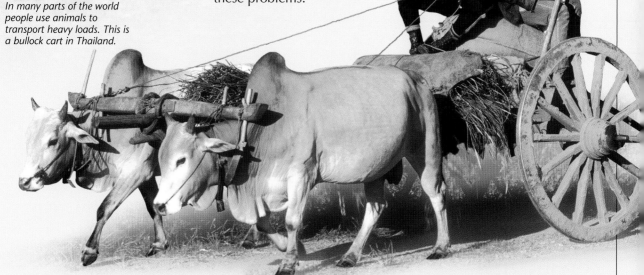

# GLOBAL CITIZENSHIP

Global citizenship is about being interested in the wider world and thinking about the ways that different countries affect one another. It involves people everywhere becoming aware of global issues, such as poverty, the environment and human rights.

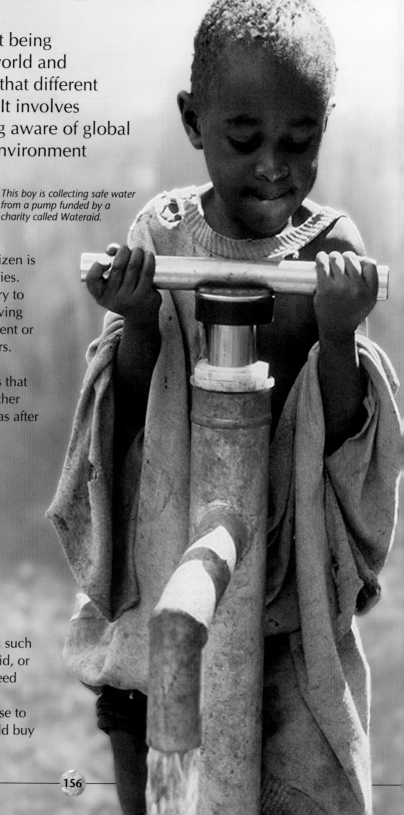

*This boy is collecting safe water from a pump funded by a charity called Wateraid.*

## Giving aid

An important part of being a global citizen is wanting to help people in other countries. People in richer countries sometimes try to help poorer countries to develop by giving aid. This may be money, food, equipment or expert help from engineers and teachers.

However, it is not only richer countries that give aid. Poorer countries often help other countries in times of emergency, such as after a flood or an earthquake.

## Kinds of aid

There are two main kinds of aid. Short-term aid may involve sending supplies to help a country after an emergency. Long-term aid aims to improve the quality of life of people in poorer countries, for example, through building and healthcare projects.

There can be problems with giving aid, such as countries becoming dependent on aid, or money not reaching the people who need help. Sometimes, in return for aid, rich countries make poorer countries promise to buy goods from them, even if they could buy them more cheaply elsewhere.

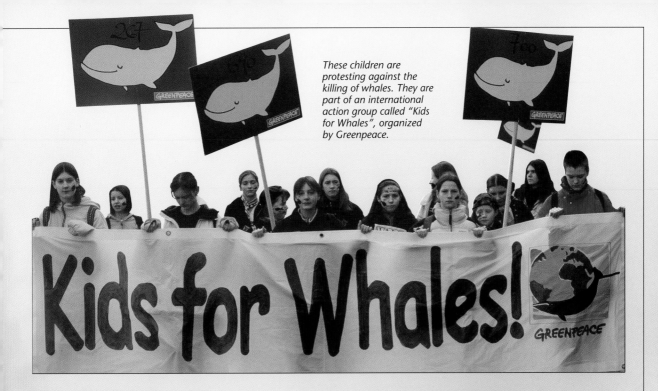

*These children are protesting against the killing of whales. They are part of an international action group called "Kids for Whales", organized by Greenpeace.*

## Internet links

**Website 1** A guide to aid, what it is, who needs it and how it is given.

**Website 2** Find ideas for ways to make the world a better place.

For links to these websites go to **www.usborne-quicklinks.com**

## Human rights

A vital part of being a global citizen is believing that everyone has the same right to food, water, education, health, security and justice. People may choose to work for human rights by campaigning about a particular issue. However, it's important that they are well informed about the complexities of the situation and the effects of their actions.

## The environment

Environmental problems not only affect the country which causes them, they can affect the whole world. For example, burning fossil fuels or chopping down trees in one country can lead to global warming*.

Being a global citizen is about learning how to take care of the world. Many people do this by joining environmental organizations, or by changing their lifestyles to help the environment, for example by using trains or buses instead of cars, or recycling household waste.

*This boy is protesting against French nuclear tests on Cook Island, in the Pacific.*

American football fans wave pom-poms at the Rose Bowl stadium, Los Angeles, California

# PEOPLES OF
# NORTH AMERICA

# NORTH AMERICA

The name "North America" can be used to mean several different things. In this book, the northern part of the American continent begins with Panama in the south and stretches up to Canada and Greenland in the north. It includes the U.S.A., Mexico, Central America and the Caribbean.

*This carved, painted pillar is part of a totem pole. Some Native American groups used these as community symbols or in memory of someone who had died.*

## Native Americans

Native Americans are the people who lived in North America before European explorers arrived. Each Native American group had its own lifestyles and customs and was governed by a chief.

In the 19th century, the European settlers forced Native Americans to live on areas of land called reservations and tried to force them to adopt European lifestyles. Many Native American traditions were forgotten. Now languages are being revived and Native Americans make and sell traditional pottery, baskets or textiles. However, people also lead modern lifestyles – for example some groups run casinos.

*This modern Native American is wearing traditional clothes, reflecting the interest in reviving traditional culture. But the Christian monument he is leaning against is a sign of the influence of European culture.*

### Internet links

**Website 1** Explore some Native American communities of today.

**Website 2** Canada's aboriginal peoples.

**Website 3** Browse an online encyclopedia guide to North America.

For links to these websites go to
**www.usborne-quicklinks.com**

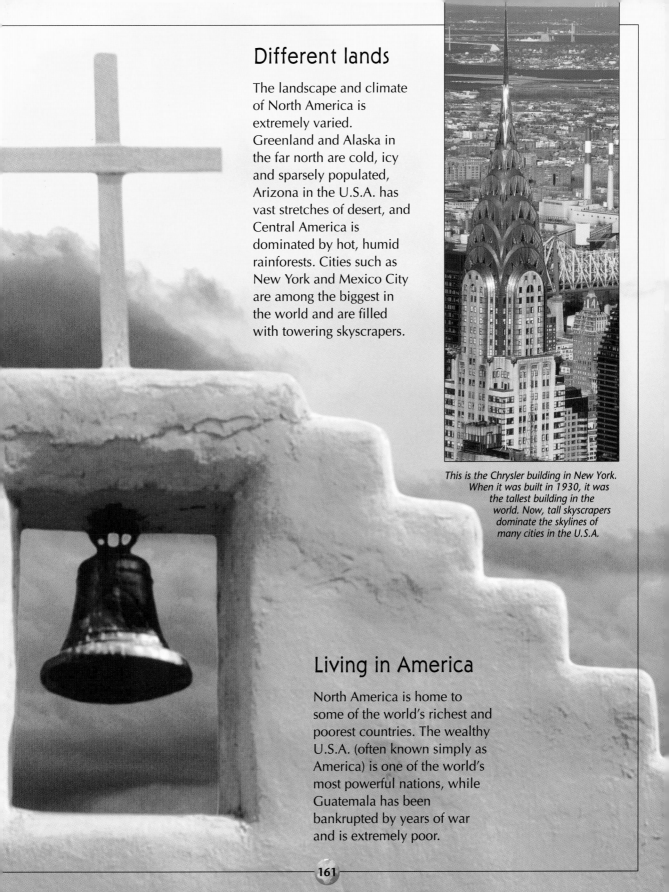

## Different lands

The landscape and climate of North America is extremely varied. Greenland and Alaska in the far north are cold, icy and sparsely populated, Arizona in the U.S.A. has vast stretches of desert, and Central America is dominated by hot, humid rainforests. Cities such as New York and Mexico City are among the biggest in the world and are filled with towering skyscrapers.

*This is the Chrysler building in New York. When it was built in 1930, it was the tallest building in the world. Now, tall skyscrapers dominate the skylines of many cities in the U.S.A.*

## Living in America

North America is home to some of the world's richest and poorest countries. The wealthy U.S.A. (often known simply as America) is one of the world's most powerful nations, while Guatemala has been bankrupted by years of war and is extremely poor.

# THE U.S.A.

The United States of America, also known as the U.S.A. or America, is a huge country, although it's not much more than half the size of Russia, the biggest country. The U.S.A. is very rich and has immense political and cultural influence worldwide.

## Land and law

The U.S.A. is divided into 50 states. Power is shared between state governments and a central federal government based in the capital, Washington D.C. The southern states are warm, green and rich in oil, while the main farming areas are in the western states. The northeast is the main business region. Manufacturing has moved more to the southern states in recent years. Many computer companies are located in Silicon Valley in California.

*The U.S.A. has hundreds of large theme parks with huge rides like this roller coaster.*

## The 'American Dream'

People from all over the world have moved to the U.S.A., and a million new immigrants arrive each year.
Many are following the 'American Dream': the belief that, in America, anyone can become rich and successful. However, many Americans are still very poor.

The mixture of peoples gives the U.S.A. a rich, diverse culture. Jazz and blues music, for instance, developed out of rhythms brought to the U.S.A. from Africa, while cheesecake and bagels were originally Jewish foods.

*Dr. Martin Luther King Jr., the leader of the 1960s Civil Rights movement for equality for black Americans, speaks at a "March against Fear" rally in 1966.*

*The crowned figure in the background is the Statue of Liberty in New York. It is a symbol of the political freedom enshrined in the Constitution of the U.S.A.*

### Internet links

**Website 1** Learn about the U.S.A. with video clips, songs and an interactive map.

**Website 2** Fascinating facts, games and quizzes about the U.S.A.

**Website 3** A guide to the U.S. government.

**Website 4** Discover festivals across the Americas.

For links to these websites, go to **www.usborne-quicklinks.com**

## Entertainment

Entertainment is big business in the U.S.A. The country's main movie-making area, Hollywood, in California, produces films that can cost many millions of dollars to make, but which earn even more. Theme parks are also very popular.

## Science and power

The U.S.A. is the leading political world power, and science and technology have played an important part in its success. Nuclear science, which can be used to make powerful bombs, has helped give the U.S.A. political strength. As a result, the U.S.A. now plays a big part in making wars and keeping peace around the world. The nation's wealth and success also owe a lot to computer science, and the U.S.A. dominates Internet technology. American English is the main language of the Internet.

*Minnie Mouse posing for a photo with a young boy in Disney World, a theme park based on famous characters from the cartoons of Walt Disney*

*The reusable Space Shuttle spacecraft is part of America's world-famous multi-billion dollar space exploration industry.*

# THE FAR NORTH

In Canada, people ski in resorts where there are ski lifts and other facilities, but people also ski cross country just to get from place to place.

The far north of North America is taken up by Greenland, Canada and Alaska (part of the U.S.A.). This is a vast area: Canada is the second largest country in the world, and Greenland is the world's biggest island.

## Many cultures

Canada is divided into ten provinces and three territories: the Yukon, Nunavut and the Northwest Territories.

Many Canadians have British, French or Native American ancestors and the offical languages are English and French. French culture is strong in the province of Quebec where cafes and shops reflect its influence.

Skiers swoop down a slope in Banff National Park, Alberta, Canada. Many tourists visit Canada for its natural beauty and outdoor activities.

## Natural resources

Most Canadians live in large cities along the border with the U.S.A. The rest of the country has a varied landscape, including lakes, mountains, forests and grasslands, or prairies. These provide rich natural resources such as timber, water power, gas, oil and minerals. Outside the cities, many people's jobs are based around mining and forestry.

## Winter sports

Outdoor sports and activities such as canoeing, riding horses and rafting are popular in Canada. But the country is particularly known for its winter sports, especially ice hockey which can be played on frozen ponds and lakes.

Snowmobiling at a winter sports festival in Canada

# Greenland

Although Greenland is the world's largest island, its population is very small because conditions there are so harsh. Most of Greenland lies within the Arctic Circle, and its central region is covered by a layer of ice that never melts.

The island has a small road network, but planes and dog sleds provide a flexible and reliable way of getting around. The majority of Greenlanders live along the coast, where the climate is mildest, making a living from catching fish, shrimps and seals.

## Inuit people

The Inuit are the native people of northern Canada. In 1999, the Canadian government made part of the Northwest Territories into a new Inuit territory, giving back land which the Inuit had lost to settlers. The new territory is called Nunavut, which means "our land" in Inukitut, the Inuit language.

The Inuit keep their traditions alive by speaking Inukitut, hunting for food, and making wood and bone carvings. They also take advantage of modern technology, using snowmobiles, telephones and computers.

Villages in Greenland are small. This one has about 500 human residents and 2,000 sled dogs, which are used for hunting and transportation.

These Inuit people are wearing heavy animal-skin coats to keep warm.

## Internet links

**Website 1** Discover more about Nunavut and Inuit culture.

**Website 2** Explore the landscape of Canada with a clickable map.

**Website 3** Virtual tours of Alaska and Canada

For links to these websites, go to **www.usborne-quicklinks.com**

# MEXICO

Mexico is a big country between the U.S.A. and Central America. It is very mountainous, but most Mexicans live in towns and cities in the middle of the country, where the land is flat.

## The Aztecs

From the early-14th century, Mexico was ruled by the Aztecs, a Native American people. They built an empire with a capital city called Tenochtitlan and ruled over many Native American peoples. The empire ended when the Spanish conquered Mexico in 1521. Today's Mexicans are mainly *mestizos*, of mixed Spanish and Native American descent.

## Hot and spicy

Mexican food is popular all over the world. *Guacamole* (mashed avocados), *tortillas* (flat bread), and meat and beans cooked in tomato sauce with hot chillies* are typical Mexican dishes. Over 60 different kinds of chillies are grown in Mexico. In some areas, people eat salads made out of cactus plants.

*Corn tortilla chips are eaten with Mexican-style dips around the world.*

## Mexico City

Mexico City, the capital of Mexico, was built directly over the ruins of the Aztec capital. Today, it is one of the world's biggest cities, with around 18 million people. The majority of the country's business is there, and the city is extremely busy, with lots of noise and traffic. It lies in a valley overlooked by volcanoes, and is regularly affected by earthquakes. The soil beneath it is so soft and swampy that the city sinks a little each year.

*Tomatoes, chillies* and beans are key ingredients in many Mexican dishes.*

*Chilies (U.S.A.)

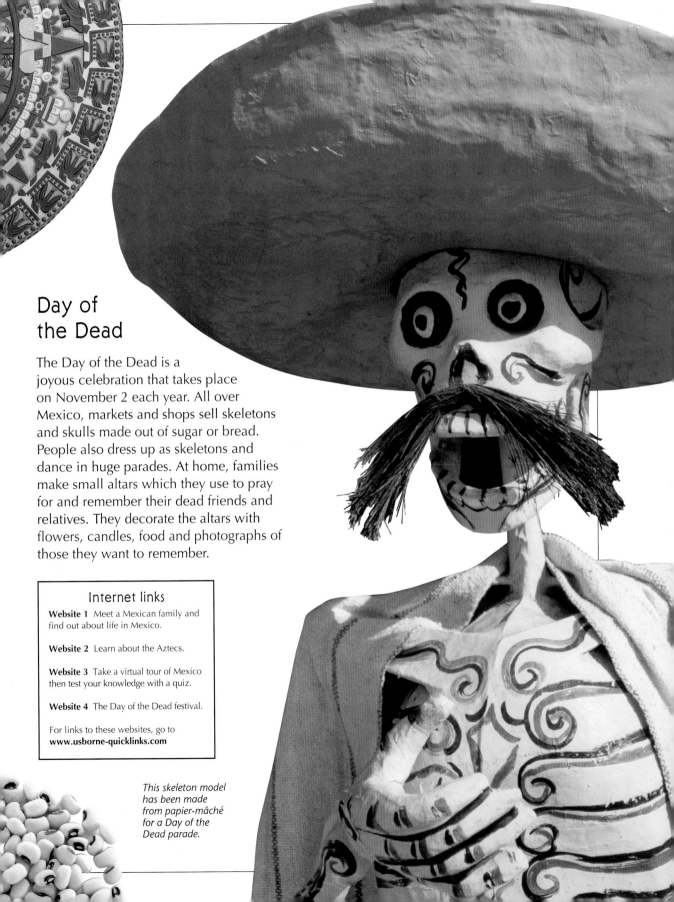

# Day of the Dead

The Day of the Dead is a joyous celebration that takes place on November 2 each year. All over Mexico, markets and shops sell skeletons and skulls made out of sugar or bread. People also dress up as skeletons and dance in huge parades. At home, families make small altars which they use to pray for and remember their dead friends and relatives. They decorate the altars with flowers, candles, food and photographs of those they want to remember.

### Internet links

**Website 1**  Meet a Mexican family and find out about life in Mexico.

**Website 2**  Learn about the Aztecs.

**Website 3**  Take a virtual tour of Mexico then test your knowledge with a quiz.

**Website 4**  The Day of the Dead festival.

For links to these websites, go to **www.usborne-quicklinks.com**

*This skeleton model has been made from papier-mâché for a Day of the Dead parade.*

# CENTRAL AMERICA

Central America is the narrow strip of land, or isthmus, connecting North and South America. The landscape of Central America is mainly made up of mountains and volcanoes and people's lives are affected by frequent earthquakes and volcanic eruptions.

*These girls are dressed as angels to take part in a religious procession in El Salvador. Religious festivals are common in Central America.*

## Takeover

The Spanish arrived in Central America 500 years ago, and many people living there today are of mixed Spanish and Native American descent. But each country has its own mix of peoples. As well as Native Americans and people of European descent, there are people of African descent along the Caribbean coast.

## Land of the Maya

The Maya had a powerful empire around AD200–900, when they built great cities. The empire covered most of Guatemala, and parts of Belize, Mexico, Honduras and El Salvador. Ruined cities can still be found in the jungles of Guatemala. The Maya are no longer powerful, but they still make up nearly half of Guatemala's population.

*This Mayan girl in Guatemala is carrying a younger child on her back, wrapped in a traditional Mayan shawl.*

### Internet links

**Website 1** Learn how to make a worry doll.

**Website 2** An online adventure in the land of the Maya.

**Website 3** Watch animations of how the Panama Canal works.

**Website 4** Find Guatemala on a map and read about children in Guatemala.

For links to these websites, go to **www.usborne-quicklinks.com**

## The Soccer War

Central America has suffered from decades of civil wars and conflict between countries. One war broke out between El Salvador and Honduras in 1969, after they had played soccer against each other in the World Cup. The real reasons, however, were disagreements over land, trade, and Salvadorean refugees in Honduras.

## Worry dolls

Children in Central America sometimes make tiny, bright dolls called worry dolls. There is a legend that if they tell the dolls their worries at night and then place them under their pillows, by morning all their worries will have disappeared.

*These tiny dolls are worry dolls. Their clothes are made by wrapping thread around the bodies.*

## The Panama Canal

The Panama Canal is one of the most important waterways in the world. It is a channel of water around 65km (40 miles) long that cuts through Panama, linking the Atlantic Ocean with the Pacific Ocean. Each vessel that uses the canal must pay a fee according to its weight. This means that while ships pay thousands of dollars, Richard Halliburton, who swam through the canal in 1928, only paid 36 cents.

*A thatched bohio, or hut, in a rainforest clearing in Panama. Huts like these are the homes of the Guaymi people, who live on the border between Panama and Costa Rica.*

## Rainforest life

A large area of Central America is covered by rainforest, which is home to a huge variety of plants and animals. But the rainforest is being devastated and many plants and animals may die out as trees are cut down to make timber for export, and to clear land for farming.

# THE CARIBBEAN

A rich variety of fruit is grown on the tropical islands of the Caribbean.

Pineapple

The Caribbean is the name given to the chain of hundreds of tropical islands stretching from North America to South America across the Caribbean Sea.

Plantains are green fruits which belong to the same family as bananas.

## Slavery

From around 1500, Europeans fought with each other over possession of the Caribbean islands. They brought slaves from Africa, the Middle East, the Far East and India to work on sugar, tobacco and cocoa plantations. Many of today's inhabitants are descendants of these slaves. Languages from around the world have combined to form unique regional dialects known as *creoles*.

Mango

## Tourism

The Caribbean islands are known for their white sandy beaches, clear blue sea and tropical sunshine. Their beauty and isolation has given them a reputation of being a "paradise on earth". As a result, tourism is one of the Caribbean's most important industries.

Papaya

Tourists often go diving in the clear blue sea of the Caribbean. This boy is looking at a shell he has found while diving at Virgin Gorda, in the British Virgin Islands.

## Hard work

Although the Caribbean may be seen as a paradise by people who go there as tourists, life is not always easy for its inhabitants. Many of those who do not work in the tourist industry make a living growing sugar cane, the Caribbean's main export, and other crops such as bananas, coffee and tobacco. Some of the poorest countries, such as Haiti, suffer from severe unemployment. Many Haitians have to cross the border into the wealthier Dominican Republic to find work.

## Music

Africa has had an important influence on the music of the Caribbean. Many Caribbean musical styles, such as reggae, conga, cha-cha-cha, plena and calypso, have African roots. Calypso, which originated in Trinidad, is the music style most associated with the Caribbean. Calypso songs are often improvised and tend to focus on social and political subjects.

## Street parties

Carnivals held to mark religious festivals are an important part of island life. The main carnival season takes place before Lent (the period of 40 days leading up to Easter in the Christian calendar). The streets are filled with parades, loud music, and people singing and dancing in bright costumes.

*Junkanoo is a huge festival in the Bahamas. People make flamboyant costumes like this to take part in parades.*

A busy outdoor market in Zumbahua, Ecuador

# PEOPLES OF
# SOUTH AMERICA

# SOUTH AMERICA

The people of South America have a huge range of origins. Over the centuries, settlers have arrived from Europe, Africa and Asia to join the Native Americans who have lived there for thousands of years.

*A pair condors flying high in the Andes, the mountain range that runs most of the length of South America*

## Empty and crowded

Much of South America is covered in rainforest, mountains and deserts where it can be hard to survive. Many people live in small villages and work as farmers. Yet along the coast are some of the world's biggest cities, with towering skyscrapers and crowded shanty towns.

### Internet links

**Website 1** Visit South American countries.

**Website 2** Meet a family in Peru and learn about weaving in the Andes Mountains.

**Website 3** Fascinating facts about the ancient Americas.

For links to these websites, go to **www.usborne-quicklinks.com**

*The Inca people had a powerful empire in South America around five hundred years ago. This watchtower is part of Inca ruins at Machu Picchu, in the Andes mountains.*

## Native Americans

Experts think the first South Americans came from Asia. They probably walked across a strip of land in the north that once joined what are now Russia and Alaska. Their descendants now live mostly in South America's mountainous countries, such as Colombia, Bolivia, Ecuador and Peru.

## Religions

Over 90% of the people in South America are Roman Catholics. This form of Christianity was introduced by Spanish and Portuguese invaders who took control of the continent in the 1500s.

Many South Americans also worship traditional Native American or African gods and spirits. Some traditional religions have priests called shamans, who are believed to have magical powers.

## Latin languages

South America is sometimes called Latin America, because most South Americans speak the Latin-based languages Spanish and Portuguese. These were brought by the European invaders. However, many people speak Native American languages, such as Quechua and Aymara.

*Christian festivals are important to many South Americans. This Brazilian pilgrim is carrying a cross in an Easter procession in Jerusalem.*

# IN THE MOUNTAINS

The vast Andes mountain range snakes down the western side of South America, through Colombia, Ecuador, Peru, Bolivia, Chile and Argentina. Despite dangers from volcanoes and earthquakes, the Andes are home to millions of miners, farmers, craftspeople and city-dwellers.

*This young boy from Ecuador is harnessing a llama to lead it to market.*

## Fertile farms

The peaks of the Andes are covered in snow, but the lower slopes are good for growing crops. Mountain farmers grow corn, coffee and other crops on small plots of land, sometimes with terraces to stop the soil from being washed away. If the land is not good enough for crops, they keep herds of mountain animals, such as llamas and alpacas, which provide milk and wool, and which may also be used to transport goods.

## Craft work

Many Native Americans live in villages in the Andes. Some earn a living from traditional crafts. They weave brightly striped shawls, blankets and hats. These are used by local people as well as being sold to tourists and exported around the world.

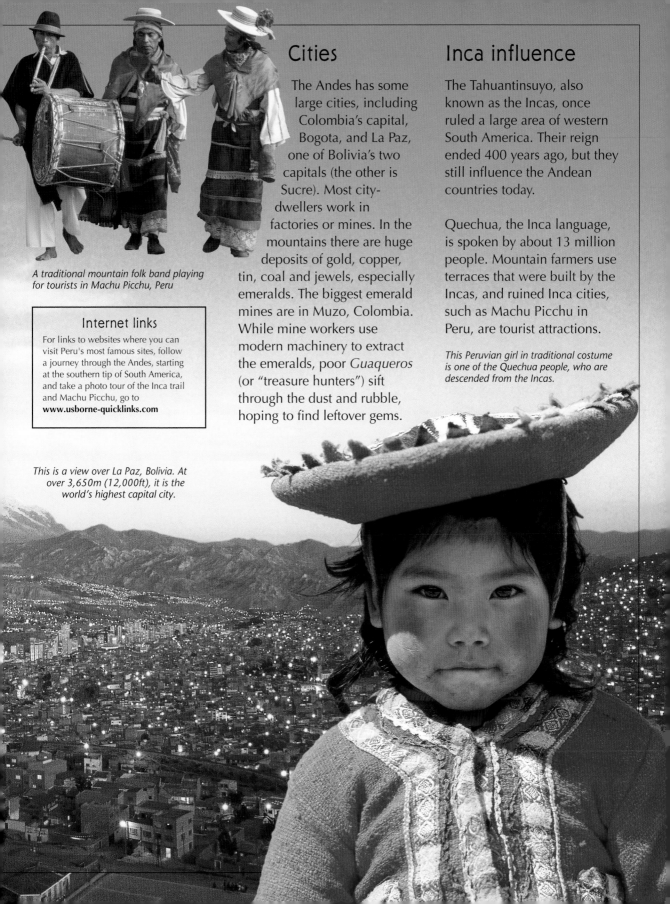

_A traditional mountain folk band playing for tourists in Machu Picchu, Peru_

## Cities

The Andes has some large cities, including Colombia's capital, Bogota, and La Paz, one of Bolivia's two capitals (the other is Sucre). Most city-dwellers work in factories or mines. In the mountains there are huge deposits of gold, copper, tin, coal and jewels, especially emeralds. The biggest emerald mines are in Muzo, Colombia. While mine workers use modern machinery to extract the emeralds, poor _Guaqueros_ (or "treasure hunters") sift through the dust and rubble, hoping to find leftover gems.

## Inca influence

The Tahuantinsuyo, also known as the Incas, once ruled a large area of western South America. Their reign ended 400 years ago, but they still influence the Andean countries today.

Quechua, the Inca language, is spoken by about 13 million people. Mountain farmers use terraces that were built by the Incas, and ruined Inca cities, such as Machu Picchu in Peru, are tourist attractions.

_This Peruvian girl in traditional costume is one of the Quechua people, who are descended from the Incas._

### Internet links

For links to websites where you can visit Peru's most famous sites, follow a journey through the Andes, starting at the southern tip of South America, and take a photo tour of the Inca trail and Machu Picchu, go to **www.usborne-quicklinks.com**

_This is a view over La Paz, Bolivia. At over 3,650m (12,000ft), it is the world's highest capital city._

# RAINFOREST PEOPLES

South America's huge Amazon valley is covered in millions of square miles of thick, humid rainforest. The Amazon rainforest is so big that it contains over a third of the world's trees. For thousands of years, it has also been the home of Native American peoples.

*Leaders of the Kayapo people of Brazil sometimes wear lip-plates like this which emphasize their roles as public speakers.*

## Traditional lives

The rainforest is so vast that groups of people living in it have been cut off from the rest of the world for centuries. Some have only recently been discovered by outsiders. There may be others who have never had contact with the outside world. Rainforest peoples such as the Jivaro, Txikao and Kayapo have their own languages and customs. But many of them share similar lifestyles, surviving by hunting animals, gathering fruits and nuts, and growing crops in forest clearings.

## Losing lifestyles

As new roads are built into the rainforest, the people who live there have more contact with outsiders. They may even lose their homes when parts of the rainforest are cut down. To make a living, they may have to learn more widely spoken languages or move away from the forest into towns and cities, leaving their old traditions and lifestyles behind.

### Internet links

**Website 1** Watch video clips of rainforest peoples and learn about the threats to their survival.

**Website 2** Explore the Amazon rainforest and play an interactive game where you try to run an ecotourism project.

For links to these websites, go to **www.usborne-quicklinks.com**

*This man playing a wooden flute is one of the Jivaro people of the Amazon.*

## Clearing the forest

Rainforest trees provide all kinds of useful products, such as brazil nuts, cashew nuts, wax and rubber. At one time these things were simply collected from the forest, but now they are mostly farmed on plantations.

Traditionally, rainforest peoples cleared small areas of land to grow crops, and moved on after a few years. Because the cleared areas were tiny, this method, called shifting agriculture, did not harm much of the forest, and the trees eventually grew back. But since the 1960s, more rainforest has been cut down, for timber and to make space for farms, mines and factories. So the amount of rainforest is decreasing.

*These are rainforest plants in Ecuador. Many rainforest plants can be used to make medicines.*

## Forest food

Although most rainforest peoples grow crops, they can also find food in the rainforest. Hunting and fishing provide them with a wide range of meat, including monkeys, toucans and caimans, which are reptiles similar to alligators. The Piaroa people of Venezuela sometimes eat tarantulas (a type of spider), cooking them by squeezing their insides onto a leaf and baking it over a fire.

*Many rainforest peoples grow just enough food to supply their village. This woman is processing locally-grown manioc (a plant a little like a potato) to make flour.*

179

# COMBINED CULTURES

South American culture is influenced by the traditions of the different types of people who live there. For example, many South Americans love soccer, which came from Europe; samba music from Africa; and foods that combine Spanish, African and Native American influences.

## Party!

Carnivals and costume parades take place frequently all over South America. Most of them celebrate Christian festivals, such as Lent, Easter and Christmas. They are lively occasions, with plenty of loud music, dancing, dressing up, eating and drinking. Many cities, towns and villages also hold their own local religious or historical celebrations.

## Delicious dishes

All kinds of foods are eaten in South America. Argentinians and Uruguayans eat lots of meat, and Bolivians have dozens of varieties of potatoes. A typical meal in the Andes consists of fried beef, beans, a fried egg, rice and a slice of avocado. This type of dish is called *churrasco* in Ecuador and *bandeja paisa* in Colombia. Local delicacies include *cuy* (guinea pig) and *hormiga culona* (fried ants) in Colombia, and iguana (a type of lizard) in Guyana.

*This Peruvian woman is preparing guinea pigs for roasting.*

*These costumed dancers are taking part in a parade in Venezuela, held to mark the Catholic feast of Corpus Christi.*

## Soccer fever

Soccer is the biggest sport in South America, and national team members are heroes. Uruguay hosted and won the first ever soccer World Cup in 1930 and Argentina and Brazil have since won it several times. Children play soccer in the streets all over South America. Most towns and villages have local teams, and even rainforest-dwellers have a patch of land set aside for soccer games.

### Internet links

For links to websites where you can learn about the influences that have shaped the festivals, religion and music of Latin America, and follow the progress of South American soccer teams, go to
**www.usborne-quicklinks.com**

*These children are playing informal games of soccer by an old fort at Sacsahuaman, near Cusco in Peru.*

## African influence

Culture along the east coast of South America has a strong African element. People from West Africa arrived as slaves hundreds of years ago, to work in mines and on sugar plantations for the area's European rulers. Their beliefs, music and culture had an important influence, which is still present today. African rhythms blended with Spanish, Portuguese and Native American sounds to produce musical styles such as samba and salsa. Many Brazilians follow a spiritual religion called Candomblé, which is based on African traditions.

*This dancer represents the God of Medicine in the Candomblé religion.*

# BRAZIL

Brazil is the biggest country in South America. It contains most of the Amazon rainforest and also has some of the world's largest cities. In many ways it is a very modern country, with futuristic buildings and high-tech industries, but a lot of its people are still poor.

*This 30m (100ft) high statue of Christ stands on Corcovado Hill above Rio de Janeiro. Its shape can be seen from far out at sea.*

## Portugal and Brazil

Unlike the rest of South America, Brazil was once ruled by Portugal, and its main language is Portuguese. This happened because just before 1500, news reached Europe that the Spanish had discovered lands not previously known to Europeans, which they called the "New World". Portugal wanted some of the land for itself, so the two countries agreed that Portugal could take over the eastern side of the continent. Brazil has been independent from Portugal since 1822.

## Carnaval

Brazil is famous for its festivals, music and nightclubs. The most famous event is Carnaval (the Brazilian spelling of "carnival"). Carnaval celebrations are held all over Brazil every February or March, to mark the start of Lent.

The celebrations go on for five days, with feasting, dancing, a huge costume parade and samba competitions. Samba is a type of percussion music popular in Brazil. There are special samba schools where people can learn samba music and dancing.

*A samba dancer twirls at Rio's famous Carnaval.*

## A new capital

In 1956 the Brazilian government began to build a new capital city, Brasilia. Brasilia was planned as a modern, hi-tech city and it is still known for its space-age buildings. It was designed to be fast and easy to drive around, so it had no traffic lights. But when people moved in, they complained that it was too hard to cross the roads, so the design was changed.

### Internet links

For links to websites where you can take a fun journey through Brazil and find out more about the people, music and food and Brazil's fast-growing cities, go to
**www.usborne-quicklinks.com**

*This is the Metropolitan Cathedral in Brasilia. It is a good example of the city's modern architecture.*

## Cities out of control

The populations of many of Brazil's cities, such as Sao Paulo and Rio de Janeiro, are rising fast as more and more people from rural areas arrive, looking for jobs and homes.

Often there is not enough housing for the new arrivals, and so shanty towns develop on the outskirts of cities. These are made up of makeshift houses built out of scrap metal and junk. The shanty towns are nicknamed *favelas* after a type of hillside flower.

*Shanty towns, like this one in Sao Paulo, often develop on hillsides, where the land is too steep to build bigger houses.*

# ARGENTINA

Argentina is the second biggest country in South America. It ranges from lakes and glaciers in the south, across flat grasslands, known as the Pampas, to mountains in the west and rainforest in the north. However, more than a third of the population lives in or around the capital city, Buenos Aires.

*This is the Avenida 9 de Julio, Buenos Aires. It is the widest street in the world.*

## Invaders

The first people to live in Argentina were Native American groups who farmed the land. But then in 1516 a Spanish explorer named Juan de Solis arrived and claimed the land for the Spanish. The Spanish named the country Argentina, which means "Land of Silver", and ruled there until 1810.

*This is La Boca, a district in Buenos Aires made up of brightly painted metal houses.*

## Buenos Aires

Around 12 million people live in Buenos Aires, making it one of the largest cities in the world. It is also Argentina's main port, and its inhabitants are known as *porteños*, or port people.

Buenos Aires is sometimes called the "Paris of South America", as its architecture is very European. In the 19th and 20th centuries people from all over Europe moved to Argentina, and most settled in Buenos Aires. Many of the immigrants lived together in districts called *barrios*. Today, you can still see these districts and each one has its own individual style and character.

## Gauchos

Gauchos are Argentinian cowboys. The first gauchos lived in the 18th century and worked on the Pampas, taming wild horses and using them to catch cattle. Then, in the 1800s, Argentina's cattle industry began to develop. The Pampas were fenced into huge cattle ranches called *estancias* and gauchos became farmhands.

### Internet links

For links to websites where you can explore the mountains, beaches and parks of Patagonia then test your knowledge with a quiz or take a tour of Argentina's famous sites, go to **www.usborne-quicklinks.com**

## The tango

Argentina is famous for the dance and music known as the tango. It began in the mid-19th century in the poor immigrant areas of Buenos Aires, as a mixture of Italian, Spanish and African music. At first, people found the tango shocking because the dancers' bodies were very close together, but by the 1900s it had become a craze in fashionable European circles. The tango is still danced today in many parts of the world. Finland has more than 2,000 tango clubs.

*Professional dancers perform the tango in a street in Argentina.*

## Patagonia

With 90% of Argentinians living in cities, much of the country is wilderness. Patagonia, in the south, is one of the least populated regions in the world. It is home to many kinds of animals, such as elephant seals and some of the world's rarest birds.

Two girls in front of their thatched house in Samoa

# PEOPLES OF AUSTRALASIA AND OCEANIA

# AUSTRALASIA AND OCEANIA

The definitions of what makes up Australasia and Oceania vary, but Australasia usually refers to Australia and New Zealand and Oceania to the three main groups of Pacific Islands: Melanesia, Micronesia and Polynesia.

## Small populations

Australasia and Oceania are not very heavily populated. The Pacific islands, including Papua New Guinea, are home to around eight million people, 20 million people live in Australia and four million in New Zealand.

## Land masses

Australia is more than three times the size of Greenland, the world's largest island. It is too large to be called an island, so it is usually described as a continent, or land mass. It is home to many unusual animals, such as kangaroos, wombats and koalas. There are thousands of tiny islands in the Pacific. Many have been formed by erupting volcanoes under the sea*.

*Kangaroos belong to a group of animals called marsupials, most of which carry their young in pouches like this. Most marsupials live in Australasia and Oceania.*

*This tiny islet is part of the group of Pacific islands known as Micronesia.*

*Volcanic islands, 44

## Europeans arrive

In 1606, a Dutchman named Willem Jantszoon became the first European in Australia. In 1642, his countryman Abel Tasman was the first European to see New Zealand.

An English explorer, James Cook, landed at Botany Bay, on the east coast of Australia in 1770. Eighteen years later the British established a colony there for prisoners. During the 19th century, many parts of the Pacific were colonized by European countries. Today, most Pacific nations have gained independence.

## Internet links

For links to websites where you can find facts, maps and information about explorers of Australia and Oceania, and take a virtual tour of Australasia, go to **www.usborne-quicklinks.com**

*This is part of a wooden pillar of Maori carvings. Traditionally, the Maoris often used carvings to record details of real events.*

## Early explorers

The first people to explore and inhabit Australasia and Oceania came originally from Southeast Asia. They include the Aborigines, who arrived in Australia between 40,000 and 60,000 years ago, the peoples who arrived on the Pacific islands about 7,000 years ago, and the Maoris, who arrived in New Zealand a little over 1,000 years ago.

*This man from Papua New Guinea is holding the paddle of a traditional wooden canoe.*

# AUSTRALIA

Australia is bordered by the Pacific Ocean on one side and the Indian Ocean on the other. It is almost as big as Europe, yet has less than 3% of the population Europe has. Most Australians live on the country's eastern and southeastern coasts.

*Many people in the outback live a long way from a hospital, so a medical service known as the Flying Doctors rescues sick people by plane.*

## Australia's people

For many thousands of years the Aborigines and Torres Strait islanders were the only inhabitants of Australia. British colonists arrived in Australia in the 18th century, and in the 1850s gold was discovered. This brought a rush of people from Europe, China and the U.S.A., all hoping to make their fortunes by mining. In 1901 Australia ceased to be a set of colonies and became a federation.

## City life

Over 80% of Australia's population lives in cities and towns along the coast, as this is where jobs are to be found. Canberra is the capital, but Sydney is the biggest city. Around four million people, a fifth of Australia's total population, live there. The other major Australian cities are Melbourne, Perth, Brisbane, Adelaide, Hobart and Darwin.

## The outback

The vast desert area in the middle of Australia, known as the outback, is one of the hottest, driest places in the world. The soil is too dry for crops, but farmers keep sheep and cattle on enormous farms called stations, which can have 15,000 sq km (5,800 sq miles) or more of land. With farms and towns so far apart, people living in the outback can lead isolated lives. Children often live so far from the nearest school that lessons have to be held via the Internet, or transmitted by TV or radio.

*Sydney's opera house sits on the edge of Sydney Harbour. Its roof mirrors the shape of the boats that sail past.*

## The first Australians

When the Aboriginal peoples came to Australia, they spread gradually across the country in large, nomadic groups, hunting animals and gathering plants. Sometimes they settled for quite long periods in some places. They believed that the land and its wildlife were sacred. When Europeans arrived, they seized much of the land for themselves, destroying many Aboriginal sacred places.

Today, less than 2% of the Australian population is Aboriginal, and many no longer have a traditional lifestyle. They are just as likely to live in cities and have modern jobs. However, most Aboriginal peoples want to preserve their culture and, after years of campaigning, some traditional lands are now being returned to their original owners.

*The coral reefs that make up the Great Barrier Reef support a huge variety of underwater life.*

*This Aboriginal man has painted his body and face as Aboriginal peoples have done for thousands of years. Body painting is a group activity and is usually done for special ceremonies.*

## Sun, sea and sports

Australians enjoy their warm, sunny climate and spend a lot of time outdoors, playing sports, swimming, surfing and sailing. The climate and range of outdoor activities available also make Australia attractive as a tourist destination. Swimming and diving at Australia's Great Barrier Reef are especially popular, although scientists are concerned that too much tourism will damage the wildlife living around the reef.

### Internet links

**Website 1** Go sightseeing in Australia and learn some Australian slang.

**Website 2** Watch a presentation about the Great Barrier Reef.

**Website 3** More on Aboriginal peoples.

For links to these websites, go to
**www.usborne-quicklinks.com**

# NEW ZEALAND

New Zealand lies in the South Pacific, about 1,500km (1,000 miles) southeast of Australia. The country is made up of two main islands, known as the North Island and the South Island, and several smaller ones. Much of New Zealand is wild and mountainous, and the country is sparsely populated, with fewer than four million people.

## A young nation

New Zealand was one of the last places in the world to be inhabited. The first settlers, the Maoris, arrived just over 1,000 years ago, migrating from islands farther north. Europeans started to arrive in the late 18th century, and in 1840 New Zealand came under British rule. Today, it is an independent state. The majority of New Zealanders are still of British descent. The rest are mostly Maoris and South Sea islanders.

*An experienced shearer can shear a sheep in just a few minutes. Wool is one of New Zealand's most important exports.*

## Important industries

Many New Zealanders make their living from farming. Over half the land is used for sheep farming and this is the country's biggest industry. Wool and lamb are major exports. Other exports include dairy products, wine, vegetables and fruit, such as oranges, lemons, grapefruits and kiwi fruit. New Zealand used to trade mainly with Britain, but today much of its trade is with Australia and Asian countries. Non-agricultural exports include wood and paper products, textiles and machinery.

*This is a typical New Zealand sheep farm, stretching over a vast area.*

*These tourists are photographing a geyser spouting hot water in Waiotapua Thermal Park.*

## Clean and green

New Zealand does not use nuclear power, and has little heavy industry and relatively small towns and cities. As a result, it is one of the world's least polluted countries. Its beautiful scenery attracts many tourists. In the North Island, active volcanoes and spouting geysers can be seen, and in the South Island, there are spectacular mountains with huge glaciers.

### Internet links

**Website 1** Take part in a "powhiri", a Maori welcome ceremony.

**Website 2** Go on a photo tour of New Zealand.

For links to these websites, go to **www.usborne-quicklinks.com**

## The Maoris

When they first arrived in New Zealand, the Maoris lived a traditional lifestyle. They hunted, fished and grew crops, and lived in small ethnic groups ruled by chiefs. Then in the 18th century, British colonists arrived. Battles raged over who owned the land and many Maoris were killed. Most of those that were left were forced to move to the new towns and cities.

*This Maori man has tattoos known as Ta Moko on his face. He is carrying a club called a wahaika, to take part in a traditional dance.*

## Modern Maoris

Today, Maoris make up about 10% of the population of New Zealand and their culture is being re-established. The Maori language is taught in schools and traditional arts such as tattooing (*Ta Moko*) have been revived. But many Maoris are still campaigning for the return of lands they lost. Their name for New Zealand is *Aotearoa*, which means "land of the long white clouds".

# PAPUA NEW GUINEA

New Guinea, the world's second largest island after Greenland, lies in the Pacific Ocean, to the north of Australia. Its western half, called Irian Jaya, is part of Indonesia*. Its eastern half, together with around 600 small islands, makes up the country of Papua New Guinea.

### Internet links

**Website 1** Watch a slide show about Papua New Guinea masks and artifacts.

**Website 2** Papua New Guinea fact file.

For links to these websites, go to **www.usborne-quicklinks.com**

## Peoples of Papua

Most Papua New Guineans are of Papuan or Melanesian* origin, although there are also people of European, Polynesian* and Chinese origin. The first inhabitants migrated from Southeast Asia over 40,000 years ago. They lived in small groups and found food by hunting and gathering.

The country is dominated by mountains and thick rainforests. This has meant that groups often became isolated. Today, there are still hundreds of different ethnic groups living in Papua New Guinea.

## Languages

Because there are so many separate groups, many different languages have developed in Papua New Guinea. There are more than 700 in total, a huge number of languages for a population of less than five million. The different groups communicate with each other in a language called Hiri Motu, or in pidgin English, which is a mixture of English and local languages. The official language is English, but in fact only 2% of the population can speak it.

*This Waghi boy, from the eastern mountains of Papua New Guinea, is wearing a traditional feather headdress for a festival at his high school.*

*Indonesia, 213; Melanesia, 196; Polynesia, 196

## Village life

About a fifth of Papua New Guinea's people live in towns, where many have moved to find work. The rest still have a traditional lifestyle, similar to that of their ancestors. They live in villages, grow fruit and vegetables, catch fish and keep pigs and poultry. Some farmers sell their produce at local markets. Villagers eat a diet based on starchy crops such as sweet potatoes in the highland areas, and sago in the lowlands.

*A father and son display their catch of fish for sale to passers-by.*

*These are men from a village called Asaro. They are wearing mud masks and their bodies are covered in mud too. Warriors of Asaro are said to have once dressed like this in order to win a battle, and villagers still sometimes dress like this today for tourists.*

## Art and life

The art of Papua New Guinea is a key part of local life, history and culture. Traditions vary from region to region and most forms of art have a practical or religious function.

In Malangan culture, people make wooden masks to commemorate a death. The people of Kambot carve wooden story boards showing incidents from village life. Around the Gulf Province, shield-like objects called gope boards are hung outside houses. They are said to contain protective spirits which ward off sickness and evil. Many Papuan peoples also carve elaborate prows for canoes.

# OCEANIA

Scattered over the vast Pacific Ocean are more than 20,000 islands, which are collectively known as Oceania. Some, such as New Guinea, are huge, but many are little more than specks in the ocean. Only a few thousand of the islands are inhabited.

*This brightly-painted building is a Hindu temple in Nadi, Fiji.*

## Pacific peoples

The original inhabitants of the Pacific islands migrated from Southeast Asia about 7,000 years ago. They made long sea journeys and, over many generations, settled one group of islands after another. Later, in the 16th century, European explorers started to discover the Pacific islands. Colonists began to arrive, and by the 1800s many islands were under the control of other countries. Today, some Pacific islands are independent and others are still ruled by states such as the U.S.A., France and New Zealand.

## Island groups

There are three main Pacific island groups: Melanesia, Polynesia and Micronesia. Polynesia means "many islands" and Micronesia means "small islands". Melanesia means "black islands"; it got its name because the people there tend to have darker skin than elsewhere in the Pacific.

*These French Polynesian girls are wearing traditional flower garlands, known as* leis.

## Tourism

Some of the Pacific islands, such as those that make up Fiji, Tonga and Samoa, are among the most beautiful in the world. This, together with their tropical climate, makes them popular tourist destinations. Tourism brings money to the islands but too many tourists can also damage the environment.

### Internet links

**Website 1** Find out about the people, everyday life, geography and climate of the islands in the South Pacific Ocean.

**Website 2** Feather money, masks, shields and other items made by Pacific peoples.

For links to these websites, go to **www.usborne-quicklinks.com**

*Huts cluster along the beach on Mana Island, one of the many islands that make up Fiji.*

## Island life

On more developed Pacific islands, many people live in urban areas and work in mining and tourism. However, traditional village life is still strong. Fishing is common, crops such as cassava, yams and sweet potatoes are grown and families often keep livestock – for example, chickens and pigs. On some islands, people live in large, extended families, and community and religious life is often important.

## Testing weapons

Because of their remote locations, the Pacific islands have been used by the U.K., France and the U.S.A. for testing nuclear weapons. In 1946, an atom bomb was detonated on Bikini, one of the Marshall Islands in Micronesia, and many islanders had to leave their homes. Some underground tests continue today in French Polynesia, despite protests from conservation groups and local people worried about the environment.

*This man is fishing by standing on a ledge jutting out just over the water and stabbing at fish with his spear.*

Children carry balloons and flowers at the opening ceremony of a school in Hanoi, Vietnam

# PEOPLES
# OF ASIA

# ASIA

Asia is the world's biggest continent. It covers almost a third of the Earth's land surface, and over 60% of the world's people live there. Asian peoples are very diverse, with many different cultures, lifestyles, religions and political systems.

*A farm worker picking tea leaves in Malaysia. Tea is an important crop in Asia.*

## New states

Since 1991, Asia has gained several new states, including Tajikistan, Kyrgyzstan and Kazakhstan. These were once part of the U.S.S.R. (Union of Soviet Socialist Republics), a huge country governed from Moscow. In 1991 the U.S.S.R. dissolved into a number of independent states, including Russia.

## Fishing and farming

Asia has thousands and thousands of miles of coastline, especially in the southeast, where there are over 15,000 islands. Because of this, fishing is a vital source of food and work for millions of Asians.

The continent also has vast areas of fertile farmland, with millions of tiny farms where poor families grow food for their own use. But Asia also has large farms that export crops such as rice, rubber, tea and coffee.

# Trade and industry

Asia is also home to some of the world's biggest banking, manufacturing and trading nations. Wealthy cities such as Hong Kong, Singapore, Tokyo and Dubai tower with gleaming skyscrapers.

Many of the things you own, especially clothes, computers, toys, phones and CDs, have probably been made in Asia. Millions of factory workers in countries such as China, Taiwan and Japan make goods to be exported and sold all over the world.

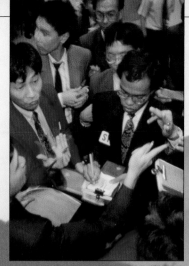

*Trade is important for many Asian nations. Here you can see people trading in the stock exchange in Malaysia.*

## Internet links

**Website 1** Explore an interactive map of Asia, with sound clips and facts.

**Website 2** Take a lesson in Japanese and find out more about everyday life.

**Website 3** Build a rice paddy online and learn about the importance of rice.

**Website 4** Learn about Buddhism, tour a temple and meet some monks.

For links to these websites, go to
**www.usborne-quicklinks.com**

*The Buddhist religion plays a central role in the lives of many people throughout Southeast Asia and boys are encouraged to spend some time as monks. These boys are young Buddhist monks.*

# A RANGE OF RELIGIONS

All the world's major religions started in Asia. The continent still has a wide range of religions and many of them, such as Christianity, Islam and Judaism, have also spread around the world. For billions of Asians, religious rituals are an essential everyday activity.

## Holy places

Important holy sites are found all over Asia. They include places where prophets were born or died, places where religions began, and cities, mountains and rivers that are believed to be sacred. Millions of people from all over the world make religious journeys, or pilgrimages, to these sites every year.

## Holy water

The Ganges River in northern India is sacred to Hindus, who make up more than 80% of India's population. Pilgrims visit the Ganges to purify themselves by bathing in its waters, and religious ceremonies are held on its banks.

*These women are bathing at dawn in the Ganges River at Varanasi, India. Steps have been built there so pilgrims can get in and out of the water safely.*

## A trip to Mecca

All Muslims are expected to make a pilgrimage (or *Hajj*) to the holy city of Mecca, in Saudi Arabia, at least once in their lives. It is the birthplace of Mohammed, the prophet of Islam. When they arrive, the pilgrims walk around a shrine called the Ka'bah, which is said to have been built by the prophet Ibrahim.

## Jerusalem

Jerusalem is a holy city for Jews, Christians and Muslims. It contains the Western Wall, the remains of a Jewish temple, and the Dome of the Rock, a shrine marking the spot where the Islam prophet Mohammed is said to have risen into heaven. It is also where Christians believe Jesus Christ, the central figure of Christianity, was crucified.

### Internet links

**Website 1** Make your own pilgrimage to Mecca.

**Website 2** Learn more about Jerusalem's holy sites.

For links to these websites, go to
**www.usborne-quicklinks.com**

*The silhouette in the background is part of the huge Borobudur Buddhist temple in Java, Indonesia.*

*Jewish pilgrims visit the Western Wall to mourn the destruction of their temple, and to insert prayers into cracks in the wall. In the background is the Dome of the Rock, part of a Muslim shrine.*

## Beautiful buildings

There are beautiful religious buildings all over Asia: Muslim mosques, Sikh gurdwaras, Christian churches, Hindu temples, and Buddhist pagodas. Many of these holy buildings have been created by the very best craftspeople, using expensive and gorgeous materials. Their impressive shapes often dominate cities' skylines.

## Spiritual sounds

In Asia, many people take part in regular religious chanting, praying or singing. For example, Muslims are called to prayer five times a day, many Buddhists chant verses every day, and dancing and singing are an important part of Hindu ceremonies.

*This man is calling Muslims to prayer. An official who does this is called a muezzin.*

# RUSSIA

Russia is the world's biggest country. It covers 11% of the Earth's land surface, is divided into 11 time zones and straddles two continents: Europe and Asia. It takes over a week to travel by train from St. Petersburg in the west to Vladivostok in the east.

*These are matryoshka dolls, which open up into halves so that several dolls can fit one inside the other. The word matryoshka means mother in Russian.*

## City culture

Russia's cities are famous across the world for their art and culture. Moscow and St. Petersburg (which are both in European Russia) have dozens of beautiful museums and palaces. Russia is also home to world-famous orchestras and ballet companies such as Moscow's Bolshoi Ballet.

*This is St. Basil's Cathedral, Moscow. The beautiful onion-shaped domes are characteristic of Russian church architecture.*

## Big changes

The independent country of Russia, officially known as the Russian Federation, has only existed since 1991. Before that, it belonged to the U.S.S.R. This was an even bigger country, created in 1917 when a Communist revolution overthrew the Russian czar, or king. For most of the 20th century, Communists ran the U.S.S.R.

## Communism

Communism is a way of running a country. Under Communism, the state owns everything, including railways, roads, factories and houses, and it distributes things like food, money and medicine among the people. It is the opposite of Capitalism, in which people can own their own houses and run their own businesses. The government which ruled the U.S.S.R. from 1917 to 1991 was the world's best-known Communist system.

*This girl is playing outside the tent where her family lives, in Chukchi, in the far northeast of Russia.*

## Size matters

Russia stretches 7,700km (4,800 miles) along the Arctic Circle. When it's bedtime in the west, people in the east are just waking up. People in different parts of the country have very different lifestyles, depending on the climate and landscape where they live, and the influence of nearby countries. In the north, Russia extends beyond the Arctic Circle, but few people live there because it's too cold. There is a central government in Moscow, but many regions have their own laws, parliaments and languages.

*In some parts of Russia it can be extremely cold. These children live in the Kamchatka region where the average temperature is -40°C (-40°F).*

## New freedoms

Under Communism there were strict rules. Books and newspapers were tightly regulated, religion was suppressed and it was hard to leave the country. In 1991, the Communists were defeated and the U.S.S.R. broke up into 15 new countries. Many of the old rules were relaxed. However, the new freedoms also meant that crime increased. Many people are poorer than they were under Communism, because the state no longer looks after everyone.

## Varied literature

Russian literature is well-known around the world. Russia's most famous writers include Dostoevsky, Tolstoy and Pushkin; they wrote realist novels. However Russia also has a rich tradition of magical folk tales and fairy tales, which have been passed down orally for centuries.

### Internet links

**Website 1** Take a virtual journey around Russia with a clickable map.

**Website 2** Discover key facts about Russia.

**Website 3** Go sightseeing in Moscow, the capital of Russia.

**Website 4** Meet the people and wildlife of eastern Siberia.

For links to these websites, go to
**www.usborne-quicklinks.com**

# THE MIDDLE EAST

The Middle East is famous for its beautiful old buildings and wealthy modern cities, and the hospitality of its peoples. It was where Sumer, the home of the first civilization, was; and it is the nucleus of the world's oil industry. It is sometimes seen as a trouble spot, because of the many wars and revolutions that have taken place there.

*These are Marsh Arabs, a people from Iraq who live in houses built on floating platforms of reeds. They are loading mats made from reeds onto a truck.*

*This woman in Oman is wearing a mask to cover her face. Some Islamic women cover their faces in public to protect their modesty.*

## What is the Middle East?

The Middle East is usually said to include the area between the Red Sea and the Persian Gulf, as well as Israel, Jordan, Syria, Lebanon, Iran and Iraq. It was named the Middle East by Europeans, because it is east of Europe, but not as far away as other Asian countries such as China and Japan (often referred to as the Far East).

## Different peoples

The peoples of the Middle East belong to four main groups: Arabs, Persians, Turks and Jews. The area's Arabic countries (Bahrain, Saudi Arabia, Yemen, Oman, Qatar, Kuwait and United Arab Emirates) lie in and around the peninsula of Arabia. Their people are Muslims and speak Arabic languages. But Iran, once known as Persia, is not Arabic, and nor is Turkey, although they too are mainly Muslim. Israel is a Jewish state which was created in 1948. Many Arabs claim that Israel's land belongs to an Arabic people, the Palestinians.

## Desert life

Stretching across the Middle East are vast deserts which contain important oil reserves. Few people live in these areas. However, some Bedouin herders still travel across the desert from one oasis to the next with their animals. They use either camels or four-wheel-drive vehicles to carry their tents and possessions.

*Bedouin people are nomads who traditionally live in the desert. These Bedouins are leading a train of camels.*

## Ancient and modern

When oil was discovered in the Middle East, it made many nations rich. They were able to rebuild their cities with new apartments and skyscrapers, and to provide for new banks and businesses. But most cities still have old areas with narrow streets and traditional markets, called souks.

*These huge towers in Kuwait are for water storage. Kuwait is a desert nation with no rivers or lakes, so sea water has to be processed to make it safe to drink, then stored.*

## Coffee and small talk

Coffee probably first came from Yemen, in southern Arabia, and it is still an important part of life in the Middle East. When Middle Eastern people have visitors, they usually offer them coffee, along with dates or pieces of cake called baklava. Then, even if there is something important to discuss, it is polite to make small talk over coffee before getting down to business.

*This is the traditional Middle Eastern way of pouring coffee, holding the pot up high to create a long, fine flow.*

### Internet links

For links to websites where you can find out about Middle Eastern countries and meet a boy from Kuwait, go to **www.usborne-quicklinks.com**

# CHINA

Nearly a quarter of the people on Earth are Chinese, and China is one of the world's oldest nations. It has existed for about 2,000 years, and had one of the earliest civilizations. The ancient Chinese invented paper, silk, gunpowder and seismology, the science of predicting earthquakes.

## Ancient arts

China has a lot of traditional art and culture, including opera, pottery (known as china), kite making and jade carving. A type of beautiful writing known as calligraphy is also considered a form of art. It usually consists of black letters painted using a brush.

*In Chinese cities people often use pedal power to get around. These children are riding in a wooden trailer on the back of a tricycle.*

## Population explosion

In 1982, China became the first country to have over a billion people. It now has around 1.2 billion. It is hard for China to provide enough food, schools and doctors for all its people. Since the 1950s, the government has tried to slow down the population increase. Couples are encouraged to get married later in life, and to have only one child.

## Farming nation

Even though China has a lot of big cities, nearly three-quarters of its people live in the countryside and survive by farming. Their main crops are rice, wheat and millet.

China is mountainous, and only about 10% of its land is fertile, so all the soil has to be used carefully. Terraces built into hillsides allow farmers to grow crops on steep slopes. Throughout China, farmland is irrigated, or watered, using systems of canals and streams.

*Chinese opera costumes are very elaborate and performers often wear heavy make-up.*

## Chinese beliefs

Many people in China follow Confucianism, a way of behaving based on the ideas of Confucius, who lived in the area 2,500 years ago. He taught that people should be polite and considerate and obey their elders.

The ancient Chinese worshipped their ancestors and various gods. These old beliefs are remembered at certain times of the year. For example, many families keep a picture of the kitchen god next to the kitchen stove. Just before the New Year, they take it down and smear honey and wine on the god's lips to keep him happy. When the New Year arrives, a new picture is put up.

*This is a holder for burning incense sticks. Incense gives off a scent which is said to attract the attention of the gods.*

## New Year

The start of the Chinese year, which is usually in February, is marked with celebrations, including fireworks, parades and feasts. People decorate their homes with symbols of good fortune and unmarried people receive red envelopes containing money for good luck.

### Internet links

**Website 1** Explore an online guide to China, see famous landmarks and try a quiz.

**Website 2** See your name in Chinese and find out how Chinese numbers are written.

For links to these websites, go to **www.usborne-quicklinks.com**

## Spellings

Chinese writing uses symbols, or characters, to represent words. In other languages, Chinese words have to be written down as they sound. Recently these spellings have been changed to make them more consistent, so you might see different spellings in different books.

*The Chinese characters on the right spell out the phrase "Peoples of the World".*

*The final day of Chinese New Year celebrations culminates in the Lantern Festival, where elaborate lanterns like this dragon lantern are carried along in a night-time procession.*

世界各民族

# INDIA AND PAKISTAN

India and Pakistan straddle the area where, around 4,500 years ago, a complex ancient society began in and around the Indus Valley. The two countries are now both modern states, but many of their people also follow ancient traditions and beliefs.

Pakistani truck, van and bus drivers are proud of their hand-decorated vehicles, like this truck covered in patterns and symbols.

## Dividing into states

India and Pakistan used to be one country, which was ruled by Britain in the 19th century. Britain agreed to grant India its independence in 1947, but Hindus and Muslims wanted their own separate states. So the country was divided into two parts: Pakistan for the Muslims, and India for the more numerous Hindus. At first, Bangladesh was part of Pakistan, but it too became independent in 1971.

## East and West

Britain's influence can be seen all over India and Pakistan. European-style buildings from the time of British rule stand among mosques and temples. Cricket, originally an English game, is an important sport in both India and Pakistan.

Indians and Pakistanis wear a mixture of European-style clothes and traditional dress, such as the *shalwar kameez* (baggy shirt and trousers) in Pakistan and the sari, a wrap-around gown, in India.

Women from Rajasthan, in India, carrying heavy loads on their heads

The building in the background is the Taj Mahal, near the city of Agra. It is an elaborate tomb built by a 17th-century Indian emperor, Shah Jahan, for his wife.

# Film fanatics

India has the world's biggest film industry, based in Mumbai (Bombay) and known as "Bollywood". Bollywood films are usually love stories or historical dramas, with lots of songs and dance routines. The top film stars and singers are incredibly rich and famous.

# Getting around

In crowded cities such as Lahore and Calcutta, the streets are full of buses, trams, taxis, rickshaws and bikes jostling for space with pedestrians and market stalls. In India, cows wander the streets as well. Hindus regard cows as sacred animals and no one is allowed to harm them, so they slow down the traffic as everyone tries to keep out of their way.

*Posters advertising Bollywood films*

## Internet links

**Website 1** Facts on the people and places of India and Pakistan.

**Website 2** Find an online guide to Bollywood, with photographs and a quiz.

For links to these websites, go to **www.usborne-quicklinks.com**

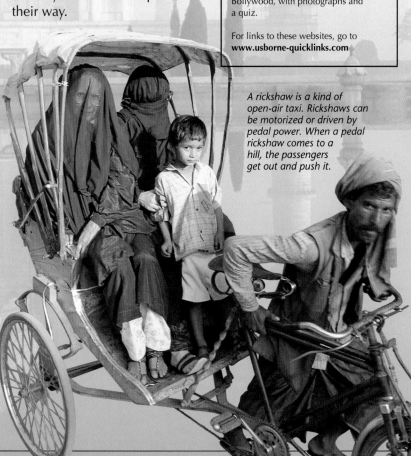

*A rickshaw is a kind of open-air taxi. Rickshaws can be motorized or driven by pedal power. When a pedal rickshaw comes to a hill, the passengers get out and push it.*

# Caste

In Indian tradition, most people are born with a *Jati*, or caste, an inherited status. In ancient India, it determined the job you did, and you could only marry someone from the same group. *Jati* is still important to many people and people of the same *Jati* support each other. But some of the old laws have been abolished, so that Indians from all levels of society can hold positions of power.

# Curry craze

Spicy food from Pakistan and India is popular across the globe. Its name "curry" comes from *kari*, from the Tamil language of southern India. Curry is usually vegetables or meat with a sauce, eaten with rice or bread. Hindus avoid eating meat, so Indian food is often vegetarian.

# SOUTHEAST ASIA

Southeast Asia stretches out into the sea to the south of China and Japan. The countries there, including Thailand, Vietnam, Laos, Malaysia and Indonesia, are spread out over a long peninsula and a series of hilly, forested islands.

*This girl is performing a traditional dance, called the Legong, from Bali, in Indonesia.*

## Performing arts

Southeast Asia has a rich tradition of performing arts, often combining music, dance and drama. Performances are visually stunning, making use of masks and elaborate costumes.

In Indonesia, an unusual form of storytelling has developed which uses shadow puppets to tell the stories. The puppets are two-dimensional figures moved using rods. During a show, a light and a screen are placed behind them, so you can just see their silhouettes. A puppet's features reveal its character and status, so the audience is able to recognize key character types.

*This is an Indonesian shadow puppet. It is moved using the rods attached to its arms and head.*

## Temples and mosques

In Southeast Asia, many different religions exist side by side, usually peacefully. Some countries, such as Burma, are mainly Buddhist; others, such as Indonesia, are mainly Muslim; but other religions such as Christianity and Hinduism are also common. Temples, mosques and churches are found everywhere. There are also many ruined temples which have now been abandoned.

### Internet links

For links to websites where you can take virtual tours of Vietnam, Thailand and South Korea and watch an introduction to shadow puppets, go to **www.usborne-quicklinks.com**

# Nations in pieces

Malaysia, Indonesia and the Philippines stretch across a vast archipelago (a network of islands) southeast of the Asian mainland. Even within the same country, different islands can be very unlike each other.

For example, Bali, one of Indonesia's most populated islands, is small and crowded, with farms, towns and a big tourist industry. Its main religion is a type of Hinduism, and it has thousands of temples.

Irian Jaya, part of the much bigger island of New Guinea, is very remote, with thick forests. Most of its peoples live by farming, fishing and hunting. Some have converted to Christianity, while others worship the spirits of their ancestors.

*On the marshy eastern coast of Sumatra in Indonesia, men and boys spend part of the year fishing from huts on tall stilts built up to 10km (6 miles) out at sea.*

# Rice and spice

Although Southeast Asia has some big cities, most of its people are farmers and live in the countryside. Rice is their main crop and it forms a part of almost every meal.

Thailand and Indonesia are famous for their spicy food. Spices are not a major crop now, but hundreds of years ago they made this part of the world rich. Merchants came from India, Arabia, Europe and China to buy cloves, mace and nutmeg, which were more valuable than gold.

# Elephant work

On the Southeast Asian mainland, elephants are used to transport people and for moving heavy loads, such as logs. Sometimes they are also dressed up in glittery costumes for parades and special occasions.

In Laos (which was once known as the Land of a Million Elephants) and Thailand, each working elephant has its own trainer, or mahout. One mahout may spend his whole life caring for the same animal.

*A mahout starts working with an elephant while it is still young. Over the years they build up a close relationship. These baby elephants are just starting to be trained.*

# BIG BUSINESS

Although many Asians are poor and live by farming, Asia is also home to some of the world's biggest banking, trading and manufacturing nations.

*A farm worker in India gathers crocuses to collect saffron from them. Saffron is added to food and can be used as a yellow dye.*

## Trading history

Some of the reasons for the success of Asian cities are historical. Hong Kong, Singapore and Dubai are ancient ports on trading routes that have been used for centuries. The Chinese, in particular, have a long history of trading. They invented paper money in the 9th century.

## New resources

As the population of Asia has risen, some countries have been unable to make enough money from traditional industries such as farming, so they have turned to business and services instead. For example, Japan has very little fertile land, but banking and manufacturing have allowed it to become rich without relying on its natural resources.

*These are banknotes from Singapore. Singapore is one of Asia's "Four Tigers" – countries which became known for their fast-growing economies.*

## Money from oil

In some parts of Asia, especially the Middle East, a lot of wealth comes from selling oil. The money can then be lent to other businesses and used to build hotels, restaurants and new apartments. This type of financial service is provided by banks called merchant banks, which can become very rich in the process. In this way, these countries provide for when the oil runs out.

# Ways of working

Some people suggest that business in Asia is successful because the culture places a positive emphasis on working hard, giving Asian peoples a strong "work ethic".

For example, many Japanese people have a strong work ethic, believing you should work long hours if necessary, and be loyal to your company. Singapore, meanwhile, is famous for its culture of honesty, making it a popular place for other countries to trade with.

# Big buildings

Big businesses need big office blocks, and the money they make means they can afford to build new, expensive skyscrapers. Asian countries compete with each other to create the most amazing modern architecture and the tallest skyscrapers. The Petronas Towers building in Kuala Lumpur, Malaysia, is currently the tallest building in the world.,

*This is a view of Kuala Lumpur, in Malaysia. In the middle, you can see the impressive twin towers of the Petronas Towers building. They are 452m (1,483ft) high.*

## Internet links

**Website 1** Discover more about Petronas Towers, the world's tallest building.

**Website 2** Read about the role of oil in the development of the Middle East.

For links to these websites, go to **www.usborne-quicklinks.com**

*This robot was developed by a Japanese electronics company. Japan is one of the world leaders in developing new technology.*

Masked partygoers at the Venice Carnival in Italy

PEOPLES OF
EUROPE

*This is a picture of St. John from a 12th century Christian manuscript.*

# EUROPE

Although Europe is the second smallest continent in the world, it contains over 40 countries, and its peoples speak more than 50 different languages. Throughout history there have been many migrations* within, to and from Europe.

## Ancient Europe

For nearly six centuries, until around 1,500 years ago, the Romans ruled much of Europe. Today, there are similarities in law, language, architecture and education across the continent that date back to the Romans. You can still see the ruins of Roman towns throughout Europe. The Romans took many of their ideas from the Greeks, who had their own powerful empire and culture.

## Christianity

Christianity has been the main religion in Europe since the days of the Roman Empire. Today, many Europeans do not go to church regularly, and many others follow different religions. Yet the influence of Christianity on art, architecture and culture can be seen all over Europe.

### Internet links

For links to websites where you can find out more about the history, geography and peoples of Europe, explore a clickable map and test your knowledge with online games and quizzes, go to **www.usborne-quicklinks.com**

*Migrations, 142; U.S.S.R., 204*

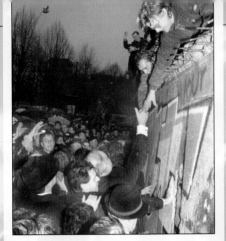

*People climbing on the Berlin Wall in 1989*

## European arts

Europe has produced many great artists, composers and writers. The ancient Greek poet Homer and the English playwright Shakespeare, composers like Bach, Mozart and Beethoven, and artists such as Michelangelo and Picasso are famous around the world. Europe also attracts millions of tourists every year to see its ancient ruins, beautiful architecture and fine art galleries.

## Europe divided

After the Second World War, much of eastern Europe was under the control of the Communist U.S.S.R.* Political differences between the U.S.S.R. and the non-Communist west increased until Europe split in two. In 1961, East German authorities built a wall in the German city of Berlin to prevent people fleeing from east to west. The wall was guarded by armed soldiers. In 1989, protests against the lack of freedom led to the destruction of the Berlin Wall.

*As well as having a great history of art, Europe still produces a wide range of art today. This is a modern sculpture, known as the "Angel of the North", in the north of England. Its huge steel structure is 20m (65ft) tall.*

# WESTERN EUROPE

In western Europe, most people live in cities or towns. City life can be fast and exciting and most western European cities have lots of stores, restaurants, cinemas, concert halls and museums. But many cities are also crowded and polluted.

*Pasta is popular around the world, but it is particularly associated with Italy. Here are some of the different pasta shapes.*

## Food culture

The food of western Europe is extremely varied and many countries are known for particular foods or ways of eating. For example, Italy is known for pizzas and pasta, Germany for sausages, Greece for kebabs and France for breads and cheeses. Many Spanish bars serve small snacks called tapas with drinks. These foods are popular in other countries around the world too.

## Work in industry

Many western Europeans have jobs in manufacturing industries, designing and making products such as cars and clothes. However, as more factories use machines and computers to make their products, more people are getting jobs in service industries. These are jobs which involve doing things for other people. Hotel staff, bank managers and TV presenters are examples of service jobs.

## Rural life

In a few parts of western Europe, farmers still use oxen to pull farm machinery, and harvest their crops by hand. But in most areas, only large, industrialized modern farms can survive, so smaller farms are disappearing.

## The Mediterranean

The northern coast of the Mediterranean Sea forms the southern border of Europe. People who live there enjoy long, hot, dry summers, which make the Mediterranean area a popular tourist destination. Many of the people living around the coast work in the tourist industry.

### Internet links

**Website 1** Take virtual tours of countries in Europe and see many famous landmarks.

**Website 2** View photo galleries of Venice.

**Website 3** Browse online guides to the UK, France and Spain for lots of facts and figures.

**Website 4** See some photos of festivals held in Spain.

**Website 5** Watch a video clip about a cheese-rolling festival near Gloucester, England.

For links to these websites, go to **www.usborne-quicklinks.com**

These are small ornamental masks sold as souvenirs in Venice. Full-size masks like these are worn by "masqueraders" at Venice's annual carnival.

## A watery city

Western Europe has many impressive historical cities, but one of the most unusual is Venice in Italy, which is divided into more than a hundred tiny islands by a network of canals. No cars are allowed in Venice's old town, so people get around on foot or by boat. There are special boats that provide public transportation and long, narrow boats called gondolas which tourists take rides in.

The Arc de Triomphe in Paris, France's capital, is a war monument which was commissioned by Napoleon in 1806. Today it is surrounded by huge, traffic-filled roads.

## Unusual festivals

Western Europeans celebrate many festivals including religious and national holidays, but there are also many unusual regional celebrations. For example, near Gloucester, England, there is a competition where people chase cheeses down a hill.

A dancer in Madrid, Spain, performs a traditional flamenco dance, involving dramatic stamping and twirling movements.

At the Sylvesterchlausen New Year celebration in Urnasch, Switzerland, people wearing masks go from house to house ringing bells and dancing. Spain has lots of local festivals. In Bunol, there is a huge annual tomato fight, and in Catalonia people make human castles by standing on one another's shoulders. Pamplona has a festival where people run through the streets ahead of bulls.

# EASTERN EUROPE

*This is a corridor in a school near Chernobyl which was evacuated after a nuclear disaster.*

**U**ntil the 1990s much of eastern Europe was ruled by the former Communist power the U.S.S.R.* But in the late 1980s and the 1990s, people rebelled against their Communist leaders, and today the area is a patchwork of independent states.

## Peoples at war

Over the centuries, eastern Europe has seen many wars. In recent years, fighting broke out when small ethnic groups demanded more freedom from the people who ruled over them. For example, Yugoslavia, now called Serbia and Montenegro, was once much bigger. It contained many peoples: Serbs, Bosnians, Croats, Slovenes, Montenegrins, Albanians and Macedonians. Since the Communist collapse in 1990, wars have raged in the area as ethnic groups have fought to set up their own states.

## Pollution

Pollution is a big problem in eastern Europe. Many factories, set up under Communism, still use old-fashioned fuels and methods which allow toxic gases to escape. In 1986, an accident at a nuclear power station in Chernobyl, Ukraine, sent radioactive dust into the air, polluting large areas of Europe. Hundreds of people had to leave their villages and the radiation made many people ill.

## Trade links

The collapse of the U.S.S.R. and Communism has led to an explosion of trade between eastern Europe and the rest of the world. As well as selling products such as wine and factory goods, eastern European countries have become major buyers of new technology such as computing systems and mobile phones.

*This is a statue from Statue Park, in Hungary. The park contains Communist statues that once stood in public places.*

*Communism, U.S.S.R., 204

## Spa towns

Spas are springs containing minerals. During the 19th century, it became fashionable throughout Europe to drink and bathe in spa waters. Many resorts were developed to cater for visitors. There are numerous spas throughout eastern Europe which remain popular today, such as those in Budapest in Hungary, and Karlovy Vary and Marianske Lazne in the Czech Republic. People can still go to these places to drink the waters.

### Internet links

**Website 1** Take a photo tour of Prague's buildings, including the "Ginger and Fred".

**Website 2** Find out what happened at Chernobyl and the aftermath of the world's worst nuclear accident.

For links to these websites, go to **www.usborne-quicklinks.com**

## Old age record

Georgia has more people who live to be over 100 than any other country. Many Georgians suggest this is due to their outdoor lifestyle, gentle climate and fertile farmland. According to Georgian legend, when God created the Georgians, he didn't have any land left for them to live on. So he had to give them the piece of land he had saved for himself, which was the best in the world.

## Architecture

Many cities of eastern Europe, such as Prague, Krakow and Budapest, have well-preserved old towns. These have winding cobbled streets and a wide variety of architecture, including impressive churches and castles. Some houses are made from wood and many larger houses have distinctive painted facades, or fronts. However, some cities, such as Warsaw in Poland, which had to be heavily rebuilt after the Second World War, are dominated by modern apartment buildings.

*This modern building in Prague was designed by an architect named Frank Gehry. It is nicknamed "Ginger and Fred" after the dancers Ginger Rogers and Fred Astaire, because its shape looks a little like a dancing couple.*

# NORTHERN EUROPE

Denmark, Sweden, Norway and Finland form the area known as Scandinavia. Together with the volcanic island of Iceland, they make up northern Europe. There is very little poverty in Scandinavia and Iceland, and their clean cities and countryside are envied by many.

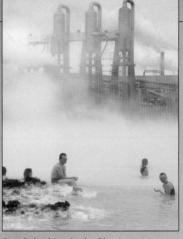

*People bathing in the Blue Lagoon, a warm spring near Keflavik in Iceland*

## Land of the Midnight Sun

The northern part of Scandinavia juts far into the Arctic, the area around the North Pole. In midwinter, for about a month, the people who live there see no daylight at all, while from the end of May until the end of July the Sun never sets. Because of this, it is sometimes known as the Land of the Midnight Sun.

*This hotel in Sweden is made entirely of ice. Every summer it melts and has to be rebuilt the following winter. Even the glasses people drink from are made of ice.*

*Skiing is a popular leisure activity in Scandinavia. In winter, it's also a way of getting to and from school and work.*

## Winter months

During the winter, much of northern Europe is covered in snow. In many places, skiing becomes the easiest way of getting around. Children often learn to ski as soon as they can walk, and some ski to school every morning. Many places hold annual ski competitions.

## The environment

Many children and adults in Scandinavia belong to "green" groups that try to protect the environment by looking after the countryside and preventing pollution. Governments run recycling projects to collect reusable products from people's homes, and Scandinavia leads the way in building eco-friendly homes which use solar panels and insulation to save energy.

## Lapland

Lapland, in the far north of Scandinavia, is one of the last areas of wilderness in Europe. It stretches from northern Russia across the north of Finland, and through parts of Sweden and Norway. It is home to the Sami, a people with their own language and culture. Some of the Sami still live a traditional lifestyle and herd reindeer. Their traditional homes are conical tents called *kota*. But these days most Sami live in houses, grouped together in small villages.

*A Sami reindeer herder in northern Norway tends a newborn reindeer calf.*

### Internet links

**Website 1** Explore a hotel built of ice and snow in Sweden.

**Website 2** Find facts about Scandinavia with a clickable map.

**Website 3** Go on a virtual sightseeing tour of Iceland.

For links to these websites, go to **www.usborne-quicklinks.com**

## Daring design

Scandinavia is famous for its exciting design styles. Scandinavian companies are renowned for making everyday objects, like chairs, tables and cars, that are simple to use yet beautiful to look at. The Scandinavian style is now copied all over the world.

# A UNITING EUROPE

Most of Europe's countries belong to organizations such as the European Union and the Council of Europe, in which several states band together to support each other. Many Europeans feel this has major advantages, although others worry that countries may lose their individuality.

*Representatives of E.U. states meet in Strasbourg, France.*

## What is the E.U.?

The E.U., or European Union, is the most important European organization. It dates from 1957, when Belgium, France, Italy, Germany, Luxembourg and the Netherlands formed the E.E.C. (European Economic Community) to improve trade and cooperation between their countries. The group changed over the years, and in 1993 it became known as the European Union. By the year 2000 it had 15 members, with more applying to join.

**Internet links**

**Website 1** Explore an online guide to the E.U.

**Website 2** Key E.U. facts and figures.

**Website 3** A brief guide to the euro.

For links to these websites, go to **www.usborne-quicklinks.com**

## Free trade

The E.U. has set up laws to allow its member states to trade with each other easily. The E.U. also has laws to regulate measuring systems and safety standards for its workers, and workers from any E.U. state can work in any other without a visa or work permit.

*The E.U. flag and the flags of its member states. Can you identify which country each flag belongs to?*

## Single currency

In the 1990s, the European Union began to introduce a single currency called the Euro. Eventually it is intended to replace the national currencies of all the member states. However, some countries did not join the single currency immediately. It was launched on January 1, 1999, with 11 member states taking part.

*These are 50-cent coins, part of the new Euro currency. There are 100 cents in one Euro.*

## The Council of Europe

The Council of Europe is not part of the E.U. It is a European organization that exists to protect human rights in Europe. It has 41 members, many more than the E.U. The citizens of any of its member states can appeal to the European Court, run by the Council of Europe, if they feel they are not being treated fairly by the legal system in their own country.

*The E.U. flag has 12 stars representing the 12 states which were members when the E.U. was named in 1993.*

## Euro-skeptics

Although belonging to European organizations brings benefits, it may also have disadvantages. Some people in Europe are worried that the increasing power of European organizations could threaten the unique culture of individual countries. In several countries, political activists, sometimes called Euro-skeptics, campaign to stop their governments from signing up to European laws and joining the single currency.

*These are farmers from all over Europe protesting in Strasbourg against some of the European Union's agricultural policies.*

# EUROPE AND THE WORLD

Over the centuries, European countries have explored and dominated many other lands, imposing their languages, customs and cultures. Europe itself has also been greatly influenced by the cultures it has come into contact with.

**Internet links**

For links to websites where you can see how World War Two affected the history of the UK and find out more about European explorers and the colonization of Africa, go to **www.usborne-quicklinks.com**

*This cloud was produced by the atomic bomb that was dropped on Nagasaki, in Japan, on August 9, 1945. Five days later Japan surrendered, ending the Second World War.*

## Two world wars

The First and Second World Wars of the 20th century both began in Europe. They grew larger as nations around the world became involved. Both wars spread as far as Africa and the Far East.

The Second World War in particular had a huge impact on the world. It began in 1939 after German troops, under the leadership of Adolf Hitler, began invading other European countries. Nations worldwide took sides in the conflict, and the war only ended in 1945, after the U.S.A. used newly invented nuclear weapons against two Japanese cities, Hiroshima and Nagasaki.

## Science

Europe's inventors and scientists have changed the world. The idea that the world was round and not flat began in ancient Greece. When it was finally proved in the 15th century, it spurred European explorers to discover and colonize other continents.

Europeans also invented machines such as the steam engine, which led to the Industrial Revolution in the 18th century. This meant goods began to be mass-produced in factories instead of being made by individual craftspeople. Colonization ensured that European-style factories soon spread around the world.

## Cultural exchanges

In the past, many Europeans saw it as their right to spread European culture in the places they colonized. For example, Spanish missionaries spread Catholicism in South America, and British educational and political systems were put in place in India. Most former European colonies are now independent, but some aspects of European culture, such as religions and clothes styles, remain behind. These former colonies have also had an influence on European culture and some people from them have moved to Europe.

*This is the Royal Pavilion in Brighton, in the south of England. The design of the building was influenced by architecture in India, a former British colony.*

*These young Indian boys are learning to play cricket, which was brought to India from Britain.*

## Colonization

Like other peoples around the world, Europeans have been exploring for thousands of years. On many expeditions, European explorers also attempted to colonize the places they found, and bring them under European control.

From the 1500s onwards, Spain and Portugal ruled much of South America, Britain colonized India, and several European nations claimed parts of Africa. During the 18th and 19th centuries, European countries ruled over more than half the people in the world.

Zulu men wearing traditional headdresses for a celebration in Durban, South Africa

# PEOPLES OF
# AFRICA

# AFRICA

Africa is a huge continent, the second biggest in the world. It contains more than 50 countries, many hundreds of peoples and many different religions and ways of life. Yet many Africans also have a sense of belonging together as one big group, especially in the part of the continent south of the Sahara Desert.

These women are collecting water from a village well in Burkina Faso.

## Freedom

In the 15th century, Europeans began to transport people from West Africa to Europe and North and South America to work as slaves.

Slavery was abolished in the 19th century, but European countries then began to take over Africa for themselves. Most of the continent was divided into colonies ruled by Portugal, Belgium, Italy, France, Britain and Germany. The African peoples resisted foreign rule, and most African countries became independent in the 1960s and 1970s.

# 1,000 languages

Over 1,000 languages are spoken in Africa. Countries with lots of languages usually have an official language as well, so that everyone can communicate with each other easily.

Most people learn the official language for use at work and at school, but may speak other languages at home and with their friends.

## Internet links

**Website 1** Find facts about African countries with a clickable map.

**Website 2** Travel through the history of Africa with an interactive timeline.

**Website 3** Explore a timeline of the life of an African slave.

**Website 4** Take a photo tour of Africa.

For links to these websites, go to **www.usborne-quicklinks.com**

*Two Masai\* women, wearing traditional dress, talk together. The language they speak is also called Masai. The Masai people live in Kenya and Tanzania.*

*A Herero woman milks a cow in her village in Botswana. Herero women wear bright dresses with full skirts, and skilfully arranged headscarves called* taku *or distinctive hats.*

# Africa's peoples

Africa's largest populations are mainly in its capital cities, but Africa as a whole is sparsely populated and many of its people lead rural lives. Around three thousand different ethnic groups have been classified. One country can contain many different peoples, while a single ethnic group can spread across several countries.

*\*Masai, 241*

# PEOPLES AND POWER

Africa was once made up of ethnic kingdoms, each with its own language and culture. But when European powers split Africa into countries, the new borders ran across the kingdoms of peoples such as the Tuareg and the Masai, dividing up their homelands.

*This woman is one of the Berber people of northern Africa. She is spinning wool in the traditional way.*

## Ethnic emphasis

Africans often feel that their ethnic group is just as important as their nationality. Instead of just being Ghanaian or Kenyan, for example, Africans may introduce themselves as Yoruba, Bantu, Mundani, !Kung San, Berber, or one of hundreds of other groups.

## Wars and civil wars

After countries such as Chad, Nigeria and Angola gained independence from Europe, different ethnic groups began to fight for power. Many of the wars still going on in Africa are based on ethnic disagreements. Often, as in the conflict between Hutu and Tutsi peoples in Rwanda and Burundi in the 1990s,

people on the losing side are forced to flee across borders to nearby countries for safety. These people are called refugees*. When there are large numbers of refugees they may have to live in temporary refugee camps.

*This is a refugee camp in Rwanda. It provided a temporary shelter for thousands of people who were forced to leave home by the war there in 1994.*

*Refugees, 142

## Local leaders

Although African countries are ruled by their governments, many villages and ethnic groups also have their own local leaders, or chiefs. A chief has the power to settle disputes, and presides over ceremonies and official celebrations. The role of chief is usually passed from father to son.

*This is a leader of the Anlo-Ewe people of Ghana, dressed in ceremonial clothing.*

### Internet links

**Website 1** Find lots of information about life in Africa today.

**Website 2** Read about the problem of drought facing Africa.

**Website 3** Meet Asamoah, a cocoa producer in Ghana.

**Website 4** Visit four different schools in Africa.

For links to these websites, go to **www.usborne-quicklinks.com**

## The Nanas Benz of Togo

Women rarely gain political power in African governments. But some African peoples have matriarchal societies. This means that power is passed from mother to daughter. In parts of Togo, for example, rich female cloth traders called "Nanas Benz" are the most powerful people in their communities. They pass on their businesses and their wealth to their daughters. If they only have sons, they pass everything to their nieces instead.

# DESERT LANDS

The Sahara, the world's biggest desert, divides northern Africa from the rest of the continent. The Mediterranean countries (Morocco, Algeria, Tunisia, Libya and Egypt) are Muslim nations. They tend to have more in common with the Middle East than with the rest of Africa.

*These pendants represent the Hand of Fatima, the daughter of Mohammed who is the main prophet of Islam.*

## Life in the desert

The Sahara takes up most of northern Africa, though only a few people live there. These include the Tuareg, a nomadic people who looked after trade routes in the desert in ancient times. Because of severe droughts in the last few decades, many desert people have had to abandon their old lifestyles and move to the cities.

## Fatima's hand

In Northern Africa, the Muslim religion is very important. Most people pray several times each day. They also protect themselves from bad luck with images of a patterned hand, called the Hand of Fatima. It is said to ward off the "evil eye", which means a curse caused by a jealous glance.

*Traditionally, Tuareg men wear veils like these, which show only the eyes, in the presence of women and strangers.*

## Walled cities

In some modern northern African cities, such as Marrakesh in Morocco and Tunis in Tunisia, there are still old medieval towns, or *medinas*. Surrounded by tall, thick walls, these old towns are crammed with tiny winding streets, along which markets, or *souks,* are held. Different kinds of goods are sold or made in different areas of the town. For example, noisy or smelly trades such as leather-making take place near the edge of the town, while crafts such as bookbinding are close to the main mosque.

*These impressive walls surround the old town of Marrakesh in Morocco. Most of the city's modern buildings lie outside these walls.*

## Ancient history

There have been big cities and advanced civilizations in northern Africa for thousands of years, and there are now hundreds of ancient ruins all over the area. The most famous monuments are the pyramids, built by the ancient Egyptians as tombs for their pharaohs, or kings. There are also lots of amazing ruins in Tunisia, including a huge Roman colosseum at El Jem.

### Internet links

**Website 1** Find out about the Sahara desert and the Tuareg who live there.

**Website 2** Try activities about ancient Egypt's pyramids, temples and more. For links to these websites, go to

**www.usborne-quicklinks.com**

*A statue of Tutankhamun, a pharaoh of ancient Egypt, found in his tomb in the Valley of the Kings*

## Along the Nile

Egypt is not as dry as the rest of the Sahara, as it has the Nile, the longest river in the world, running through it. The Nile floods every spring, making the area along its banks very fertile. Rice, wheat and oranges are grown there.

The flooding is now regulated by a huge dam, the Aswan High Dam, completed in 1968. Thousands of local Nubian people had to leave their homes to make space for the large lake that the dam created.

# WEST AND CENTRAL AFRICA

The countries of West and Central Africa are tightly packed around a huge bay known as the Gulf of Guinea. Nigeria, right in the middle of this region, is Africa's most populous country. This part of the world is characterized by its diversity of peoples, cultures and religions, and its thriving art and music scene.

## The Sahel

The Sahel is a strip of dry land south of the Sahara Desert. Countries there, such as Chad, Niger and Mali, are cut off from the coast and have little fertile land. Bad droughts happen every few years. Nomadic herders, such as the Tuareg, live in the north of the Sahel. In the south, the land is greener and people live by farming and fishing.

*Left: Dogon people dance on stilts at a traditional celebration in the village of Sangha, Mali.*

## Along the coast

The small countries along the western African coast, such as Ghana and Senegal, are among Africa's wealthier nations. As well as farming and fishing, many of them mine valuable deposits of iron ore, diamonds and gold. Having been ruled by Europe, these countries gained their independence in the mid-20th century. But some, such as Sierra Leone, have been damaged by wars between groups battling for power.

# Nigeria

Nigeria is a land of huge diversity, from the high-rise coastal city of Lagos to tropical forests in the east, and dusty plains and mud-walled villages in the central regions. Nigeria also has many different peoples, belonging to over 250 ethnic groups. The biggest groups are the mainly-Muslim Hausa and Fulani peoples of the north, the Christian Igbo of the south, and the southwestern Yoruba people, most of whom follow traditional local religions.

This statue is part of a Yoruba shrine in Oshogbo, southwestern Nigeria, dedicated to a river goddess called Oshun.

## Internet links

**Website 1** Find out about the extreme conditions of the Sahel and the problems of the people who live there.

**Website 2** Take a sightseeing trip of Nigeria.

For links to these websites, go to **www.usborne-quicklinks.com**

A street in Lagos, Nigeria's biggest city, crammed with cars, buses, pedestrians and busy markets

These Buduma people are fishing from a papyrus reed boat. The Buduma live on a series of islands in Lake Chad, which is bordered by Chad, Niger, Nigeria and Cameroon.

## Diverse religions

Across Africa, many ancient, local belief systems are still strong. They often involve animism, a belief in spirits belonging to plants or animals. The spirit world is believed to exist alongside the physical world and to be able to affect it in various ways.

# LANDSCAPES OF THE EAST

Africa's most famous landscapes are found along its eastern side, where deserts in the north give way to grasslands, lakes and wildlife reserves in the Great Rift Valley. This region has been influenced by many peoples, including Indians, Arabs, and local ethnic groups such as the Masai.

*Eastern Africa has huge expanses of open grasslands which are home to many large animals, such as lions.*

## The Horn of Africa

The Horn of Africa is a hook-shaped piece of land sticking out into the sea just south of Arabia. The countries there, such as Ethiopia, Djibouti and Somalia, are hot and dry, and most people live by herding cattle from place to place.

Recently Ethiopia and Somalia have suffered from famines, triggered by droughts which have killed crops and farm animals. Money has often been spent on wars instead of food, and areas have become so dangerous that aid workers are unable to reach them.

## Ecotourism

In Kenya and Tanzania, the Great Rift Valley's grassy plains teem with leopards, lions, antelopes and other wildlife. These countries have set aside huge national parks and reserves, which not only protect the animals, but also make money from tourism. In the past, people paid to hunt these animals, but now tourists go on safaris to spot and photograph them.

*The round, thatched huts in this farming village near Belet Weyne, Somalia, are typical traditional East African homes. There is also a pen for the cattle.*

## Losing a lake

The peoples who live around Lake Victoria, which straddles Uganda, Tanzania and Kenya, have fished in the lake and used it as a way to get around for centuries. But recently Lake Victoria has been polluted by fertilizers running into it from coffee and tea fields, and the amount of fish in it has fallen.

## Great Rift Valley

The Great Rift Valley is made up of a huge series of valleys and lakes which stretch all the way down East Africa. The lakes and fertile hillsides make this a good area for fishing and farming. Archaeologists searching there have found skulls and tools which suggest that East Africa was the home of the first ever human beings.

## The Masai

East Africa is home to many local ethnic groups. The Masai, who live in Tanzania and Kenya, are proud of their nomadic cattle-herding lifestyle. They rarely slaughter their cattle for food. Instead, they get protein by drinking milk and blood drawn from the cattle.

Today, Masai people also visit towns to sell their cattle and buy goods. Some also make money by selling their famous beadwork and posing in traditional dress for tourists.

### Internet links

**Website 1** Meet a young Masai boy called Dita and read a report about his daily life.

**Website 2** Take a photo tour of the Serengeti National Park in Tanzania.

**Website 3** Find out about life in Kenya.

For links to these websites, go to **www.usborne-quicklinks.com**

*A young Masai woman dressed up in a traditional beadwork headdress, necklaces and earrings*

# SOUTHERN AFRICA

S outhern Africa is a region of rich farmland, dusty deserts, beautiful coasts and steamy swamps. It is dominated by South Africa, Africa's richest country. South Africa's mines, farms and factories provide work for many people from other southern African countries. Yet South Africa itself is in the midst of huge changes.

*The mining of precious stones such as diamonds creates jobs for many people in South Africa.*

## Divisions and inequality

In 1994, South Africa held its first free election after more than 40 years of a regime known as apartheid. Under apartheid (which means "apartness"), only white people could vote. They ruled the country, and the main ethnic groups were forced to live separately from each other.

At the election, a party called the African National Congress was voted into power and things began to change. People of all ethnic groups can now live and work together. But there are big inequalities, and many South Africans still struggle with poverty, violence and a high crime rate.

*Nelson Mandela was a leading member of South Africa's anti-apartheid movement. He was the country's president from 1994 to 1999.*

## Diamonds and gold

A lot of southern Africa's wealth comes from its rich deposits of valuable minerals. The world's biggest goldfield is in Witwatersrand, near Johannesburg in South Africa, and thousands of people across southern Africa work in mines extracting precious stones and metals.

### Internet links

**Website 1** Tour South Africa and read an interview with Nelson Mandela.

**Website 2** Meet the Xhosa, Zulu and San peoples of South Africa.

For links to these websites, go to **www.usborne-quicklinks.com**

## !Kung San

The Kalahari is a stony desert which occupies parts of Botswana, South Africa and Namibia. It has been home to the !Kung San people for several thousand years. Many have moved to the cities, but a few still live as hunter-gatherers. The men hunt wild animals, while the women and children collect nuts, fruit and honey.

The !Kung San, along with many other southern African peoples, speak a language belonging to a group called Khoisan languages. As well as vowels and consonants, these languages include clicking noises made with the tongue. The ! sign stands for just one of many different types of click.

*Hunter-gatherers, like these !Kung San picking berries in the Kalahari, have one of the world's oldest lifestyles.*

## Island life

*Two young boys from Madagascar carrying a fishing net. Fishing is an important part of island life.*

To the east of southern Africa lie the islands of Madagascar, Mauritius, Comoros and the Seychelles. The first people to live there came from Southeast Asia, over 4,000km (2,500 miles) away across the Indian Ocean. Today, the people are a mix of African, south Asian and Arabic ethnic groups. They make a living from fishing and tourism, and from growing spices.

# AFRICAN ART

**A**frica is famous for its arts and crafts of all kinds: sculpture and mask-making, painting, beadwork, pottery and carving. Traditionally, African artworks were used in religious ceremonies or worn on special occasions. Today, they are also sold to tourists, exported, or shown in art galleries.

## Prehistoric pictures

8,000-year-old rock paintings and engravings found in the Sahara Desert are the earliest examples of African art. The hunting scenes in these pictures suggest that the Sahara was once much greener than it is today, with more people and wildlife living in it.

*A prehistoric rock painting found in Tassili, Algeria, showing people with a herd of cattle.*

## Masks and statues

Masks and statues are much more common in African art than pictures of landscapes or objects. This is because African art is often designed for use in ceremonies. Masks and statues can show gods, spirits, or images of perfect beauty, and can also be used for good luck. Some Ashanti women in Ghana, for example, carry a figure of a baby as a charm to help them have healthy children.

*This mask is from Zimbabwe. It is part of a ceremonial dancing costume.*

# Symbolic coffins

In Accra, Ghana's capital city, an unusual art form has developed. Those who can afford it can be buried in special coffins built to represent their lifestyles. For example, a businessman might have a car-shaped coffin or a fisherman could have a fish or boat-shaped coffin.

*This chicken-shaped coffin was probably built for a farmer.*

## Internet links

**Website 1** Learn about life in Africa by looking at artwork.

**Website 2** Find out about Adinkra, an African fabric.

**Websites 3 and 4** Design an African mask and learn how to draw like an Egyptian.

For links to these websites, go to **www.usborne-quicklinks.com**

# Body art

Earrings and nose rings, face painting and elaborate hairstyles are vital elements of many traditional ceremonies. Some peoples also use tattooing and scarification (marking the skin with scars) to create a kind of body art.

*Women of the Nuer people of southern Sudan have their faces patterned with scars to mark their passage into adulthood.*

*Ancient Egyptian artworks, like this carving in Saqqara, attract many tourists to Africa every year.*

This map projection is called Boggs Eumorphic. It is a modified cylindrical
projection. This type of map reduces the distortion of land areas.

# ATLAS OF THE WORLD

# WHAT IS A MAP?

A map is an image that represents a particular area of the Earth's surface, usually from above and at a reduced size. A map can show the whole world or just a street. There can be many kinds of maps of the same place, each giving different types of information.

## What maps show

Unlike an aerial photograph, which shows exactly what an area looks like from above, a map can show features of the area in a clearer, simplified way. It can also give different kinds of information about the area, such as the names of places, the position of borders between countries, or the types of crops that grow there.

*This map was drawn in 1584. Although people at this time knew much less about the shapes and locations of countries, they still created many maps of the world.*

*On the left is a simple map of Baltimore Harbor, U.S.A. It just shows the area's main streets.*

*On this aerial photograph of the same area it's difficult to see the streets.*

## Internet links

**Website 1** Look at physical and political maps of different countries.

**Websites 2** Find out more about maps, map symbols and scale, with online quizzes.

For links to these websites, go to **www.usborne-quicklinks.com**

## Map features

Maps are designed to be clear, so most of them use conventions to help us recognize certain features. Land is often shown as green, and seas, rivers and lakes are usually shown as blue. Symbols can also be used to represent features. The meanings of the symbols are usually explained in a key.

Mountain vegetation

Coniferous forest

Deciduous forest

Grassland

Scrubland

This is a thematic map that shows Europe's natural vegetation. The key above indicates the type of land that the different shading represents.

# Kinds of maps

There are many different kinds of maps. Physical maps focus on natural features such as mountains, rivers and lakes. Political maps focus on the division of the Earth's surface into separate states*. Some maps are thematic. This means that only certain information, such as climate types or population, is represented. Thematic maps can help us make comparisons between the features of different areas.

# Which way is up?

Although the Earth doesn't have a top and a bottom, north is usually at the top of maps. But it is sometimes more convenient to reposition a map, so north might not necessarily be at the top. Some maps have a compass symbol that indicates where north lies.

# Scale

The size of a map in relation to the area it shows is called its scale. Some maps have a scale bar, which is a rule with measurements. It tells you how many miles or km are represented by a certain distance on the map. Other maps show this ratio in numbers. The figure 1:100 may mean, for example, that 1cm on the map represents 100cm on the Earth's surface. The scale of a map depends on its purpose. A map showing the whole world is on a very small scale, but a town plan is on a much larger scale so that features, such as roads and buildings, can be shown clearly.

1:80,000,000

0    1,000    2,000    3,000km

0              1,000        2,000 miles

This map of Europe is on a small scale so that it all fits onto one small map.

1:7,000,000

0        100      200      300km

0                100            200 miles

This map of Denmark is on a larger scale to show more detail.

*States, 256

# DIVIDING LINES

We divide up the Earth with imaginary lines to help us measure distances and find where places are. There are two sets of lines, called latitude and longitude.

This arctic fox lives in northern Canada, very near the Arctic Circle line of latitude.

## Latitude lines

Lines of latitude run around the globe. They are parallel to each other and get shorter the closer they are to the two poles. The latitude line that runs around the middle of the Earth is called the Equator. It is the most important line of latitude as all other lines are measured north or south of it.

*Latitude lines*     *Longitude lines*

## Longitude lines

Lines of longitude run from the North Pole to the South Pole. All the lines are the same length, and they all meet at the North and South Poles.

The most important line of longitude is the Prime Meridian Line, which runs through Greenwich, in England. All other lines of longitude are measured east or west of this line.

## Other lines

The Equator is not the only named latitude line. The Tropic of Cancer is a line north of the Equator. The Tropic of Capricorn is at the same distance south of the Equator. Between these lines is the hottest, stormiest part of the world. It is called the tropics.

The Arctic Circle is a latitude line far north of the Equator. The area north of this includes the North Pole and is called the Arctic. On the other side of the globe is the Antarctic Circle. The area south of this includes the South Pole and is known as the Antarctic.

*Here is a drawing of the Earth, showing the main lines of latitude and longitude.*

North Pole

Arctic Circle (66°30'N)

Prime Meridian Line (0°)

Tropic of Cancer (23°27'N)

Equator (0°)

Lines of longitude

Lines of latitude

Tropic of Capricorn (23°27'S)

South Pole

### Internet links

**Website 1** Find out more about latitude and longitude and the other lines on a map.

**Website 2** Play a latitude and longitude game.

For links to these websites go to **www.usborne-quicklinks.com**

250

## Using the lines

Lines of latitude and longitude are measured in degrees (°). We describe the positions of places according to which lines of latitude and longitude are nearest to them. For example, a place with a location of 50°S and 100°E has a latitude 50 degrees south of the Equator, and a longitude 100 degrees east of the Prime Meridian Line.

## Exact locations

The distance between degrees is divided up to give even more precise measurements. Each degree is divided into 60 minutes ('), and each minute is divided into 60 seconds ("). The subdivisions allow us to locate any place on Earth. For example, the city of New York, U.S.A., is at 40°42'51"N and 74°00'23"W.

*The steamy rainforests of Malaysia lie near the Equator. Many orangutans, like the one shown here, live in these rainforests.*

## Using a grid

Lines of latitude and longitude form grids on maps. The maps in this book look similar to the one on the left. The vertical columns formed by lines of longitude are marked with letters, and the horizontal rows formed by lines of latitude are numbered.

All the places listed in the map index on page 376 have a letter and a number reference that tell you where to find them on a particular page. For example, on the map on the left, the city of Christchurch would have a grid reference of C3.

*This is a map of New Zealand, with a grid formed by lines of latitude and longitude.*

A   B   C   D

2

1

Auckland
Hamilton   North Island

*Tasman Sea*

Lake
Taupo

2

3

South Island   ■Wellington

**NEW
ZEALAND**

Christchurch

Dunedin

3

4

Chatham Islands
(New Zealand)

B   C   D   E

# LOOKING AT THE EARTH

**M**odern technology has enabled scientists to make more accurate maps of the world than ever before. Even remote places, such as deserts, ocean floors and mountain ranges, have been mapped in detail using information from satellites that observe the Earth from space.

## What is a satellite?

Artificial satellites are machines that orbit, or travel around, the Earth. They observe the Earth using a technique called remote sensing. Instruments on the satellite monitor the Earth without touching it, and send back pictures of its surface. Satellites also monitor moons and other planets.

*This satellite monitors the Earth 24 hours a day. It uses powerful radar that pierces through clouds. This means that the satellite can provide images of the Earth in all weather conditions.*

## Satellite movement

Some satellites orbit the Earth at a height of between 5km (3 miles) and 1,500km (930 miles), providing views of different parts of the planet. Others stay above the same place all the time, moving at the same speed as the Earth rotates to give a constant view of a particular area. These are called geostationary satellites. They travel at a height of around 36,000km (22,370 miles).

### Internet links

**Website 1** Zoom in and take a closer look at satellite pictures of the Earth.

**Website 2** Find out about navigation satellites and global positioning.

**Website 3** Learn what geographical information systems (GIS) are used for.

For links to these websites, go to **www.usborne-quicklinks.com**

This satellite image of Sicily was taken in July 2001. It shows the volcano Mount Etna erupting. You can see smoke from the volcano on the right of the picture.

## Satellite uses

The information provided by satellites helps scientists to produce accurate maps. Satellite pictures can also be used to help predict and monitor natural hazards such as volcanic eruptions or earthquakes. Some satellites monitor the weather*. Satellite images can also show the effects that people have on their environment, for example the destruction of rainforests in South America.

## Remote sensing

Satellites use a range of remote sensing techniques. One type is radar, which can provide images of the Earth even when it is dark or cloudy. Radar works by reflecting radio waves off a target object. The time it takes for a wave to bounce back indicates how far away the object is.

Powerful cameras provide pictures of the Earth's surface. Often, infrared cameras are used. Different surfaces reflect the infrared rays differently, so infrared images of the Earth are able to show its various types of land surfaces, such as deserts, grasslands and forests.

This satellite image of the Earth shows different types of land. Deserts and other dry regions are red, and areas with lots of vegetation are orange and yellow.

253

*Weather satellites, 90

# HOW MAPS ARE MADE

The process of making maps is called cartography. Map-makers, or cartographers, compile each map by gathering information about the area and representing it on paper as accurately as possible.

### Internet links

**Website 1** Find out more about map projections with interactive diagrams.

**Website 2** Watch video clips about map-making.

For links to these websites, go to **www.usborne-quicklinks.com**

## Creating maps

Many sources are used to create maps. These include satellite images and aerial photographs. Cartographers often visit the area to be mapped, where they take many extra measurements.

In addition, cartographers use statistics, such as population figures, from censuses* and other documents. As the maps are being made, many people check them to make sure they are accurate and up-to-date.

## Map projections

Cartographers can't draw maps that show the world exactly as it is, because it is impossible to show a curved surface on a flat map without distorting (stretching or squashing) some areas. A representation of the Earth on a map is called a projection. Projections are worked out using complex mathematics.

There are three basic types of projections – cylindrical, conical and azimuthal, but there are also variations on these. They all distort the Earth's surface in some way, either by altering the shapes or sizes of areas of land or the distance between places.

*A cartographer uses an electronic distance measurer to check the measurements of an area of land.*

# Cylindrical projections

A cylindrical projection is similar to what you would get if you wrapped a piece of paper around a globe to form a cylinder and then shone a light inside the globe. The shapes of countries would be projected onto the paper. Near the middle they would be accurate, but farther away they would be distorted.

Cartographers often alter the basic cylindrical projection to make the distortion less obvious in certain areas, but they can never make a map that is completely accurate.

*This picture of a piece of paper wrapped around a globe illustrates how a cylindrical projection is made.*

*Below is a type of cylindrical projection called the Mercator projection, which was invented in 1596 by a cartographer called Gerardus Mercator. It makes countries the right shape, but makes those near the poles too big.*

*This cylindrical projection makes countries the right size in relation to each other, but some parts are too long. The projection was created in 1973 by Arno Peters. It is called the Peters Projection.*

# Conical projections

A conical projection is similar to the image you would get if you wrapped a cone of paper around part of a globe, then shone a light inside the globe. Where the cone touches the globe, the projection will be most accurate.

*This picture of a cone of paper over a globe illustrates how a conical projection is made.*

*This is a conical projection. The land nearest the top is the most distorted in shape.*

# Azimuthal projections

An azimuthal projection is like an image made by holding paper in front of a globe, and shining a light through it. Land projected onto the middle of the paper would be accurate, but areas farther away would be distorted.

*This picture of a piece of paper placed in front of a globe illustrates how an azimuthal projection is made.*

*This is an azimuthal projection. The farther away land is from the middle, the more distorted it is.*

# STATES AND BORDERS

The world's main land masses, which are called continents, are divided into independent states and dependent territories. The different areas are separated by borders.

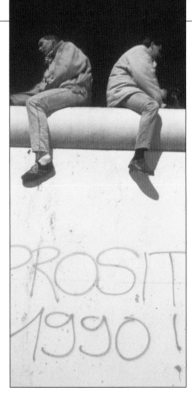

## What is a state?

A state is an area of land that has its own government* and is fully independent. Independent states are also known as countries.

Some large countries, such as the U.S.A., are split into several regions. Each region has its own government, which is responsible for the affairs of that region. In the U.S.A. these regions are also known as states.

## Changing states

States don't always stay the same. They can divide or merge. For example, Germany was split into two states after the Second World War, and was then reunited in 1990. Sometimes an area becomes independent and a new state is formed. For example, Georgia was once part of the USSR but became a separate state when the USSR dissolved in 1991.

The picture above shows people sitting on the Berlin Wall. The wall formed a border between East and West Berlin when East and West Germany were separate states. It has now been pulled down.

## What is a territory?

A dependent territory is an area of land that has a very limited government or no government at all. Instead, the land is owned and governed by a separate, independent state. For example, French Guiana in South America is a dependent territory of France.

# Border disputes

Sometimes states disagree about where the border between them should be. This can lead to long conflicts, such as the war between Eritrea and Ethiopia. Eritrea was once part of Ethiopia but became an independent state in 1993. The two countries are still disputing the position of the border between them. Thousands of people have been killed in the conflict.

*Borders often follow natural features such as rivers or mountain ranges. The Danube River separates several countries. Above, it is shown separating Serbia (left) and Romania (right).*

## Internet links

For links to websites with test-yourself puzzles and quizzes on the world's continents and countries, with facts and print-outs, go to **www.usborne-quicklinks.com**

*Some borders are marked by barriers. Guards check that anyone crossing from one state to another is permitted to do so. This barrier marks the border between Belarus and Poland.*

# HOW TO USE THE MAPS

The maps in this book are divided up by continent. At the beginning of each section there is a political map showing the whole continent. The rest of the maps are larger scale maps showing more detailed views of the region.

## Political maps

The shading on the political maps in this book is there to help you see clearly the different countries that make up each continent. The main purpose of these maps is to show country borders and capital cities. Alongside them there are facts and figures about the continents and their features.

*This is a section of the political map of South America. You can see the whole map on pages 276–7.*

## Environmental maps

The majority of the maps in this book are environmental maps, like the one on the right. The shading on these maps shows different types of land, or environments, such as desert, mountain or wetland.

The main key on the opposite page shows what the different shading means. It also shows the symbols used to represent towns, cities and other features. There is a smaller key on each environmental map repeating the most important information from this key.

## Finding places

To find a particular place or feature on the environmental maps, look up its name in the index on pages 376–389. Its page number and grid reference is given next to the name. You can find out how to use the grid on page 251.

*The map on the right is part of the environmental map of the U.S.A. The numbered labels at the top explain some important features of these maps.*

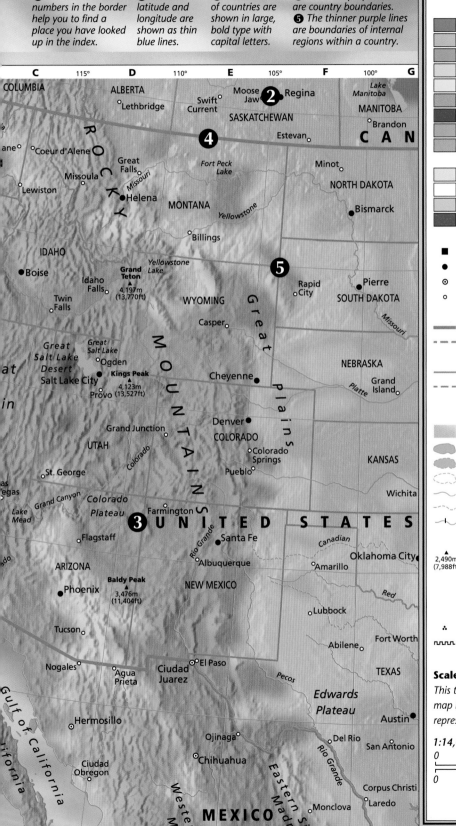

① *The letters and numbers in the border help you to find a place you have looked up in the index.*

② *Lines of latitude and longitude are shown as thin blue lines.*

③ *The names of countries are shown in large, bold type with capital letters.*

④ *The thick purple lines are country boundaries.*
⑤ *The thinner purple lines are boundaries of internal regions within a country.*

## Main key

**Land cover:**

Boreal forest
Temperate forest
Tropical forest
Temperate grassland
Savanna
Semi-desert and scrub
Hot desert
Wetland
Mountain (Only high mountains are marked.)
Tundra
Ice
Cultivation
Urban

**Cities and towns:**

■ National capital
● Internal capital
⊙ Major city or town
○ Other town

**Boundaries:**

International boundary
International boundary through water
Internal boundary
Internal boundary through water

**Water features:**

Sea
Lake or reservoir
Seasonal lake
Dry lake/salt pan
River
Seasonal river
Waterfall/dam

**Other features:**

▲ 2,490m (7,988ft) Height above or below sea level (Only a selection of elevation points are given. Places below sea level have a minus sign in front of the height.)

∴ Ruin or other place of interest
ⵊⵊⵊ Ancient wall

**Scale:**

*This tells you the size of the map in relation to the area it represents. For example:*

**1:14,000,000**

0     200     400km

0   100   200   300 miles

160°  140°  120°  100°  80°  60°  40°  20° W  0°

80°

**GREENLAND**
(Denmark)

Arctic Circle

ALASKA
(U.S.A.)

60°

**C A N A D A**

ICELAND

NOR

DEN
UNITED
KINGDOM    NE
IRELAND    BEL
L
S
FRANC

40°

**UNITED STATES
OF AMERICA**

*Azores*
(Portugal)

PORTUGAL    **SPAIN**

TU

**MOROCCO**

*Canary Islands*
(Spain)

**WESTERN SAHARA**
(Morocco)

**ALGER**

Tropic of Cancer

THE BAHAMAS

20°
N

*Hawaiian
Islands*
(U.S.A.)

**MEXICO**

**CUBA**

DOMINICAN
REPUBLIC

HAITI

JAMAICA

BELIZE

GUATEMALA    HONDURAS

EL SALVADOR    NICARAGUA

*Caribbean Sea*

DOMINICA

**MAURITANIA**

**MALI**

NI

SENEGAL

**CAPE VERDE**

THE GAMBIA
GUINEA-BISSAU

BURKINA
FASO

BENI

GUINEA    TOGO    NIG

**P A C I F I C**

COSTA RICA

PANAMA

TRINIDAD AND TOBAGO

**VENEZUELA**

GUYANA

SURINAM

FRENCH GUIANA
(France)

SIERRA LEONE    IVORY
COAST    GHANA

LIBERIA    EQUATC
GU

**COLOMBIA**

SAO TOME AND
PRINCIPE

*Galapagos Islands*
(Ecuador)

**ECUADOR**

**O C E A N**

KIRIBATI

0°  Equator

**A T L A N T I C**

**B R A Z I L**

**PERU**

**O C E A N**

*Cook
Islands*
(New Zealand)

*French
Polynesia*
(France)

**BOLIVIA**

20°
S

*Pitcairn
Islands*
(U.K.)

Tropic of Capricorn

**PARAGUAY**

**CHILE**

**URUGUAY**

**ARGENTINA**

40°

1:93,200,000

0    1,000    2,000    3,000    4,000    5,000km

0    1,000    2,000    3,000 miles

*Falkland Islands*
(U.K.)

*South Georgia*
(U.K.)

60°

Antarctic Circle

*Weddell
Sea*

80°

160°  140°  120°  100°  80°  60°  40°  20° W  0°

Abbreviations used on map:

| | |
|---|---|
| ARM. | ARMENIA |
| AUST. | AUSTRIA |
| AZER. | AZERBAIJAN |
| BELG. | BELGIUM |
| B.H. | BOSNIA AND HERZEGOVINA |
| CRO. | CROATIA |
| CZECH REP. | CZECH REPUBLIC |
| LEB. | LEBANON |
| LUX. | LUXEMBOURG |
| MAC. | MACEDONIA |
| NETH. | NETHERLANDS |
| SLOV. | SLOVENIA |
| S.M. | SERBIA & MONTENEGRO |
| SWITZ. | SWITZERLAND |
| U.A.E. | UNITED ARAB EMIRATES |

ARCTIC OCEAN

Svalbard
(Norway)

RUSSIA

Arctic Circle

80°

60°

SWEDEN  FINLAND
ESTONIA
LATVIA
RUSSIA  LITHUANIA
GERMANY  BELARUS
POLAND
CZECH REP.
SLOVAKIA  UKRAINE
HUNGARY  MOLDOVA
ROMANIA
B.H.  S.M.  BULGARIA
ITALY  MAC.
ALBANIA
GREECE  TURKEY
CYPRUS  SYRIA
ISRAEL  LEB.
Mediterranean Sea  JORDAN
LIBYA  EGYPT

KAZAKHSTAN

MONGOLIA

40°

NORTH
KOREA

SOUTH
KOREA

JAPAN

PACIFIC

OCEAN

Black Sea
Caspian
Sea
GEORGIA
ARM.  AZER.
UZBEKISTAN
KYRGYZSTAN
TURKMENISTAN
TAJIKISTAN

CHINA

IRAQ  IRAN
KUWAIT
BAHRAIN
QATAR
U.A.E.
SAUDI
ARABIA
OMAN

AFGHANISTAN

PAKISTAN

NEPAL  BHUTAN
BANGLA-
DESH
BURMA
(MYANMAR)

INDIA

LAOS
THAILAND
VIETNAM
CAMBODIA

TAIWAN

Tropic of Cancer

20°
N

Northern
Mariana
Islands
(U.S.A.)

MARSHALL
ISLANDS

CHAD
SUDAN
ERITREA
YEMEN
DJIBOUTI
CENTRAL
AFRICAN
REPUBLIC
CAMEROON
ETHIOPIA
SOMALIA

PHILIPPINES

SRI LANKA

MALDIVES

BRUNEI

MALAYSIA
SINGAPORE

PALAU

FEDERATED STATES
OF MICRONESIA

Equator  0°

GABON
CONGO
CONGO
(DEMOCRATIC
REPUBLIC)
UGANDA
RWANDA  KENYA
BURUNDI
TANZANIA

SEYCHELLES

INDIAN

OCEAN

INDONESIA

PAPUA
NEW GUINEA

NAURU

SOLOMON
ISLANDS

KIRIBATI

TUVALU

ANGOLA
ZAMBIA  MALAWI

ZIMBABWE

NAMIBIA
BOTSWANA
MOZAMBIQUE

COMOROS

MADAGASCAR  MAURITIUS

Reunion
(France)

Coral Sea
Islands
Territory
(Australia)
New
Caledonia
(France)

VANUATU

SAMOA

FIJI  TONGA

20°
S

SWAZILAND
LESOTHO
SOUTH AFRICA

Tropic of Capricorn

AUSTRALIA

Kerguelen Islands
(France)

NEW
ZEALAND

40°

SOUTHERN OCEAN

60°

Antarctic Circle

ANTARCTICA

The shading on this map is there to help
you see the different countries clearly.

80°

0° E  40°  60°  80°  100°  120°  140°  160°  180°

261

160°  140°  120°  100°  80°  60°  40°  20° W  0°

80°

Beaufort
Sea

Ellesmere
Island

Queen
Elizabeth
Islands

Greenland

Greenland
Sea

Victoria
Island

Baffin
Island

Baffin
Bay

Iceland

Arctic Circle
Alaska
Mount McKinley
▲
6,194m
(20,321ft)

60°

Yukon

Hudson
Bay

Labrador
Sea

British
Isles

Nor
Se

Aleutian Islands

Gulf of Alaska

NORTH
AMERICA

Great
Lakes

Newfoundland

40°

Rocky Mountains

Great Plains

Appalachian Mountains

Azores

Mississippi

Canary
Islands

Atlas Mount

Tropic of Cancer

Gulf of
Mexico

S

20°
N

Cuba

West Indies

Cape Verde
Islands

S

Hawaiian
Islands

Greater Antilles

Caribbean
Sea

Lesser
Antilles

Guiana
Highlands

0°  Equator

PACIFIC

Galapagos
Islands

Amazon
Basin

Amazon

ATLANTIC

Polynesia

OCEAN

Selvas

SOUTH
AMERICA

OCEAN

Tahiti

Andes

20°
S

Tropic of Capricorn

Easter Island

Atacama Desert

Aconcagua
▲
6,959m
(22,831ft)

Pampas

40°

1:93,200,000
0    1,000   2,000   3,000   4,000  5,000km

Patagonia

Falkland Islands

0        1,000        2,000        3,000 miles

South Georgia

Cape Horn

60°

Antarctic Circle

Antarctic
Peninsula

Weddell
Sea

80°

160°  140°  120°  100°  80°  60°  40°  20° W  0°

ARCTIC OCEAN

Svalbard
North Cape
Scandinavia
Barents Sea
Novaya Zemlya
Kara Sea
Severnaya Zemlya
Laptev Sea
New Siberia Islands
East Siberian Sea
80°
Verkhoyansk Range
Arctic Circle
60°

North European Plain
Ob
Yenisey
Siberia
Ural Mountains
Volga
EUROPE
Danube
Black Sea
Mount Elbrus
5,642m
(18,510ft)
Caspian Sea
Aral Sea
ASIA
Altai Mountains
Gobi Desert
Lake Baikal
Sea of Okhotsk
Kamchatka Peninsula
Hokkaido
40°

Mediterranean Sea
Zagros Mountains
Himalayas
Huang He (Yellow)
Chang Jiang (Yangtze)
Sea of Japan
Honshu
Yellow Sea
East China Sea
Taiwan
Nile
Red Sea
Arabian Peninsula
ara
Sahel
Mount Everest
8,850m
(29,035ft)
Ganges
Tropic of Cancer
20° N

AFRICA
Ethiopian Highlands
Arabian Sea
Deccan Plateau
Bay of Bengal
Mekong
South China Sea
Philippine Islands
Micronesia
PACIFIC OCEAN

Lake Victoria
Kilimanjaro
5,895m
(19,340ft)
Sri Lanka
Celebes Sea

Congo Basin
Rift Valley
Congo
Seychelles
Sumatra
Borneo
Greater Sunda Islands
Java
New Guinea
Mount Wilhelm
4,509m
(14,793ft)
Solomon Islands
Melanesia
Equator
0

INDIAN OCEAN
Comoro Islands
Arafura Sea
Lesser Sunda Islands
Coral Sea
New Caledonia
Fiji Islands
20° S

Namib Desert
Kalahari Desert
Drakensberg
Madagascar
Mauritius
Reunion
Great Sandy Desert
AUSTRALASIA AND OCEANIA
Great Barrier Reef
Great Dividing Range
Tropic of Capricorn

Cape of Good Hope
Great Victoria Desert
Tasman Sea
North Island
40°

Kerguelen Islands
Tasmania
South Island

60°

SOUTHERN OCEAN
Antarctic Circle

ANTARCTICA
See page 259 for key.
80°

20° E    40°    60°    80°    100°    120°    140°    160°    180°

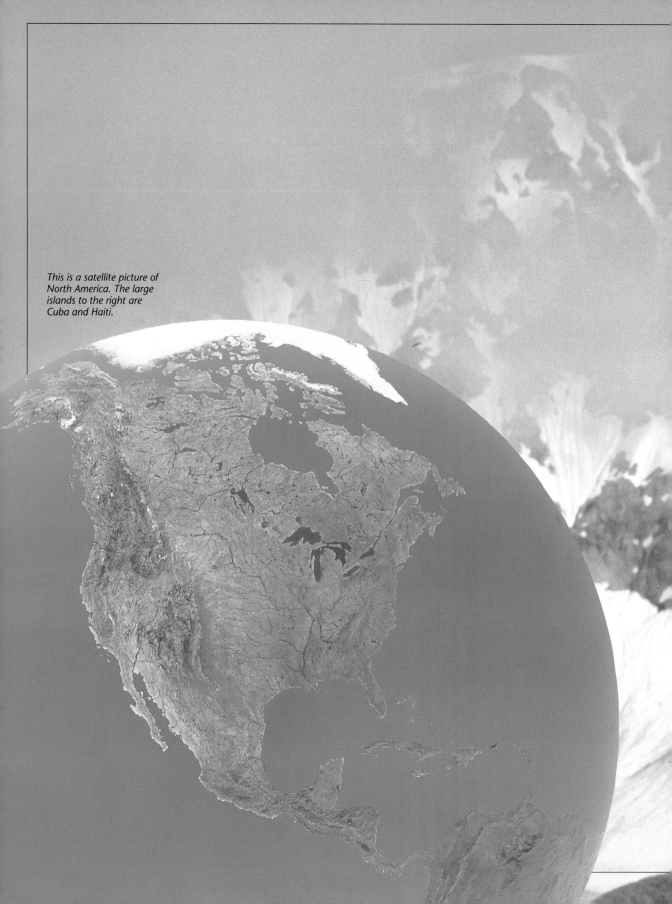

This is a satellite picture of North America. The large islands to the right are Cuba and Haiti.

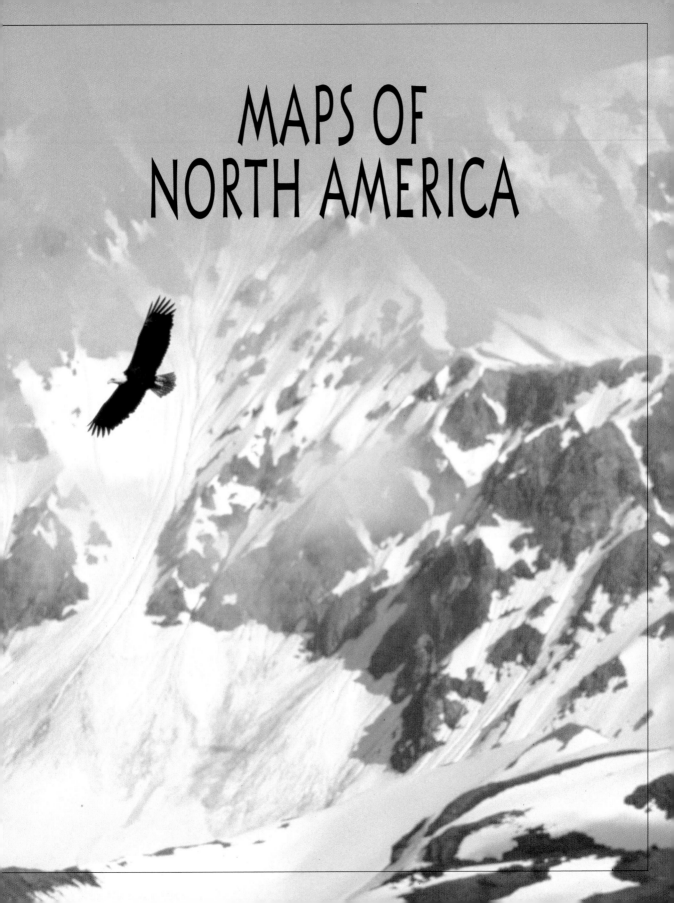

# MAPS OF
# NORTH AMERICA

In this atlas, North America includes Canada, the U.S.A., the Caribbean, and the countries of Central America, which run along the narrow strip of land between the U.S.A. and South America. This large continent contains over 20 countries, ranging from Canada, the world's second largest state, to tiny islands such as Grenada and Saint Lucia.

*These are columns of rock called hoodoos in Bryce Canyon National Park, U.S.A.*

ARCTIC OCEAN

Arctic Circle

Beaufort Sea

Bering Sea

Yukon

ALASKA (U.S.A.)

Anchorage

Victoria Island

CANADA

Vancouver

Columbia

PACIFIC OCEAN

Hawaiian Islands (U.S.A.)

UNITED STATES

Colorado

Los Angeles

Rio Grande

Tropic of Cancer

MEXICO

Mexico City

*The shading on this map is there to help you see clearly the different countries that make up the continent.*

GREENLAND
(Denmark)

*Arctic Circle*

llesmere
land

ueen
izabeth
lands

*Baffin
Island*

Godthab

*Hudson
Bay*

*Newfoundland*

*St. Lawrence*

Montreal
Ottawa

*Great
Lakes*

ATLANTIC

OCEAN

Chicago

New York

Washington D.C.

OF AMERICA

*Mississippi*

*Tropic of Cancer*

Houston

THE
BAHAMAS

*Gulf of
Mexico*

Havana

CUBA

Puerto Rico
(U.S.A.)

Guadeloupe
(France)

HAITI

DOMINICAN
REPUBLIC

DOMINICA
*Martinique* (France)

BARBADOS

JAMAICA

TRINIDAD
AND TOBAGO

BELIZE

*Caribbean Sea*

GUATEMALA

HONDURAS

EL SALVADOR

NICARAGUA

COSTA RICA

PANAMA

# Facts

**Total land area** 22,656,190 sq km (8,745,289 sq miles)

**Total population** 487 million

**Biggest city** Mexico City, Mexico

**Biggest country** Canada 9,970,610 sq km (3,849,653 sq miles)

**Smallest country** Saint Kitts and Nevis 269 sq km (104 sq miles)

**Highest mountain** Mount McKinley, Alaska, U.S.A. 6,194m (20,321ft)

**Longest river** Mississippi/Missouri, U.S.A. 6,019km (3,741 miles)

**Biggest lake** Lake Superior, between the U.S.A. and Canada 82,414 sq km (31,820 sq miles)

**Highest waterfall** Yosemite Falls, on the Yosemite Creek, California, U.S.A. 739m (2,425ft)

**Biggest desert** Great Basin Desert, U.S.A. 492,000 sq km (190,000 sq miles)

**Biggest island** Greenland 2,175,600 sq km (840,000 sq miles)

**Main mineral deposits** Silver, gold, copper, lead, zinc, graphite, molybdenum, nickel

**Main fuel deposits** Oil, coal, natural gas, uranium

*The bald eagle is the national bird of the U.S.A. It is not really bald, but has white feathers on its head.*

ARCTIC OCEAN

**Canada and Alaska**

- Boreal forest
- Temperate forest
- Tropical forest
- Temperate grassland
- Savanna
- Semi-desert and scrub
- Hot desert
- Wetland
- Mountain
- Tundra
- Ice
- Cultivation
- Urban

■ National capital
● Internal capital
⊙ Major city or town
○ Other town

International boundary
Internal boundary
▲ 2,490m (7,988ft) Height above or below sea level

*See also main key on page 259.*

1:18,600,000

| 0 | 200 | 400 | 600km |
| 0 | 100 | 200 | 300 | 400 miles |

Chukchi Sea
Wainwright
Point Barrow
Bering Strait
St. Lawrence Island
Bering Sea
Teller
Seward Peninsula
Prudhoe Bay
Beaufort Sea
Brooks Range
Mackenzie Bay
McClure Strait
Melville Island
Banks Island
Viscount Melville Sound
Queen Elizabeth
Parr
McClintock Chann
Nunivak Island
Bethel
Yukon
ALASKA (U.S.A.)
Mount McKinley ▲ 6,194m (20,321ft)
Fairbanks
Yukon
Inuvik
Amundsen Gulf
Victoria Island
Bristol Bay
Iliamna Lake
Alaska Range
Anchorage
Dawson
Mackenzie Mountains
Mackenzie
Great Bear Lake
NORTHWEST TERRITORIES
Alaska Peninsula
Seward
Kodiak Island
Gulf of Alaska
Mount Logan ▲ 5,959m (19,551ft)
YUKON TERRITORY
Whitehorse
Yellowknife
Dubawnt Lake
PACIFIC
OCEAN
Watson Lake
Fort Providence
Great Slave Lake
Juneau
Alexander Archipelago
Dease Lake
Coast Mountains
Fort Nelson
Fort Chipewyan
Lake Athabasca
Wollaston Lake
Prince Rupert
Queen Charlotte Islands
BRITISH COLUMBIA
Fort St. John
Peace River
Fort Vermilion
Fort McMurray
ALBERTA
Reindeer Lake
R O C K Y
Prince George
Mount Robson ▲ 3,954m (12,972ft)
Grande Prairie
Athabasca
Whitecourt
Hinton
Edmonton
Flin Flon
Ced
Lak
Port Hardy
Williams Lake
Lloydminster
Prince Albert
Saskatoon
Vancouver Island
Port McNeill
Kamloops
Red Deer
Lak
Winnipegos
C A N
Nanaimo
Vancouver
Revelstoke
Calgary
SASKATCHEWAN
Victoria
Bellingham
Kelowna
Moose Jaw
Regina
Seattle
Lethbridge
Swift Current
Olympia
Mount Rainier ▲ 4,392m (14,409ft)
WASHINGTON
Estevan
M O U N T A I N S
Salem
Columbia
Cascade Range
Coast Ranges
Helena
MONTANA
Missouri
NORTH
Bismarck
UNITED  STATES  OF
OREGON
IDAHO
Boise
Grand Teton ▲ 4,197m (13,770ft)
WYOMING
SOUTH
Pierr
CALIFORNIA    NEVADA

K 90° L 80° M 70° N 60° P 50° Q 40° R 30° S 60°

*Ellesmere Island*

Baffin

Bay

Devon Island

Lancaster Sound

Somerset Island

1

Gulf of Boothia

Boothia Peninsula

King William Island

Melville Peninsula

Baffin Island

Foxe Basin

NUNAVUT

Southampton Island

Foxe Peninsula

Nettilling Lake

Amadjuak Lake

Iqaluit

Hudson Strait

Cumberland Peninsula

Ivujivik

Ungava Peninsula

Ungava Bay

All islands within Hudson Bay, James Bay and Ungava Bay lie within Nunavut.

Inukjuak

Kuujjuaq

Churchill

Hudson Bay

Belcher Islands

MANITOBA

Thompson

Fort Severn

La Grande Reservoir

James Bay

Radisson

QUEBEC

Lake Mistassini

ADA

Lake Winnipeg

Grand Rapids

Fort Albany

Waskaganish

Lake Manitoba

Winnipeg

Lake of the Woods

Dryden

Kenora

Brandon

Thunder Bay

Marathon

ONTARIO

Lake Nipigon

Kirkland Lake

Val-d'Or

Chicoutimi

Baie-Comeau

Manicouagan Reservoir

Lake Superior

DAKOTA

MINNESOTA

AMERICA

St. Paul

Minneapolis

Mississippi

WISCONSIN

Madison

MICHIGAN

Lansing

Lake Huron

Lake Michigan

Sudbury

Sault Ste. Marie

Owen Sound

Toronto

Hamilton

London

Detroit

Windsor

Huntsville

Kingston

Lake Ontario

Niagara Falls

Buffalo

Lake Erie

Erie

Cleveland

North Bay

**Ottawa**

Montreal

Trois-Rivieres

Quebec

St. Lawrence

Montpelier

VERMONT

NEW HAMPSHIRE

MAINE

Augusta

Concord

Albany

NEW YORK

Hartford

CONNECTICUT

Boston

MASSACHUSETTS

Providence

RHODE ISLAND

New York

Trenton

NEW JERSEY

Philadelphia

Dover

DELAWARE

Harrisburg

PENNSYLVANIA

Pittsburgh

Annapolis

**Washington D.C.**

Chicago

ILLINOIS

INDIANA

OHIO

Columbus

70°

N

90°

80°

K

## Inset map (Aleutian Islands)

A 180° B 170°W C 160°

Bering Sea

55°N

55°N

Shishaldin Volcano

2,857m (9,372ft)

Unimak Island

3

Attu Island

Near Islands

Aleutian Islands

Fox Islands

Unalaska Island

Umnak Island

3

Rat Islands

Andreanof Islands

Atka Island

Umnak Island

Same scale as main map

A 180° B 170°W C

GREENLAND (Denmark)

Cape Farewell

2

Davis Strait

Labrador Sea

ATLANTIC

OCEAN

3

Cape Chidley

Nain

Makkovik

Cartwright

Kuujjuaq

NEWFOUNDLAND

Happy Valley-Goose Bay

Smallwood Reservoir

Churchill Falls

Labrador City

Gander

St. John's

*Newfoundland*

Corner Brook

50°

Anticosti Island

Gulf of St. Lawrence

St. Pierre and Miquelon (France)

4

Gaspe

PRINCE EDWARD ISLAND

Sydney

Charlottetown

Edmundston

NEW BRUNSWICK

Moncton

Bathurst

Fredericton

Saint John

Halifax

NOVA SCOTIA

Yarmouth

40°

5

3

4

United States of America map (western region)

**Grid coordinates (top):** A 125°W · B 115° C · D 110° · E 105° · F 100°

**Grid coordinates (rows):** 1, 2, 3, 4, 5, 6

Vancouver Island
Nanaimo
Vancouver
Victoria
Bellingham
BRITISH COLUMBIA
ALBERTA
Lethbridge
Swift Current
Moose Jaw
Regina
SASKATCHEWAN
Lake Manitoba
MANITOBA
Brandon
C A

Seattle
Tacoma
Olympia
Mount Rainier 4,392m (14,409ft) ▲
Spokane
Coeur d'Alene
Columbia
WASHINGTON
Great Falls
Fort Peck Lake
Estevan
Minot
NORTH DAKOTA
Bismarck

Portland
Salem
Columbia
Missoula
Lewiston
Helena
MONTANA
Billings
Yellowstone

45°N

Eugene
OREGON
IDAHO
Boise
Idaho Falls
Grand Teton 4,197m (13,770ft) ▲
Yellowstone Lake
WYOMING
Rapid City
Pierre
SOUTH DAKOTA
Missouri

Medford
Harney Basin
Goose Lake
Twin Falls
Casper

Mount Shasta 4,317m (14,163ft) ▲
Redding
Chico
Reno
Carson City
Great Salt Lake Desert
Great Salt Lake
Ogden
Salt Lake City
Kings Peak 4,123m (13,527ft) ▲
Provo
Cheyenne
NEBRASKA
Great Plains
Grand Island
Platte

40°N

Sacramento
Great Basin
NEVADA
Denver
COLORADO
KANSAS

San Francisco
San Jose
Salinas
Fresno
Sierra Nevada
Yosemite Falls
Grand Junction
Colorado
Colorado Springs
Pueblo

35°

Mount Whitney 4,418m (14,494ft) ▲
Death Valley -86m (-282ft)
St. George
UTAH
Wichi

San Luis Obispo
Bakersfield
Las Vegas
Grand Canyon
Lake Mead
Colorado Plateau
Farmington
Santa Fe
Rio Grande
Canadian
Oklahoma Ci
Amarillo

CALIFORNIA
Mojave Desert
Pasadena
Los Angeles
Channel Islands
Riverside
Colorado
Flagstaff
U N I T E D   S T A T E S
Albuquerque

40°

Salton Sea
ARIZONA
Phoenix
Baldy Peak 3,476m (11,404ft) ▲
NEW MEXICO
Lubbock
Red
Fort Wor
TEXAS

San Diego
Tijuana
Mexicali

PACIFIC

30°

Tucson
Nogales
Agua Prieta
Ciudad Juarez
El Paso
Pecos
Abilene

OCEAN

Guadalupe Island (Mexico)

Edwards Plateau
Austin

Del Rio
San Antoni

25°

Ojinaga
Chihuahua
Rio Grande
Corpus Chris
Laredo

Western Sierra Madre
Eastern Sierra Madre

MEXICO
Monclova

Torreon
Saltillo
Monterrey
Brownsvi
Matamoro

**Legend:**

# United States of America

- Boreal forest
- Temperate forest
- Tropical forest
- Temperate grassland
- Savanna
- Semi-desert and scrub
- Hot desert
- ━━ International boundary
- ── Internal boundary
- ▲ 2,490m (7,988ft) Height above or below sea level

- Wetland
- Mountain
- Tundra
- Ice
- Cultivation
- Urban

- ■ National capital
- ● Internal capital
- ⊙ Major city or town
- ○ Other town

*See also main key on page 259.*

1:14,000,000

0    200    400km
0   100   200   300 miles

120°W · 115° C · 110° D · 105° E · 100° F

95°  H  90°  J  85°  K  80°  L  75°  M  70°  N  65°

**1**

Lake Winnipeg

nnipeg  Kenora  Dryden  Marathon  ONTARIO  Gouin Reservoir  QUEBEC  Chicoutimi  Bathurst  Edmundston  NEW BRUNSWICK

D A  Lake of the Woods  Lake Nipigon  Kirkland Lake  Val-d'Or  Quebec  Fredericton  MAINE  Saint John

Thunder Bay  Cabonga Reservoir  Trois-Rivieres  St. Lawrence  St. Stephen  45° N

and Forks  Lake Superior  Sault Ste. Marie  Sudbury  North Bay  Huntsville  Ottawa  Montreal  Bangor  Augusta

argo  Duluth  MINNESOTA  Montpelier  VERMONT  Portland  Gulf of Maine

**2**

MINNESOTA  Green Bay  MICHIGAN  Owen Sound  Toronto  Lake Ontario  Kingston  NEW YORK  Concord  NEW HAMPSHIRE  Boston  Cape Cod

Minneapolis  St. Paul  WISCONSIN  Grand Rapids  Hamilton  Niagara Falls  Rochester  Syracuse  Albany  MASSACHUSETTS  Providence

oux Falls  Mississippi  Milwaukee  Lake Michigan  Lansing  London  Buffalo  Jamestown  Springfield  Hartford  RHODE ISLAND

Sioux City  Madison  Rockford  Detroit  Windsor  Lake Erie  Erie  CONNECTICUT  40°

Cedar Rapids  Chicago  South Bend  Toledo  Cleveland  PENNSYLVANIA  Newark  New York  **3**

IOWA  Des Moines  Peoria  Fort Wayne  OHIO  Pittsburgh  Harrisburg  Trenton  Philadelphia  NEW JERSEY

Omaha  INDIANA  Columbus  Baltimore  Dover  Atlantic City

Lincoln  ILLINOIS  Indianapolis  Cincinnati  WEST VIRGINIA  MARYLAND  Annapolis  DELAWARE

Kansas City  Springfield  St. Louis  Frankfort  Charleston  Charlottesville  Washington D.C.

opeka  Jefferson City  Evansville  Lexington  Ohio  VIRGINIA  Richmond  35°

MISSOURI  KENTUCKY  Roanoke  Virginia Beach

Springfield  Cape Girardeau  Kentucky Lake  Nashville  Knoxville  Greensboro  Raleigh  Cape Hatteras

OF  A M E R I C A  Ozark Plateau  Jonesboro  Jackson  Chattanooga  TENNESSEE  Charlotte  NORTH CAROLINA  **ATLANTIC**  **4**

Tulsa  Little Rock  Memphis  Huntsville  Clark Hill Lake  Columbia  **OCEAN**

KLAHOMA  ARKANSAS  Tupelo  Birmingham  Atlanta  SOUTH CAROLINA

Texarkana  Greenville  Tuscaloosa  Macon  Charleston

Dallas  Shreveport  MISSISSIPPI  ALABAMA  GEORGIA  Savannah

co  Vicksburg  Meridian  Montgomery  Columbus  Albany  **5**

LOUISIANA  Hattiesburg  Jackson  Valdosta  Jacksonville

Sam Rayburn Reservoir  Toledo Bend Reservoir  Mobile  Tallahassee

Beaumont  Baton Rouge  Pensacola  Apalachee Bay  Daytona Beach

ouston  New Orleans  Orlando  Cape Canaveral

Galveston  Mississippi Delta  FLORIDA

**Gulf of Mexico**  St. Petersburg  Tampa  Lake Okeechobee  Grand Bahama  Abaco  **THE BAHAMAS**  25°

Fort Lauderdale  Freeport City  Eleuthera

The Everglades  Miami  **Nassau**  Cat Island

Key West  Florida Keys  Andros  Tropic of Cancer  **6**

Straits of Florida  Long Island  Acklins Island

Matanzas

95°  H  90°  J  **Havana**  **CUBA**  Santa Clara  75°

85°  Cienfuegos  Ciego de Avila

Pinar del Rio  80°  Camaguey

Hawaiian Islands inset:
160°W  Same scale as main map  **Hawaiian Islands**

**7**  Kauai  Oahu  Molokai  **7**

Honolulu  Kahului  Maui

HAWAII (U.S.A.)  4,205m (13,796ft)  20°N  20°N

PACIFIC OCEAN  **8**  Hilo  **8**

160°W  P  Hawaii  155°

A 120°W | 115° B | 110° C | 105° D | 100° E | 95° F | 90°

**UNITED STATES OF AMERICA**

CALIFORNIA
San Diego
Tijuana
Mexicali
Phoenix
ARIZONA
Tucson
Nogales
Agua Prieta
El Paso
Ciudad Juarez
NEW MEXICO
Lubbock
OKLAHOMA
Little Rock
ARKANSAS
Tupelo
Texarkana
MISSISSIPPI
Fort Worth
Dallas
Shreveport
Jackson
Abilene
TEXAS
Waco
LOUISIANA
Hattiesburg
Austin
Houston
Baton Rouge
San Antonio
Galveston
New Orleans

Guadalupe Island (Mexico)
Cedros Island
Point Eugenia
Gulf of California
Lower California
Western Sierra Madre
Hermosillo
Ciudad Obregon
Ojinaga
Chihuahua
Edwards Plateau
Rio Grande
Pecos
Laredo
Corpus Christi
Brownsville
Matamoros
Mississippi Delta

Tropic of Cancer
La Paz
Cape San Lucas
Los Mochis
Culiacan
Durango
Mazatlan
Plateau of Mexico
Torreon
Matehuala
San Luis Potosi
Monclova
Saltillo
Monterrey
4,054m (13,300ft)
Ciudad Victoria
Eastern Sierra Madre
Gulf of Mexico
Tampico

**MEXICO**
Aguascalientes
Puerto Vallarta
Guadalajara
Leon
Celaya
Morelia
Colima
Uruapan
Acapulco
Teotihuacan
**Mexico City**
Puebla
Orizaba 5,610m (18,405ft)
Tehuacan
Veracruz
Oaxaca
Coatzacoalcos
Villahermosa
Juchitan
Isthmus of Tehuantepec
Gulf of Tehuantepec
Southern Sierra Madre
Bay of Campeche
Merida
Yucatan Peninsula
Campeche
Ciudad del Carmen
Tuxtla Gutierrez
Belmopan
BELIZE
Tikal
Tajumulco 4,220m (13,845ft)
GUATEMALA
Quezaltenango
Tapachula
**Guatemala City**
**San Salvador**
EL SALVADOR

*Gulf of Mexico*

*PACIFIC OCEAN*

Galapagos Islands (Ecuador)

Equator

Puerto Ayora

---

L 65°W | M | N 60°

*ATLANTIC OCEAN*

Virgin Islands (U.K.)
Anguilla (U.K.)
Leeward Islands
St. Martin (France and Netherlands)
San Juan
Puerto Rico (U.S.A.)
Virgin Islands (U.S.A.)
**ANTIGUA AND BARBUDA**
**Basseterre**
**ST. KITTS AND NEVIS**
**St. John's**
Montserrat (U.K.)
Guadeloupe (France)
Basse-Terre
**DOMINICA**
**Roseau**

1:9,300,000

0   100   200km
0   50   100 miles

*Caribbean Sea*
Martinique (France)
Fort-de-France
**Castries**
**ST. LUCIA**
**BARBADOS**
**Kingstown**
**ST. VINCENT AND THE GRENADINES**
**Bridgetown**
**St. George's**
**GRENADA**
Windward Islands
Lesser Antilles
Margarita Island
Porlamar
Tobago
**Port-of-Spain**
**TRINIDAD AND TOBAGO**
Cumana
**VENEZUELA**
Trinidad

L 65°W | M | N 60°

115°W B | 110° C | 105° D | 100° E | 95° F | 90°

## Central America and the Caribbean

**Legend:**
- Boreal forest
- Temperate forest
- Tropical forest
- Temperate grassland
- Savanna
- Semi-desert and scrub
- Hot desert
- Wetland
- Mountain
- Tundra
- Ice
- Cultivation
- Urban
- International boundary
- Internal boundary
- ▲ 2,490m (7,988ft) Height above or below sea level
- ■ National capital
- ● Internal capital
- ⊙ Major city or town
- ○ Other town

*See also main key on page 259.*

1:18,600,000

| 0 | 200 | 400 | 600km |
| 0 | 100 | 200 | 300 | 400 miles |

**ATLANTIC OCEAN**

Tropic of Cancer

NORTH CAROLINA
Columbia
SOUTH CAROLINA
Atlanta
GEORGIA
Macon
Columbus
ntgomery
Savannah
Albany
Charleston
Tallahassee
FLORIDA
Daytona Beach
Apalachee Bay
Orlando
Cape Canaveral
St. Petersburg
Tampa
Lake Okeechobee
The Everglades
Miami
Key West
Florida Keys
Straits of Florida

Grand Bahama
Freeport City
Abaco
Eleuthera
Nassau THE BAHAMAS
Cat Island
Andros
Long Island
Acklins Island
Great Inagua
Turks and Caicos Islands (U.K.)

Havana
Pinar del Rio
Matanzas
Santa Clara
Cienfuegos
CUBA
Camaguey
Holguin
Bayamo
Guantanamo
Santiago de Cuba
Isle of Youth
Cayman Islands (U.K.)
ancun
Swan Islands (Honduras)

Windward Passage
Cap-Haitien
Gonaives
Hispaniola
HAITI
Les Cayes
Port-au-Prince
Montego Bay
Greater Antilles
JAMAICA
Kingston

DOMINICAN REPUBLIC
Santiago
La Romana
Santo Domingo
Virgin Islands (U.K.)
San Juan
Ponce
Puerto Rico (U.S.A.)
ST. KITTS AND NEVIS
ANTIGUA AND BARBUDA
Leeward Islands
Guadeloupe (France)
DOMINICA
Martinique (France)
ST. LUCIA
Windward Islands
ST. VINCENT AND THE GRENADINES
BARBADOS
GRENADA

**Caribbean Sea**

Aruba (Netherlands)
Netherlands Antilles (Netherlands)
Cape Gallinas
Willemstad
Margarita Island
Port-of-Spain
TRINIDAD AND TOBAGO
Maturin
Orinoco Delta

NDURAS
gucigalpa
Puerto Cabezas
Matagalpa
NICARAGUA
Managua
Lake Nicaragua
eria
ntarenas
OSTA RICA San Jose
Limon
Gulf of Mosquitos
Almirante
Colon
PANAMA
Panama City
Panama Canal
David
Santiago
La Palma
Gulf of Panama
Coiba Island

San Andres Island (Colombia)
Riohacha
Santa Marta
Cristobal Colon
Barranquilla
Cartagena
5,775m (18,947ft)
Paraguaipoa
Gulf of Venezuela
Maracaibo
Lake Maracaibo
Valera
Valencia
Maracay
Caracas
Barcelona
Cumana
Barquisimeto
VENEZUELA
Ciudad Bolivar
Ciudad Guayana
Georgetown
GUYANA

Gulf of Darien
Sincelejo
Dabeiba
Cordillera
Quibdo
Medellin
Manizales
Pereira
Ibague
Buenaventura
Cali
Neiva
5,750m (18,865ft)
Popayan
Pasto
Tumaco
olpiales

Bolivar Peak
5,007m (16,427ft)
Cucuta
San Fernando de Apure
San Cristobal
Pamplona
Bucaramanga
Tunja
Western Cordillera
Eastern Cordillera
Bogota
COLOMBIA
Llanos
Orinoco
Puerto Paez
Guaviare
Puerto Inirida
San Jose del Guaviare
Florencia

Angel Falls
Guiana Highlands
Mount Roraima 2,810m (9,219ft)
Santa Elena
Boa Vista

BRAZIL
Negro

Esmeraldas
ECUADOR Quito
Ibarra
Puerto Leguizamo
Equator

273

Copyright © Usborne Publishing Ltd.

*A parrot snake*

# MAPS OF SOUTH AMERICA

This is a satellite image of South America. The brown, mottled streak along the west coast is the Andes mountain range.

Triangle-shaped South America is made up of only 12 independent countries, along with French Guiana, which belongs to France. A huge part of this continent is taken up with the Amazon rainforest, which covers the Amazon basin with over a third of the world's trees. South America also has dusty deserts, towering mountains and, in Venezuela, the world's highest waterfall - Angel Falls.

*This is a guanaco. Guanacos are members of the camel family that live in South America. Guanaco hair is used to make textiles.*

Caribbean Sea

Caracas

VENEZUELA

Medellin○   ■ Bogota

COLOMBIA

Orinoco

Quito

ECUADOR

Man

Galapagos
Islands
(Ecuador)

Equator

Guayaquil○

PERU

Lima ■

BOLIVIA

■ La Paz

■ Sucre

Tropic of Capricorn

CHILE

PACIFIC

OCEAN

Santiago ■   ○ Mendoza

ARGENTIN

Cape Horn

Drake Passag

*The shading on this map is there to help you see clearly the different countries that make up the continent.*

Georgetown
Paramaribo
YANA  Cayenne
SURINAM  FRENCH
GUIANA
(France)

azon

Equator

Recife

B R A Z I L

Brasilia

Belo Horizonte

Parana

RAGUAY  Sao Paulo  Rio de Janeiro

Tropic of Capricorn

Asuncion

Porto Alegre

ATLANTIC

URUGUAY

Montevideo  OCEAN

Buenos Aires

Falkland Islands
(U.K.)

*This is a red-eyed tree frog. These frogs live in rainforests in South and Central America.*

# Facts

**Total land area** 17,866,130 sq km (6,898,113 sq miles)

**Total population** 346 million

**Biggest city** Sao Paulo, Brazil

**Biggest country** Brazil *8,547,400 sq km (3,300,151 sq miles)*

**Smallest country** Surinam *163,270 sq km (63,039 sq miles)*

**Highest mountain** Aconcagua, Argentina *6,959m (22,831ft)*

**Longest river** Amazon, mainly in Brazil *6,440km (4,000 miles)*

**Biggest lake** Lake Maracaibo, Venezuela *13,312 sq km (5,140 sq miles)*

**Highest waterfall** Angel Falls, on the Churun River, Venezuela *979m (3,212ft)*

**Biggest desert** Patagonian Desert, Argentina *673,000 sq km (260,000 sq miles)*

**Biggest island** Tierra del Fuego *46,360 sq km (17,900 sq miles)*

**Main mineral deposits** Copper, tin, molybdenum, bauxite, emeralds

**Main fuel deposits** Oil, coal

# NORTHERN SOUTH AMERICA

A 85°W    B    80°    C    75°    D    70°    E    65°    F

Liberia
Puntarenas    Limon
San Jose
Aruba
Cape Gallinas
Netherlands Antilles (Netherlands)
Lesser Antilles
GRENADA
Riohacha
Santa Marta
Barranquilla
Cartagena
Cristobal Colon 5,775m (18,947ft)
Gulf of Venezuela
Paraguaipoa
Maracaibo
Willemstad
Coro
Tortuga Island
Margarita Island
TRINIDAD AND TOBAGO
Maracay    Caracas    Cumana    Guiria    Port-o Spain

COSTA RICA
Almirante
David
Santiago
Penonome
Colon
Panama City
Gulf of Darien
Sincelejo
Magangue
La Palma
Turbo
Caceres
Dabeiba
Medellin
Duitama
Tunja
Nuqui
Quibdo
Manizales
Pereira
Buga    Ibague    Bogota

Lagunillas
Lake Maracaibo
Barquisimeto
Valera
Araure
Zaraza
Barcelona
Maturin
Tucupita

Cucuta
Pamplona
Bucaramanga
Bolivar Peak 5,007m (16,427ft)
San Cristobal
San Fernando de Apure
Caicara
Valencia
VENEZUELA
Ciudad Bolivar
Ciudad Guayana
Orinoco Del

Cravo Norte
Puerto Paez
Guiana Highlands
Angel Falls
Mount Roraim 2,810m (9,219ft)
Santa Elena

PANAMA
Gulf of Panama
Coiba Island
Puerto Armuelles
Gulf of Mosquitos

Western Cordillera
Eastern Cordillera
Llanos

5°N
Buenaventura
Cali
Neiva
5,750m (18,865ft)
Popayan
Tumaco
Florencia
COLOMBIA
San Jose del Guaviare
Guaviare
Puerto Inirida
Orinoco
Boa Vista

Malpelo Island (Colombia)

Esmeraldas
Cape San Francisco
Ibarra
Quito
Santo Domingo de los Colorados
Equator
Ipiales    Pasto
Nueva Loja
Puerto Leguizamo
La Chorrera
Japura
Negro

Manta
Quevedo
Ambato 6,310m (20,702ft)
ECUADOR
Babahoyo
Montalvo
Amazon
Iquitos
Amazon

La Libertad
Guayaquil
Cuenca
Gulf of Guayaquil
Tumbes
Machala
Loja
Leticia
Atalaia do Norte
Selvas

Talara
Sullana
Piura
Zumba
Maranon
Central Cordillera
Yurimaguas
Moyobamba
Ucayali
Jurua

Cape Negro
Chiclayo
Pacasmayo
Cajamarca
PERU
Pucallpa
Cruzeiro do Sul
Purus
Madeira

Trujillo
Huacrachuco
Chimbote
Mount Huascaran 6,746m (22,132ft)
Huanuco
Rio Branco
Porto Velho

PACIFIC OCEAN
Cerro de Pasco
La Oroya
Lima
Huancayo
Mala
Andes Western Cordillera
Quillabamba
Ayacucho
Machu Picchu
Cusco
Eastern Cordillera
Puerto Maldonado
Cobija
Riberalta
Rurrenabaque
Magdalena
Trinidad

Chincha Alta
Ica
Nazca
Chala
Mount Coropuna 6,425m (21,079ft)
Sicuani
Juliaca
Puno
Lake Titicaca
La Paz
BOLIVIA
Concepcion

Mollendo
Arequipa
Mount Illimani 6,402m (21,004ft)
Cochabamba
Oruro
Santa Cruz
San Jose de Chiquito

Tacna
Arica
Gulf of Arica
Lake Poopo
Challapata
Sucre
CHILE
Potosi
Charagua
Camiri

## Galapagos Islands inset
N    90°W    P
Same scale as main map
Galapagos Islands (Ecuador)
9        9
Equator    0°
Fernandina
Isabela
San Salvador
Santa Cruz
Puerto Ayora
San Cristobal
10        10
PACIFIC OCEAN
N    90°W    P

## Northern South America

**Legend:**
- Boreal forest
- Temperate forest
- Tropical forest
- Temperate grassland
- Savanna
- Semi-desert and scrub
- Hot desert
- Wetland
- Mountain
- Tundra
- Ice
- Cultivation
- Urban
- ■ National capital
- ● Internal capital
- ⊙ Major city or town
- ○ Other town

— International boundary
▲— Internal boundary

*See also main key on page 259.*

2,490m (7,988ft) Height above or below sea level

1:16,300,000

0    200    400km

0    100    200    300 miles

ATLANTIC OCEAN

Equator 0°

Georgetown
New Amsterdam
Nieuw Nickerie
Brokopondo
**GUYANA**
**SURINAM**
Paramaribo
Sinnamary
Cayenne
Regina
Cape Orange
**FRENCH GUIANA** (France)

5° N

Macapa
Amazon Delta
Braganca
Belem
Cameta
Balbina Reservoir
Amazon
anaus
Santarem
Altamira
Itaituba
Tapajos
Xingu
Tocantins
Tucurui Reservoir
Maraba
Imperatriz
Sao Luis
Parnaiba
Sobral
Bacabal
Teresina
Fortaleza
Cape Sao Roque
Mossoro
Natal

4°

5° S

**B R A Z I L**
Araguaina
Urucui
Floriano
Juazeiro do Norte
Campina Grande
Joao Pessoa
Recife
Caruaru
Floresta
Maceio
Arapiraca

Sao Francisco
Petrolina
Juazeiro
Sobradinho Reservoir
Aracaju

10°

*P l a t e a u   o f*
Araguaia
Tocantins
Gurupi
Barreiras
Morpara
Feira de Santana

*M a t o   G r o s s o*
Salvador (Bahia)
Ilheus

15°

Cuiaba
Caceres
Rondonopolis
Espinosa
Vitoria da Conquista
**Brasilia**
Montes Claros
*B r a z i l i a n*
Goiania
Jatai
*H i g h l a n d s*
Teofilo Otoni

Puerto Suarez
Corumba
Patos de Minas
Governador Valadares
Linhares

Uberlandia
Uberaba
Tres Marias Reservoir
Belo Horizonte
Vitoria
Cachoeiro de Itapemirim

20°

Parana
Sao Jose do Rio Preto
Ribeirao Preto
Furnas Reservoir
Barbacena

BRAZIL

Plateau of Mato Grosso

Brazilian Highlands

Brasilia

Goiania

PERU

BOLIVIA

Sucre

La Paz

PARAGUAY

Asuncion

URUGUAY

CHILE

Santiago

Andes

Gran Chaco

Atacama Desert

Sobradinho Reservoir
Morpara
Feira de Santana
Espinosa
Montes Claros
Barreiras
Patos de Minas
Tres Marias Reservoir
Uberaba
Uberlandia
Jatai
Rondonopolis
Caceres
Cuiaba
Campo Grande
Sao Jose do Rio Preto
Presidente Prudente
Londrina
Dourados
Ponta Pora
Pedro Juan Caballero
Concepcion
Vilarrica
Foz do Iguacu
Iguacu Falls
Eldorado
Ciudad del Este
Cascavel
Guarapuava
Curitiba
Paranagua
Itajai
Florianopolis
Criciuma
Passo Fundo
Caxias do Sul
Porto Alegre
Patos Lagoon
Rio Grande
Santa Maria
Bage
Pelotas
Melo
Mitim Lake
Rivera
Tacuarembo
Paysandu
Durazno
Minas
Salto
Concordia
Gualeguaychu
San Nicolas de los Arroyos
Cherbura
Santa Fe
Rufino
Reconquista
Formosa
Corrientes
Posadas
Encarnacion
Uruguaiana
Paraguay
Parana
Pilcomayo
Salado
Santiago del Estero
San Miguel de Tucuman
Catamarca
La Rioja
Cordoba
San Francisco
Villa Maria
Rio Cuarto
Venado Tuerto
Rosario
San Luis
Villa Mercedes
San Juan
Mendoza
Merlo
Aconcagua 6,959m (22,831ft)
Rancagua
Valparaiso
Coquimbo
Ovalle
Illapel
Vallenar
Copiapo
Chanaral
Taltal
Antofagasta
Mount Ojos del Salado 6,908m (22,664ft)
Calama
San Pedro de Atacama
Salta
San Salvador de Jujuy
Tartagal
Tarija
Camiri
Charagua
Uyuni
Tupiza
Ollague
Lake Poopo
Oruro
Challapata
Potosi
Pica
Iquique
Arica
Lake Titicaca
Mount Illimani 6,402m (21,004ft)
Cochabamba
Concepcion
Santa Cruz
San Jose de Chiquitos
Puerto Suarez
Corumba
Trinidad
Magdalena
Rurrenabaque
Riberalta
Cobija
Rio Branco
Puerto Maldonado
Cobija
Juliaca
Puno
Tacna

Tocantins
Araguaia
Parana
Paraguay

Ilheus
Vitoria da Conquista
Teofilo Otoni
Governador Valadares
Linhares
Cachoeiro de Itapemirim
Vitoria
Campos
Macae
Belo Horizonte
Barbacena
Juiz de Fora
Rio de Janeiro
Nova Iguacu
Tropic of Capricorn
Mount Agulhas Negras 2,787m (9,144ft)
Furnas Reservoir
Ribeirao Preto
Pocos de Caldas
Sao Paulo
Araraquara
Campinas
Marilia
Itapetininga
Gurupi

280

# MAPS OF
# AUSTRALASIA
# AND OCEANIA

*A school of barracuda fish*

*This is a satellite image of Australasia, which includes Australia and New Zealand, and Oceania, which is the name given to the other islands in the Pacific Ocean.*

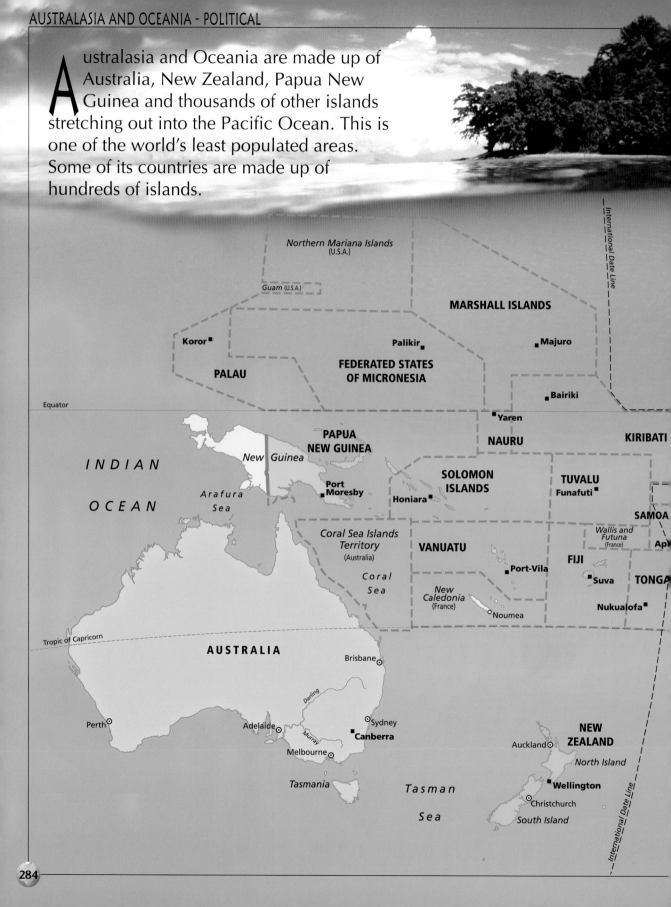

Australasia and Oceania are made up of Australia, New Zealand, Papua New Guinea and thousands of other islands stretching out into the Pacific Ocean. This is one of the world's least populated areas. Some of its countries are made up of hundreds of islands.

Northern Mariana Islands (U.S.A.)

Guam (U.S.A.)

MARSHALL ISLANDS

Koror ■

Palikir ■

■ Majuro

PALAU

FEDERATED STATES OF MICRONESIA

■ Bairiki

Equator

■ Yaren

PAPUA NEW GUINEA

NAURU

KIRIBATI

INDIAN

New Guinea

OCEAN

Arafura Sea

Port Moresby

Honiara ○

SOLOMON ISLANDS

TUVALU
Funafuti ■

SAMOA

Coral Sea Islands Territory (Australia)

VANUATU

Wallis and Futuna (France)

Ap

Coral Sea

Port-Vila ■

FIJI

New Caledonia (France)

■ Suva

TONGA

○ Noumea

Nukualofa ■

Tropic of Capricorn

AUSTRALIA

Brisbane ○

Darling

Sydney ○

Perth ○

Adelaide ○

Canberra ■

NEW ZEALAND

Auckland ○

Murray

Melbourne ○

North Island

Tasmania

Tasman

■ Wellington

Sea

○ Christchurch

South Island

International Date Line

International Date Line

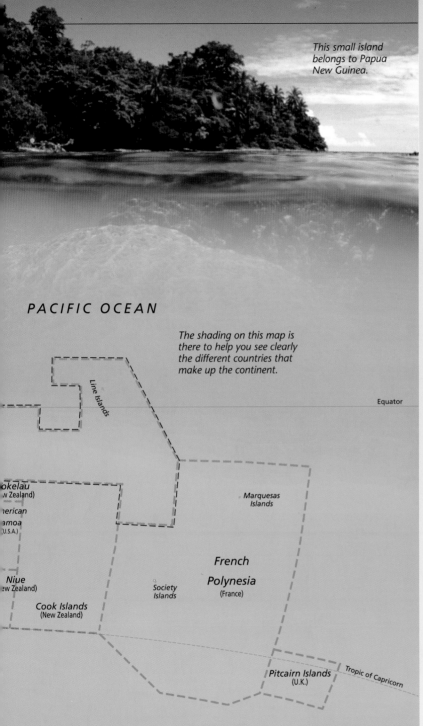

This small island belongs to Papua New Guinea.

PACIFIC OCEAN

The shading on this map is there to help you see clearly the different countries that make up the continent.

Line Islands

Equator

okelau
(New Zealand)

merican
amoa
(U.S.A.)

Marquesas
Islands

Niue
(New Zealand)

Society
Islands

French
Polynesia
(France)

Cook Islands
(New Zealand)

Pitcairn Islands
(U.K.)

Tropic of Capricorn

# Facts

**Total land area** 8,564,400 sq km (3,306,715 sq miles)

**Total population** 31 million

**Biggest city** Sydney, Australia

**Biggest country** Australia 7,686,850 sq km (2,967,124 sq miles)

**Smallest country** Nauru 21 sq km (8 sq miles)

**Highest mountain** Mount Wilhelm, Papua New Guinea 4,509m (14,793ft)

**Longest river** Murray/Darling River, Australia 3,718km (2,310 miles)

**Biggest lake** Lake Eyre, Australia 9,000 sq km (3,470 sq miles)

**Highest waterfall** Sutherland Falls, on the Arthur River, New Zealand 580m (1,904ft)

**Biggest desert** Great Victoria Desert, Australia 388,500 sq km (150,000 sq miles)

**Biggest island** New Guinea 800,000 sq km (309,000 sq miles) (Australia is counted as a continental land mass and not as an island.)

**Main mineral deposits** Iron, nickel, precious stones, lead, bauxite

**Main fuel deposits** Oil, coal, uranium

The Moorish idol fish is found in shallow waters throughout the Pacific. It has very bold stripes and a long, distinctive snout.

Tokyo

*Honshu*

JAPAN

*Kyushu*

30°

*Bonin Islands*
*(Japan)*

2

Tropic of Cancer

20°

*Northern Mariana Islands*
*(U.S.A.)*

*Wake Island*
*(U.S.A.)*

*Johnston Atoll*
*(U.S.A.)*

3

○ Chalan
Kanoa

*Guam*
*(U.S.A.)*

MARSHALL ISLANDS

*Ratak*
*Islands*

10°
N

M i c r o n e s i a

*Ralik Islands*

Majuro

*Palmyra Atoll*
*(U.S.A.)*

Koror

*Caroline Islands*

Palikir

PALAU

FEDERATED STATES
OF MICRONESIA

M e l a n e s i a

Bairiki

0° Equator

*Gilbert*
*Islands*

KIRIBATI

*Jayapura*

PAPUA NEW GUINEA

Yaren

NAURU

INDONESIA

○ *Wewak*

○ *Rabaul*   *New Ireland*

TUVALU

*New Guinea*

Mount
Hagen  ▲ Mount Wilhelm
4,509m
(14,793ft)
○ Lae

*New*
*Britain*

SOLOMON
ISLANDS

Funafuti ■

*Tokelau*
*(New Zealand)*

10°
S

*Arafura*
*Sea*

*Cape York*

Port
Moresby

Honiara

*American*
*Samoa*
*(U.S.A.)*

SAMOA

Apia

6

*Gulf of*
*Carpentaria*

*Coral Sea*

*Coral Sea Islands*
*Territory*
*(Australia)*

VANUATU

*Wallis and*
*Futuna*
*(France)*

FIJI

○ *Cairns*

Port-Vila ■

Suva ■

TONGA

*Niue*
*(New Zealand)*

○ *Townsville*

*New Caledonia*
*(France)*

20°

Nukualofa ■

*Cook Islands*
*(New Zealand)*

Tropic of Capricorn

○ *Noumea*

*Rockhampton*

7

*Simpson*
*Desert*

AUSTRALIA

*Great Dividing Range*

*Norfolk Island*
*(Australia)*

*Kermadec Islands*
*(New Zealand)*

30°

*Darling*

*Lord Howe Island*
*(Australia)*

○ *Newcastle*

8

○ *Sydney*

*Tasman Sea*

NEW
ZEALAND

*Adelaide* ○

*Murray*

Canberra ■

*Great Barrier Reef*

Auckland ○   *North Island*

○ Hamilton

170°E   180°

**Oceania**

- Boreal forest
- Temperate forest
- Tropical forest
- Temperate grassland
- Savanna
- Semi-desert and scrub
- Hot desert
- —— International boundary
- --- International boundary in water
- —— Internal boundary
- ▲ 2,490m (7,988ft) Height above or below sea level

- Wetland
- Mountain
- Tundra
- Ice
- Cultivation
- Urban

- ■ National capital
- ● Internal capital
- ⊙ Major city or town
- ○ Other town

*See also main key on page 259.*

1:35,000,000

0    500    1,000km

0   200   400   600 miles

H  150°  J  140°  K  130°  L  120°  M  110°  N  100°  P

1 — 30°
2 — 20°
10° N
4 — 
Equator 0°
5 — 
10° S
6 — 
20°
Tropic of Capricorn
7 — 
30°
8

*Hawaiian Islands*

○ Honolulu

*Hawaii*

**HAWAII**
(U.S.A.)

*Line Islands*

PACIFIC OCEAN

*Marquesas
Islands*

*P o l y n e s i a*

*Society
Islands*

**French**

*Papeete* ○ *Tahiti*

*Tuamotu
Archipelago*

**Polynesia**

(France)

*Tubuai Islands*

**Pitcairn Islands**
(U.K.)

*Easter Island*
(Chile)

**SOLOMON ISLANDS**

*Coral Sea*

*Rennell Island*

*Santa Cruz Islands*

10° S

**TUVALU**

*Coral Sea Islands Territory* (Australia)

**VANUATU**

*Banks Islands*

*Espiritu Santo*

○Luganville

*Malakula*

15°

*Efate* ■ **Port-Vila**

**FIJI**

*Vanua Levu*

Lautoka○

○**Suva**

*Viti Levu*

○Mackay

arrier Reef

*Chesterfield Islands*

*New Caledonia* (France)

20°

hampton

○Gladstone

Noumea○

*Loyalty Islands*

Bundaberg○

*Fraser Island*

Gympie○

*PACIFIC OCEAN*

Tropic of Capricorn

4

oowoomba○

●Brisbane
○Gold Coast

*Norfolk Island* (Australia)

25°

oree○

○Grafton

○Armidale

*Lord Howe Island* (Australia)

ubbo○

○Port Macquarie

5

Newcastle◎

Great Dividing Range

●Sydney
◎Wollongong

*Kermadec Islands* (New Zealand)

30°

■**Canberra**
AUSTRALIAN CAPITAL TERRITORY
**Mount** ciuszko
29m 43ft)

*Tasman Sea*

*North Cape*

6

inders and

○Whangarei

◎Auckland

*North Island*

35°

Hamilton○

New Plymouth○

○Rotorua

*East Cape*

*Lake Taupo*

*Cape Farewell*

○Napier

Nelson○

7

*South Island*

Cook Strait

■**Wellington**

**NEW ZEALAND**

**Aoraki (Mount Cook)** ▲ 3,754m (12,316ft)

○Christchurch

*Sutherland Falls*

40°

*Cape Providence*

Invercargill○

○Dunedin

*Chatham Islands* (New Zealand)

*Stewart Island*

*South West Cape*

8

A satellite image of Earth, focusing on Asia. You can also see the Arctic at the top, the Indian Ocean (lower middle), Pacific Ocean (right) and some of the Pacific islands.

# MAPS OF ASIA

Asia is the world's largest continent and has over 40 countries, including Russia, the biggest country in the world. As well as large land masses, it has thousands of islands and inlets, giving it over 160,000km (100,000 miles) of coastline. Asia also contains the Himalayas, the world's highest mountain range. Turkey and Russia are part in Europe and part in Asia, but both are shown in full on this map.

The shading on this map is there to help you see clearly the different countries that make up the continent.

A type of Chinese sailing boat called a junk in the port at Singapore

ARCTIC OCEAN

Franz Josef Land

Novaya Zemlya

Barents Sea

Kara S

Moscow

R U S

Ob

Volga

Black Sea

Ankara

TURKEY

GEORGIA

Caspian Sea

Astana

KAZAKHSTAN

Aral Sea

CYPRUS

ARMENIA

AZERBAIJAN

UZBEKISTAN

LEBANON

SYRIA

Beirut

Damascus

TURKMENISTAN

Tashkent

Bishkek

KYRGYZSTAN

Jerusalem

Amman

Ashgabat

Dushanbe

ISRAEL

JORDAN

Baghdad

Tehran

TAJIKISTAN

IRAQ

IRAN

Kabul

Tropic of Cancer

KUWAIT

AFGHANISTAN

Islamabad

SAUDI ARABIA

BAHRAIN

QATAR

PAKISTAN

Riyadh

Doha

Abu Dhabi

Indus

New Delhi

NEPAL

Kathmandu

UNITED ARAB EMIRATES

Muscat

Ganges

Thim

BANGLAD

Sana

OMAN

Arabian Sea

INDIA

YEMEN

Socotra (Yemen)

Bay o Benga

INDIAN OCEAN

Equator

Sri Jayewardenepura Kotte

SRI LANKA

Colombo

MALDIVES

Male

## Map labels

Wrangel Island
Bering Sea
East Siberian Sea
New Siberia Islands
Severnaya Zemlya
Laptev Sea
Sea of Okhotsk
Lena
A
Lake Baikal
Hokkaido
Sea of Japan
Ulan Bator ■
MONGOLIA
NORTH KOREA
JAPAN
Tokyo ■
Pyongyang ■
Seoul ■
Beijing ■
Honshu
SOUTH KOREA
C H I N A
Huang He (Yellow)
East China Sea
Chang Jiang (Yangtze)
Tropic of Cancer
Taipei ■
TAIWAN
TAN
(Irrawaddy)
aka
PACIFIC
OCEAN
BURMA (MYANMAR)
LAOS
Hanoi ■
Vientiane ■
South China Sea
PHILIPPINES
Mekong
goon
THAILAND
VIETNAM
Manila ■
Philippine Sea
Bangkok ■
CAMBODIA
Andaman Islands (India)
Phnom Penh ■
Nicobar Islands (India)
BRUNEI
Equator
M A L A Y S I A
New Guinea
Kuala Lumpur ■
SINGAPORE
Borneo
Celebes
Sumatra
INDONESIA
Dili ■ EAST TIMOR
Arafura Sea
Jakarta ■
Java

## Facts

**Total land area** 44,537,920 sq km (17,196,090 sq miles)

**Total population** 3.8 billion (including all of Russia)

**Biggest city** Tokyo, Japan

**Biggest country** Russia *Total area: 17,075,200 sq km (6,592,735 sq miles) Area of Asiatic Russia: 12,780,800 sq km (4,934,667 sq miles)*

**Smallest country** Maldives *300 sq km (116 sq miles)*

**Highest mountain** Mount Everest, Nepal/China border *8,850m (29,035ft)*

**Longest river** Chang Jiang (Yangtze), China *6,380km (3,964 miles)*

**Biggest lake** Caspian Sea, western Asia *370,999 sq km (143,243 sq miles)*

**Highest waterfall** Jog Falls, on the Sharavati River, India *253m (830ft)*

**Biggest desert** Arabian Desert, in and around Saudi Arabia *2,230,000 sq km (900,000 sq miles)*

**Biggest island** Borneo *751,100 sq km (290,000 sq miles)*

**Main mineral deposits** Zinc, mica, tin, chromium, iron, nickel

**Main fuel deposits** Oil, coal, uranium, natural gas

*These are lotus flowers, Asian water lilies known for their beauty. In China they are associated with purity and for Buddhists they are sacred.*

## Southern Southeast Asia

| | | |
|---|---|---|
| Boreal forest | Wetland | ■ National capital |
| Temperate forest | Mountain | ● Internal capital |
| Tropical forest | Tundra | ⊙ Major city or town |
| Temperate grassland | Ice | ○ Other town |
| Savanna | Cultivation | **See also main key** |
| Semi-desert and scrub | Urban | **on page 259.** |
| Hot desert | | |

International boundary

Internal boundary

▲ 2,490m (7,988ft) Height above or below sea level

**1:14,000,000**

0    200    400km

0   100   200   300 miles

Qui Nhon

**VIETNAM**

*South China*

*Sea*

Nha Trang

*Spratly Islands*

**THAILAND**

*Andaman*

Hat Yai

Yala

*Sea*

Alor Setar

Kota Bharu

Banda Aceh

Lhokseumawe

George Town (Penang)

Kuala Terengganu

**M A L A Y S I A**

Kota Kinabalu

**Bandar Seri Begawan**

**BRUNEI** ■

Taiping

*Gunung Tahan*

▲ 2,187m (7,175ft)

Ipoh

Langsa

Kuantan

Miri

Medan

Bintulu

Natuna Islands

*Anambas Islands*

Sibu

Tarak

Pematangsiantar

**Kuala Lumpur** ■

Seremban

Melaka

Kuching

▲ 2,988m (9,803ft)

Tanjungred

*Lake Toba*

*Strait of Malacca*

Sibolga

Johor Bahru

**Singapore** ■

**SINGAPORE**

*Nias*

*Simeulue*

Pekanbaru

*Riau Islands*

Pontianak

*Borneo*

Samarinda

*Equator*

Padango

*Sumatra*

*Gunung Kerinci*

▲ 3,805m (12,483ft)

Jambi

*Bangka*

Pangkalpinang

Palangkaraya

Balikpapan

Banjarmasin

*Belitung*

Martapura

Palembang

Bengkulu

Lahat

Baturaja

*G r e a t e r   S u n d a   I s l a n d s*

**I N D O N E S I A**

*Mentawai Islands*

*Java Sea*

Tanjungkarang-Telukbetung

*Krakatoa*

▲ 813m (2,667ft)

**Jakarta** ■

Serang

Bogor

Tegal

Semarang

*Lesse*

Bandung

Surakarta

Surabaya

Cilacap

Yogyakarta

Jember

*Lombok*

Malang

*Bali*

Matara

Denpasar

*Sumba*

*INDIAN*

*OCEAN*

*Christmas Island (Australia)*

*J a v a*

## Grid references (top)
A 90°E B 95° C 100° D 105° E

*Brahmaputra*

Lhasa

**Himalayas**

Mount Everest
8,850m
(29,035ft)

**NEPAL**
Darjeeling
Biratnagar

**Thimphu**
**BHUTAN**

**INDIA**

Dibrugarh
Jorhat

*Brahmaputra*

Rangpur

Guwahati

Shillong

Darbhanga

Bhagalpur

*Ganges*

Rajshahi Sylhet

**BANGLADESH**
**Dhaka**

Imphal

Asansol

Jamshedpur

Kolkata
(Calcutta)

Khulna

Aizawl

Chittagong

*Mouths of the Ganges*

Monywa

Mandalay

Mount
Victoria
3,053m
(10,016ft)

**BURMA**
**(MYANMAR)**

Lashio

Myitkyina

Baoshan

Dali

Meiktila

Taunggyi

Sittwe

Pyinmana

*Bay of Bengal*

Sandoway

Pye

*Irrawaddy*

Henzada

Pegu

Thaton

Pathein

**Rangoon**

Moulmein

*Mouths of the*
*Irrawaddy*

Chiang Mai

**INDIAN**
**OCEAN**

*Salween*

Phitsanulok

Nakhon Sawan

**THAILAND**

Nakhon Ratchasima

Tavoy

**Bangkok**

Pattaya

*Andaman*
*Islands*
(India)

*Andaman*
*Sea*

Mergui

Port Blair

*Little*
*Andaman*

Prachuap
Khiri Khan

*Mergui*
*Archipelago*

Chumphon

Kampong Saom

*Ten Degree Channel*

*Gulf of Thailand*

*Nicobar Islands*
(India)

Nakhon Si
Thammarat

*Con Son*

Hat Yai

Yala

Banda Aceh

Alor Setar

Kota Bharu

Lhokseumawe

**George Town**
(Penang)

Kuala Terengganu

*Sumatra*

Langsa

Taiping

Ipoh

Gunung
Tahan
2,187m
(7,175ft)

**MALAYSIA**

**INDONESIA**

*Natuna*
*Islands*
(Indonesia)

Chengdu

Wanxian

Ensh

Gongga Shan
7,556m
(24,790ft)

Leshan

Neijiang

Chongqing

Luzhou

Yibin

Xichang

Zhaotong

**C H**

Zunyi

Huaih

Panzhihua

Guiyang

Anshun

Kunming

Liuzhou

*Red*

Kaiyuan

Gejiu

Nanni

Simao

Ha Giang

Lao Cai

Phongsali

Thai Nguyen

Qinzhou

Son La

**Hanoi**

Hai Phong

*Mekong*

Louangphrabang

Thanh Hoa

*Gulf of*
*Tonkin*

**LAOS**

Vinh

**Vientiane**

Sanya

Udon Thani

Savannakhet

Khon
Kaen

Hue

Da Nan

Ubon
Ratchathani

Pakxe

Attapu

Stoeng Treng

Qui Nhon

Angkor
*Tonle Sap*

**VIETNAM**

Batdambang

**CAMBODIA**

Buon Me
Thuot

Kampong
Chhnang

Kampong
Cham

Da Lat

Nh
Tra

Krong
Kaoh Kong

**Phnom**
**Penh**

Bien Hoa

*Mekong*

Ho Chi Minh City
(Saigon)

Long Xuyen

Can Tho

Bac Lieu

## Latitude (left side)
2, 25°N, 3, 20°, 4, 15°, 5, 10°, 6, 5°, 7

## Grid references (bottom)
A 90°E B 95° C 100° D 105° E

296

F  G  120°  Nantong  125°  J  130°  K

Luan  Hefei  Nanjing  Wuxi
Wuhu  Shanghai
Yichang  Wuhan  Anqing  *Chang Jiang (Yangtze)*  Tai Lake
Huangshi  Hangzhou
Yueyang  *Poyang Lake*  Quzhou  Ningbo
*Dongting Lake*  Nanchang  Jinhua  East
ngde  A  Changsha  Linchuan  China
Zhuzhou  Wenzhou  Sea
Shaoyang  2
Hengyang  Nanping  25°N
Chenzhou  Yongan  Fuzhou  *Ryukyu Islands (Japan)*
ilin  Ganzhou  Quanzhou  Chilung  *Sakishima Islands*  Tropic of Cancer
Shaoguan  Zhangzhou  Xiamen  Taipei  3
Wuzhou  Meizhou  Changhua  Taichung
*Xi Jiang*  Canton  Shantou  **Yu Shan** 3,997m  TAIWAN
(Guangzhou)  Tainan  (13,113ft)
Macau  Kaohsiung
hanjiang  Hong Kong  *Batan Islands*  20°
(Xianggang)
aikou  *Luzon Strait*
*Babuyan Islands*  4
Hainan

*Paracel Islands*  Laoag  Aparri
Tuguegarao
Ilagan
**Mount Pulog** 2,930m  15°
(9,613ft)
Dagupan  Cabanatuan
*Luzon*  Quezon City
South China  Olongapo  *Philippine*
Manila  Lucena  *Sea*  PACIFIC
Sea  Naga
Calapan  Legaspi  5
*Mindoro*  Masbate  PHILIPPINES  OCEAN
*Masbate*  Calbayog
*Calamian Group*  Roxas  *Samar*
*Panay*  Iloilo  Tacloban
Taytay  Bacolod  10°
Cebu
*Spratly Islands*  *Negros*  Surigao
*Bohol*
*Palawan*  Puerto  Dumaguete  Butuan
Princesa  Cagayan de Oro
Iligan  6
*Sulu Sea*  Pagadian  *Mindanao*
Davao
Zamboanga
General Santos
MALAYSIA  Jolo
**Bandar Seri**  Kota  Sandakan  *Sulu*  7
**Begawan**  Kinabalu  *Archipelago*  *Talaud Islands*
**BRUNEI**  *Celebes Sea*
Miri  Tawau
INDONESIA  120°  H  125°  J  130°  K
Bintulu  115°  *Borneo*  Tarakan

**Northern Southeast Asia**

- Boreal forest
- Temperate forest
- Tropical forest
- Temperate grassland
- Savanna
- Semi-desert and scrub
- Hot desert
- Wetland
- Mountain
- Tundra
- Ice
- Cultivation
- Urban

■ National capital
● Internal capital
◉ Major city or town
○ Other town
━━ International boundary
━━ Internal boundary
▲ 2,490m (7,988ft) Height above or below sea level

**See also main key on page 259.**

1:14,000,000

0   200   400km
0  100  200  300 miles

KAZAKHSTAN

Almaty

Lake Issyk

KYRGYZSTAN

▲ Pik Pobedy
7,439m
(24,406ft)

Aksu

Karamay

Yining

Kuytun

Shihezi

Urumqi

Turpan

Korla

Bosten Lake

-154m
(-505ft)

Turpan Depression

Hami

*Tien Shan*

*Dzungarian Basin*

Altay

*Altai Mountains*

Bulgan

■ Ulan Bator

MONGOLIA

Erenh

*Gobi Desert*

Mogao Caves

Yumen

5,547m
(18,199ft)

*The Great Wall of China*

Baotou

Hohho

Wuhai

Yinchuan

Taiyu

Hotan

*Tarim Basin*

*Taklimakan Desert*

Lop Lake

*Altun Mountains*

*Kunlun Mountains*

*Qaidam Basin*

Golmud

Qinghai Lake

Xining

Huang He (Yellow)

Lanzhou

CHINA

*Plateau of Tibet*

Siling Lake

TIBET

Nam Lake

Brahmaputra

Lhasa

*Himalayas*

NEPAL

■ Kathmandu

▲ Mount Everest
8,850m
(29,035ft)

Darjeeling

Darbhanga

Patna

Biratnagar

Ganges

Bhagalpur

Rangpur

■ Thimphu

BHUTAN

Brahmaputra

Dibrugarh

Guwahati

Shillong

Yushu

*Salween*

*Mekong*

*Chang Jiang (Yangtze)*

Chengdu

Gongga Shan
7,556m
(24,790ft)

Leshan

Chongqing

Xichang

*Chang Jiang (Yangtze)*

Luzhou

Zunyi

Baoji

Mount Li
(Terracotta A

Xian

Shiyan

Xiangfa

Yichang

Changde

Huaihua

Hengy

India

Ranchi

Asansol

Rajshahi

Sylhet

Tropic of Cancer

BANGLADESH

Dhaka ■

Kolkata
(Calcutta)

Khulna

Chittagong

Cuttack

*Mouths of the Ganges*

*Bay of Bengal*

Imphal

Aizawl

Myitkyina

Dali

Panzhihua

*Irrawaddy*

Kunming

Guiyang

Guilin

Liuzhou

Wuzhou

Yulin

Nanning

Sittwe

Monywa

Mount Victoria
3,053m
(10,016ft)

BURMA
(MYANMAR)

Lashio

Mandalay

Simao

Gejiu

Lao Cai

Son La

Taunggyi

Phongsali

*INDIAN*

*OCEAN*

Sandoway

Pye

Henzada

Pathein

Pegu

■ Rangoon

Pyinmana

*Salween*

*Irrawaddy*

Chiang Mai

THAILAND

*Mekong*

Louangphrabang

LAOS

■ Vientiane

Udon Thani

Phongsali

Thai Nguyen

■ Hanoi

Hai Phong

Thanh Hoa

*Gulf of Tonkin*

VIETNAM

Vinh

Zhanjian

Haikou

Hainan

Sanya

*Mouths of the Irrawaddy*

Moulmein

Q

Hailar

Hulun
Lake

Qiqihar

Yichun
Hegang

Amur

Jiamusi

Daqing

RUSSIA

La Perouse Strait

Kuril
Islands
(Russia)

2

Asahikawa

Hokkaido

Kushiro

Ulanhot

Harbin

Jixi

Sapporo

Tomakomai

Mudanjiang

Lake
Khanka

Hakodate

MANCHURIA

Changchun

Jilin

Vladivostok

Nakhodka

40°

Xilinhot

Tongliao

Yanji

Aomori

INNER
ONGOLIA

Liaoyuan

Chongjin

Akita

Chifeng

Fuxin

Fushun

Hyesan

Sea of Japan

Sikhote Alin Range

3

Shenyang

Kanggye

Kimchaek

Sendai

Jinzhou

Anshan

NORTH
KOREA

Niigata

Fukushima

lf of China

Zhangjiakou

Dandong

Hamhung

Honshu

Datong

Qinhuangdao

Sinuiju

Wonsan

Utsunomiya

Beijing

Tangshan

Korea Bay

Pyongyang

Toyama

JAPAN

Tokyo

35°

Baoding

Tianjin

Gulf of
Chihli

Dalian

Nampo

Kanazawa

Mount Fuji

Shijiazhuang

Yantai

Inchon

Seoul

Fukui

3,776m
(12,388ft)

Suwon

Shizuoka

Handan

Zibo

Weifang

Chongju

Nagoya

Hamamatsu

angzhi

Taian

Qingdao

Yellow

Taejon

SOUTH
KOREA

Taegu

Kyoto

Osaka

Jining

Kwangju

Sea

Pusan

Okayama

Wakayama

4

Zhengzhou

Grand Canal

Lianyungang

Korea Strait

Hiroshima

Matsuyama

Xuzhou

Fukuoka

Kitakyushu

Shikoku

Pingdingshan

Yancheng

Cheju

Nagasaki

Kumamoto

Huang He (Yellow)

Cheju

Kyushu

Kagoshima

Nanjing

Hefei

Wuxi

30°

Tai Lake

Shanghai

Chang Jiang (Yangtze)

Wuhan

Anqing

Hangzhou

Poyang
Lake

Ningbo

East

Amami

5

ngting
ke

Nanchang

Jinhua

China

hangsha

Linchuan

Wenzhou

Sea

Ryukyu Islands
(Japan)

Okinawa

huzhou

Nanping

25°

Ganzhou

Yongan

Fuzhou

enzhou

Taipei

Chilung

6

Quanzhou

Sakishima
Islands

Tropic of Cancer

Shaoguan

Xiamen

Taichung

Meizhou

Changhua

Yu Shan

TAIWAN

Canton
(Guangzhou)

Shantou

Tainan

3,997m
(13,113ft)

20°

Kaohsiung

Hong Kong
(Xianggang)

Batan
Islands

PACIFIC

OCEAN

South China Sea

Luzon Strait

7

Babuyan
Islands

PHILIPPINES

Laoag

Aparri

Luzon

Tuguegarao

## China, Korea and Japan

Boreal forest
Temperate forest
Tropical forest
Temperate grassland
Savanna
Semi-desert and scrub
Hot desert
Wetland  Miyamae
Mountain
Tundra
Ice
Cultivation
Urban

■  National capital
●  Internal capital
⊙  Major city or town
○  Other town

International boundary
Internal boundary

▲ 2,490m
(7,988ft)  Height above or below sea level

See also main key on page 259.

1:16,300,000

0        200      400km

0    100    200    300 miles

1    45°N    2    40°    3    35°    4

30°

**H**

Altay

Altai Mountains    **MONGOLIA**

95°

Hami

Mogao Caves∴

Qaidam Basin

Golmud

90°    Turpan

Turpan Depression

-154m (-505ft)

Altun Mountains    **CHINA**

Salween

Dibrugarh    Jorhat

Brahmaputra    Guwahati

Urumqi    Shihezi

Dzungarian Basin    Kuytun

Bosten Lake

Lop Lake    Nam Lake    Lhasa    Rangpur

85°    Karamay    Korla    Siling Lake    **Thimphu** ■    Darjeeling

Kunlun Mountains    **TIBET**    **■BHUTAN**

Plateau of Tibet    Birathagar

Altay    Kashi    Brahmaputra    Pokhara    **NEPAL**    Patna

Lake Zaysan    Yining    Tarim Basin    Mount Everest    **Kathmandu**■    Darbhanga

Taklimakan Desert    8,850m (29,035ft)    Gorakhpur    Ganges

80°    Shan    Hotan    Himalayas    Lucknow    Kanpur

Tien    ▲ Pik Pobedy    Bareilly

**KYRGYZSTAN**    7,439m (24,406ft)    Saharanpur    Meerut    Agra    Taj Mahal

Aksu    Chandigarh    Aligarho    Gwalior

Lake Balkhash    Almaty    Ludhiana    Jaipur

Karakol    Ajmer

Taldyqorghan    Lake Issyk    ▲ Kongur Shan    Delhi■

75°    Balqash    Karakol    7,719m (25,325ft)    **New Delhi**■

**Bishkek** ■    K2    **JAMMU**

Kara-Balta    8,611m (28,251ft)    Srinagar    **AND**    Bikaner

Karakorum Range    Gilgit    **KASHMIR**

**KAZAKHSTAN**    Taraz    Jammu

Qyzylorda    Shieli    Jalal-Abad    Osh    Sialkot

Turkistan    Namangan    Gujrat    Gujranwala

70°    Shymkent    Fargona    Communism Peak    Peshawar    Amritsar

Jizzax    Khujand    7,495m (24,590ft)    Khorugh    Lahore

**TASHKENT**■    Angren    **TAJIKISTAN**    ■Islamabad    Faisalabad    Sahiwal

Navoiy    Samarqand    **Dushanbe**■    Kulob    Jalalabad    Sargodha    Multan

**UZBEKISTAN**    Ourghonteppa    Konduz    **Kabul**■    Bahawalpur    **PAKISTAN**

Buxoro    Hindu Kush    5,143m (16,873ft)    Dera Ghazi Khan    Rahimyar Khan

Syr Darya    Mazar-e Sharif    Quetta    Larkana    Sukkur

65°E    Turkmenabat    Amu Darya    **AFGHANISTAN**    Jodhpur    **Thar Desert**

**TURKMENISTAN**    Kandahar    Nawabshah

Urganch    Mary    Herat    Panjgur

Aral Sea

45°N    300    35°    30°    **5**

**A**    **B**    **C**

300

# India and Central Asia

Boreal forest
Temperate forest
Tropical forest
Temperate grassland
Savanna
Semi-desert and scrub
Hot desert
Wetland
Mountain
Tundra
Ice
Cultivation
Urban

■ National capital
● Internal capital
⊙ Major city or town
○ Other town

— International boundary
— Internal boundary

▲ 2,490m
(7,988ft) Height above or below sea level

**See also main key on page 259.**

**1:14,000,000**

0   100   200   300 miles
0   200   400km
70°E

Copyright © Usborne Publishing Ltd.

301

**INDIA**

Rann of Kutch

*Arabian Sea*

Porbandar
Jamnagar
Bhavnagar
Rajkot
Ahmadabad
Vadodara
Surat
Mumbai (Bombay)
Pune
Nashik
Kolhapur
Belgaum
Mangalore
Kozhikode (Calicut)
Hubli
Dhule
Malegaon
Aurangabad
Nanded
Solapur
Bhopal
Indore
Jabalpur
Raipur
Nagpur
Amravati
Akola
Chandrapur
Warangal
Gulbarga
Hyderabad
Godavari
Krishna
*Deccan Plateau*
Davangere
Bangalore
Mysore
Salem
Coimbatore
Madurai
Trivandrum
Kochi (Cochin)

*Western Ghats*
*Eastern Ghats*

Nellore
Chennai (Madras)
Tiruchchirappalli
Jaffna
Mannar
Palk Strait

Vijayawada
Rajahmundry
Vishakhapatnam
Brahmapur
Cuttack
Sambalpur
Jamshedpur
Ranchi
Asansol
Kolkata (Calcutta)
**BANGLADESH**
Khulna
**Dhaka** ■
Chittagong

*Mouths of the Ganges*

**BURMA (MYANMAR)**
Aizawl
Monywa
▲ Mount Victoria 3,053m (10,016ft)
Sittwe
Sandoway
Pathein
Pye
*Irrawaddy*

*Mouths of the Irrawaddy*

*Bay of Bengal*

Andaman Islands (India)
Port Blair
Little Andaman
*Ten Degree Channel*
Nicobar Islands (India)

**INDIAN OCEAN**

**SRI LANKA**
Trincomalee
Kandy
Colombo ● ■ **Sri Jayewardenepura Kotte**
Negombo
Galle
*Gulf of Mannar*

**MALDIVES**
**Male** ■

Tropic of Cancer

PAKISTAN

Helmand
Zabol
Zahedan
Iranshahr
Panjgur
Turbat

30°
25°

7
20°
8
15°
9
H
60°

Tropic of Cancer
Masirah Island

Kerman
Bandar-e Abbas
Sirjan
Strait of Hormuz
Sur

Gulf of Oman

Muscat

Suhar

Zagros Mountains
Shiraz
Persepolis
Bushehr
Sharjah
Dubai
OMAN
Al Ayn

OMAN

G
55°

Busehr

Persian Gulf
(The Gulf)

Manama
BAHRAIN
Doha
QATAR
Abu Dhabi

UNITED ARAB
EMIRATES

Salalah

ARABIAN SEA

A r a b i a n   S e a

I N D I A N

O C E A N

Socotra
(Yemen)

Cape Guardafui

F
50°

Ahvaz
Abadan
Basra
Al Amarah
Tigris
An Nasiriyah
Euphrates

Kuwait City
KUWAIT

Ad Dammam
Al Mubarrez
Haradh

Riyadh

SAUDI ARABIA

A r a b i a n

P e n i n s u l a

R u b   a l
K h a l i

( E m p t y   Q u a r t e r )

Hadhramaut
Al Mukalla

YEMEN

Gulf of Aden

SOMALIA

Hail

Buraydah

Najran
Sadah
Marib
Dhamar
Ibb
Taizz

Sana
3,760m
(12,336ft)

Abha
3,133m
(10,279ft)

Aden
Bab al Mandab
Berbera
Hargeysa
45°

DJIBOUTI
Djibouti
Dikhil

Medina
Mecca
At Taif

A s i r

Farasan
Islands

Al Hudaydah

Assab
Kobar
Sink
-116m
(-381ft)

Dire Dawa
40°

Jedda

R e d   S e a

Karora
Keren
Massawa
Asmara

Mekele
Ras Dashen
4,620m
(15,157ft)

Gonder
Lake Tana
Dese

ETHIOPIA

Ethiopian
Highlands

Blue Nile
Bahir Dar

Amman
ISRAEL JORDAN
Jerusalem
Gaza
Beer Sheva
Maan
Al Aqaba
Petra
Elat
Sharm el Sheikh
Tabuk

H e j a z

Port Sudan

SUDAN

ERITREA

Teseney
Kassala
Wad Medani
Gedaref

Atbarah
Nubian Desert
Nile

EGYPT
Cairo
El Mansura
Ismailia
Suez Canal
Suez
Pyramids of Giza
Beni Suef
El Minya
Asyut
Sohag
Qena
Valley of
the Kings
Luxor

A r a b i a n   D e s e r t

S i n a i
Mount
Sinai
2,285m
(7,497ft)

Hurghada

Aswan
Aswan High Dam
Tropic of Cancer
Lake
Nasser

Syrian Desert

Delta
Port Said
Nile
Gaza

30°
25°

6
7
20°
8
15°
9
35°E

303

Copyright © Usborne Publishing Ltd.

UNITED
KINGDOM
London
*North
Sea*
*Norwegian
Sea*
Arctic Circle
*Svalbard*
(Norway)
20°
B
ARCTI
NORWAY
Oslo
Paris
BELGIUM
NETHERLANDS
LUXEMBOURG
FRANCE
DENMARK
SWEDEN
40°
*Franz Josef
Land*
C
60°
D
80°
GERMANY
Berlin
Stockholm
FINLAND
*North Cape*
Murmansk
*Barents
Sea*
*Novaya
Zemlya*
*Baltic
Sea*
Helsinki
*Kola
Peninsula*
*Kara
Sea*
CZECH
REPUBLIC
AUSTRIA
POLAND
Warsaw
LITHUANIA
LATVIA
Vilnius
ESTONIA
*Lake
Ladoga*
St. Petersburg
Arkhangelsk
SLOVAKIA
Budapest
HUNGARY
Minsk
BELARUS
*Lake
Onega*
Cherepovets
Vorkuta
Noril
Lviv
Moscow
Ukhta
*Ural Mountains*
Novyy Urengoy
ROMANIA
Kiev
MOLDOVA
Chisinau
UKRAINE
Ryazan
Nizhniy Novgorod
*West Siberian*
*Ob*
Kharkiv
Odesa
Voronezh
*Volga*
Kazan
Perm
*Plain*
Surgut
*Yenisey*
Dnipropetrovsk
Simferopol
Samara
Yekaterinburg
*Ob*
40°
N
*Black
Sea*
Rostov
Volgograd
Krasnodar
Oral
Orenburg
Chelyabinsk
*Irtysh*
Omsk
R     U
Ankara
Mount Elbrus
5,642m
(18,510ft)
Astrakhan
*Volga*
Aqtobe
Tomsk
Krasnoya
TURKEY
Adana
GEORGIA
Tbilisi
Atyrau
KAZAKHSTAN
Astana
Pavlodar
Novosibirsk
Barnaul
Aba
Aleppo
ARMENIA
Yerevan
AZERBAIJAN
Baku
Aqtau
Qaraghandy
Uskemen
Kyz
SYRIA
Mosul
Tabriz
*Caspian Sea*
*Aral
Sea*
Nukus
Qyzylorda
Balqash
*Lake
Balkhash*
Altay
*Altı*
Baghdad
IRAQ
Damavand
5,604m
(18,386ft)
Dasoguz
UZBEKISTAN
Shymkent
Almaty
Urumqi
4
Tehran
Ashgabat
(Ashkhabad)
TURKMENISTAN
Tashkent
Bishkek
KYRGYZSTAN
*Tien Shan*
Ahvaz
Esfahan
Mashhad
Turkmenabat
Samarqand
Osh
Dushanbe
Aksu
Kuwait City
KUWAIT
*Persian
(The Gulf)*
Shiraz
Herat
Mazar-e Sharif
TAJIKISTAN
*Tarim Basin*
*Taklimakan Desert*
SAUDI
ARABIA
IRAN
AFGHANISTAN
Hotan
Riyadh
Manama
QATAR
Doha
Abu Dhabi
Bandar-e
Abbas
Zahedan
Kandahar
Kabul
Islamabad
K2
8,611m
(28,251ft)
Srinagar
PAKISTAN
*Indus*
Lahore
INDIA
*Plateau of Tibet*

ALASKA
(U.S.A.)
60°

Chukchi
Sea

Wrangel
Island

East Siberian
Sea

St. Lawrence
Island

Gulf of
Anadyr

Bering Sea

Anadyr

CEAN

J
160°

H
140°

G
120°

F

Severnaya
Zemlya

New Siberia
Islands

Taimyr
eninsula

Laptev Sea

Aleutian Islands
(U.S.A.)

3

Kolyma Range

Verkhoyansk Range

Lena

2,959m
(9,708ft)

Kamchatka
Peninsula

Magadan

Petropavlovsk-Kamchatskiy

PACIFIC

OCEAN

40°
N

ntral Siberian

Plateau

Yakutsk

Lena

Sea of
Okhotsk

S I A

Kuril Islands

Tynda

Komsomolsk

Sakhalin

Amur

Yuzhno Sakhalinsk

Lake
Baikal

Blagoveshchensk

Khabarovsk

Hokkaido

Irkutsk

Ulan Ude

Jiamusi

Sapporo

Hakodate

Manzhouli

JAPAN

Vladivostok

Sendai

Changchun

Chongjin

Sea of
Japan

Honshu

4

Ulan Bator

MONGOLIA

ountains

Gobi Desert

The Great Wall of China

Baotou

Beijing

The Great Wall of China

Huang He (Yellow)

Qinghai
Lake

Lanzhou

Zhengzhou

CHINA

20°

## Northern Eurasia

| | | |
|---|---|---|
| Boreal forest | Wetland | ■ National capital |
| Temperate forest | Mountain | ● Internal capital |
| Tropical forest | Tundra | ⊙ Major city or town |
| Temperate grassland | Ice | ○ Other town |
| Savanna | Cultivation | |
| Semi-desert and scrub | Urban | *See also main key on page 259.* |
| Hot desert | | |

International boundary

Internal boundary

2,490m
(7,988ft) Height above or below sea level

1:28,000,000

0        400        800km

0    200    400    600 miles

# MAPS OF EUROPE

This is a satellite image of
Europe. You can see how
the continent joins on
to Asia to the east.

This is a red squirrel, a species which is widespread throughout Europe but declining in numbers in Britain.

Europe is a small continent, packed with over 40 countries and more than 700 million people. It has no deserts, but its geography ranges from high mountain ranges to icy tundra, rocky islands and lush farmland. With dozens of islands and peninsulas, many of Europe's countries are largely surrounded by sea.

*The shading on this map is there to help you see clearly the different countries that make up the continent.*

Arctic Circle

ARCTIC OCEAN

Reykjavik
ICELAND

Norwegian
Sea

Faroe Islands
(Denmark)

Shetland
Islands

Orkney
Islands

SWEDEN

NORWAY

Oslo

Stockholm

North
Sea

DENMARK
Copenhagen

Ba
Se

IRELAND
Dublin

UNITED
KINGDOM

London

The
Hague

Amsterdam
NETHERLANDS

Berlin

POLA

Brussels
BELGIUM Bonn

GERMANY

Prague
CZECH
REPUBLIC

Paris

LUXEMBOURG
Luxembourg

Rhine

Vienna
Bratislava

ATLANTIC

OCEAN

Bay
of
Biscay

FRANCE

Bern
SWITZERLAND

LIECHTENSTEIN
Vaduz

AUSTRIA Budape

SLOVENIA
Ljubljana

Zagre
CROAT

HUNGA

MONACO

ANDORRA

Andorra
la Vella

SAN MARINO

BOSNIA AN
HERZEGOVI
Sarajevo

PORTUGAL

Lisbon

Madrid

SPAIN

Corsica

ITALY

Rome

VATICAN CITY

ALBA
Tira

Sardinia

Balearic
Islands

Mediterranean Sea

Sicily

MALTA
Valletta

Barents Sea

Murmansk

Arctic Circle

Arkhangelsk

FINLAND

Isinki

St. Petersburg

Tallinn
ESTONIA

RUSSIA

Nizhniy Novgorod

Kazan

Riga  LATVIA

Moscow

LITHUANIA
Vilnius
IA

Volga

Minsk

BELARUS

Warsaw

Kiev

Volgograd

UKRAINE

Dnieper

VAKIA

MOLDOVA

Chisinau

ROMANIA

grade

Bucharest

Danube

Black Sea

A &
EGRO  BULGARIA

Sofia

Skopje

ACEDONIA   TURKEY

REECE

Athens

Crete

## Facts

**Total land area**  10,205,720 sq km (3,940,428 sq miles) (including European Russia)
**Total population**  727 million (including all of Russia)
**Biggest city**  Paris, France
**Biggest country**  Russia  *Total area: 17,075,200 sq km (6,592,735 sq miles)  Area of European Russia: 4,294,400 sq km  (1,658,068 sq miles)*
**Smallest country**  Vatican City  *0.44 sq km (0.17 sq miles)*

**Highest mountain**  Elbrus, Russia  *5,642m (18,510ft)*
**Longest river**  Volga  *3,700km (2,298 miles)*
**Biggest lake**  Lake Ladoga, Russia  *17,700 sq km (6,834 sq miles)*
**Highest waterfall**  Utigard, on the Jostedal Glacier, Norway  *800m (2,625ft)*
**Biggest desert**  No deserts in Europe
**Biggest island**  Great Britain  *229,870 sq km (88,753 sq miles)*

**Main mineral deposits**  Bauxite, zinc, iron, potash, fluorspar
**Main fuel deposits**  Oil, coal, natural gas, peat, uranium

*A dairy cow in Devon, in the south of England*

Hameenlinna   Paijanne Lake   Mikkeli
Turku   Lahti   Pihlaja Lake
**FINLAND**
Kouvola   Lappeenranta   Saimaa Lake
Espoo   Helsinki   Kotka   Vyborg
Aland Islands   **Helsinki**
Baltic Sea   Gulf of Finland   Lake Ladoga   Lake Onega   Konosha
Hiiumaa   **Tallinn**
Haapsalu   Kohtla-Jarve   Zelenogorsk   St. Petersburg   White Lake
Kuressaare   Narva   Kingisepp   Pushkin   Volkhov
Saaremaa   **ESTONIA**   Gatchina   Tikhvin
Parnu   Kirishi
Ventspils   Gulf of Riga   Tartu   Lake Peipus   Novgorod   Cherepovets   Vologda
Jurmala   Cesis   Voru   Lake Pskov   Borovichi   Rybinsk Reservoir
Jelgava   **Riga**   Pskov   Lake Ilmen   Vyshniy Volochek   Rybinsk
Siauliai   **LATVIA**   Aluksne   Opochka   Valdai Hills   Kostroma
Jekabpils   Ludza   Velikiye Luki   343m (1,125ft)   Yaroslavl   Kineshma   Volga
Panevezys   Daugavpils   Tver   Ivanovo   Gorki Reservoir
**LITHUANIA**   Rzhev   Seme
Kaunas   Navapolatsk   Polatsk   Zelenograd   Sergiyev Posad   Vladimir   Nizhni Novg
Marijampole   Western Dvina   Vitsyebsk   Podolsk   **Moscow**   Murom   Arzam
Alytus   **Vilnius**   Maladzyechna   Orsha   Dnieper   Smolensk   Obninsk   Kolomna
Hrodna   Lida   Barysaw   Kaluga   Serpukhov   Ryazan
**Minsk**   Zhodzina   Roslavl   Oka   **Tula**   Sarans
Baranavichy   **BELARUS**   Mahilyow   Oka
Slutsk   Babruysk   Bryansk   293m (961ft)
Pinsk   Pripet Marshes   Salihorsk   Zhlobin   Klintsy   Desna   Orel   Yelets   Michurinsk   Kamenka
Svyetlahorsk   Lipetsk   Tambov   Penz
Mazyr   Homyel   Rechytsa   Central   Kursk
Lutsk   Chernihiv   Staryy Oskol   Voronezh
Rivne   Korosten   Russian
Shepetivka   Kievske Reservoir   Sumy
Zhytomyr   **Kiev**   Uplands
417m (1,368ft)
Khmelnytskyy   Bila Tserkva   Dnieper   Lubny   Kharkiv   Kamys
Vinnytsya   Cherkasy   Kremenchukske Reservoir   Poltava
Kamyanets-Podilskyy   Uman   **UKRAINE**   Kremenchuk   Slovyansk   Lysychansk
Botosani   Balti   Dniester   Kirovohrad   Oleksandriya   Kramatorsk   Donets   Volgograd
Iasi   Rabnita   Dniprodzerzhynsk   Dnipropetrovsk   Horlivka   Luhansk
**MOLDOVA**   Yuzhnoukrayinsk   Kryvyy Rih
**Chisinau**   Tiraspol   Nikopol   Zaporizhzhya   **Donetsk**   Tsimlyansk Reservoir
Tighina   Mykolayiv   Kakhovske Reservoir   Mariupol   Novocherkassk   Don
**ROMANIA**   Bilhorod Dnistrovskyy   Odesa   Dnieper   Kherson   Melitopol   Rostov   Volgodonsk
Galati   Berdyansk
Braila   Mouths of the Danube   **Black Sea**   Sea of Azov
Tulcea

2

55° N

3

50°

4

45°

F | 50° | G | 55° | H | 60° | J | 65° | K | 70° | L

*West Siberian Plain*

Kotlas
Syktyvkar
Ivdel
Uray

Solikamsk
Berezniki
*Kama Reservoir*
Serov
*Irtysh*
Tobolsk

2

Kirov
Glazov
Perm
Nizhniy Tagil
Tyumen

*Ural Mountains*

**R U S S I A**
Yekaterinburg
*Tobol*

55° N

Izhevsk
Votkinsk
Kurgan

Yoshkar-Ola
Sarapul
Zlatoust
Chelyabinsk

Cheboksary
*Belaya*
Ershovka

Kazan
Naberezhnyye Chelny
*Uy*

Buinsk
*Kuybyshev Reservoir*
Almetyevsk
Ufa
**Yamantau** ▲ 1,640m (5,381ft)
Komsomolets
Qostanay

Ulyanovsk
Oktyabrskiy
Beloretsk
Rudnyy
Semiozernoe

3

*Volga Uplands*
Tolyatti
Sterlitamak
Magnitogorsk
Tobyl

Syzran
*Saratov Reservoir*
Samara
*Belaya*
Zhetiqara

Buzuluk
Zhayylma

Balakovo
Orenburg
*Ural*
Orsk
Tolybay

Saratov
Engels
Oral
Aqsay
Torghay

*Volgograd Reservoir*
Aqtobe

**K A Z A K H S T A N**

50°

Chapaev

Kaztalovka
*Ural*

4

Zhanibek
Inderbor

Topoli

Balkuduk
*Volga*

*Caspian Depression*

Atyrau

Astrakhan
*Caspian Sea*

50°

45°

55° | H | 60° | J

## Eastern Europe

| | | |
|---|---|---|
| ■ Boreal forest | ■ Wetland | ■ National capital |
| ■ Temperate forest | ■ Mountain | ● Internal capital |
| ■ Tropical forest | ■ Tundra | ◉ Major city or town |
| ■ Temperate grassland | ☐ Ice | ○ Other town |
| ■ Savanna | ■ Cultivation | |
| ■ Semi-desert and scrub | ■ Urban | ***See also main key on page 259.*** |
| ■ Hot desert | | |

— International boundary
— Internal boundary
▲ 2,490m (7,988ft) Height above or below sea level

**1:8,200,000**

0    100    200    300km

0         100         200 miles

M 40° L 36° K 32° G 28° 24° G 20° F 16° E 12° D 8° C 4°E B 0° A 4°W

1 68°N 2 64° 3 60° 4

Barents Sea

Kola Peninsula

White Sea

RUSSIA

North Cape
Soroya
Vadso
Hammerfest
Kirkenes
Severomorsk
Severomorsk
Murmansk
Monchegorsk
▲1,191m 3,907ft
Apatity
Kandalaksha
Belomorsk
Lake Onega
Tikhvin
Volkhov
Borovichi
Kirishi

Arctic Circle

Lake Top
Lake Pya
Lake Kuyto
Lake Vyg
Lake Seg
Petrozavodsk
Medvezhyegorsk
Lake Ilmen
Novgorod
Lake Peipus

Alta
Utsjoki
Sevettijarvi
Kaamanen
Lake Inari
Lokan Reservoir
Sodankyla
Kostomuksha
Kuhmo
Lieksa
Lake Ladoga
St. Petersburg
Pushkin
Gatchina
Kingisepp
Narva
ESTONIA

Tromso
Kiruna
Boden
Rovaniemi
Oulu Lake
Kajaani
Pielis Lake
Kiuruvesi
Varkaus
Hauki Lake
Pihlaja Lake
Vyborg
Zelenogorsk
Kotka
Kohtla-Jarve
Haapsalu
Hiiumaa

Lapland

Narvik
Kebnekaise
▲2,114m (6,935ft)
Stora Lule Lake
Tornio
Oulu
Raahe
Kuopio
Saimaa Lake
Lappeenranta
Kouvola
Helsinki
Tallinn

Svolvaer
Horn Lake
Storavan Lake
Skelleftea
Ume
Umea
Jyvaskyla
Mikkeli
Pajanne Lake
Lahti
Espoo
Turku
Gulf of Finland

Lofoten
Vesteralen
Mo-i-Rana
Bodo
Sundsvall
Hudiksvall
Vaasa
Nasi Lake
Tampere
Hameenlinna
Pori
Rauma
Aland Islands

Vestfjorden
Ostersund
Indals
Gavle
Uppsala
Stockholm
Sodertalje

Norwegian Sea

Namsos
Steinkjer
Vikna
Trondheim
Stor Lake
Borlange
Eskilstuna
Orebro
Lake Malar

FINLAND
Kokkola
Kurikka
Saarijarvi
Alavus
Vyborg
Puula Lake
Pielis Lake

Gulf of Bothnia

SWEDEN
NORWAY

Oppdal
Lillehammer
Karlstad
Lake Vaner
Lidkoping

Froya
Hitra
Smola
Kristiansund
Honefoss
Drammen
Oslo
Fredrikstad
Larvik
Arendal

Galdhopiggen
▲2,469m (8,100ft)
Alesund
Bergen
Odda
Stavanger
Kristiansand

Sula
Sotra
Karmoy
Varhaug

Klar
Glama
Glama

ICELAND

A 0° B 20°W C 16° 16°E Q
N P Q

Langanes
Isafjordur
Siglufjordur
Seydhisfjordhur
Reykjavik
Keflavik
Faxafloi
Vatnajokull
Hvannadalshnukur
▲2,119m (6,952ft)

Same scale as main map

Arctic Circle
ATLANTIC OCEAN

64°N
68°N
24°W 20°W

# WESTERN EUROPE

NORWAY

Lerwick
Shetland Islands

Karmoy
Stavanger
Varhaug

Drammen
Larvik
Arendal
Kristiansand

Orebro
Karlstad
Fredrikstad

Linkoping
Lidkoping
Lake Vatter

Lake Vaner
Uddevalla
Jonkoping
Gothenburg
Varberg
Halmstad
Vaxjo

SWEDEN

Skagerrak
Skagen
Viborg
Jutland
Randers
Arhus

Kattegat

Alborg

DENMARK
Kolding
Esbjerg
North Frisian Islands

Copenhagen
Zealand
Odense
Fyn
Flensburg
Lolland
Nykobing

Karlshamn
Helsingborg
Malmo

Baltic Sea

Rostock
Schwerin

Kiel
Cuxhaven
Bremerhaven
Bremen

Hamburg
Elbe
Hannover

Gorzow
Wielkopolski
Potsdam

Berlin

Cottbus
Dresden
Chemnitz
Gera

Most
Prague
Karlovy Vary
Pilsen
CZECH
REPUBLIC

Wels
AUSTRIA
Salzburg

Magdeburg
Leipzig
Erfurt

Gottingen
Kassel

GERMANY
Frankfurt
Wurzburg
Mannheim

Nuremberg
Regensburg

Ingolstadt
Augsburg
Munich
Kempten

Stuttgart
Winterthur

Karmoy

NORTH SEA

North
Sea

Shetland Islands

Orkney Islands
Kirkwall
Wick

Stornoway
Hebrides
(Western Isles)

SCOTLAND
Aberdeen
Ben Nevis
1,343m
(4,406ft)
Dundee
Edinburgh
Glasgow
Stranraer

Londonderry
NORTHERN
IRELAND
Belfast

IRELAND
Sligo
Galway
Limerick
Tralee
Cork
Waterford

Irish Sea

Dublin

Celtic Sea

Isle of Man
Blackpool
Liverpool
Colwyn Bay
Aberystwyth
WALES
Swansea
Cardiff
Newport

Stornoway

Carlisle
Newcastle upon Tyne
Sunderland
Middlesbrough

UNITED
KINGDOM

Leeds
Hull
Manchester
Sheffield
Stoke-on-Trent
Nottingham
ENGLAND
Birmingham
Gloucester
Severn
Bristol
Swindon

Norwich
Ipswich
Cambridge
Oxford
London
Southend-on-Sea

Land's End
Penzance
Exeter
Plymouth
Southampton
Portsmouth
Poole
Isle of Wight

Dover
Strait of Dover
Calais

Groningen
Leeuwarden
Frisian Islands

NETHERLANDS
Amsterdam
Haarlem
The Hague
Rotterdam
Arnhem
Enschede

Eindhoven
Bruges
Antwerp
Gent
BELGIUM
Brussels
Charleroi
Namur
Liege
Maastricht

Osnabruck
Munster
Bielefeld
Essen
Duisburg
Dusseldorf
Cologne
Bonn
Koblenz
Rhine

LUXEMBOURG
Luxembourg
Saarbrucken

Metz
Nancy
Reims
Amiens
Troyes

Calais
Dover
Cherbourg
Le Havre
Rouen
Caen
Le Mans

Seine
Paris
Evry
Orleans

St. Malo
Rennes
Quimper
Brest

Channel Islands
(U.K.)
St. Helier

English Channel

ATLANTIC
OCEAN

A 0° B 4°E C 8° D 12° E 16°

Cherbourg
Le Havre
Rouen
Caen
Amiens
Charleroi
Namur
**BELGIUM**
Koblenz
Erfurt
Gera
Chemnitz
Dresden
Wroclaw
Walbrzyc

**Paris**
Evry
Reims
**LUXEMBOURG**
■ **Luxembourg**
Frankfurt
Wurzburg
Karlovy
Vary
Most
Liberec
Hradec Kralove
■ **Prague**

1

48°
N
Le Mans
Troyes
Metz
Nancy
Saarbrucken
Mannheim
Karlsruhe
**GERMANY**
Nuremberg
Regensburg
Pilsen
Karlovy
Vary
**CZECH REPUBLIC**
Olomouc
Brno
Zli

Angers
Tours
Orleans
Nevers
Dijon
Strasbourg
Stuttgart
Ingolstadt
Danube
Augsburg
Munich
Ceske
Budejovice
Wels
Linz
St. Polten
**Vienna**
Trn

Poitiers
Limoges
**FRANCE**
Besancon
Chalon-
sur-Saone
Biel
**Bern** ■
**SWITZERLAND**
Lucerne
Winterthur
Zurich
Freiburg
Ulm
Kempten
Salzburg
St. Polten
Bratisla

2

Clermont-Ferrand
Lyon
Geneva
Lausanne
Lake Geneva
**Vaduz**
**LIECHTENSTEIN**
Innsbruck
**AUSTRIA**
Grossglockner
3,798m
(12,461ft)
S
p
Villach
Klagenfurt
Knittelfeld
Graz
Szombathe
Gyo
Bala

St. Etienne
*Massif
Central*
Mont Blanc
4,807m
(15,771ft)
Grenoble
A
l
Lake
Como
Trento
Bolzano
Kranj
**SLOVENIA**
Maribor
Zalaegers
**Ljubljana** ■
Novo
Mesto
**Zagreb** ■
**CROATIA**

44°
Montauban
Toulouse
Garonne
Novara
Bergamo
Milan
Brescia
Verona
Vicenza
Po
Turin
**Rhone**
Parma
Venice
Trieste
Rijeka
Karlovac
Slavor
B

Montpellier
Nimes
Beziers
**Andorra la Vella** ■
**MONACO**
Aix-en-
Provence
San Remo
Nice
Cannes
*Gulf of
Genoa*
Genoa
Modena
Bologna
Ferrara
Ravenna
Pula
Zadar
**BOSNIA
AND
HERZEGOVID**
Banja Luka
*Dinaric
Alps*
Ze

*Gulf of
Lions*
**Marseille**
Toulon
**ITALY**
Pisa
Livorno
Florence
**SAN MARINO**
Rimini
Ancona
Split
Mo

3
*Ligurian Sea*
Bastia
Elba
Perugia
Terni
Pescara
*A
d
r
i
a
t
i
c

S
e
a*

**Southern Europe**

Boreal forest
Temperate forest
Tropical forest
Temperate grassland
Savanna
Semi-desert and scrub
Hot desert
Wetland
Mountain
Tundra
Ice
Cultivation
Urban
■ National capital
● Internal capital
⊙ Major city or town
○ Other town
—— International boundary
--▲-- Internal boundary
2,490m
(7,988ft) Height above or below sea level
**See also main key on page 259.**
1:8,200,000

0   100   200   300km
0        100       200 miles

Ajaccio
*Corsica*
(France)
**VATICAN CITY**
**Rome** ■
Porto-Vecchio
Foggia
Bari

40°
Olbia
Sassari
*A
p
e
n
n
i
n
e
s*
Naples
Pompeii
Salerno
Taranto

*Sardinia*
(Italy)
*Tyrrhenian*
Oristano

*Sea*
Cosenza

4
Cagliari
Catanzar

*M e d i t e r r a n e a n   S e a*
*Lipari
Islands*

Trapani
Palermo
Messina

36°
Annaba
Menzel
Bourguiba
Bizerte
*Sicily*
Mount Etna
3,323m
(10,902ft)
Catania
Syracuse

Guelma
Carthage
**Tunis** ■
Agrigento
Ragusa

**See also main key on page 259.**

Souk Ahras
**TUNISIA**
Nabeul
*Pantelleria*
(Italy)
**MALTA**

5
Tebessa
Kairouan
Sousse
Monastir
*Pelagian Islands*
(Italy)
**Valletta** ■

Kasserine
El Jem
Biskra

B 4°E C 8° D 12° E 16°

African elephants in Amboseli National Park, Kenya

*This satellite image of Africa shows how the continent is dominated by deserts, particularly the Sahara in the north, which are represented here in yellow.*

# MAPS OF AFRICA

Africa is the second-biggest continent and has 53 countries altogether. More than a quarter of them are landlocked, with no access to the sea except through other countries. Africa is home to the world's longest river, the Nile, and its largest desert, the Sahara. It also has vast amounts of natural resources, such as gold, copper and diamonds. Many of them have not yet begun to be used.

*A group of Masai people from East Africa silhouetted against a sunset over the flat grasslands*

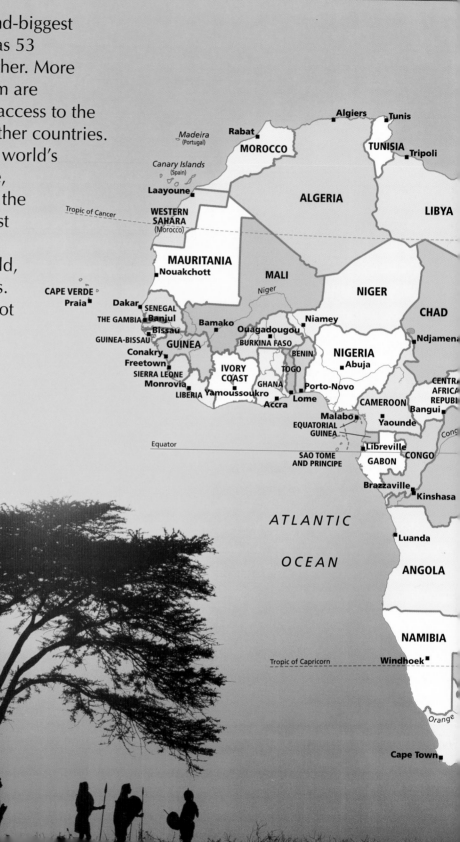

Madeira
(Portugal)

Algiers  Tunis

Rabat

MOROCCO

TUNISIA
Tripoli

Canary Islands
(Spain)

Laayoune

ALGERIA

LIBYA

Tropic of Cancer

WESTERN
SAHARA
(Morocco)

MAURITANIA
Nouakchott

MALI

NIGER

CHAD

Niger

CAPE VERDE
Praia

Dakar
SENEGAL

Niamey

Ndjamena

THE GAMBIA  Banjul

Bamako

GUINEA-BISSAU  Bissau

Ouagadougou
BURKINA FASO

Conakry
GUINEA

BENIN

NIGERIA

Freetown

Abuja

IVORY
COAST

TOGO

SIERRA LEONE

Monrovia

GHANA

Porto-Novo

CENTRAL
AFRICAN
REPUBLIC

LIBERIA  Yamoussoukro

Lome

CAMEROON

Accra

Bangui

Malabo

EQUATORIAL
GUINEA

Yaounde

Congo

Equator

Libreville
CONGO

SAO TOME
AND PRINCIPE

GABON

Brazzaville

Kinshasa

ATLANTIC

Luanda

OCEAN

ANGOLA

NAMIBIA

Tropic of Capricorn  Windhoek

Orange

Cape Town

*The shading on this map is there to help you see clearly the different countries that make up the continent.*

Cairo ■

EGYPT

Tropic of Cancer

Nile

Khartoum ■

ERITREA
Asmara ■

SUDAN

DJIBOUTI ■ Djibouti

Addis Ababa ■ SOMALIA

ETHIOPIA

NGO

UGANDA
Kampala ■

Mogadishu ■

KENYA

Equator

Kigali ■

EM.

Nairobi ■

RWANDA
BURUNDI
Bujumbura ■

KEP.)

Dodoma ■

TANZANIA ■ Dar es Salaam

Victoria ■
SEYCHELLES

*INDIAN*

MALAWI

Moroni ■
COMOROS

AMBIA
Lusaka ■

Lilongwe ■

*OCEAN*

Zambezi

Harare ■
ZIMBABWE

MOZAMBIQUE

Antananarivo ■

MAURITIUS
■ Port Louis

SWANA

MADAGASCAR

Reunion
(France)

Tropic of Capricorn

borone

Pretoria ■
Mbabane ■ Maputo ■
SWAZILAND
Lobamba ■

emfontein ■ Maseru ■

LESOTHO

UTH
RICA

## Facts

**Total land area** 30,311,690 sq km (11,703,343 sq miles)

**Total population** 794 million

**Biggest city** Cairo, Egypt

**Biggest country** Sudan *2,505,810 sq km (967,493 sq miles)*

**Smallest country** Seychelles *455 sq km (176 sq miles)*

**Highest mountain** Kilimanjaro, Tanzania *5,895m (19,340ft)*

**Longest river** Nile, running from to Burundi to Egypt *6,671km (4,145 miles)*

**Biggest lake** Lake Victoria, between Tanzania, Kenya and Uganda *69,215 sq km (26,724 sq miles)*

**Highest waterfall** Tugela Falls, on the Tugela River, South Africa *610m (2,000ft)*

**Biggest desert** Sahara, North Africa *9,100,000 sq km (3,500,000 sq miles)*

**Biggest island** Madagascar *587,040 sq km (226,656 sq miles)*

**Main mineral deposits** Gold, copper, diamonds, iron ore, manganese, bauxite

**Main fuel deposits** Coal, uranium, natural gas

*A greater flamingo in the Transvaal National Park*

A  0°  B  5°E

Annaba
Bizerte
Menzel
Bourguiba
Carthage
**Tunis**

Sicily
(Italy)
Catania
Syracuse

20°

**GREECE**  Ath

Saida

Djelfa
Batna
Tebessa
Kairouan
Sousse
Monastir
El Jem

Pantelleria
(Italy)

Pelagian
Islands
(Italy)

**MALTA**
**Valletta**

Biskra

*Atlas Mountains*

Ghardaia
Touggourt
El Oued
Gafsa
Tozeur
Sfax
Kerkenah
Islands

*M e d i t e r r a n e a*

2

Chott
el Jerid
Gabes
Gulf of Gabes
Jerba

Ouargla

Tataouine

**TUNISIA**

Al Khums
**Tripoli**
Leptis Magna
Gharyan
Misratah

Cyrene
Al Bayda
Darnah

30°
N

*Tademait
Plateau*

Ghadamis

Surt
Benghazi
Tubruq

*Gulf of
Sidra*
Ajdabiya

*Great
Eastern Erg*

3

**ALGERIA**

Illizi

Sabha

**LIBYA**

*Libya*

25°

Murzuq

*Ahaggar
Mountains*

Ghat

Tropic of Cancer

Mount Tahat
2,918m
(9,573ft)

4

Al Jaw

Tamanrasset

*Djado
Plateau*

*Tibesti
Mountains*

20°

Emi Koussi
3,415m
(11,204ft)

**MALI**  S  A  H  A  R  A

5

Agadez
**NIGER**

*Bodele
Depression*

Faya-Largeau

*Ennedi
Plateau*

15°

Tahoua

S  A  H  E  L

**CHAD**

Dosso
Maradi
Zinder
Mao
Abeche

**Mount M**
3,08
(10,1.

6

Sokoto
Birnin-Kebbi
Katsina
Katsina
Gusau
Kano

*Lake Chad*

Kandi

Zaria
Potiskum
Maiduguri
**Ndjamena**
Mongo

10°

*Kainji
Reservoir*
Kaduna
**NIGERIA**

Am Timan

7

Saki
Minna
Bida
*Niger*
Jos
Kumo
Maroua
**CAMEROON**  Bongor

Birao
Nya

**Abuja**

322

B  5°E  C  10°  D  15°  E  20°  F

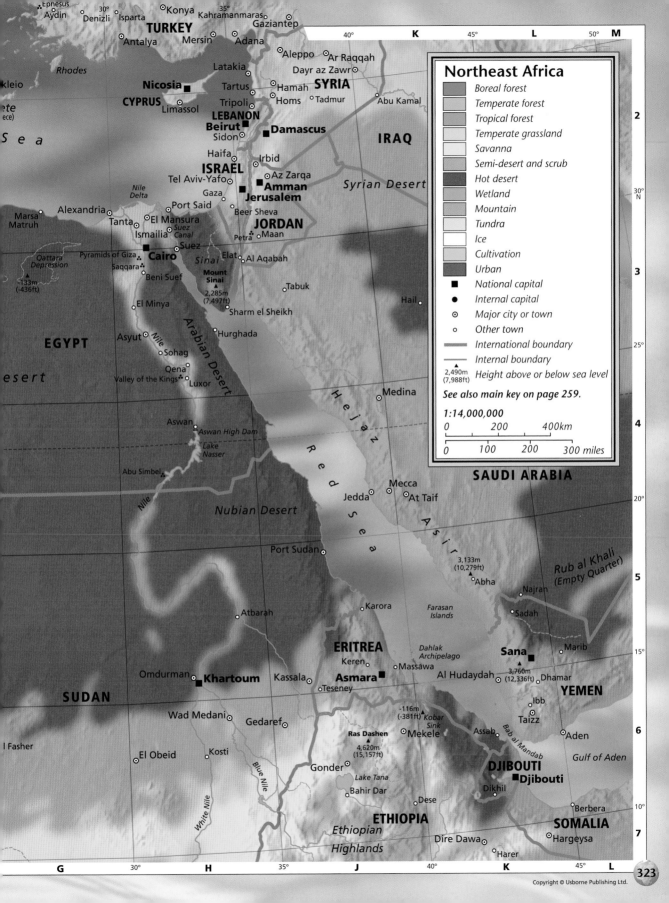

## Northeast Africa

**Legend:**
- Boreal forest
- Temperate forest
- Tropical forest
- Temperate grassland
- Savanna
- Semi-desert and scrub
- Hot desert
- Wetland
- Mountain
- Tundra
- Ice
- Cultivation
- Urban
- ■ National capital
- ● Internal capital
- ⊙ Major city or town
- ○ Other town
- ── International boundary
- ── Internal boundary
- ▲ 2,490m (7,988ft) Height above or below sea level

*See also main key on page 259.*

1:14,000,000

0    200    400km

0    100    200    300 miles

---

Epnesus
Aydin
Konya
Kahramanmaras
TURKEY
Denizli    Isparta    30°    35°    Gaziantep
Antalya    Mersin    Adana
Rhodes    Aleppo    Ar Raqqah
Latakia    Dayr az Zawr
Nicosia    Tartus    Hamah    SYRIA    Abu Kamal
CYPRUS    Tripoli    Homs    Tadmur
Limassol    Beirut    Damascus    IRAQ
LEBANON    Sidon
kleio    Haifa    Irbid
rte    ISRAEL    Az Zarqa
ece)    Tel Aviv-Yafo    Amman
Sea    Gaza    Jerusalem
Alexandria    Port Said    Beer Sheva    JORDAN
Marsa Matruh    Tanta    El Mansura    Petra    Maan
Ismailia    Suez Canal
Pyramids of Giza    Cairo    Suez    Elat    Al Aqabah
Qattara Depression    Saqqara    Sinai
-133m (-436ft)    Beni Suef    Mount Sinai    Tabuk
2,285m (7,497ft)
El Minya    Sharm el Sheikh    Hail
EGYPT    Asyut    Nile    Hurghada
Sohag
desert    Qena    Arabian Desert
Valley of the Kings    Luxor
Medina
Aswan
Aswan High Dam
Lake Nasser
Red Sea    Mecca    At Taif
Abu Simbel    Jedda
Nile    SAUDI ARABIA
Nubian Desert
3,133m (10,279ft)    Rub al Khali (Empty Quarter)
Port Sudan    Abha
Najran
Atbarah    Karora    Sadah
Farasan Islands
ERITREA    Dahlak Archipelago    Sana    Marib
Keren    Massawa
Omdurman    Khartoum    Kassala    Asmara    Al Hudaydah    Dhamar    YEMEN
SUDAN    Teseney    3,760m (12,336ft)
Wad Medani    -116m (-381ft)    Kobar Sink    Ibb
Gedaref    Assab    Taizz
Ras Dashen    Mekele    Aden
El Fasher    Kosti    4,620m (15,157ft)    Gulf of Aden
El Obeid    Gonder    DJIBOUTI
Blue Nile    Lake Tana    Dikhil    Djibouti
Bahir Dar    Berbera
White Nile    Dese    SOMALIA
ETHIOPIA    Dire Dawa    Hargeysa
Ethiopian    Harer
Highlands

323

Copyright © Usborne Publishing Ltd.

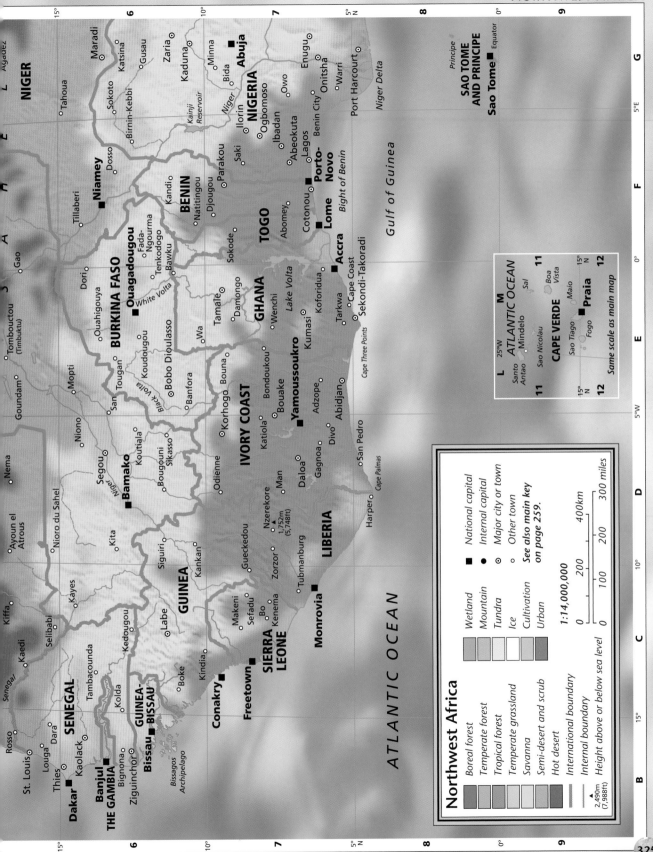

## Northwest Africa

Boreal forest
Temperate forest
Tropical forest
Temperate grassland
Savanna
Semi-desert and scrub
Hot desert

International boundary
Internal boundary

▲ 2,490m
(7,988ft) Height above or below sea level

■ National capital
● Internal capital
◉ Major city or town
○ Other town
See also main key
on page 259.

1:14,000,000

0   100   200   300 miles
0   200   400km

**Countries and places:**

NIGER
Agadez
Maradi
Tahoua
Katsina
Gusau
Birnin-Kebbi
Sokoto
Zaria
Kaduna
Minna
Bida
Abuja
Niamey
Tillaberi
Dosso
Gao
Kandio
BENIN
Natitingou
Djougou
Parakou
Saki
Ilorin
Ogbomoso
Ibadan
Abeokuta
Owo
Enugu
Onitsha
Benin City
Lagos
Porto-Novo
Cotonou
Lome
Warri
Port Harcourt
Niger Delta
NIGERIA
Kainji Reservoir

SAO TOME
AND PRINCIPE
Principe
Sao Tome
Equator

Tombouctou (Timbuktu)
Goundam
Mopti
Niono
Nema
Ayoun el Atrous
Nioro du Sahel
Kita
BURKINA FASO
Ouagadougou
Ouahigouya
Dori
Fada-Ngourma
Tenkodogo
Bawku
White Volta
Koudougou
Bobo Dioulasso
Banfora
Tougan
San
Segou
TOGO
Sokode
Dapango
Damongo
Tamale
Wa
GHANA
Wenchi
Lake Volta
Kumasi
Koforidua
Accra
Cape Coast
Sekondi-Takoradi
Tarkwa
Cape Three Points

Gulf of Guinea
Bight of Benin

ATLANTIC OCEAN
CAPE VERDE
Santo Antao
Sao Nicolau
Mindelo
Sal
Boa Vista
Maio
Sao Tiago
Praia
Fogo
Same scale as main map

Rosso
St. Louis
Louga
Thies
Dakar
Kaolack
Banjul
THE GAMBIA
Ziguinchor
Bignona
GUINEA-BISSAU
Bissau
Bissagos Archipelago
SENEGAL
Kaedi
Kiffa
Selibabi
Dara
Tambacounda
Kolda
Kayes
Kedougou
Boke
Kindia
Labe
Siguiri
Kankan
GUINEA
Conakry
Freetown
SIERRA LEONE
Makeni
Sefadu
Kenema
Bo
Gueckedou
Zorzor
Nzerekore
1,752m (5,748ft)
Tubmanburg
Monrovia
LIBERIA
Harper
Cape Palmas
BAMAKO
Segou
Bougouni
Sikasso
Koutiala
IVORY COAST
Odienne
Korhogo
Bouna
Katiola
Bouake
Bondoukou
Man
Daloa
Gagnoa
Divo
Adzope
Abidjan
Yamoussoukro
San Pedro
Adzope

ATLANTIC OCEAN

See also main key on page 259.

Copyright © Usborne Publishing Ltd.

325

Mao

Lake Chad

Kano

Maiduguri

Potiskum

**Ndjamena**

Mongo

**CHAD**

Mount Marra
3,088m
(10,131ft)

El Fasher

Nyala

NIGERIA

Jos

Kumo

Maroua

Bongor

Garoua

Lai

Sarh

Birao

SUDAN

Makurdi

Doba

Moundou

Lagdo
Reservoir

Ndele

Ouadda

Wau

Ngaoundere

Bossangoa

Bozoum

**CENTRAL AFRICAN
REPUBLIC**

Bria

Djema

Bamenda

Foumban

Bouar

Bossembele

Bafoussam

**CAMEROON**

Obo

Calabar

Nkongsamba

Bertoua

Berberati

Bangassou

Kumba

Cameroon Mountain
4,095m
(13,435ft)

Douala

**Yaounde**

**Bangui**

Uele

**Malabo**

Gemena

Buta

Isiro

Bioco
(Equatorial
Guinea)

Ebolowa

Bata

**EQUATORIAL
GUINEA**

Oyem

Ouesso

Ubangi

Congo

Kisangani

Margherita P
5,1
(16,76

Makokou

Butembo

Equator

**Libreville**

Mbandaka

Lake
Edward
4,507m
(14,787ft)

Cape
Lopez

**GABON**

Lastoursville

Owando

**CONGO
(DEMOCRATIC
REPUBLIC)**

Goma
Lake Kivu

**RWAND**

Port-
Gentil

Lambarene

Moanda

Franceville

Djambala

Lake
Mai-Ndombe

Kindu

Bukavu

Buta

Tchibanga

Mossendjo

Bandundu

**Bujumbura**

Sibiti

Congo

Kasai

Ilebo

**BURUN**

Loubomo

**Brazzaville**

Madingou

Kinkala

**Kinshasa**

Kikwit

Kigoma

Pointe-Noire

**CABINDA**
(Angola)

Kananga

Kalemie

Tshikapa

Kabinda

*Lake
Tanganyika*

Mbuji-Mayi

Mwene-Ditu

**Luanda**

Marimba

Kamina

Mitwaba

Pwe

Kamina

Kilwa

Lake
Mwe

Cape Ledo

Ndalatando

Malanje

Saurimo

Kafakumba

Sampwe

Kawambwa

*ATLANTIC*

Dondo

**ANGOLA**

Dilolo

Mutshatsha

Kolwezi

*Bangwe

*OCEAN*

Quirima

Luacano

Likasi

Mansa

2,620m
(8,596ft)

Kasai

Luena

Mwinilunga

Kipushi

Lubumbash

Benguela

Kuito

Munhango

Zambezi

Solwezi

Chingola

Mufulira

Kabun

*Bie
Plateau*

Huambo

Lumbala
Kaquengue

Chavuma

**ZAMBIA**

Kitwe

Ndola

Luanshya

Mku

Obeid
Kosti
White Nile
Blue Nile
Ras Dashen
4,620m
(15,157ft)
Mekele
Gonder
Lake Tana
Bahir Dar
Dese
Assab
Taizz
YEMEN
Aden
Gulf of Aden
Cape Guardaful
Boosaaso
DJIBOUTI
Dikhil
Djibouti
Berbera

1

Ethiopian
Highlands
Dire Dawa
Harer
Hargeysa
SOMALIA
Malakal
Nekemte
Addis Ababa
Debre Zeyit
Nazret
ETHIOPIA
Gambela
Jima
Eyl

2

White Nile
Awasa
Lake
Abaya
Gode

Juba
Beledweyne

5°
N

Lake
Turkana
Moyale
Mandera
Juba
Baydhabo

3

Gulu
UGANDA
Soroti
Mount Elgon
4,321m
(14,176ft)
Mbale
Kitale
Eldoret
KENYA
Baardheere
Mogadishu
Marka
Lake
Albert
Lake
Kyoga
Kampala
Jinja
Kisumu
Nakuru
Meru
Kirinyaga
(Mount Kenya)
5,199m
(17,057ft)
Garissa
Entebbe
Masaka
Mbarara
Kisii
Nyeri
Nairobi
Thika
Machakos
Kismaayo

0°

igali
Lake Victoria
Great Rift Valley
Kilimanjaro
5,895m
(19,340ft)
Moshi
Arusha
Malindi

4

Mwanza
Mombasa
Tabora
Tanga
Pemba Island
INDIAN

5°
S

OCEAN
Dodoma
Zanzibar
Zanzibar Island
TANZANIA
Morogoro
Dar es Salaam
Mafia
Island
Great Rift Valley
Lake Rukwa
Iringa
Mbeya
Makumbako
Ilonga
Njinjo
Liwale
Lindi

bala
Tunduma
Kasama
Karonga
Songea
Masasi
Mtwara
Palma
Cape Delgado
COMOROS
Grand Comoro
(Njazidja)

10°

Isoka
ZAMBIA
Mpika
Mzuzu
Lake Nyasa
(Lake Malawi)
Ruvuma
Tunduru
Mecula
Mueda
Pemba
Moroni
Anjouan
Island
(Nzwani)
Mutsamudu
Fomboni
Mohilla Island
(Mwali)
Mamoudzou
Mayotte
(France)

6

Lundazi
MALAWI
MOZAMBIQUE
Kasungu
Lichinga
Nungo
Chipata
Lilongwe
Luangwa
Petauke
Cuamba

### Central Africa

| | |
|---|---|
| | Boreal forest |
| | Temperate forest |
| | Tropical forest |
| | Temperate grassland |
| | Savanna |
| | Semi-desert and scrub |
| | Hot desert |
| | Wetland |
| | Mountain |
| | Tundra |
| | Ice |
| | Cultivation |
| | Urban |
| ■ | National capital |
| ● | Internal capital |
| ◉ | Major city or town |
| ○ | Other town |
| | International boundary |
| | Internal boundary |
| 2,490m<br>(7,988ft) | Height above or below sea level |

See also main key on page 259.

1:14,000,000

0   200   400km

0   100   200   300 miles

Mbeya
Makumbako
duma
Ilonga
Njinjo
Karonga
Liwale
a
TANZANIA
Lindi
Mtwara
Masasi
Mzuzu
Songea
Tunduru
Palma
Ruvuma
Cape Delgado
Lundazi
Lupilichi
Mueda
Lake Nyasa
(Lake Malawi)
Mecula
Kasungu
Lichinga
ata
Nungo
Pemba
Lilongwe
MALAWI
Cuamba
Zomba
Lake
Chilwa
ngo
Nampula
Nacala
Blantyre
Milange
Mozambique
te
Zambezi
Angoche
Mocuba
ngani
92m
04ft)
Quelimane
tare
MOZAMBIQUE
manimani
Beira
pungabera
Nova
Mambone
assangena
Bassas da India
(Reunion)
Chigubo
Barra Falsa Point
Massinga
Barra Point
Inhambane
Xai-Xai
aputo

SEYCHELLES
Aldabra Group
St. Pierre
Cosmoledo Group
Assumption
Astove
Farquhar
Group
Providence
Bancs
Providence

Grand
Comoro
(Njazidja)
COMOROS
Glorioso Islands
(Reunion)
Moroni
Anjouan Island
(Nzwani)
Mutsamudu
Cape Amber
Fomboni
Mohilla Island
(Mwali)
Mamoudzou
Antsiranana
Mayotte
(France)
Nosy Be
Ambilobe
Ambanja
Cape Melamo
Analalava
Bealanana
Antalaha
Nampula
Mahajanga
Mandritsara
Maroantsetra
Cape St. Andrew
Besalampy
Maevatanana
Nosy
Boraha
Juan de Nova
(Reunion)
Ikopa
Antsalova
Tsiroanomandidy
Toamasina
Belo-
Tsiribihina
Antananarivo
Mania
Malaimbandy
Antsirabe
Ambositra
Bassas da India
(Reunion)
MADAGASCAR
Morombe
Manja
Beroroha
Fianarantsoa
Europa
Island
(Reunion)
Ihosy
Manakara
St. Denis
Reunion
(France)
2,658m
(8,720ft)
Toliara
Betroka
Bekily
Tropic of Capricorn
Androka
Tolanaro
Cape St. Mary

INDIAN

OCEAN

St. Lucia

### Southern Africa

| | | |
|---|---|---|
| Boreal forest | Wetland | ■ National capital |
| Temperate forest | Mountain | ● Internal capital |
| Tropical forest | Tundra | ⊙ Major city or town |
| Temperate grassland | Ice | ○ Other town |
| Savanna | Cultivation | |
| Semi-desert and scrub | Urban | See also main key on page 259. |
| Hot desert | | |
| International boundary | | |
| Internal boundary | 1:14,000,000 | |

2,490m
(7,988ft) Height above or below sea level

0   200   400km
0   100   200   300 miles

K   55°E   L
INDIAN OCEAN
3       3
MAURITIUS
Port Louis
20°S       20°S
St. Denis
4       4
Reunion
(France)
Same scale as main map
K   55°E   L

# MAPS OF THE ARCTIC AND ANTARCTICA

*This is a satellite image of the Arctic. The area in white is the Arctic icecap.*

This is a satellite image of Antarctica with its permanent white icecap.

Adelie penguins in Antarctica

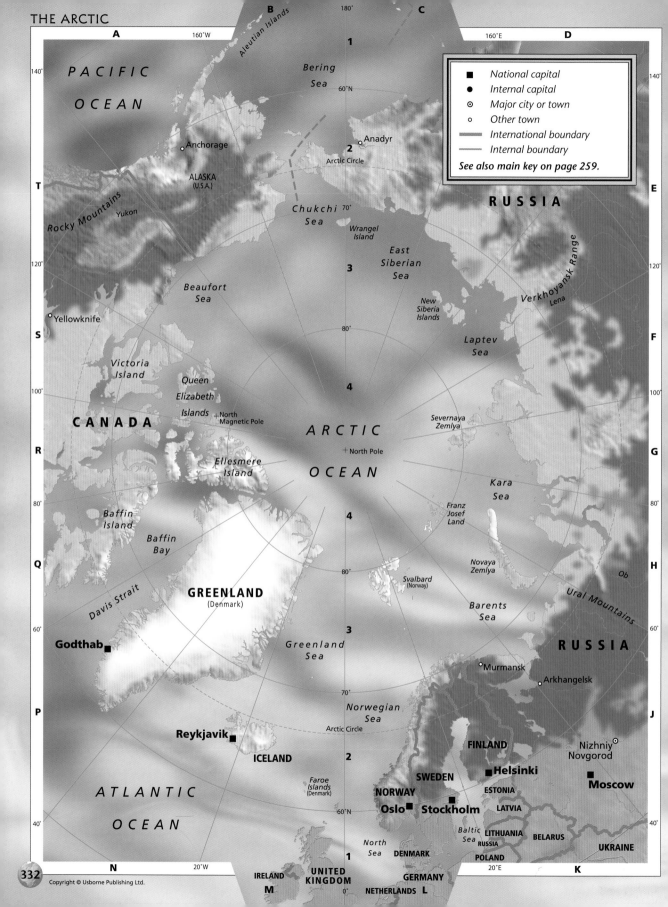

**Key**

- ■ National capital
- ● Internal capital
- ⊙ Major city or town
- ○ Other town
- ▬ International boundary
- ▬ Internal boundary

*See also main key on page 259.*

**A** 160°W **B** 180° **C** 160°E **D**

140°

PACIFIC OCEAN

Aleutian Islands

Bering Sea

60°N

**1**

Anadyr

**2**

Arctic Circle

Anchorage

ALASKA (U.S.A.)

**T**

Rocky Mountains

Yukon

Chukchi Sea

70°

Wrangel Island

RUSSIA

**E**

120°

Beaufort Sea

East Siberian Sea

New Siberia Islands

Verkhoyansk Range

Lena

**3**

Yellowknife

**S**

Victoria Island

Queen Elizabeth Islands

North Magnetic Pole

80°

**4**

Laptev Sea

Severnaya Zemlya

**F**

100°

CANADA

ARCTIC

OCEAN

**R**

Ellesmere Island

+ North Pole

Kara Sea

**G**

80°

Baffin Island

Franz Josef Land

80°

**4**

Ural Mountains

Ob

**H**

Baffin Bay

Novaya Zemlya

**Q**

Davis Strait

GREENLAND (Denmark)

Svalbard (Norway)

Barents Sea

60°

**3**

RUSSIA

**J**

Godthab ■

Greenland Sea

Murmansk ⊙

Arkhangelsk ○

70°

**P**

Reykjavik ■

ICELAND

Norwegian Sea

Arctic Circle

**2**

FINLAND

Nizhniy Novgorod ⊙

40°

ATLANTIC OCEAN

Faroe Islands (Denmark)

60°N

SWEDEN

Helsinki ■

ESTONIA

Moscow ■

**K**

North Sea

NORWAY

Oslo ■ Stockholm ■

LATVIA

Baltic Sea

LITHUANIA RUSSIA

BELARUS

20°W

DENMARK

20°E

UKRAINE

**N** **M** **L** 0° **K**

IRELAND

UNITED KINGDOM

GERMANY

NETHERLANDS

POLAND

**A** 20°W **B** 0° **C** 20°E **D**

1

60°S

**ATLANTIC OCEAN**

South Sandwich
Islands
(U.K.)

South Georgia
(U.K.)

2

Antarctic Circle

**T** **E**

South Orkney Islands
(U.K.)

70°

**S** **F**

South Shetland Islands
(U.K.)

3

*Weddell
Sea*

Queen Maud Land

Enderby
Land

Coats
Land

80°

**ANTARCTICA**

*East
Antarctica*

**INDIAN
OCEAN**

*Antarctic
Peninsula*

Ronne
Ice Shelf

4

**Bellingshausen
Sea**

**Vinson Massif**
5,140m
(16,863ft)

+ South Pole

*Ellsworth
Land*

**R** **G**

100°

*West
Antarctica*

*Transantarctic Mountains*

*Wilkes Land*

*Marie Byrd Land*

4

*Amundsen
Sea*

Ross
Ice Shelf

**Q** **H**

80°

**P A C I F I C**

Ross Sea

3

120°

**O C E A N**

*Victoria
Land*

+ South Magnetic
Pole

70°

**P** **J**

Antarctic Circle

2

60°S

1

**N** 160°W **M** 180° **L** 160°E **K**

*Scale: 1:35,000,000*

0    500    1,000km

0    200    400    600 miles

| Legend | |
|---|---|
| Boreal forest | Wetland |
| Temperate forest | Mountain |
| Tropical forest | Tundra |
| Temperate grassland | Ice |
| Savanna | Cultivation |
| Semi-desert and scrub | Urban |
| Hot desert | |

▲ 2,490m
(7,988ft)   Height above or below sea level

*See also main key on page 259.*

*Stalactites and stalagmites in the Cave of the Winds,
Colorado Springs, U.S.A.*

# FACT FILE

# GEOGRAPHERS AND SCIENTISTS

Geography is the scientific study of the Earth. *Geo* is Greek for "Earth", and "graphy" comes from the Greek "graphein", which means "to write". Sciences that relate to the Earth are known as Earth sciences or geosciences.

Many geographers and scientists are involved in studying different aspects of the Earth. The table below lists some of these areas of study, the scientists and geographers who study them and the area each one deals with.

| Name of study | Name of scientist/geographer | What is it? |
| --- | --- | --- |
| Biogeography | Biogeographer | The study of the distribution of plants and animals |
| Geography | Geographer | The study of the Earth's features and processes, climates, resources and the way people relate to the Earth |
| Historical geography | Historical geographer | The geographic study of a place or region at a specific time in the past, or the study of geographic change over a period of time |
| Regional geography | Regional geographer | The study of the interrelationship between human and physical geography in a particular region |
| Urban geography | Urban geographer | The geographical study of cities |
| Geology | Geologist | The study of planet Earth, what it is made of, how it formed and how it is changing |
| Mineralogy | Mineralogist | The study of minerals |
| Geomorphology | Geomorphologist | The study of landforms (the shapes and features on the Earth's surface) and the processes which cause them |
| Volcanology | Volcanologist | The study of volcanoes |
| Seismology | Seismologist | The study of earthquakes and earth tremors |
| Oceanography | Oceanographer | The study of seas and oceans and the seabed |
| Meteorology | Meteorologist | The study of the weather and weather forecasting |
| Climatology | Climatologist | The study of climates past and present |
| Ecology | Ecologist | The study of the relationship between living things (including humans) and their surroundings on Earth |
| Pedology | Pedologist | The study of soil, which is also often known as soil science |
| Cartography | Cartographer | The science of designing and making maps, and collecting the information needed to make them |

These are some of the famous scientists and geographers who have contributed to our understanding of how the Earth and its processes work, and explored other aspects of geography.

**al-Idrisi (c.1100–c.1165)**
Arabic geographer and author who explored the Mediterranean region, created an early map of the world, and wrote a book, *The Book of Roger*, describing his travels.

**Aristotle (384BC–322BC)**
Greek scientist and philosopher who wrote on many subjects. He realized that the Earth was a sphere, although it took a long time for everyone to accept this. (Until about AD1500, many people still thought the world was flat.)

**Darwin, Charles (1809–1882)**
English scientist who developed the theory of natural selection, which argues that plant and animal species change, or evolve, over long periods of time. This theory was controversial, partly because it suggested that the Earth was much older than many people believed.

**Davis, William Morris (1850–1934)** American geologist and meteorologist who founded the science of geomorphology. He developed a theory of how the process of erosion forms a cycle and was famous for his detailed diagrams showing how features of the Earth's crust are formed.

**Democritus (c.460BC–c.370BC)**
Greek philosopher who was the first to claim that all matter was made up of tiny particles, or atoms. He also studied earthquakes, volcanoes, the water cycle and erosion.

**Eratosthenes (c.276BC–c.196BC)**
Greek scientist and geographer who made the first measurement of the distance around the Earth, using the stars as a guide. He was the first person to use the word *geography*.

**Gould, Stephen Jay (born 1941)**
American geologist and paleontologist (person who studies fossils) who built on the theories of Charles Darwin. He has written many popular books, such as *Wonderful Life* (1989).

**Hartshorne, Richard (1899–1992)**
A leading American philosopher of geography. His major work was *Perspective on the Nature of Geography*, published in 1939, in which he argued for the study of specific places and regions.

**Henry the Navigator (1394–1460)**
A prince of Portugal who planned and paid for many journeys of exploration to Africa. He opened a school which taught explorers how to navigate (find their way) and record their discoveries.

**Herodotus (c.484BC–c.425BC)**
Greek historian known as the "father of history", but also regarded as the founder of geography because he was the first person to put historical events in a geographical setting.

**Humboldt, Alexander von (1769–1859)**
German explorer who contributed to geography, geology, meteorology and oceanography. He explored South America and wrote *Kosmos* (The Cosmos), in 1844, describing the geography and geology of the world.

**Hutton, James (1726–1797)**
Scottish scientist who studied rocks and minerals, and is sometimes called "the father of geology". He said that the Earth's crust changed gradually through erosion, volcanic eruptions and other processes.

**Kant, Immanual (1724–1804)**
Famous German philosopher who taught physical geography.

**Lyell, Sir Charles (1797–1875)**
Scottish geologist who developed the theories of James Hutton. He was also a friend of Charles Darwin and his ideas helped Darwin with his theory of natural selection.

**Mackinder, Sir Halford J. (1861–1947)**
Leading British geographer in the early 20th century. He was head of the first university geography department in the United Kingdom.

**Ptolemy (c.AD100–c.AD170)**
Egyptian geographer and astronomer. He devised an early system of latitude and longitude and used it to create many maps.

**Ritter, Carl (1779–1859)**
German geographer who was the first professor of geography at Berlin University. He wrote his major work, the 19-volume *Erdkunde* (Earth Science), in 1817 and is seen as the founder of modern regional geography.

**Strabo (c.64BC–c.AD20)**
Greek historian and geographer. He wrote *Geography*, a 17-volume book which provides geographical information on the Roman Empire.

**Varenius, Bernhardus (1622–1650)**
Dutch geographer. He wrote a major book, *Geographia Generalis* (General Geography) in 1650, in which he was one of the first people to distinguish between physical and human geography.

**Wegener, Alfred (1880–1930)**
German meteorologist who claimed that the Earth's continents were once joined together in one big continent, which he named Pangaea. His theories were not widely accepted until the 1960s when they were used to develop the theory of plate tectonics.

# WORLD RECORDS

Here are some of the Earth's longest rivers, highest mountains and other amazing world records. But the world is always changing; mountains wear down, rivers change shape, and new buildings are constructed. Ways of measuring things can also change. That's why you may find slightly different figures in different books.

| Highest mountains | |
| --- | --- |
| Everest, Nepal/China | 8,850m (29,035ft) |
| K2, Pakistan/China | 8,611m (28,251ft) |
| Kanchenjunga, India/Nepal | 8,597m (28,208ft) |
| Lhotse I, Nepal/China | 8,511m (27,923ft) |
| Makalu I, Nepal/China | 8,481m (27,824ft) |
| Lhotse II, Nepal/China | 8,400m (27,560ft) |
| Dhaulagiri, Nepal | 8,172m (26,810ft) |
| Manaslu I, Nepal | 8,156m (26,760ft) |
| Cho Oyu, Nepal/China | 8,153m (26,750ft) |
| Nanga Parbat, Pakistan | 8,126m (26,660ft) |

| Longest rivers | |
| --- | --- |
| Nile, Africa | 6,671km (4,145 miles) |
| Amazon, South America | 6,440km (4,000 miles) |
| Chang Jiang (Yangtze), China | 6,380km (3,964 miles) |
| Mississippi/Missouri, U.S.A. | 6,019km (3,741 miles) |
| Yenisey/Angara, Russia | 5,540km (3,442 miles) |
| Huang He (Yellow), China | 5,464km (3,395 miles) |
| Ob/Irtysh/Black Irtysh, Asia | 5,411km (3,362 miles) |
| Amur/Shilka/Onon, Asia | 4,416km (2,744 miles) |
| Lena, Russia | 4,400km (2,734 miles) |
| Congo, Africa | 4,374km (2,718 miles) |

| Biggest natural lakes | |
| --- | --- |
| Caspian Sea | 370,999 sq km (143,243 sq miles) |
| Lake Superior | 82,414 sq km (31,820 sq miles) |
| Lake Victoria | 69,215 sq km (26,724 sq miles) |
| Lake Huron | 59,596 sq km (23,010 sq miles) |
| Lake Michigan | 58,016 sq km (22,400 sq miles) |
| Lake Tanganyika | 32,764 sq km (12,650 sq miles) |
| Lake Baikal | 31,500 sq km (12,162 sq miles) |
| Great Bear Lake | 31,328 sq km (12,096 sq miles) |
| Lake Nyasa | 29,928 sq km (11,555 sq miles) |
| Aral Sea | 28,600 sq km (11,042 sq miles) |

| Deepest ocean |
| --- |
| The Mariana Trench, part of the Pacific Ocean, is the deepest part of the sea at 11,022m (36,740ft) deep. |

| Deepest lake |
| --- |
| Lake Baikal in Russia is the deepest lake in the world. At its deepest point it is 1,637m (5,370ft) deep. |

| Biggest islands | |
| --- | --- |
| Greenland | 2,175,600 sq km (840,000 sq miles) |
| New Guinea | 800,000 sq km (309,000 sq miles) |
| Borneo | 751,100 sq km (290,000 sq miles) |
| Madagascar | 587,040 sq km (226,656 sq miles) |
| Baffin Island | 507,451 sq km (195,928 sq miles) |
| Sumatra | 437,607 sq km (184,706 sq miles) |
| Great Britain | 234,410 sq km (90,506 sq miles) |
| Honshu | 227,920 sq km (88,000 sq miles) |
| Victoria Island | 217,290 sq km (83,896 sq miles) |
| Ellesmere Island | 196,236 sq km (75,767 sq miles) |

| Tallest inhabited buildings | |
| --- | --- |
| Petronas Towers, Malaysia | 452m (1,483ft) |
| Sears Tower, U.S.A. | 443m (1,454ft) |
| Jin Mao Building, China | 420m (1,378ft) |
| CITIC Plaza, China | 391m (1,283ft) |
| Shun Hing Square, China | 384m (1,260ft) |
| Plaza Rakyat, Malaysia | 382m (1,254ft) |
| Empire State Building, U.S.A. | 381m (1,250ft) |
| Central Plaza, China | 373m (1,227ft) |
| Bank of China, China | 368m (1,209ft) |
| Emirates Tower, U.A.E. | 350m (1,148ft) |

| Biggest cities/urban areas | |
| --- | --- |
| Tokyo, Japan | 26.4 million |
| Mexico City, Mexico | 18.1 million |
| Bombay, India | 18.1 million |
| Sao Paulo, Brazil | 17.8 million |
| New York, U.S.A | 16.6 million |
| Lagos, Nigeria | 13.4 million |
| Los Angeles, U.S.A. | 13.1 million |
| Calcutta, India | 12.9 million |
| Shanghai, China | 12.9 million |
| Buenos Aires, Argentina | 12.6 million |

| Famous waterfalls | Height |
| --- | --- |
| Angel Falls, Venezuela | 979m (3,212ft) |
| Sutherland Falls, New Zealand | 580m (1,904ft) |
| Mardalfossen, Norway | 517m (1,696ft) |
| Jog Falls, India | 253m (830ft) |
| Victoria Falls, Zimbabwe/Zambia | 108m (355ft) |
| Iguacu Falls, Brazil/Argentina | 82m (269ft) |
| Niagara Falls, Canada/U.S.A. | 57m (187ft) |

# Natural disasters

Natural disasters can be measured in different ways. For example, some earthquakes score highly on the Richter scale, while others cause more destruction. The earthquakes, volcanic eruptions, floods, hurricanes and tornadoes listed here are among the most famous and destructive disasters in history.

| Earthquakes | Richter scale | Disastrous effects |
|---|---|---|
| San Francisco, U.S.A., 1906 | 7.9 | 3,000 died in resulting fire |
| Messina, Italy, 1908 | 7.5 | More than 70,000 people died |
| Tokyo-Kanto, Japan, 1923 | 8.3 | Great Tokyo Fire; 142,807 died |
| Quetta, Pakistan, 1935 | 7.5 | 30-60,000 died; city destroyed |
| Concepcion, Chile, 1960 | 8.7 | 2,000 died; strongest quake ever |
| Alaska, U.S.A., 1964 | 8.6 | 125; strongest U.S. quake ever |
| Tangshan, China, 1976 | 7.9 | More than 655,000 people died |
| Manjil-Rudbar, Iran, 1990 | 7.7 | 50,000 died; cities destroyed |
| Kobe, Japan, 1995 | 6.8 | 6,400; over $147bn damage |
| Gujarat, India, 2001 | 8.0 | 20,085 died; 2nd strongest Indian quake |

| Volcanic eruptions | Disastrous effects |
|---|---|
| Mount Vesuvius, Italy, AD79 | Pompeii flattened; up to 20,000 died |
| Tambora, Indonesia, 1815 | 92,000 people starved to death |
| Krakatau, Indonesia, 1883 | 36,500 drowned in resulting tsunami |
| Mount Pelee, Martinique, 1902 | Nearly 30,000 people buried in ash flows |
| Kelut, Indonesia, 1919 | Over 5,000 people drowned in mud |
| Agung, Indonesia, 1963 | 1,200 people suffocated in hot ash |
| Mount St. Helens, U.S.A., 1980 | Only 61 died but a large area was destroyed |
| Ruiz, Colombia, 1985 | 25,000 people died in giant mud flows |
| Mt. Pinatubo, Philippines, 1991 | 800 killed by collapsing roofs and disease |
| Island of Montserrat, 1995 | Volcano left most of the island uninhabitable |

| Floods | Disastrous effects |
|---|---|
| Holland, 1228 | 100,000 drowned by a sea flood |
| Kaifeng, China, 1642 | 300,000 died after rebels destroyed a dyke |
| Johnstown, U.S.A., 1889 | 2,200 killed in a flood caused by rain |
| Italy, 1963 | Vaoint Dam overflowed; 2–3,000 killed |
| East Pakistan, 1970 | Giant wave caused by cyclone killed 250,000 |
| Bangladesh, 1988 | 1,300 died, 30m homeless in monsoon flood |
| Southern U.S.A., 1993 | $12bn of damage after Mississippi flooded |
| China, 1998 | Chang Jiang overflow left 14m homeless |
| Papua New Guinea, 1998 | Tsunamis killed 2,000 people |
| Venezuela, 1999 | Floods and mudslides killed 5,000-20,000 |

| Storms | Disastrous effects |
|---|---|
| Caribbean "Great Hurricane", 1780 | Biggest ever hurricane killed over 20,000 |
| Hong Kong typhoon, China, 1906 | 10,000 people died in this giant hurricane |
| Killer tornado, U.S.A., 1925 | Up to 700 people died in Ellington, Missouri |
| Tropical Storm Agnes, U.S.A., 1972 | $3.5bn damage, 129 dead |
| Hurricane Fifi, Honduras, 1974 | 8,000 people died and 100,000 left homeless |
| Hurricane Georges, U.S.A., 1998 | Caribbean and U.S.A. hit; $5bn of damage |
| Hurricane Mitch, C. America, 1998 | Over 9,000 killed across Central America |

## Amazing Earth facts

The Earth is 12,103km (7,520 miles) across. Its circumference (the distance around the Equator) is 38,022km (23,627 miles) and it is 149,503,000 km (92,897,000 miles) away from the Sun.

To make one complete orbit around the Sun, the Earth has to travel 938,900,000km (583,400,000 miles). To do this in just a year, it has to travel very fast. Because of the atmosphere surrounding the Earth, you can't feel it moving. But in fact you are zooming through space faster than any rocket.

- **Orbit speed** The Earth travels around the Sun at a speed of about 106,000kph (65,868mph).

- **Spinning speed** The Earth also spins around an axis, but the speed you are spinning at depends on where you live. Places on the Equator move at 1,600kph (995mph). New York moves at around 1,100kph (684mph). Near the poles, the spinning is not very fast at all. (You can see how this works by looking at a spinning globe.)

- **Solar System speed** The whole Solar System, including the Sun, the Earth and its moon, and the other planets and their moons, is moving at 72,400kph (45,000 mph) through the galaxy.

- **Galaxy speed** Our galaxy, the Milky Way, whizzes through the universe at a speed of 2,172,150kph (1,350,000mph).

# CYCLES OF PLANET EARTH

The Earth is constantly going through repeated processes, or cycles, such as the orbit of the Earth around the Sun, the way it spins and tilts as it moves through space, the orbit of the Moon around the Earth, and the sequence of the tides.

## Days and years

Days and years are created by the movement of the Earth in relation to the Sun. Here are some facts and figures about the Earth's orbit.

• One **day** is the amount of time it takes the Earth to spin around on its axis. We divide each day into 24 hours of 60 minutes each.

• The exact amount of time it takes the Earth to make one complete orbit around the Sun is 365.26 days. This is known as a **solar year**.

• Instead of having 365.26 days, a normal **year** on Earth has exactly 365 days (because this is easier for us). Every four years another day is added to make up the difference. A year with an extra day in it is called a **leap year**. The extra day is added to February, so in leap years February has 29 days instead of 28.

• Making every fourth year a leap year does not even things out exactly, so some leap years are missed. Usually, every fourth year is a leap year, such as 1988, 1992 and 1996. But century years, such as 1700, 1800 and 1900, are not leap years. However, millennium years, such as the year 2000, are leap years

## Calendars

A **calendar** is a system of measuring years, months, weeks and days. People don't all agree when the world began, so years cannot be measured from then. Several different calendars, mostly based on religious beliefs, are used today.

| Years ago | Christian calendar | Muslim calendar | Chinese calendar | Hebrew calendar |
|---|---|---|---|---|
| 5,800 | | | | |
| 5,600 | | | | *This is when Jews believe the world began.* |
| 5,400 | | | | |
| 5,200 | | | | |
| 5,000 | | | | |
| 4,800 | | | | |
| 4,600 | | | | |
| 4,400 | | | *Emperor Huang Di is said to have invented the Chinese calendar 4,600 years ago.* | |
| 4,200 | | | | |
| 4,000 | | | | |
| 3,800 | | | | |
| 3,600 | | | | |
| 3,400 | | | | |
| 3,200 | | | | |
| 3,000 | | | | |
| 2,800 | | | | |
| 2,600 | | | | |
| 2,400 | | | | |
| 2,200 | | | | |
| 2,000 | | | | |
| 1,800 | *The Christian calendar begins with the birth of Jesus Christ.* | | | |
| 1,600 | | | | |
| 1,400 | | | | |
| 1,200 | | *This is when the Muslim prophet Mohammed fled from Mecca to Medina.* | | |
| 1,000 | | | | |
| 800 | | | | |
| 600 | | | | |
| 400 | | | | |
| 200 | | | | |
| 0 | | | | |

*This chart shows how many years ago the different calendars began. When the Christian calendar is on the year 2000, the Muslim calendar is on the year 1378, and so on.*

...moon is a ball of rock orbiting (moving around) a planet. The Earth only has one moon, but some planets have more. Saturn, for example, has at least 30 moons.

Our Moon orbits the Earth once every 27 days, 7 hours and 43 minutes. The Moon "shines" because it is reflecting light from the Sun. Whether we see a full moon, a thin crescent moon, or something in between, depends on what position the Moon is in and how much sunlight it can reflect onto the Earth. These different shapes are called the phases of the Moon.

This diagram shows the phases of the Moon as it orbits the Earth.

• A new moon does not shine at all. The Moon's cycle begins when the Moon is between the Earth and the Sun, so none of the light it reflects can reach the Earth.

• A half moon appears when the Moon has moved around and is alongside the Earth. We see half of it reflecting the Sun.

• A full moon is what you see when the Moon is on the opposite side of the Earth from the Sun. When the Moon is in this position, you can see sunlight reflecting off the whole of the surface facing Earth.

• When the Moon is moving away from the Sun and growing fuller, it is waxing. When it moves around toward the Sun again and seems to be getting smaller, it is waning.

• A crescent moon is between a new moon and a half moon, and looks like a crescent or C-shape.

• A gibbous moon is between a half moon and a full moon, and is a fat oval shape.

• A lunar month is the amount of time it takes the Moon to complete its cycle: 29 days, 12 hours and 44 minutes. This is longer than the orbit time, because while the Moon is making its orbit around the Earth, the Earth is moving around the Sun and so changing its own position.

• Like the Earth, the Moon spins around on its axis. It does this every 27 days, 7 hours and 43 minutes. This is exactly the same amount of time as the time it takes to travel around the Earth, which means we always see the same side of the Moon from Earth. However, we can see the other side of the Moon in pictures taken by spacecraft.

• The Moon is 3,476km (2,160 miles) across, about a quarter of the width of the Earth. Its circumference is 10,927km (6,790 miles) and its distance away from the Earth varies between 356,399 and 384,403km (221,456 and 238,857 miles). It orbits the Earth at about 3,700kph (2,300mph).

• A month on Earth is a period of time based on the Moon's cycle. But to make 12 months fit into a year, an average month is about 30 days long, slightly longer than a lunar month.

• A blue moon happens when there are two full moons within one Earth month. The second full moon of the two is called the blue moon.

Light rays from the Sun

Half moon
New moon
Full moon
Half moon

1. New moon    3. Half moon    5. Full moon    7. Half moon

2. Waxing crescent    4. Waxing gibbous    6. Waning gibbous    8. Waning crescent

## Tides

The water in the Earth's seas and oceans rises and falls twice a day. These movements are called tides, and they are caused by the gravity of the Moon.

As the Earth spins, different parts of its surface move past the Moon. The part nearest the Moon has a high tide, when the water rises as the Moon pulls it.

At the same time, a high tide also happens on the opposite side of the Earth, because of a reaction called centrifugal force, created by the way the Earth and the Moon move around each other.

While this is happening, there is a low tide on the parts of the Earth's surface that are not facing or opposite the Moon. Each part of the world has two high tides and two low tides every day.

# TIME ZONES

When it's midday in Rio de Janeiro, it's midnight in Tokyo. This is because we divide the Earth into different time zones. Within each zone, people usually set their clocks to the same time. If you fly between two zones, you change your watch to the time in the new zone.

## Summer time

Some countries adjust their clocks in summer. For example, in the U.K. everybody's clocks go forward one hour. This is known as Daylight Saving Time or Summer Time. It is a way of getting more out of the days by giving people an extra hour of daylight in the evening. It reduces energy use because people don't use as much electricity for lights.

## Dividing up time

There are 25 different time zones. They are separated by one-hour intervals and there is a new time zone roughly every 15 degrees of longitude*. The zones are measured in hours ahead of or behind Greenwich Mean Time, or GMT, which is the time at the Prime Meridian Line*.

Governments can change their countries' time zones. So, for convenience, whole countries usually keep the same local time instead of sticking to the zones exactly. For example, China could be divided into several time zones, but instead the whole country keeps the same time. A few areas, such as India, Iran and parts of Australia, use non-standard half hour deviations.

## Changing dates

On the opposite side of the world from the Prime Meridian Line is the International Date Line, which runs mostly through the Pacific Ocean and bends to avoid the land. Places to the west of it are 24 hours ahead of places to the east. This means that if you travel east across it you lose a day and if you travel west across it you gain a day.

*This map shows the different time zones. The times at the top of the map tell you the time it is in the different zones when it is noon at the Prime Meridian Line. The numbers in circles tell you how many hours ahead of or behind Greenwich Mean Time an area is.*

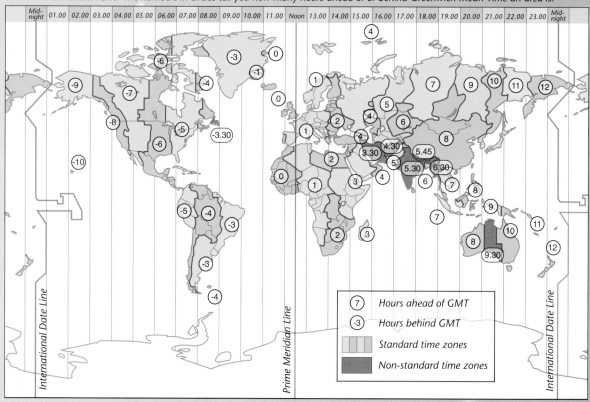

*Longitude, 250; Prime Meridian Line, 250

# LOOKING AT THE STARS

On a clear night you can see a huge number of stars from Earth. If you look carefully, you will soon be able to recognize individual stars and groups of stars, known as constellations. The star maps on the following pages will show you which stars to look for.

## Internet links

**Website 1** Read the stories behind the names of stars and constellations.

**Website 2** Browse a clickable list of the 88 constellations.

**Website 3** Try a constellation quiz.

For links to these websites, go to **www.usborne-quicklinks.com**

*Pegasus*

## Constellations

To make it easier to find and identify different stars, people divided them into constellations and gave them names, often based on characters in stories. The constellations on the star maps in this book appear in capital letters and some have been joined together with lines to make them easier to recognize.

*Andromeda*

*Perseus*

*In these pictures, the red dots show the stars that make up a constellation and the white outlines show the figures they are supposed to represent.*

## Star maps

On the next eight pages there are star maps for each season. This is because as the Earth orbits the Sun, the part of the sky that we can see changes. In addition, many of the stars you can see from the northern hemisphere are different from the ones you can see from the southern hemisphere, so there are different maps for each of these.

*You can observe the stars with your naked eye, but binoculars or a telescope like this one will make them look much bigger and brighter.*

## Using the maps

To use the star maps, choose the right hemisphere and season and look in the direction indicated at the bottom of the map. You will find it easiest to see stars on a clear, dark night, away from city lights. You can look at them with just your naked eye or you can use binoculars or a telescope to see the fainter ones more clearly. On each pair of star maps there is a note of the dates and times when the star maps will match up exactly with the night sky.

# THE NIGHT SKY IN SPRING

## Star maps for the northern hemisphere

The only star in the sky that doesn't seem to change its position is Polaris, in the middle of the top map. Polaris is flanked by Capella and Aldebaran on its left, and Deneb and Vega on its right.

*Look out for Ursa Major (the Great Bear) overhead and Taurus (the Bull) in the west. The bright streak in the sky is the starry trail of the Milky Way.*

March 15th 11:00pm
April 15th 10:00pm
May 15th 9:00pm

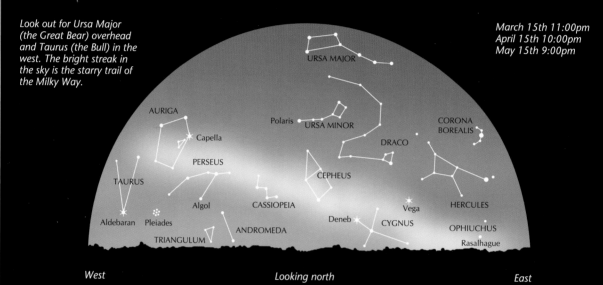

West          Looking north          East

*Regulus is the bright star in the middle of the sky. It is part of the constellation of Leo (the Lion).*

East          Looking south          West

## Star maps for the southern hemisphere

The most famous constellation is Crux, or the Southern Cross. It can never be seen from the northern hemisphere. Facing north, the constellations of Pegasus and Andromeda dominate the sky.

### Internet links

**Website 1** Find tips on how to observe the night sky.

**Website 2** Print out night sky maps for the current month.

For links to these websites, go to **www.usborne-quicklinks.com**

*M31, just above the horizon, is a spiral-shaped galaxy.*

*September 15th 11:00pm*
*October 15th 10:00pm*
*November 15th 9:00pm*

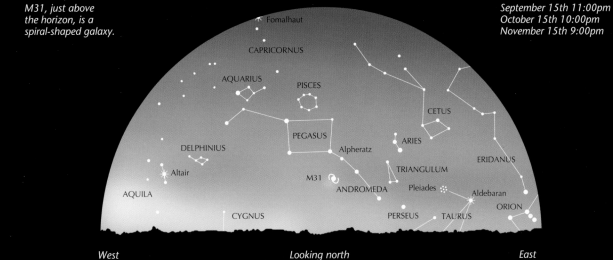

West     Looking north     East

*Sirius is the brightest star in the sky. Canopus is the second brightest.*

East     Looking south     West

# THE NIGHT SKY IN SUMMER

## Maps for the northern hemisphere

The sky never really gets dark in summer, so only the brightest stars show up clearly. If the sky is clear on August 12th, stay up to watch shooting stars coming from the constellation of Perseus.

*Capella, Regulus and Deneb are the brightest stars in the northern sky at this time of year.*

*June 15th 11:00pm*
*July 15th 10:00pm*
*August 15th 9:00pm*

West    Looking north    East

*Look out for Antares shining brightly above the southern horizon.*

East    Looking south    West

## Maps for the southern hemisphere

Facing north, the easiest constellations to spot are Orion and Canis Major (the Great Dog) and over to the east you can see Leo (the Lion). Sirius (the Dog Star), one of the stars in Canis Major, is the brightest star in the sky.

### Internet links

**Website 1** See a different NASA picture of the universe each day, accompanied by a brief explanation by a professional astronomer.

**Website 2** Try to spot constellations in a fun online game.

For links to these websites, go to **www.usborne-quicklinks.com**

*Look out for the cluster of stars known as Pleiades, or Seven Sisters, in the constellation of Taurus.*

*December 15th 11:00pm*
*January 15th 10:00pm*
*February 15th 9:00pm*

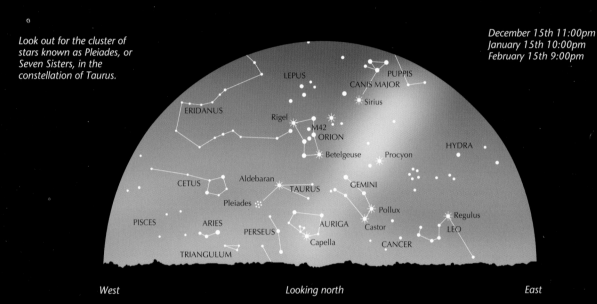

West — Looking north — East

*LMC and SMC stand for Large and Small Magellanic Cloud. These are small galaxies.*

East — Looking south — West

# THE NIGHT SKY IN AUTUMN

## Maps for the northern hemisphere

Facing north, look for Ursa Major, which is below Polaris and parallel with the horizon. Looking south, you should be able to see Pegasus (the Winged Horse), which has a square of stars in the middle.

*In the east, the winter stars are beginning to rise, including the red star Aldebaran.*

*September 15th 11:00pm*
*October 15th 10:00pm*
*November 15th 9:00pm*

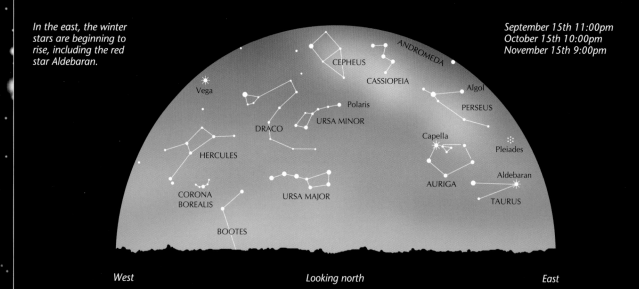

West — Looking north — East

*This is the best time to see M31, a huge distant galaxy. It is just visible with the naked eye, but binoculars will show it as a misty oval.*

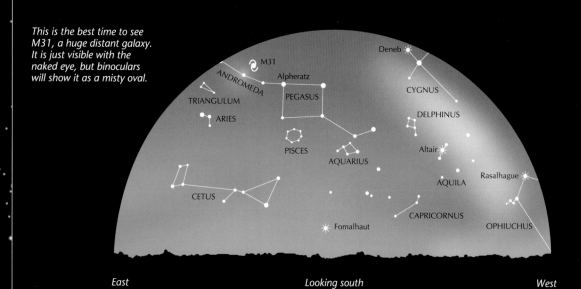

East — Looking south — West

## Maps for the southern hemisphere

Facing north, a triangle of three bright stars dominates the sky: Regulus, which is blue, yellow Arcturus and blue-white Spica. Facing south, the Milky Way crosses the sky in a wide band.

### Internet links

**Website 1** Find star-gazing tips and play a space object matching game.

**Website 2** Spot meteors, comets and other objects in the night sky.

**Website 3** Constellations in autumn.

For links to these websites, go to
**www.usborne-quicklinks.com**

*Look out for the constellations of Virgo (the Virgin) and Leo (the Lion).*

*March 15th 11:00pm*
*April 15th 10:00pm*
*May 15th 9:00pm*

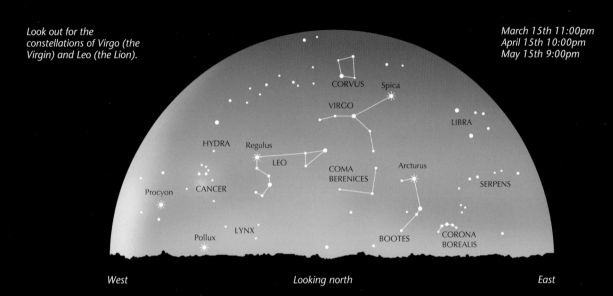

*West*     Looking north     *East*

*Above Crux (the Southern Cross) is Centaurus (the Centaur). A centaur was a mythical creature that was half man and half horse.*

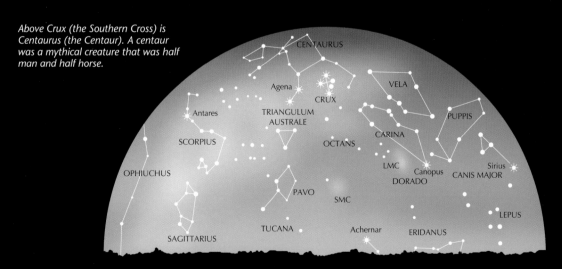

*East*     Looking south     *West*

# THE NIGHT SKY IN WINTER

## Maps for the northern hemisphere

Winter is a good time to look for shooting stars. Set your alarm for just before dawn on December 14th to see shooting stars coming from Gemini. Looking south, you can see Orion, one of the brightest constellations.

*Facing north, look for Ursa Major balancing on its tail, and Cygnus (the Swan).*

*December 15th 11:00pm*
*January 15th 10:00pm*
*February 15th 9:00pm*

PERSEUS

CASSIOPEIA

Polaris

Alpheratz

CEPHEUS

URSA MINOR

URSA MAJOR

PEGASUS

Deneb

DRACO

LEO

CYGNUS

Vega

West          Looking north          East

*If you find the bright constellation of Orion, it will help you to locate the other constellations.*

Capella

AURIGA

Algol

ANDROMEDA

PERSEUS

Castor

Pollux   GEMINI

TAURUS

Pleiades

TRIANGULUM

CANCER

Betelgeuse

Aldebaran

ARIES

Regulus   HYDRA

Procyon

M42

ORION

Rigel

Sirius

CETUS

PISCES

Alphard

CANIS MAJOR

ERIDANUS

East          Looking south          West

## Maps for the southern hemisphere

There are plenty of bright stars to look for at this time of the year. Try to spot Deneb, Spica, Altair, Vega and Fomalhaut. The Milky Way is seen at its best, cutting the sky in half.

### Internet links

**Website 1** Find out about the different equipment you can use for star gazing.

**Website 2** Watch a movie about this month's constellations.

For links to these websites, go to **www.usborne-quicklinks.com**

*Look out for Ophiuchus (the Serpent Bearer), a very large group of stars, and Hercules, named after a Greek hero.*

*June 15th 11:00pm*
*July 15th 10:00pm*
*August 15th 9:00pm*

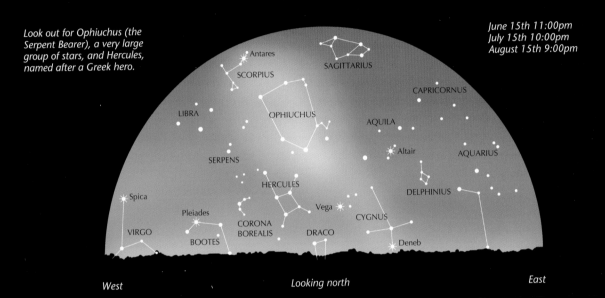

West    Looking north    East

*The Milky Way runs through Crux (the Southern Cross) and Centaurus (the Centaur).*

East    Looking south    West

# MEASUREMENTS

Measuring things – distance, area, weight, volume, time and temperature – is one of the most important parts of science. There are two main systems of measurement: metric and imperial. This page shows how each measuring system works, and also how to convert from one into the other.

## Imperial

This system of measurement is very old, dating from the 12th century or even earlier. It can be hard to use because it is not based on the decimal (base 10) system which we use for numbers. Some of the units have symbols or abbreviations. For example, the symbol for an inch is ".

### Length and distance

12 inches (") = 1 foot (')
3 feet = 1 yard (yd)
1,760 yards = 1 mile
3 miles = 1 league

### Weight

16 drams (dr) = 1 ounce (oz)
16 ounces = 1 pound (lb)
14 pounds = 1 stone
2,240 pounds (160 stone) = 1 ton
2,000 pounds = 1 short ton

### Area

144 square inches = 1 square foot
9 square feet = 1 square yard
4,840 square yards = 1 acre
640 acres = 1 square mile

### Volume and capacity

1,728 cubic inches = 1 cubic foot (ft³)
27 cubic feet = 1 cubic yard (yd³)
5 fluid ounces (fl oz) = 1 gill (gi)

20 fluid ounces = 1 pint (pt) (U.K.)
16 fluid ounces = 1 pint (U.S.)
2 pints = 1 quart (qt)
8 pints (4 quarts) = 1 gallon (gal)

### Temperature

The imperial unit of temperature is one degree (°) Fahrenheit (F). The freezing point of water is 32° F and the boiling point of water is 212° F.

## Metric

The metric or decimal system is based on the metre or meter, a unit of measurement which was first used in France in the 1790s. Metric units are multiples of each other by 10, 100 or 1,000. Countries around the world are gradually switching from imperial to metric. Many of the metric units have both U.S. spellings (-er) and European spellings (-re).

### Length and distance

10 millimeters/millimetres (mm) =
      1 centimeter/centimetre (cm)
100 cm = 1 meter/metre (m)
1,000 m = 1 kilometer/kilometre (km)

### Weight

1,000 grams (g) = 1 kilogram (kg)
1,000 kilograms = 1 tonne (t)

### Area

100 square mm (mm²) =
      1 square cm (cm²)
10,000 square cm =
      1 square m (m²)
10,000 square m = 1 hectare
1,000,000 square m = 1 square
      kilometer/kilometre (km²)

### Volume and capacity

1 cubic cm (cc or cm³) = 1
      milliliter/millilitre (ml)
1,000 ml = 1 liter/litre (l)
1,000 l = 1 cubic m (m³)

### Temperature

The metric temperature unit is one degree (°) Celsius (C). Water freezes at 0°C and boils at 100° C.

## Conversion tables

You can convert between metric and imperial with this table. Use a calculator to do the multiplications.

| To convert | into | multiply by |
|---|---|---|
| cm | inches | 0.394 |
| m | yards | 1.094 |
| km | miles | 0.621 |
| grams | ounces | 0.35 |
| kilograms | pounds | 2.205 |
| tonnes | tons | 0.984 |
| square cm | square inches | 0.155 |
| square m | square yards | 1.196 |
| square km | square miles | 0.386 |
| hectares | acres | 2.471 |
| liters/litres | pints | 1.76 |
| inches | cm | 2.54 |
| yards | m | 0.914 |
| miles | km | 1.609 |
| ounces | grams | 28.35 |
| pounds | kilograms | 0.454 |
| tons | tonnes | 1.016 |
| square inches | square cm | 6.452 |
| square yards | square m | 0.836 |
| square miles | square km | 2.59 |
| acres | hectares | 0.405 |
| pints | liters/litres | 0.5683 |

# TYPES OF GOVERNMENTS

Most states have one main leader along with a parliament or assembly of politicians. The main types of governments are listed and explained below. A state can have a combination of more than one of these types of governments. For example, the United States of America is a federal republic.

### Anarchy
Anarchy means a situation where there is no government. This can happen after a civil war, when a government has been destroyed and rival groups are battling to take its place.

### Capitalist state
In a Capitalist or free-market state, people can own their own businesses and property, and buy services such as healthcare privately. However, most Capitalist governments also provide national health, education and welfare services.

### Commonwealth
This word is sometimes used to mean a democratic republic, in which all the state's citizens are seen as having an equal interest in the functioning of the state.

### Communist state
Under Communism, the state owns things like factories, farms and businesses, and provides healthcare, welfare and education for its people.

### Democracy
In a democracy, the government is elected by the people, using a voting system.

### Dictatorship
This is a state run by a single, unelected leader, who may use force to keep control. In a military dictatorship, the army is in power.

### Federal government
In a federal system, such as that of the U.S.A., a central government shares power with a number of smaller regional governments.

### Monarchy
A monarchy is a state with a king or queen. In some traditional monarchies, the monarch has complete power. A constitutional monarchy, however, also has a separate, usually democratic, government and the monarch's powers are limited.

### Regional or local government
A government that controls a smaller area within a state. Some regional governments have very limited powers, and are largely directed by the central government. Others, such as the regional governments in the U.S.A., have much more power and can make their own laws.

### Republic
A republic is a state with no monarch. The head of state is usually an elected president.

### Revolutionary government
After a revolution, when a government is overthrown by force, the new regime is sometimes called a revolutionary government.

### Totalitarian state
This is a state with only one political party, in which individuals are forced to obey the government and may also be prevented from leaving the country.

### Transitional government
A government that is changing from one system to another is known as a transitional government. For example, a dictatorship may become a democracy after the dictator dies, but the transition between the systems can take several years.

# GAZETTEER OF STATES

Afghanistan

Albania

Algeria

Andorra

Angola

Antigua and Barbuda

• Argentina

This gazetteer lists the world's 193 independent states, along with key facts about each one. In the lists of languages, the language that is most widely spoken is given first, even if it is not the official language. In the lists of religions, the one followed by the most people is also placed first. Every state has a national flag, which is usually used to represent the country abroad. A few states also have a state flag which they prefer to use instead. The state flags appear here with a dot beside them.

Armenia

Australia

Austria

Azerbaijan

Bahamas, The

Bahrain

Bangladesh

**AFGHANISTAN (Asia)**
**Area:** 647,500 sq km (249,935 sq miles)
**Population:** 25,838,797
**Capital city:** Kabul
**Main languages:** Dari, Pashto
**Main religion:** Muslim
**Government:** transitional
**Currency:** 1 afghani = 100 puls

**ALBANIA (Europe)**
**Area:** 28,750 sq km (11,100 sq miles)
**Population:** 3,510,484
**Capital city:** Tirana
**Main language:** Albanian
**Main religions:** Muslim, Albanian Orthodox
**Government:** emerging democracy
**Currency:** 1 lek = 100 qintars

**ALGERIA (Africa)**
**Area:** 2,381,740 sq km (919,589 sq miles)
**Population:** 31,193,917
**Capital city:** Algiers
**Main languages:** Arabic, French, Berber dialects
**Main religion:** Sunni Muslim
**Government:** republic
**Currency:** 1 Algerian dinar = 100 centimes

**ANDORRA (Europe)**
**Area:** 468 sq km (181 sq miles)
**Population:** 67,627
**Capital city:** Andorra la Vella
**Main languages:** Catalan, Spanish
**Main religion:** Roman Catholic
**Government:** parliamentary democracy
**Currency:** 1 euro = 100 cents

**ANGOLA (Africa)**
**Area:** 1,246,700 sq km (481,351 sq miles)
**Population:** 10,366,031
**Capital city:** Luanda
**Main languages:** Kilongo, Kimbundu, other Bantu languages, Portuguese
**Main religions:** indigenous, Roman Catholic, Protestant
**Government:** transitional
**Currency:** 1 kwanza = 100 lwei

**ANTIGUA AND BARBUDA (North America)**
**Area:** 442 sq km (171 sq miles)
**Population:** 66,970
**Capital city:** Saint John's
**Main languages:** Caribbean Creole, English
**Main religion:** Protestant
**Government:** constitutional monarchy
**Currency:** 1 East Caribbean dollar = 100 cents

**ARGENTINA (South America)**
**Area:** 2,780,400 sq km (1,073,512 sq miles)
**Population:** 36,955,182
**Capital city:** Buenos Aires
**Main language:** Spanish
**Main religion:** Roman Catholic
**Government:** republic
**Currency:** 1 peso = 100 centavos

**ARMENIA (Asia)**
**Area:** 29,800 sq km (11,506 sq miles)
**Population:** 3,336,100
**Capital city:** Yerevan
**Main language:** Armenian
**Main religion:** Armenian Orthodox
**Government:** republic
**Currency:** 1 dram = 100 luma

**AUSTRALIA (Australasia/Oceania)**
**Area:** 7,686,850 sq km (2,967,124 sq miles)
**Population:** 19,357,594
**Capital city:** Canberra
**Main language:** English
**Main religion:** Christian
**Government:** federal democratic monarchy
**Currency:** 1 Australian dollar = 100 cents

**AUSTRIA (Europe)**
**Area:** 83,858 sq km (32,378 sq miles)
**Population:** 8,150,835
**Capital city:** Vienna
**Main language:** German
**Main religion:** Roman Catholic
**Government:** federal republic
**Currency:** 1 euro = 100 cents

**Barbados**

## AZERBAIJAN (Asia)
**Area:** 86,600 sq km (33,436 sq miles)
**Population:** 7,771,092
**Capital city:** Baku
**Main language:** Azeri
**Main religion:** Muslim
**Government:** republic
**Currency:** 1 manat = 100 gopiks

## BAHAMAS, THE (North America)
**Area:** 13,940 sq km (5,382 sq miles)
**Population:** 297,852
**Capital city:** Nassau
**Main languages:** Bahamian Creole, English
**Main religion:** Christian
**Government:** parliamentary democracy
**Currency:** 1 Bahamian dollar = 100 cents

**Belarus**

## BAHRAIN (Asia)
**Area:** 678 sq km (261 sq miles)
**Population:** 645,361
**Capital city:** Manama
**Main languages:** Arabic, English
**Main religion:** Muslim
**Government:** traditional monarchy
**Currency:** 1 Bahraini dinar = 1,000 fils

**Belgium**

## BANGLADESH (Asia)
**Area:** 144,000 sq km (55,598 sq miles)
**Population:** 131,269,860
**Capital city:** Dhaka
**Main languages:** Bengali, English
**Main religions:** Muslim, Hindu
**Government:** republic
**Currency:** 1 taka = 100 poisha

## BARBADOS (North America)
**Area:** 430 sq km (166 sq miles)
**Population:** 275,330
**Capital city:** Bridgetown
**Main languages:** Bajan, English
**Main religion:** Christian
**Government:** parliamentary democracy
**Currency:** 1 Barbadian dollar = 100 cents

**Belize**

## BELARUS (Europe)
**Area:** 207,600 sq km (80,154 sq miles)
**Population:** 10,350,194
**Capital city:** Minsk
**Main language:** Belarusian
**Main religion:** Eastern Orthodox
**Government:** republic
**Currency:** 1 Belarusian ruble = 100 kopecks

**Benin**

## BELGIUM (Europe)
**Area:** 30,510 sq km (11,780 sq miles)
**Population:** 10,258,762
**Capital city:** Brussels
**Main languages:** Dutch, French
**Main religions:** Roman Catholic, Protestant
**Government:** constitutional monarchy
**Currency:** 1 euro = 100 cents

**Bhutan**

## BELIZE (North America)
**Area:** 22,960 sq km (8,865 sq miles)
**Population:** 256,062
**Capital city:** Belmopan
**Main languages:** Spanish, Belize Creole, English, Garifuna, Maya

• **Bolivia**

**Main religions:** Roman Catholic, Protestant
**Government:** parliamentary democracy
**Currency:** 1 Belizean dollar = 100 cents

## BENIN (Africa)
**Area:** 112,620 sq km (43,483 sq miles)
**Population:** 6,590,782
**Capital city:** Porto-Novo
**Main languages:** Fon, French, Yoruba
**Main religions:** indigenous, Christian, Muslim
**Government:** republic
**Currency:** 1 CFA* franc = 100 centimes

## BHUTAN (Asia)
**Area:** 47,000 sq km (18,146 sq miles)
**Population:** 2,049,412
**Capital city:** Thimphu
**Main languages:** Dzongkha, Nepali
**Main religions:** Muslim, Hindu
**Government:** monarchy
**Currency:** 1 ngultrum = 100 chetrum

## BOLIVIA (South America)
**Area:** 1,098,580 sq km (424,162 sq miles)
**Population:** 8,300,463
**Capital cities:** La Paz, Sucre
**Main languages:** Spanish, Quechua, Aymara
**Main religion:** Roman Catholic
**Government:** republic
**Currency:** 1 boliviano = 100 centavos

## BOSNIA AND HERZEGOVINA (Europe)
**Area:** 51,129 sq km (19,741 sq miles)
**Population:** 3,922,205
**Capital city:** Sarajevo
**Main languages:** Bosnian, Serbian, Croatian
**Main religions:** Muslim, Orthodox, Roman Catholic
**Government:** emerging federal democracy
**Currency:** 1 marka = 100 pfenninga

## BOTSWANA (Africa)
**Area:** 600,372 sq km (231,743 sq miles)
**Population:** 1,586,119
**Capital city:** Gaborone
**Main languages:** Setswana, Kalanga, English
**Main religions:** indigenous, Christian
**Government:** parliamentary republic
**Currency:** 1 pula = 100 thebe

## BRAZIL (South America)
**Area:** 8,547,400 sq km (3,300,151 sq miles)
**Population:** 174,468,575
**Capital city:** Brasilia
**Main language:** Portuguese
**Main religion:** Roman Catholic
**Government:** federal republic
**Currency:** 1 real = 100 centavos

## BRUNEI (Asia)
**Area:** 5,770 sq km (2,228 sq miles)
**Population:** 343,653
**Capital city:** Bandar Seri Begawan
**Main languages:** Malay, English, Chinese
**Main religions:** Muslim, Buddhist
**Government:** constitutional sultanate (a type of monarchy)
**Currency:** 1 Bruneian dollar = 100 cents

**Bosnia and Herzegovina**

**Botswana**

**Brazil**

**Brunei**

**Bulgaria**

**Burkina Faso**

**Burma (Myanmar)**

*CFA = Communaute Financiere Africaine

# GAZETTEER OF STATES CONTINUED:

**Burundi**

## BULGARIA (Europe)
**Area:** 110,910 sq km (42,822 sq miles)
**Population:** 7,707,495
**Capital city:** Sofia
**Main language:** Bulgarian
**Main religions:** Bulgarian Orthodox, Muslim
**Government:** republic
**Currency:** 1 lev = 100 stotinki

## BURKINA FASO (Africa)
**Area:** 274,200 sq km (105,869 sq miles)
**Population:** 12,272,289
**Capital city:** Ouagadougou
**Main languages:** Moore, Jula, French
**Main religions:** Muslim, indigenous
**Government:** republic
**Currency:** 1 CFA* franc = 100 centimes

**Cambodia**

## BURMA (MYANMAR) (Asia)
**Area:** 678,500 sq km (261,969 sq miles)
**Population:** 50,438,300
**Capital city:** Rangoon
**Main language:** Burmese
**Main religion:** Buddhist
**Government:** military dictatorship
**Currency:** 1 kyat = 100 pyas

## BURUNDI (Africa)
**Area:** 27,830 sq km (10,745 sq miles)
**Population:** 6,223,897
**Capital city:** Bujumbura
**Main languages:** Kirundi, French, Swahili
**Main religions:** Christian, indigenous
**Government:** republic
**Currency:** 1 Burundi franc = 100 centimes

**Cameroon**

## CAMBODIA (Asia)
**Area:** 181,040 sq km (69,900 sq miles)
**Population:** 12,491 501
**Capital city:** Phnom Penh
**Main language:** Khmer
**Main religion:** Buddhist
**Government:** constitutional monarchy
**Currency:** 1 new riel = 100 sen

## CAMEROON (Africa)
**Area:** 475,440 sq km (183,567 sq miles)
**Population:** 15,803,220
**Capital city:** Yaounde
**Main languages:** Cameroon Pidgin English, Ewondo, Fula, French, English
**Main religions:** indigenous, Christian, Muslim
**Government:** republic
**Currency:** 1 CFA* franc = 100 centimes

**Canada**

## CANADA (North America)
**Area:** 9,970,610 sq km (3,849,653 sq miles)
**Population:** 31,592,805
**Capital city:** Ottawa
**Main languages:** English, French
**Main religions:** Roman Catholic, Protestant
**Government:** federal democracy
**Currency:** 1 Canadian dollar = 100 cents

**Cape Verde**

## CAPE VERDE (Africa)
**Area:** 4,033 sq km (1,557 sq miles)
**Population:** 405,163
**Capital city:** Praia
**Main languages:** Crioulo*, Portuguese

**Central African Republic**

**Main religions:** Roman Catholic, Protestant
**Government:** republic
**Currency:** 1 Cape Verdean escudo = 100 centavos

## CENTRAL AFRICAN REPUBLIC (Africa)
**Area:** 622,436 sq km (240,322 sq miles)
**Population:** 3,576,884
**Capital city:** Bangui
**Main languages:** Sangho, French
**Main religions:** indigenous, Christian, Muslim
**Government:** republic
**Currency:** 1 CFA* franc = 100 centimes

## CHAD (Africa)
**Area:** 1,284,000 sq km (495,752 sq miles)
**Population:** 8,707,078
**Capital city:** Ndjamena
**Main languages:** Arabic, Sara, French
**Main religions:** Muslim, Christian, indigenous
**Government:** republic
**Currency:** 1 CFA* franc = 100 centimes

**Chad**

## CHILE (South America)
**Area:** 756,626 sq km (292,133 sq miles)
**Population:** 15,328,467
**Capital city:** Santiago
**Main language:** Spanish
**Main religions:** Roman Catholic, Protestant
**Government:** republic
**Currency:** 1 Chilean peso = 100 centavos

**Chile**

## CHINA (Asia)
**Area:** 9,596,960 sq km (3,705,386 sq miles)
**Population:** 1,273,111,290
**Capital city:** Beijing
**Main languages:** Mandarin Chinese, Yue, Wu
**Main religions:** Taoist, Buddhist
**Government:** Communist state
**Currency:** 1 yuan = 10 jiao

**China**

## COLOMBIA (South America)
**Area:** 1,138,910 sq km (439,733 sq miles)
**Population:** 40,349,388
**Capital city:** Bogota
**Main language:** Spanish
**Main religion:** Roman Catholic
**Government:** republic
**Currency:** 1 Colombian peso = 100 centavos

**Colombia**

## COMOROS (Africa)
**Area:** 1,862 sq km (719 sq miles)
**Population:** 596,202
**Capital city:** Moroni
**Main languages:** Comorian*, French, Arabic
**Main religion:** Sunni Muslim
**Government:** republic
**Currency:** 1 Comoran franc = 100 centimes

**Comoros**

## CONGO (Africa)
**Area:** 342,000 sq km (132,046 sq miles)
**Population:** 2,894,336
**Capital city:** Brazzaville
**Main languages:** Munukutuba, Lingala, French
**Main religions:** Christian, animist
**Government:** republic
**Currency:** 1 CFA* franc = 100 centimes

**Congo**

**Congo (Democratic Republic)**

**Costa Rica**

*CFA = Communaute Financiere Africaine; Comorian = a blend of Swahili and Arabic; Crioulo = a blend of Portuguese and West African

**Croatia**

**Cuba**

**Cyprus**

**Czech Republic**

**Denmark**

**Djibouti**

**Dominica**

**CONGO (DEMOCRATIC REPUBLIC) (Africa)**
**Area:** 2,345,410 sq km (905,563 sq miles)
**Population:** 53,624,718
**Capital city:** Kinshasa
**Main languages:** Lingala, Swahili, Kikongo, Tshiluba, French
**Main religions:** Roman Catholic, Protestant, Kimbanguist, Muslim
**Government:** transitional
**Currency:** 1 Congolese franc = 100 centimes

**COSTA RICA (North America)**
**Area:** 51,100 sq km (19,730 sq miles)
**Population:** 3,773,057
**Capital city:** San Jose
**Main language:** Spanish
**Main religions:** Roman Catholic, Evangelical
**Government:** democratic republic
**Currency:** 1 Costa Rican colon = 100 centimos

**CROATIA (Europe)**
**Area:** 56,538 sq km (21,829 sq miles)
**Population:** 4,334,142
**Capital city:** Zagreb
**Main language:** Croatian
**Main religions:** Roman Catholic, Orthodox
**Government:** parliamentary democracy
**Currency:** 1 kuna = 100 lipas

**CUBA (North America)**
**Area:** 110,860 sq km (42,803 sq miles)
**Population:** 11,184,023
**Capital city:** Havana
**Main language:** Spanish
**Main religion:** Roman Catholic
**Government:** Communist state
**Currency:** 1 Cuban peso = 100 centavos

**CYPRUS (Europe)**
**Area:** 9,250 sq km (3,571 sq miles)
**Population:** 762,887
**Capital city:** Nicosia
**Main languages:** Greek, Turkish
**Main religions:** Greek Orthodox, Muslim
**Government:** republic with a self-proclaimed independent Turkish area
**Currency:** Greek Cypriot area: 1 Cypriot pound = 100 cents; Turkish Cypriot area: 1 Turkish lira = 100 kurus

**CZECH REPUBLIC (Europe)**
**Area:** 78,866 sq km (30,450 sq miles)
**Population:** 10,264,212
**Capital city:** Prague
**Main language:** Czech
**Main religion:** Roman Catholic
**Government:** parliamentary democracy
**Currency:** 1 koruna = 100 haleru

**DENMARK (Europe)**
**Area:** 43,094 sq km (16,639 sq miles)
**Population:** 5,352,815
**Capital city:** Copenhagen
**Main language:** Danish
**Main religion:** Evangelical Lutheran
**Government:** constitutional monarchy
**Currency:** 1 Danish krone = 100 oere

**DJIBOUTI (Africa)**
**Area:** 23,200 sq km (8,957 sq miles)
**Population:** 460,700
**Capital city:** Djibouti
**Main languages:** Afar, Somali, Arabic, French
**Main religion:** Muslim
**Government:** republic
**Currency:** 1 Djiboutian franc = 100 centimes

**DOMINICA (North America)**
**Area:** 751 sq km (290 sq miles)
**Population:** 70,786
**Capital city:** Roseau
**Main languages:** English, French patois
**Main religions:** Roman Catholic, Protestant
**Government:** democratic republic
**Currency:** 1 East Caribbean dollar = 100 cents

**DOMINICAN REPUBLIC (North America)**
**Area:** 48,511 sq km (18,731 sq miles)
**Population:** 8,581,477
**Capital city:** Santo Domingo
**Main language:** Spanish
**Main religion:** Roman Catholic
**Government:** democratic republic
**Currency:** 1 Dominican peso = 100 centavos

**EAST TIMOR (Asia)**
**Area:** 24,000 sq km (9,266 sq miles)
**Population:** 737,811
**Capital city:** Dili
**Main languages:** Tetun (Tetum), Bahasa Indonesia, Portuguese
**Main religions:** Roman Catholic, animist
**Government:** republic
**Currency:** 1 U.S. dollar = 100 cents

**ECUADOR (South America)**
**Area:** 283,560 sq km (109,483 sq miles)
**Population:** 13,183,978
**Capital city:** Quito
**Main languages:** Spanish, Quechua
**Main religion:** Roman Catholic
**Government:** republic
**Currency:** 1 sucre = 100 centavos

**EGYPT (Africa)**
**Area:** 1,001,450 sq km (386,660 sq miles)
**Population:** 69,536,644
**Capital city:** Cairo
**Main language:** Arabic
**Main religion:** Sunni Muslim
**Government:** republic
**Currency:** 1 Egyptian pound = 100 piasters

**EL SALVADOR (North America)**
**Area:** 21,040 sq km (8,124 sq miles)
**Population:** 6,237,662
**Capital city:** San Salvador
**Main language:** Spanish
**Main religion:** Roman Catholic
**Government:** republic
**Currency:** 1 Salvadoran colon = 100 centavos

**EQUATORIAL GUINEA (Africa)**
**Area:** 28,050 sq km (10,830 sq miles)
**Population:** 486,060
**Capital city:** Malabo
**Main languages:** Fang, Bubi, other Bantu

• **Dominican Republic**

**East Timor**

• **Ecuador**

**Egypt**

• **El Salvador**

**Equatorial Guinea**

**Eritrea**

*CFA = Communaute Financiere Africaine*

# GAZETTEER OF STATES CONTINUED:

**Estonia**

**Ethiopia**

**Federated States of Micronesia**

**Fiji**

**Finland**

**France**

**Gabon**

languages, Spanish, French, Pidgin English
**Main religion:** Christian
**Government:** republic
**Currency:** 1 CFA* franc = 100 centimes

**ERITREA (Africa)**
**Area:** 117,600 sq km (45,405 sq miles)
**Population:** 4,298,269
**Capital city:** Asmara
**Main languages:** Tigrinya, Afar, Arabic
**Main religions:** Muslim, Coptic Christian,
Roman Catholic, Protestant
**Government:** transitional
**Currency:** 1 nafka = 100 cents

**ESTONIA (Europe)**
**Area:** 45,226 sq km (17,462 sq miles)
**Population:** 1,423,316
**Capital city:** Tallinn
**Main languages:** Estonian, Russian
**Main religions:** Evangelical Lutheran,
Russian and Estonian Orthodox, other
Christian
**Government:** parliamentary democracy
**Currency:** 1 Estonian kroon = 100 senti

**ETHIOPIA (Africa)**
**Area:** 1,127,127 sq km (435,184 sq miles)
**Population:** 65,891,874
**Capital city:** Addis Ababa
**Main languages:** Amharic, Tigrinya, Arabic
**Main religions:** Muslim, Ethiopian
Orthodox, animist
**Government:** federal republic
**Currency:** 1 birr = 100 cents

**FEDERATED STATES OF MICRONESIA**
**(Australasia/Oceania)**
**Area:** 702 sq km (271 sq miles)
**Population:** 134,597
**Capital city:** Palikir
**Main languages:** Chuuk, Ponapean, English
**Main religions:** Roman Catholic, Protestant
**Government:** democracy
**Currency:** 1 U.S. dollar = 100 cents

**FIJI (Australasia/Oceania)**
**Area:** 18,270 sq km (7,054 sq miles)
**Population:** 844,330
**Capital city:** Suva
**Main languages:** Fijian, Hindustani, English
**Main religions:** Christian, Hindu
**Government:** republic
**Currency:** 1 Fijian dollar = 100 cents

**FINLAND (Europe)**
**Area:** 337,030 sq km (130,127 sq miles)
**Population:** 5,175,783
**Capital city:** Helsinki
**Main language:** Finnish
**Main religion:** Evangelical Lutheran
**Government:** republic
**Currency:** 1 euro = 100 cents

**FRANCE (Europe)**
**Area:** 547,030 sq km (211,208 sq miles)
**Population:** 59,551,227
**Capital city:** Paris
**Main language:** French

**Main religion:** Roman Catholic
**Government:** republic
**Currency:** 1 euro = 100 cents

**GABON (Africa)**
**Area:** 267,670 sq km (103,347 sq miles)
**Population:** 1,221,175
**Capital city:** Libreville
**Main languages:** Fang, Myene, French
**Main religions:** Christian, animist
**Government:** republic
**Currency:** 1 CFA* franc = 100 centimes

**GAMBIA, THE (Africa)**
**Area:** 11,300 sq km (4,363 sq miles)
**Population:** 1,411,205
**Capital city:** Banjul
**Main languages:** Mandinka, Fula, Wolof,
English
**Main religion:** Muslim
**Government:** democratic republic
**Currency:** 1 dalasi = 100 butut

**GEORGIA (Asia)**
**Area:** 69,700 sq km (26,911 sq miles)
**Population:** 4,989,285
**Capital city:** Tbilisi
**Main languages:** Georgian, Russian
**Main religions:** Georgian Orthodox, Muslim,
Russian Orthodox
**Government:** republic
**Currency:** 1 lari = 100 tetri

**GERMANY (Europe)**
**Area:** 357,021 sq km (137,846 sq miles)
**Population:** 83,029,536
**Capital city:** Berlin
**Main language:** German
**Main religions:** Protestant, Roman Catholic
**Government:** federal republic
**Currency:** 1 euro = 100 cents

**GHANA (Africa)**
**Area:** 238,540 sq km (92,100 sq miles)
**Population:** 19,894,014
**Capital city:** Accra
**Main languages:** Twi, Fante, Ga, Hausa,
Dagbani, Ewe, Nzemi, English
**Main religions:** indigenous, Muslim, Christian
**Government:** democratic republic
**Currency:** 1 new cedi = 100 pesewas

**GREECE (Europe)**
**Area:** 131,940 sq km (50,942 sq miles)
**Population:** 10,623,835
**Capital city:** Athens
**Main language:** Greek
**Main religion:** Greek Orthodox
**Government:** parliamentary republic
**Currency:** 1 euro = 100 cents

**GRENADA (North America)**
**Area:** 340 sq km (131 sq miles)
**Population:** 89,227
**Capital city:** Saint George's
**Main languages:** English, French patois
**Main religions:** Roman Catholic, Protestant
**Government:** constitutional monarchy
**Currency:** 1 East Caribbean dollar = 100 cents

**Gambia, The**

**Georgia**

**Germany**

**Ghana**

**Greece**

**Grenada**

**Guatemala**

*CFA = Communaute Financiere Africaine

**Guinea**

**Guinea-Bissau**

**Guyana**

• **Haiti**

**Honduras**

**Hungary**

**Iceland**

**GUATEMALA (North America)**
**Area:** 108,890 sq km (42,042 sq miles)
**Population:** 12,974,361
**Capital city:** Guatemala City
**Main languages:** Spanish, Amerindian languages including Quiche, Kekchi, Cakchiquel, Mam
**Main religions:** Roman Catholic, Protestant, indigenous Mayan beliefs
**Government:** democratic republic
**Currency:** 1 quetzal = 100 centavos

**GUINEA (Africa)**
**Area:** 245,860 sq km (94,927 sq miles)
**Population:** 7,613,870
**Capital city:** Conakry
**Main languages:** Fuuta Jalon, Mallinke, Susu, French
**Main religion:** Muslim
**Government:** republic
**Currency:** 1 Guinean franc = 100 centimes

**GUINEA-BISSAU (Africa)**
**Area:** 36,120 sq km (13,946 sq miles)
**Population:** 1,315,822
**Capital city:** Bissau
**Main languages:** Crioulo*, Balante, Pulaar, Mandjak, Mandinka, Portuguese
**Main religions:** indigenous, Muslim
**Government:** republic
**Currency:** 1 CFA* franc = 100 centimes

**GUYANA (South America)**
**Area:** 214,970 sq km (83,000 sq miles)
**Population:** 697,181
**Capital city:** Georgetown
**Main languages:** Guyanese Creole,English, Amerindian languages, Caribbean Hindi
**Main religions:** Christian, Hindu
**Government:** republic
**Currency:** 1 Guyanese dollar = 100 cents

**HAITI (North America)**
**Area:** 27,750 sq km (10,714 sq miles)
**Population:** 6,964,549
**Capital city:** Port-au-Prince
**Main languages:** Haitian Creole, French
**Main religions:** Roman Catholic, Protestant, Voodoo
**Government:** republic
**Currency:** 1 gourde = 100 centimes

**HONDURAS (North America)**
**Area:** 112,090 sq km (43,278 sq miles)
**Population:** 6,406,052
**Capital city:** Tegucigalpa
**Main language:** Spanish
**Main religion:** Roman Catholic
**Government:** republic
**Currency:** 1 lempira = 100 centavos

**HUNGARY (Europe)**
**Area:** 93,030 sq km (35,919 sq miles)
**Population:** 10,106,017
**Capital city:** Budapest
**Main language:** Hungarian
**Main religions:** Roman Catholic, Calvinist
**Government:** parliamentary democracy
**Currency:** 1 forint = 100 filler

**ICELAND (Europe)**
**Area:** 103,000 sq km (39,768 sq miles)
**Population:** 277,906
**Capital city:** Reykjavik
**Main language:** Icelandic
**Main religion:** Evangelical Lutheran
**Government:** republic
**Currency:** 1 Icelandic krona = 100 aurar

**INDIA (Asia)**
**Area:** 3,287,590 sq km (1,269,339 sq miles)
**Population:** 1,029,991,145
**Capital city:** New Delhi
**Main languages:** Hindi, English, Bengali, Urdu, over 1,600 other languages and dialects
**Main religions:** Hindu, Muslim
**Government:** federal republic
**Currency:** 1 Indian rupee = 100 paise

**INDONESIA (Asia)**
**Area:** 1,919,440 sq km (741,096 sq miles)
**Population:** 228,437,870
**Capital city:** Jakarta
**Main languages:** Bahasa Indonesia, English, Dutch, Javanese
**Main religion:** Muslim
**Government:** republic
**Currency:** 1 Indonesian rupiah = 100 sen

**IRAN (Asia)**
**Area:** 1,648,000 sq km (636,293 sq miles)
**Population:** 66,128,965
**Capital city:** Tehran
**Main languages:** Farsi and other Persian dialects, Azeri
**Main religions:** Shi'a Muslim, Sunni Muslim
**Government:** Islamic republic
**Currency:** 10 Iranian rials = 1 toman

**IRAQ (Asia)**
**Area:** 437,072 sq km (168,754 sq miles)
**Population:** 23,331,985
**Capital city:** Baghdad
**Main languages:** Arabic, Kurdish
**Main religion:** Muslim
**Government:** republic under a military regime
**Currency:** 1 Iraqi dinar = 1,000 fils

**IRELAND (Europe)**
**Area:** 70,280 sq km (27,135 sq miles)
**Population:** 3,840,838
**Capital city:** Dublin
**Main languages:** English, Irish (Gaelic)
**Main religion:** Roman Catholic
**Government:** republic
**Currency:** 1 euro = 100 cents

**ISRAEL (Asia)**
**Area:** 20,770 sq km (8,019 sq miles)
**Population:** 5,938,093
**Capital city:** Jerusalem
**Main languages:** Hebrew, Arabic
**Main religions:** Jewish, Muslim
**Government:** parliamentary democracy
**Currency:** 1 Israeli shekel = 100 agorot

**ITALY (Europe)**
**Area:** 301,230 sq km (116,305 sq miles)

**India**

**Indonesia**

**Iran**

**Iraq**

**Ireland**

**Israel**

**Italy**

*CFA = Communaute Financiere Africaine;
Crioulo = a blend of Portuguese and West African

# GAZETTEER OF STATES CONTINUED:

**Ivory Coast**

Population: 57,679,825
Capital city: Rome
Main language: Italian
Main religion: Roman Catholic
Government: republic
Currency: 1 euro = 100 cents

**IVORY COAST (Africa)**
Area: 322,460 sq km (124,502 sq miles)
Population: 16,393,221
Capital city: Yamoussoukro
Main languages: Baoule, Dioula, French
Main religions: Christian, Muslim, animist
Government: republic
Currency: 1 CFA* = 100 centimes

**Jamaica**

**JAMAICA (North America)**
Area: 10,990 sq km (4,243 sq miles)
Population: 2,665,636
Capital city: Kingston
Main languages: Southwestern Caribbean Creole, English
Main religion: Protestant
Government: parliamentary democracy
Currency: 1 Jamaican dollar = 100 cents

**Japan**

**JAPAN (Asia)**
Area: 377,835 sq km (145,882 sq miles)
Population: 126,771,662
Capital city: Tokyo
Main language: Japanese
Main religions: Shinto, Buddhist
Government: constitutional monarchy
Currency: 1 yen = 100 sen

**Jordan**

**JORDAN (Asia)**
Area: 92,190 sq km (35,585 sq miles)
Population: 5,153,378
Capital city: Amman
Main languages: Arabic, English
Main religion: Sunni Muslim
Government: constitutional monarchy
Currency: 1 Jordanian dinar = 1,000 fils

**Kazakhstan**

**KAZAKHSTAN (Asia)**
Area: 2,717,300 sq km (1,049,150 sq miles)
Population: 16,731,303
Capital city: Astana
Main languages: Kazakh, Russian
Main religions: Muslim, Russian Orthodox
Government: republic
Currency: 1 Kazakhstani tenge = 100 tiyn

**Kenya**

**KENYA (Africa)**
Area: 582,650 sq km (224,961 sq miles)
Population: 30,765,916
Capital city: Nairobi
Main languages: Swahili, English, Bantu languages
Main religions: Christian, indigenous
Government: republic
Currency: 1 Kenyan shilling = 100 cents

**Kiribati**

**KIRIBATI (Australasia/Oceania)**
Area: 717 sq km (277 sq miles)
Population: 94,149
Capital city: Bairiki (on Tarawa island)
Main languages: Gilbertese, English
Main religions: Roman Catholic,

Protestant
Government: republic
Currency: 1 Australian dollar = 100 cents

**KUWAIT (Asia)**
Area: 17,820 sq km (6,880 sq miles)
Population: 2,041,961
Capital city: Kuwait City
Main languages: Arabic, English
Main religion: Muslim
Government: monarchy
Currency: 1 Kuwaiti dinar = 1,000 fils

**KYRGYZSTAN (Asia)**
Area: 198,500 sq km (76,641 sq miles)
Population: 4,753,003
Capital city: Bishkek
Main languages: Kyrgyz, Russian
Main religions: Muslim, Russian Orthodox
Government: republic
Currency: 1 Kyrgyzstani som = 100 tyiyn

**LAOS (Asia)**
Area: 236,800 sq km (91,428 sq miles)
Population: 5,638,967
Capital city: Vientiane
Main languages: Lao, French, English
Main religions: Buddhist, animist
Government: Communist state
Currency: 1 new kip = 100 at

**LATVIA (Europe)**
Area: 64,589 sq km (24,938 sq miles)
Population: 2,385,231
Capital city: Riga
Main languages: Latvian, Russian
Main religions: Lutheran, Roman Catholic, Russian Orthodox
Government: parliamentary democracy
Currency: 1 Latvian lat = 100 santims

**LEBANON (Asia)**
Area: 10,400 sq km (4,015 sq miles)
Population: 3,627,774
Capital city: Beirut
Main languages: Arabic, French, English
Main religions: Muslim, Christian
Government: republic
Currency: 1 Lebanese pound = 100 piasters

**LESOTHO (Africa)**
Area: 30,350 sq km (11,718 sq miles)
Population: 2,177,062
Capital cities: Maseru, Lobamba
Main languages: Sesotho, English, Zulu, Xhosa
Main religions: Christian, indigenous
Government: constitutional monarchy
Currency: 1 loti = 100 lisente

**LIBERIA (Africa)**
Area: 111,370 sq km (43,000 sq miles)
Population: 3,225,837
Capital city: Monrovia
Main languages: Kpelle, English, Bassa
Main religions: indigenous, Christian, Muslim
Government: republic
Currency: 1 Liberian dollar = 100 cents

**Kuwait**

**Kyrgyzstan**

**Laos**

**Latvia**

**Lebanon**

**Lesotho**

**Liberia**

*CFA = Communaute Financiere Africaine

**Libya**

**LIBYA (Africa)**
**Area:** 1,759,540 sq km (679,358 sq miles)
**Population:** 5,240,599
**Capital city:** Tripoli
**Main languages:** Arabic, Italian, English
**Main religion:** Sunni Muslim
**Government:** military rule
**Currency:** 1 Libyan dinar = 1,000 dirhams

**Liechtenstein**

**LIECHTENSTEIN (Europe)**
**Area:** 160 sq km (62 sq miles)
**Population:** 32,528
**Capital city:** Vaduz
**Main languages:** German, Alemannic
**Main religion:** Roman Catholic
**Government:** constitutional monarchy
**Currency:** 1 Swiss franc = 100 centimes

**Lithuania**

**LITHUANIA (Europe)**
**Area:** 65,200 sq km (25,174 sq miles)
**Population:** 3,610,535
**Capital city:** Vilnius
**Main languages:** Lithuanian, Polish, Russian
**Main religions:** Roman Catholic, Lutheran, Russian Orthodox
**Government:** democracy
**Currency:** 1 Lithuanian litas = 100 centas

**Luxembourg**

**LUXEMBOURG (Europe)**
**Area:** 2,586 sq km (998 sq miles)
**Population:** 442,972
**Capital city:** Luxembourg
**Main languages:** Luxemburgish, German, French
**Main religion:** Roman Catholic
**Government:** constitutional monarchy
**Currency:** 1 euro = 100 cents

**Macedonia**

**MACEDONIA (Europe)**
**Area:** 25,333 sq km (9,781 sq miles)
**Population:** 2,046,209
**Capital city:** Skopje
**Main languages:** Macedonian, Albanian
**Main religions:** Macedonian Orthodox, Muslim
**Government:** emerging democracy
**Currency:** 1 Macedonian denar = 100 deni

**Madagascar**

**MADAGASCAR (Africa)**
**Area:** 587,040 sq km (226,656 sq miles)
**Population:** 15,982,563
**Capital city:** Antananarivo
**Main languages:** Malagasy, French
**Main religions:** indigenous beliefs, Christian
**Government:** republic
**Currency:** 1 Malagasy franc = 100 centimes

**Malawi**

**MALAWI (Africa)**
**Area:** 118,480 sq km (45,745 sq miles)
**Population:** 10,548,250
**Capital city:** Lilongwe
**Main languages:** Chichewa, English
**Main religions:** Protestant, Roman Catholic, Muslim
**Government:** parliamentary democracy
**Currency:** 1 Malawian kwacha = 100 tambala

**MALAYSIA (Asia)**
**Area:** 329,750 sq km (127,316 sq miles)
**Population:** 22,229,040

**Capital city:** Kuala Lumpur
**Main languages:** Bahasa Melayu, English, Chinese dialects, Tamil
**Main religions:** Muslim, Buddhist, Daoist
**Government:** constitutional monarchy
**Currency:** 1 ringgit = 100 sen

**Malaysia**

**MALDIVES (Asia)**
**Area:** 300 sq km (116 sq miles)
**Population:** 310,764
**Capital city:** Male
**Main languages:** Maldivian, English
**Main religion:** Sunni Muslim
**Government:** republic
**Currency:** 1 rufiyaa = 100 laari

**Maldives**

**MALI (Africa)**
**Area:** 1,240,000 sq km (478,764 sq miles)
**Population:** 11,008,518
**Capital city:** Bamako
**Main languages:** Bambara, Fulani, Songhai, French
**Main religion:** Muslim
**Government:** republic
**Currency:** 1 CFA* franc = 100 centimes

**Mali**

**MALTA (Europe)**
**Area:** 316 sq km (122 sq miles)
**Population:** 394,583
**Capital city:** Valletta
**Main languages:** Maltese, English
**Main religion:** Roman Catholic
**Government:** democratic republic
**Currency:** 1 Maltese lira = 100 cents

**Malta**

**MARSHALL ISLANDS (Australasia/Oceania)**
**Area:** 181 sq km (70 sq miles)
**Population:** 70,822
**Capital city:** Majuro
**Main languages:** Marshallese, English
**Main religion:** Protestant
**Government:** republic
**Currency:** 1 U.S. dollar = 100 cents

**Marshall Islands**

**MAURITANIA (Africa)**
**Area:** 1,030,700 sq km (397,953 sq miles)
**Population:** 2,747,312
**Capital city:** Nouakchott
**Main languages:** Arabic, Wolof, French
**Main religion:** Muslim
**Government:** republic
**Currency:** 1 ouguiya = 5 khoums

**Mauritania**

**MAURITIUS (Africa)**
**Area:** 1,860 sq km (718 sq miles)
**Population:** 1,189,825
**Capital city:** Port Louis
**Main languages:** Mauritius Creole French, French, Hindi, Bhojpuri, Urdu, Tamil, English
**Main religions:** Hindu, Christian, English
**Government:** parliamentary democracy
**Currency:** 1 Mauritian rupee = 100 cents

**Mauritius**

**MEXICO (North America)**
**Nationality:** Mexican
**Area:** 1,972,550 sq km (761,602 sq miles)
**Population:** 101,879,171
**Capital city:** Mexico City

*CFA = Communaute Financiere Africaine

# GAZETTEER OF STATES CONTINUED:

**Mexico**

**Main languages:** Spanish, Mayan, Nahuatl
**Main religion:** Roman Catholic
**Government:** federal republic
**Currency:** 1 New Mexican peso = 100 centavos

**MOLDOVA (Europe)**
**Area:** 33,843 sq km (13,067 sq miles)
**Population:** 4,431,570
**Capital city:** Chisinau
**Main languages:** Moldovan, Russian, Gagauz
**Main religion:** Eastern Orthodox
**Government:** republic
**Currency:** 1 Moldovan leu = 100 bani

**Moldova**

**MONACO (Europe)**
**Area:** 1.95 sq km (0.75 sq miles)
**Population:** 31,842
**Capital city:** Monaco
**Main languages:** French, Monegasque, Italian
**Main religion:** Roman Catholic
**Government:** constitutional monarchy
**Currency:** 1 euro = 100 cents

**Monaco**

**MONGOLIA (Asia)**
**Area:** 1,565,000 sq km (604,247 sq miles)
**Population:** 2,654,999
**Capital city:** Ulan Bator
**Main language:** Khalkha Mongol
**Main religion:** Tibetan Buddist Lamaist
**Government:** republic
**Currency:** 1 tugrik = 100 mongos

**Mongolia**

**MOROCCO (Africa)**
**Area:** 446,550 sq km (172,413 sq miles)
**Population:** 30,645,305
**Capital city:** Rabat
**Main languages:** Arabic, Berber, French
**Main religion:** Muslim
**Government:** constitutional monarchy
**Currency:** 1 Moroccan dirham = 100 centimes

**Morocco**

**MOZAMBIQUE (Africa)**
**Area:** 801,590 sq km (309,494 sq miles)
**Population:** 19,371,057
**Capital city:** Maputo
**Main languages:** Makua, Tsonga, Portuguese
**Main religions:** indigenous, Christian, Muslim
**Government:** republic
**Currency:** 1 metical = 100 centavos

**Mozambique**

**NAMIBIA (Africa)**
**Area:** 825,418 sq km (318,694 sq miles)
**Population:** 1,797,677
**Capital city:** Windhoek
**Main languages:** Afrikaans, German, English
**Main religions:** Christian, indigenous
**Government:** republic
**Currency:** 1 Namibian dollar = 100 cents

**Namibia**

**NAURU (Australasia/Oceania)**
**Area:** 21 sq km (8 sq miles)
**Population:** 12,088
**Capital city:** Yaren
**Main languages:** Nauruan, English
**Main religion:** Christian
**Government:** republic
**Currency:** 1 Australian dollar = 100 cents

**NEPAL (Asia)**
**Area:** 147,181 sq km (56,827 sq miles)
**Population:** 25,284,463
**Capital city:** Kathmandu
**Main languages:** Nepali, Maithili
**Main religions:** Hindu, Buddhist
**Government:** constitutional monarchy
**Currency:** 1 Nepalese rupee = 100 paisa

**NETHERLANDS (Europe)**
**Area:** 41,532 sq km (16,036 sq miles)
**Population:** 15,981,472
**Capital cities:** Amsterdam, The Hague
**Main language:** Dutch
**Main religion:** Christian
**Government:** constitutional monarchy
**Currency:** 1 euro = 100 cents

**NEW ZEALAND (Australasia/Oceania)**
**Area:** 268,680 sq km (103,737 sq miles)
**Population:** 3,864,129
**Capital city:** Wellington
**Main languages:** English, Maori
**Main religion:** Christian
**Government:** parliamentary democracy
**Currency:** 1 New Zealand dollar = 100 cents

**NICARAGUA (North America)**
**Area:** 129,494 sq km (49,998 sq miles)
**Population:** 4,918,393
**Capital city:** Managua
**Main language:** Spanish
**Main religion:** Roman Catholic
**Government:** republic
**Currency:** 1 gold cordoba = 100 centavos

**NIGER (Africa)**
**Area:** 1,267,000 sq km (489,189 sq miles)
**Population:** 10,355,156
**Capital city:** Niamey
**Main languages:** Hausa, Djerma, French
**Main religion:** Muslim
**Government:** republic
**Currency:** 1 CFA* franc = 100 centimes

**NIGERIA (Africa)**
**Area:** 923,768 sq km (356,667 sq miles)
**Population:** 126,635,626
**Capital city:** Abuja
**Main languages:** Hausa, Yoruba, Igbo, English
**Main religions:** Muslim, Christian, indigenous
**Government:** republic
**Currency:** 1 naira = 100 kobo

**NORTH KOREA (Asia)**
**Area:** 120,540 sq km (46,540 sq miles)
**Population:** 21,968,228
**Capital city:** Pyongyang
**Main language:** Korean
**Main religions:** Buddhist, Confucianist
**Government:** authoritarian socialist
**Currency:** 1 North Korean won = 100 chon

**NORWAY (Europe)**
**Area:** 324,220 sq km (125,181 sq miles)
**Population:** 4,503,440
**Capital city:** Oslo

**Nauru**

**Nepal**

**Netherlands**

**New Zealand**

**Nicaragua**

**Niger**

**Nigeria**

*\*CFA = Communaute Financiere Africaine*

**North Korea**

Main language: Norwegian
Main religion: Evangelical Lutheran
Government: constitutional monarchy
Currency: 1 Norwegian krone = 100 oere

**Norway**

**OMAN (Asia)**
Area: 212,460 sq km (82,031 sq miles)
Population: 2,622,198
Capital city: Muscat
Main languages: Arabic, English, Baluchi
Main religion: Muslim
Government: monarchy
Currency: 1 Omani rial = 1,000 baiza

**Oman**

**PAKISTAN (Asia)**
Area: 803,940 sq km (310,401 sq miles)
Population: 144,616,639
Capital city: Islamabad
Main languages: Punjabi, Sindhi, Urdu, English
Main religion: Muslim
Government: federal republic
Currency: 1 Pakistani rupee = 100 paisa

**Pakistan**

**PALAU (Australasia/Oceania)**
Area: 459 sq km (177 sq miles)
Population: 19,092
Capital city: Koror
Main languages: Palauan, English
Main religions: Christian, Modekngei
Government: democratic republic
Currency: 1 U.S. dollar = 100 cents

**Palau**

**PANAMA (North America)**
Area: 78,200 sq km (30,193 sq miles)
Population: 2,845,647
Capital city: Panama City
Main languages: Spanish, English
Main religions: Roman Catholic, Protestant
Government: democracy
Currency: 1 balboa = 100 centesimos

**Panama**

**PAPUA NEW GUINEA**
**(Australasia/Oceania)**
Area: 462,840 sq km (178,703 sq miles)
Population: 5,049,055
Capital city: Port Moresby
Main languages: Tok Pisin, Hiri Motu, English
Main religions: Christian, indigenous
Government: parliamentary democracy
Currency: 1 kina = 100 toea

**PARAGUAY (South America)**
Area: 406,750 sq km (157,046 sq miles)
Population: 5,734,139
Capital city: Asuncion
Main languages: Guarani, Spanish
Main religion: Roman Catholic
Government: republic
Currency: 1 guarani = 100 centimos

**Papua
New Guinea**

**PERU (South America)**
Area: 1,285,220 sq km (496,223 sq miles)
Population: 27,483,864
Capital city: Lima
Main languages: Spanish, Quechua, Aymara
Main religion: Roman Catholic
Government: republic
Currency: 1 nuevo sol = 100 centimos

**PHILIPPINES (Asia)**
Area: 300,000 sq km (115,830 sq miles)
Population: 82,841,518
Capital city: Manila
Main languages: Tagalog, English, Ilocano
Main religion: Roman Catholic
Government: republic
Currency: 1 Philippine peso = 100 centavos

**POLAND (Europe)**
Area: 312,685 sq km (120,727 sq miles)
Population: 38,633,912
Capital city: Warsaw
Main language: Polish
Main religion: Roman Catholic
Government: democratic republic
Currency: 1 zloty = 100 groszy

**PORTUGAL (Europe)**
Area: 92,391 sq km (35,672 sq miles)
Population: 10,066,253
Capital city: Lisbon
Main language: Portuguese
Main religion: Roman Catholic
Government: democratic republic
Currency: 1 euro = 100 cents

**QATAR (Asia)**
Area: 11,437 sq km (4,416 sq miles)
Population: 769,152
Capital city: Doha
Main languages: Arabic, English
Main religion: Muslim
Government: monarchy
Currency: 1 Qatari riyal = 100 dirhams

**ROMANIA (Europe)**
Area: 237,500 sq km (91,699 sq miles)
Population: 22,364,022
Capital city: Bucharest
Main languages: Romanian, Hungarian, German
Main religion: Romanian Orthodox
Government: republic
Currency: 1 leu = 100 bani

**RUSSIA (Europe and Asia)**
Area: 17,075,200 sq km (6,592,735 sq miles)
Population: 145,470,197
Capital city: Moscow
Main language: Russian
Main religions: Russian Orthodox, Muslim
Government: federal government
Currency: 1 ruble = 100 kopeks

**RWANDA (Africa)**
Area: 26,338 sq km (10,169 sq miles)
Population: 7,312,756
Capital city: Kigali
Main languages: Kinyarwanda, French, English, Swahili
Main religions: Roman Catholic, Protestant,
Government: transitional
Currency: 1 Rwandan franc = 100 centimes

**SAINT KITTS AND NEVIS**
**(North America)**
Area: 269 sq km (104 sq miles)
Population: 38,756
Capital city: Basseterre

**Paraguay**

• **Peru**

**Philippines**

**Poland**

**Portugal**

**Qatar**

**Romania**

# GAZETTEER OF STATES CONTINUED:

**Russia**

Main language: English
Main religions: Protestant, Roman Catholic
Government: constitutional monarchy
Currency: 1 East Caribbean dollar = 100 cents

**SAINT LUCIA (North America)**
Area: 620 sq km (239 sq miles)
Population: 158,178
Capital city: Castries
Main languages: French patois, English
Main religion: Roman Catholic
Government: parliamentary democracy
Currency: 1 East Caribbean dollar = 100 cents

**Rwanda**

**SAINT VINCENT AND THE GRENADINES
(North America)**
Area: 389 sq km (150 sq miles)
Population: 115,942
Capital city: Kingstown
Main languages: English, French patois
Main religions: Protestant, Roman Catholic
Government: parliamentary democracy
Currency: 1 East Caribbean dollar = 100 cents

**Saint Kitts
and Nevis**

**SAMOA (Australasia/Oceania)**
Area: 2,860 sq km (1,104 sq miles)
Population: 179,058
Capital city: Apia
Main languages: Samoan, English
Main religion: Christian
Government: constitutional monarchy
Currency: 1 tala = 100 sene

**SAN MARINO (Europe)**
Area: 61 sq km (24 sq miles)
Population: 27,336
Capital city: San Marino
Main language: Italian
Main religion: Roman Catholic
Government: republic
Currency: 1 euro = 100 cents

**Saint Lucia**

**SAO TOME AND PRINCIPE (Africa)**
Area: 1,001 sq km (386 sq miles)
Population: 165,034
Capital city: Sao Tome
Main languages: Crioulo* dialects, Portuguese
Main religion: Christian
Government: republic
Currency: 1 dobra = 100 centimos

**Saint Vincent and
the Grenadines**

**SAUDI ARABIA (Asia)**
Area: 2,149,690 sq km (829,995 sq miles)
Population: 22,757,092
Capital city: Riyadh
Main language: Arabic
Main religion: Muslim
Government: monarchy
Currency: 1 Saudi riyal = 100 halalah

**Samoa**

**SENEGAL (Africa)**
Area: 196,190 sq km (75,749 sq miles)
Population: 10,284,929
Capital city: Dakar
Main languages: Wolof, French, Pulaar
Main religion: Muslim
Government: democratic republic
Currency: 1 CFA* franc = 100 centimes

**• San Marino**

**SERBIA AND MONTENEGRO (Europe)**
Area: 102,350 sq km (39,517 sq miles)
Population: 10,677,290
Capital city: Belgrade
Main languages: Serbian, Montenegrin
Main religions: Orthodox, Muslim
Government: republic
Currency: 1 dinar = 100 paras (Serbia),
1 1 euro = 100 cents (Montenegro)

**SEYCHELLES (Africa)**
Area: 455 sq km (176 sq miles)
Population: 79,715
Capital city: Victoria
Main language: Seselwa
Main religion: Roman Catholic
Government: republic
Currency: 1 Seychelles rupee = 100 cents

**SIERRA LEONE (Africa)**
Area: 71,740 sq km (27,699 sq miles)
Population: 5,426,618
Capital city: Freetown
Main languages: Mende, Temne, Krio, English
Main religions: Muslim, indigenous, Christian
Government: republic
Currency: 1 leone = 100 cents

**SINGAPORE (Asia)**
Area: 648 sq km (250 sq miles)
Population: 4,300,419
Capital city: Singapore
Main languages: Chinese, Malay, English, Tamil
Main religions: Buddhist, Muslim
Government: parliamentary republic
Currency: 1 Singapore dollar = 100 cents

**SLOVAKIA (Europe)**
Area: 48,845 sq km (18,859 sq miles)
Population: 5,414,937
Capital city: Bratislava
Main languages: Slovak, Hungarian
Main religion: Roman Catholic
Government: parliamentary democracy
Currency: 1 koruna = 100 halierov

**SLOVENIA (Europe)**
Area: 20,253 sq km (7,820 sq miles)
Population: 1,930,132
Capital city: Ljubljana
Main language: Slovenian
Main religion: Roman Catholic
Government: democratic republic
Currency: 1 tolar = 100 stotins

**SOLOMON ISLANDS (Australasia/Oceania)**
Area: 28,450 sq km (10,985 sq miles)
Population: 480,442
Capital city: Honiara
Main languages: Solomon pidgin, Kwara'ae,
To'abaita, English
Main religion: Christian
Government: parliamentary democracy
Currency: 1 dollar = 100 cents

**SOMALIA (Africa)**
Area: 637,657 sq km (246,199 sq miles)
Population: 7,488,773
Capital city: Mogadishu

**Sao Tome
and Principe**

**Saudi Arabia**

**Senegal**

**Serbia and
Montenegro**

**Seychelles**

**Sierra Leone**

**Singapore**

*CFA = Communaute Financiere Africaine; Crioulo = a
blend of Portuguese and West African

**Slovakia**

**Slovenia**

**Solomon Islands**

**Somalia**

**South Africa**

**South Korea**

**Spain**

---

Main languages: Somali, Arabic, Oromo
Main religion: Sunni Muslim
Government: currently has no government
Currency: 1 Somali shilling = 100 cents

**SOUTH AFRICA (Africa)**
Area: 1,219,912 sq km (471,008 sq miles)
Population: 43,586,097
Capital cities: Pretoria, Cape Town, Bloemfontein
Main languages: Zulu, Xhosa, Afrikaans, Pedi, English, Tswana, Sotho, Tsonga, Swati, Venda, Ndebele
Main religions: Christian, indigenous
Government: republic
Currency: 1 rand = 100 cents

**SOUTH KOREA (Asia)**
Area: 98,480 sq km (38,023 sq miles)
Population: 47,904,370
Capital city: Seoul
Main language: Korean
Main religions: Christian, Buddhist
Government: republic
Currency: 1 South Korean won = 100 chun

**SPAIN (Europe)**
Area: 504,750 sq km (194,884 sq miles)
Population: 40,037,995
Capital city: Madrid
Main languages: Castilian Spanish, Catalan
Main religion: Roman Catholic
Government: constitutional monarchy
Currency: 1 euro = 100 cents

**SRI LANKA (Asia)**
Area: 65,610 sq km (25,332 sq miles)
Population: 19,408,635
Capital cities: Colombo, Sri Jayewardenepura Kotte
Main languages: Sinhala, Tamil, English
Main religions: Buddhist, Hindu
Government: republic
Currency: 1 Sri Lankan rupee = 100 cents

**SUDAN (Africa)**
Area: 2,505,810 sq km (967,493 sq miles)
Population: 36,080,373
Capital city: Khartoum
Main languages: Arabic, English
Main religions: Sunni Muslim, indigenous
Government: Islamic republic
Currency: 1 Sudanese dinar = 100 piastres

**SURINAM (South America)**
Area: 163,270 sq km (63,039 sq miles)
Population: 433,998
Capital city: Paramaribo
Main languages: Sranang Tongo, Dutch, English
Main religions: Christian, Hindu, Muslim
Government: republic
Currency: 1 Surinamese guilder, gulden or florin = 100 cents

**SWAZILAND (Africa)**
Area: 17,363 sq km (6,704 sq miles)
Population: 1,104,343
Capital cities: Mbabane, Lobamba

---

Main languages: Swati, English
Main religions: Protestant, indigenous, Muslim
Government: monarchy
Currency: 1 lilangeni = 100 cents

**SWEDEN (Europe)**
Area: 449,964 sq km (173,731 sq miles)
Population: 8,875,053
Capital city: Stockholm
Main language: Swedish
Main religion: Lutheran
Government: constitutional monarchy
Currency: 1 Swedish krona = 100 oere

**SWITZERLAND (Europe)**
Area: 41,290 sq km (15,942 sq miles)
Population: 7,283,274
Capital city: Bern
Main languages: German, French, Italian
Main religions: Roman Catholic, Protestant
Government: federal republic
Currency: 1 Swiss franc, franken or frano = 100 centimes, rappen or centesimi

**SYRIA (Asia)**
Area: 185,180 sq km (71,498 sq miles)
Population: 16,728,808
Capital city: Damascus
Main languages: Arabic, Kurdish
Main religions: Muslim, Christian
Government: republic under military regime
Currency: 1 Syrian pound = 100 piastres

**TAIWAN (Asia)**
Area: 35,980 sq km (13,892 sq miles)
Population: 22,370,461
Capital city: Taipei
Main languages: Taiwanese, Mandarin Chinese, Hakka Chinese
Main religions: Buddhist, Confucian, Daoist
Government: democracy
Currency: 1 New Taiwan dollar = 100 cents

**TAJIKISTAN (Asia)**
Area: 143,100 sq km (55,251 sq miles)
Population: 6,578,681
Capital city: Dushanbe
Main languages: Tajik, Russian
Main religion: Sunni Muslim
Government: republic
Currency: 1 somoni = 100 dirams

**TANZANIA (Africa)**
Area: 945,087 sq km (364,898 sq miles)
Population: 36,232,074
Capital cities: Dar es Salaam, Dodoma
Main languages: Swahili, English, Sukuma
Main religions: Christian, Muslim, indigenous
Government: republic
Currency: 1 Tanzanian shilling = 100 cents

**THAILAND (Asia)**
Area: 514,000 sq km (198,455 sq miles)
Population: 61,797,751
Capital city: Bangkok
Main languages: Thai, English, Chaochow
Main religion: Buddhist
Government: constitutional monarchy
Currency: 1 baht = 100 satang

---

**Sri Lanka**

**Sudan**

**Surinam**

**Swaziland**

**Sweden**

**Switzerland**

**Syria**

*CFA = Communaute Financiere Africaine

# GAZETTEER OF STATES CONTINUED:

**Taiwan**

**Tajikistan**

**TOGO (Africa)**
Area: 56,785 sq km (21,925 sq miles)
Population: 5,153,088
Capital city: Lome
Main languages: Mina, Ewe, Kabye, French
Main religions: indigenous, Christian, Muslim
Government: republic
Currency: 1 CFA* franc = 100 centimes

**TONGA (Australasia/Oceania)**
Area: 748 sq km (289 sq miles)
Population: 104,227
Capital city: Nukualofa
Main languages: Tongan, English
Main religion: Christian
Government: constitutional monarchy
Currency: 1 pa'anga = 100 seniti

**TRINIDAD AND TOBAGO (North America)**
Area: 5,128 sq km (1,980 sq miles)
Population: 1,169,682
Capital city: Port-of-Spain
Main languages: English, French, Spanish, Hindi
Main religions: Christian, Hindu
Government: republic
Currency: 1 Trinidad and Tobago dollar = 100 cents

**TUNISIA (Africa)**
Area: 163,610 sq km (63,170 sq miles)
Population: 9,705,102
Capital city: Tunis
Main languages: Arabic, French
Main religion: Muslim
Government: republic
Currency: 1 Tunisian dinar = 1,000 millimes

**TURKEY (Europe and Asia)**
Area: 780,580 sq km (301,382 sq miles)
Population: 66,493,970
Capital city: Ankara
Main language: Turkish
Main religion: Muslim
Government: democratic republic
Currency: 1 Turkish lira = 100 kurus

**TURKMENISTAN (Asia)**
Area: 488,100 sq km (188,455 sq miles)
Population: 4,603,244
Capital city: Ashgabat (Ashkhabad)
Main languages: Turkmen, Russian
Main religion: Muslim
Government: republic
Currency: 1 Turkmen manat = 100 tenesi

**TUVALU (Australasia/Oceania)**
Area: 26 sq km (10 sq miles)
Population: 10,991
Capital city: Funafuti
Main languages: Tuvaluan, English
Main religion: Congregationalist
Government: constitutional monarchy
Currency: 1 Tuvaluan dollar or 1 Australian dollar = 100 cents

**UGANDA (Africa)**
Area: 236,040 sq km (91,135 sq miles)
Population: 23,985,712
Capital city: Kampala

Main languages: Luganda, English, Swahili
Main religion: Christian, Muslim, indigenous
Government: republic
Currency: 1 Ugandan shilling = 100 cents

**UKRAINE (Europe)**
Area: 603,700 sq km (233,089 sq miles)
Population: 49,153,027
Capital city: Kiev
Main languages: Ukrainian, Russian
Main religion: Ukrainain Orthodox
Government: republic
Currency: 1 hryvnia = 100 kopiykas

**UNITED ARAB EMIRATES (Asia)**
Area: 82,880 sq km (32,000 sq miles)
Population: 2,407,460
Capital city: Abu Dhabi
Main languages: Arabic, English
Main religion: Muslim
Government: federation
Currency: 1 Emirati dirham = 100 fils

**UNITED KINGDOM (Europe)**
Area: 244,820 sq km (94,525 sq miles)
Population: 59,647,790
Capital city: London
Main language: English
Main religions: Anglican, Roman Catholic
Government: constitutional monarchy
Currency: 1 British pound = 100 pence

**UNITED STATES OF AMERICA (North America)**
Area: 9,629,091 sq km (3,717,792 sq miles)
Population: 278,058,881
Capital city: Washington D.C.
Main language: English
Main religions: Protestant, Roman Catholic
Government: federal republic
Currency: 1 U.S. dollar = 100 cents

**URUGUAY (South America)**
Area: 176,220 sq km (68,039 sq miles)
Population: 3,360,105
Capital city: Montevideo
Main language: Spanish
Main religion: Roman Catholic
Government: republic
Currency: 1 Uruguayan peso = 100 centesimos

**UZBEKISTAN (Asia)**
Area: 447,400 sq km (172,741 sq miles)
Population: 25,155,064
Capital city: Tashkent
Main languages: Uzbek, Russian
Main religions: Muslim, Eastern Orthodox
Government: republic
Currency: 1 Uzbekistani sum = 100 tyyn

**VANUATU (Australasia/Oceania)**
Area: 12,189 sq km (4,706 sq miles)
Population: 192,910
Capital city: Port-Vila
Main languages: Bislama, French, English
Main religion: Christian
Government: republic
Currency: 1 vatu = 100 centimes

**Trinidad and Tobago**

**Tunisia**

**Turkey**

**Turkmenistan**

**Tuvalu**

**Uganda**

**Ukraine**

**Tanzania**
**Thailand**
**Togo**
**Tonga**

**United Arab Emirates**

**VATICAN CITY (Europe)**
**Area:** 0.44 sq km (0.17 sq miles)
**Population:** 880
**Capital city:** Vatican City
**Main languages:** Italian, Latin
**Main religion:** Roman Catholic
**Government:** led by the Pope
**Currency:** 1 euro = 100 cents

**VENEZUELA (South America)**
**Area:** 912,050 sq km (352,143 sq miles)
**Population:** 23,916,810
**Capital city:** Caracas
**Main language:** Spanish
**Main religion:** Roman Catholic
**Government:** federal republic
**Currency:** 1 bolivar = 100 centimos

**VIETNAM (Asia)**
**Area:** 329,560 sq km (127,243 sq miles)
**Population:** 79,939,014
**Capital city:** Hanoi
**Main languages:** Vietnamese, French, English, Khmer, Chinese
**Main religion:** Buddhist
**Government:** Communist state
**Currency:** 1 new dong = 100 xu

**YEMEN (Asia)**
**Area:** 527,970 sq km (203,849 sq miles)
**Population:** 18,078,035
**Capital city:** Sana
**Main language:** Arabic
**Main religion:** Muslim
**Government:** republic
**Currency:** 1 Yemeni rial = 100 fils

**ZAMBIA (Africa)**
**Area:** 752,614 sq km (290,584 sq miles)
**Population:** 9,770,199
**Capital city:** Lusaka
**Main languages:** Bemba, Tonga, Nyanja, English
**Main religions:** Christian, Muslim, Hindu
**Government:** republic
**Currency:** 1 Zambian kwacha = 100 ngwee

**ZIMBABWE (Africa)**
**Area:** 390,580 sq km (150,803 sq miles)
**Population:** 11,365,366
**Capital city:** Harare
**Main languages:** Shona, Ndebele, English
**Main religions:** Christian, indigenous
**Government:** republic
**Currency:** 1 Zimbabwean dollar = 100 cents

**Vatican City**

**Venezuela**

**Vietnam**

**Yemen**

**Zambia**

**Zimbabwe**

**United Kingdom**

**United States of America**

**Uruguay**

**Uzbekistan**

**Vanuatu**

# The United Nations

The United Nations (U.N.) is an organization which aims to bring different countries together to work for peace and development. Of the world's 193 states, 191 are members of the U.N. Those that don't belong are Taiwan and the Vatican City.

*Kofi Annan, the Secretary-General of the U.N., with U.N. ambassador Pele*

## Internet links

For links to websites where you can take a virtual tour of the United Nations and play a flag matching game, go to **www.usborne-quicklinks.com**

# GLOSSARY

This glossary explains some of the words you may come across when reading about the Earth and its peoples. Words in *italic type* have their own entry elsewhere in the glossary.

**ablation zone** The lower end of a *glacier*, where the ice melts and flows into streams and rivers, or into the sea.

**abyssal plain** A huge, flat expanse of seabed that forms most of the ocean floor.

**accumulation zone** The top of a *glacier*, where snow falls and is gradually compacted into ice.

**acid rain** Rain containing dissolved chemicals from polluted air. The chemicals make the water acidic, which means it can eat away at rock and damage plant life.

**active volcano** An active volcano is one which might *erupt* at any time.

**adaptation** The way a plant or animal *species* develops over time to suit its *habitat*.

**aid** Any kind of help, especially that given by one country to another. The help can be money, food, equipment or expert help from teachers and engineers.

**animism** The belief that plants, stones and other natural objects have living souls or spirits.

**anticyclone** An area of high *atmospheric pressure*, which pushes winds outward. It is the opposite of a *cyclone*.

**apartheid** A system, such as the one used in South Africa until 1994, which separates people according to their race.

**aquifer** A layer of *porous* rock which can hold water and carry it along under the ground.

**arable** Arable land is suitable for growing crops (plants). Arable farming means crop farming.

**archipelago** A group of islands.

**asteroid** A small rock that *orbits* the Sun. There are thousands of asteroids in the part of the *Solar System* known as the Asteroid Belt.

**atmosphere** A layer of gases that surrounds the Earth and some other planets and stars.

**atmospheric pressure** The force the *atmosphere* exerts on Earth. It can change according to how warm the air is and how high you are above sea level.

**atom** A tiny particle. All *elements* are made up of atoms.

**aurora** Flickering lights, caused by *magnetic* particles from the Sun, that sometimes appear in the sky near the poles. The lights in the north are named the aurora borealis and those in the south are the aurora australis.

**axis** An imaginary line running through the middle of the Earth, from the *North Pole* to the *South Pole*, around which the Earth spins.

**bacterium** (plural: **bacteria**) A tiny *organism* found in the soil, in the air, and in plants and animals.

**bedrock** The solid layer of rock that lies underneath the soil, covering the Earth's surface.

**biome** An area with a *climate* that supports a particular range of plants and animals. For example, deserts, mountains and seas are all biomes.

**black smoker** A kind of *hydrothermal vent* which churns out black water containing many dissolved minerals. The minerals gradually build up around the vent, forming a chimney.

**border** A line separating political or geographical areas, especially countries. Borders are drawn up by governments and can change over time.

**camouflage** Patterns or features, that help plants and animals to look like their backgrounds and avoid being seen. For example, a tiger's stripes blend in with long grass.

**canopy** The thick upper layer of leaves and branches in a rainforest.

**carnivore** An animal or plant that feeds on animals.

**caste** An inherited class, also known as *Jati*, in traditional Indian *culture*.

**census** An official count of the number of people in a country. Other information, such as age, sex and occupation, may also be noted in a census.

**central business district (CBD)** The main business area of a city, where most of the stores, banks and offices are found.

**chlorofluorocarbon (CFC)** Any of various chemicals that are thought to damage the layer of *ozone* in the Earth's *atmosphere*.

**chlorophyll** A green chemical in plants which enables them to convert sunlight into food.

**civilization** The process of human development from small prehistoric groups to complex human societies with cities, governments, laws and communication systems.

**civil war** A war between people of the same country.

**climate** The typical or average weather conditions in a particular region.

**colonization** The process of establishing a settlement or settlements in another country. It may involve imposing a new *culture*, language or religion.

**comet** A chunk of dirty ice mixed with dust and grit which travels around the *Sun*.

**compass** A device containing a *magnetic* needle that points to the *North Pole*. A compass is used to find your direction.

**conservation** Protecting and preserving *environments,* including the plants, animals and buildings that form a part of them, and trying to reduce the damage caused to them by *pollution.*

**constellation** A group of *stars* that form a recognizable pattern.

**continent** One of the Earth's major land masses.

**continental crust** Part of the Earth's *crust* that forms land masses. Continental crust is made mostly of a rock called granite and similar light rocks.

**continental shelf** A wide shelf of seabed that surrounds most land masses, making the sea much shallower near the land than it is in the middle of the oceans.

**continental slope** The steep slope leading from the edge of the *continental shelf* down to the deeper seabed.

**coral reef** A structure made up of the skeletons of small sea animals called coral polyps. A reef builds up gradually as old polyps die and new ones grow on top.

**core** The central part of the inside of the Earth, which scientists think is made of the metals iron and nickel.

**Coriolis effect** The effect of the spinning of the Earth, which forces winds and *currents* into a spiral.

**creole** A language formed from a European language and another language. The word creole can also be used to describe a person who is descended from Europeans and another ethnic group.

**crevasse** A crack in a *glacier.*

**crop rotation** Changing the crop grown on a particular piece of land each year, to give the soil the opportunity to recover.

**crust** The Earth's solid outer layer. It consists of *continental crust* which forms the land, and *oceanic crust* which forms the seabed.

**culture** The way of life of a group of people. It includes their customs, hobbies, food, fashions and beliefs.

**current** A body of water or air which moves in a definite direction, often through a stiller surrounding body. For example, the Gulf Stream is a current that carries warm water across the Atlantic Ocean from the Caribbean to northern Europe.

**cyclone** An area of low *atmospheric pressure* where winds rotate inward.

**debris** Any kind of loose rock, mud or other matter – such as the rocks carried along by a *glacier,* or the material carried and deposited by a flowing river.

**deforestation** Reducing or removing forests by cutting down or burning trees. Soil is washed away more easily in deforested areas.

**degree** One 360th of a circle. Degrees are used with *latitude* and *longitude* to measure distance on the Earth's surface. One degree is one 360th of the distance around the Earth.

**delta** A fan-shaped system of streams, created when a river splits up into many smaller branches and deposits *debris* as it nears the sea.

**deposition** Dropping or leaving behind rocks or other *debris.*

**desertification** The process of non-desert land becoming desert.

**development** The improvement of a country's industry, wealth and standard of living.

**DNA** Material, like a set of "coded instructions", in living *organisms* that contains the information they need to function and develop.

**dormant volcano** A volcano that is temporarily inactive, but could *erupt* in the future. The word dormant means "sleeping".

**drumlin** A small hill formed from *debris* deposited by a moving *glacier,* lengthened in the direction of the movement of the glacier to form an oval shape.

**dyke** A barrier built at the coast to stop the sea from flooding the land at high *tide.*

**ecosystem** A living system that includes a group of plants and animals and the *habitat* they live in.

**ecotourism** A type of tourism that aims to protect the environment, for example by charging tourists to visit nature reserves to spot wildlife.

**element** A substance, such as iron, oxygen or silicon, made of one type of *atom*. There are over a hundred elements on Earth.

**El Niño** A weather phenomenon that sometimes makes part of the Pacific Ocean get much warmer than normal, causing severe storms.

**emergent** A tree that rises above the main *canopy* in a rainforest.

**emigration** Movement from one country to settle in another.

**environment** Surroundings, including the landscape, living things and the *atmosphere*.

**Equator** An imaginary line around the middle of the Earth, exactly halfway between the *North Pole* and the *South Pole*.

**erratic** A large boulder that has been deposited by a *glacier* and is left standing away from its source.

**eruption** The ejection of *lava*, rocks, hot ash and gases from a volcano.

**estuary** A wide channel that forms where a river joins the sea.

**ethnic group** A group of people who share things like language, *culture* and religion, and who often live together in the same area.

**Eurasia** The continent of Europe and Asia.

**evolution** The gradual development of plants and animals, over many generations, to fit in better with their *habitats*.

**exfoliation** A process which involves shedding layers. When a rock exfoliates, its outer layers peel off like the layers of an onion. This is caused by changes in temperature, which make rock shrink and expand.

**export** A product sent abroad to be sold.

**extinction** The death of a *species* of plant or animal.

**fallow** Fallow land is farmland that is being left to rest and recover between crops.

**famine** A widespread shortage of food, which can lead to starvation and the spread of diseases.

**Far East** The most easterly countries of Asia, especially China and Japan.

**fault** A crack in the Earth's *crust*.

**fault creep** The gradual movement of two pieces of the Earth's *crust* along a *fault*.

**fertile** Fertile land is land that is good for growing plants. Fertile also means able to reproduce.

**fertilizer** A substance, such as manure, that contains *nitrates* and other chemicals and is put on land to make it more *fertile*.

**fold mountains** A mountain range formed by the Earth's *crust* buckling up into folds when the *plates* of the crust push together.

**food chain** A sequence showing which *species* eat which.

**food web** A network of *food chains* showing which *species* eat each other in an *ecosystem*.

**footloose industry** An industry that does not have to locate near its raw materials, either because it hardly uses any, or because the raw materials it does use are light and easy to transport. Also known as light industry.

**fossil** The shape or remains of a plant or animal that died long ago, hardened and preserved in rock.

**fossil fuel** .A fuel, such as coal, oil or gas, made from the compressed bodies of plants and animals that died many years ago.

**freeze-thaw action** The action of water that seeps into cracks in rocks and then freezes, which makes it expand. This expansion forces the cracks apart, so they gradually get bigger.

**fungus** (plural: **fungi**) A type of *organism*, including mushrooms, that is similar to a plant but has no leaves or flowers.

**galaxy** A huge group of stars and planets. There are millions of galaxies in the universe.

**genetically modified food** Food crops which have been genetically changed. This may be to make them grow faster or resist frost or pests.

**genetic engineering** Changing the *DNA* of plants and animals to benefit medicine, farming and industry. In farming, for example, scientists can create new plant species which work better as crops.

**geostationary** Moving in such a way as to remain above the same point on the Earth's surface. For example, geostationary *satellites* orbit the Earth at the same speed as the Earth spins, so they always stay above the same part of the Earth.

**geyser** A spring that discharges water and steam, heated up inside the Earth, in bursts.

**glacial valley** A deep U-shaped valley carved by a flowing *glacier*, left behind after the glacier melts.

**glacier** A mass of ice that flows very slowly downhill.

**globalization** The organization of industry on a worldwide scale.

**global warming** The gradual warming-up of the Earth's atmosphere, possibly due to the *greenhouse effect*.

**gorge** A deep, narrow valley, shaped by a river gradually cutting down into the land it flows across.

**gravity** The pulling force that holds the *atmosphere* and objects in place on the Earth and stops them from floating out into space.

**greenhouse effect** The effect of certain gases in the *atmosphere* which trap heat from the Sun, causing the Earth to heat up.

**greenhouse gas** A gas, such as carbon dioxide, which contributes to the *greenhouse effect*.

**gross national product (GNP)** The total value of the goods and *services* produced by a nation over a year.

**groundwater** Water that has soaked into the ground and is stored inside *porous* rock.

**habitat** The place where an animal or plant *species* lives.

**hanging valley** A valley found high up the side of a *glacial valley*. Hanging valleys once contained mini-glaciers that flowed into a large glacier. When glaciers melt, hanging valleys are left behind, high up the mountainside.

**heat expansion** The increase in size of many substances, such as wood or rock, as they get warmer.

**heavy industry** An industry, such as ship-building, that uses heavy raw materials and needs large machines.

**hemisphere** Half of the Earth.

**herbivore** An animal that eats plants.

**horizon** A layer in soil. It is also the line where you can see the land meeting the sky when you look into the distance.

**hot spot** An area of the Earth's *crust* where *magma* breaks through and forms a volcano.

**hot spring** See **thermal spring.**

**Human Development Index** A system developed by the United Nations for measuring the standard of living in different countries.

**humidity** The amount of water contained in the air.

**humus** The part of soil that makes it *fertile*. Humus is made from rotted plant and animal matter.

**hunter-gatherer** Someone who survives by hunting animals and collecting wild plants, instead of by farming.

**hydroelectric power (HEP)** Power created from the energy of flowing water.

**hydrothermal vent** A hole in the seabed, through which a *thermal spring* emerges. See also **black smoker.**

**Ice age** A period when the Earth was much colder than average. There have been several major Ice ages since the Earth began.

**iceberg** A huge chunk of a *glacier* that has broken off into the sea.

**ice sheet** A sheet of ice covering a large area, such as the ice that covers Antarctica. An ice sheet is a type of large *glacier* which flows outward from the middle.

**igneous rock** Rock formed when *magma* escapes from inside the Earth, and then cools and hardens.

**immigration** Movement of people into a new country, usually to settle there permanently.

**impermeable** Not allowing water to pass through.

**import** A product or service brought into a country from another country.

**indigenous** Originating naturally in an area. Indigenous people are the people who first lived in a particular place.

**infrared** A type of energy that *radiates* from hot things. It is invisible to the human eye, but can be detected by infrared cameras.

**intensive farming** A type of farming that involves using chemicals and technology to increase *yield*.

**interglacial** A period of time within an *Ice age* when the climate gets slightly warmer for a while.

**International Date Line**  An imaginary line on the Earth's surface, to the east of which the date is one day earlier than to the west. It runs on the opposite side of the world to the *Prime Meridian Line* at 180° of *longitude*, except where it bends to avoid time change in populated areas.

**irrigation**  The artificial watering of land to help grow crops.

**isobar**  A line that links points with the same *atmospheric pressure*. The isobars on a weather map show patterns of atmospheric pressure.

**isthmus**  A narrow strip of land connecting two larger land areas. For example, Central America is an isthmus connecting North and South America.

**landslide**  A sudden slippage of rocks and soil down a hillside, usually caused by heavy rain or earthquakes.

**latitude**  A measurement of how many *degrees* a place is north or south of the *Equator*. Lines of latitude are imaginary lines around the Earth, parallel to the *Equator*.

**lava**  Hot molten rock which bursts or flows out of volcanoes. Lava also sometimes seeps out of holes in the ground, called vents.

**leap year**  A year every four years that has 366 days instead of 365. The extra day is added in February, to make February 29th.

**less developed country (LDC)**  A poor country which has not yet been industrialized and has low standards of living.

**lithosphere**  The outer layers of Earth, made up of the *crust* and upper *mantle*.

**longitude**  A measurement of how many *degrees* a place is east or west of the *Prime Meridian Line*. Lines of longitude are imaginary lines that run around the Earth from north to south.

**magma**  Hot, molten rock inside the Earth.

**magnet**  An object that has magnetic force, an invisible force that attracts iron and steel. The ends of a magnet are known as its poles.

**magnetic poles**  The Earth is like a giant *magnet*, and the ends of this magnet are called the magnetic poles. They move gradually over time, and are not in exactly the same place as the geographic *North Pole* and *South Pole*.

**malaria**  A disease, affecting millions of people, which is spread by insects called mosquitoes.

**mantle**  The thick layer of rock under the Earth's *crust*. Some of it is solid and some is *magma*.

**manufacturing industry** Industry, such as ship-building or clothes-making, that involves making new products.

**matriarchy**  A system in which women are the most powerful members of families and of society.

**meander**  A bend or long loop in a river. Meanders form when rivers flow across gently sloping land.

**Mediterranean**  A type of *climate* that has warm winters and hot summers, and is good for growing many types of crops. It is named after the region around the Mediterranean Sea, but is also found in other parts of the world.

**megacity**  A name for a city that has more than ten million people.

**mestizo**  A Spaniard or Portuguese person of mixed origin, especially with Native American ancestors.

**metamorphic rock**  Rock that has been changed by heat or pressure. For example, when a rock called shale is squashed, it hardens into a type of metamorphic rock called slate.

**meteoroid**  Dust or a small chunk of rock which *orbits* the *Sun*.

**Middle East**  An area of Asia between the Red Sea and Persian Gulf, as well as Israel, Jordan, Syria, Lebanon, Iraq and Iran.

**migration**  Moving from one place to another. Many animals migrate each season to find food.

**Milky Way**  The *galaxy* of which the *Sun* and *Solar System* are a part. It can often be seen as a broad band of light in the night sky.

**mineral**  A non-living substance found in the Earth, such as salt, iron, diamond or quartz.

**missionary**  A member of a group sent by a religious body to do religious or social work in another country.

**molecule**  Two or more *atoms* bonded together.

**monsoon**  A strong seasonal change in the weather that affects certain parts of Asia. Monsoon regions have three seasons – a long, cool, dry season, a hot, humid season and a rainy season.

**moon**  A natural *satellite* which *orbits* a *planet*. The Earth has one moon which orbits it once a month.

**moraine**  Boulders, clay and other *debris* left behind by a *glacier*.

**more developed country (MDC)** A wealthy country with well-developed industry and a high standard of living.

**national park** An area of natural beauty protected by law from building and development.

**native** Belonging to a particular place.

**natural selection** The theory that those animals and plants that are best suited to their *environment* are the most likely to survive.

**newly industrialized country (NIC)** A country that has recently increased its wealth and standard of living through the development of modern industry.

**New World** A phrase used to mean North, Central and South America. The term was first applied by European explorers.

**niche** A particular plant or animal *species*' place in an *ecosystem*.

**nitrate** Any of a group of chemicals found in soil that helps plants grow.

**nomad** Someone who has no permanent home and travels around to make a living. Many nomads herd animals.

**northern hemisphere** The half of the Earth that lies north of the *Equator*.

**North Pole** The most northern point on the Earth, and one end of the *axis* the Earth spins around.

**nuclear power** Energy produced by splitting *atoms* of a *radioactive element* called uranium.

**oasis** A *fertile* area in a desert, supplied by water from an *aquifer*.

**oceanic crust** Part of the Earth's *crust* that forms the seabed. Oceanic crust is made mostly of a rock called basalt.

**oceanic ridge** A raised ridge on the seabed, caused by the *plates* of the Earth's *crust* pulling apart and *magma* pushing up in between.

**oceanic trench** A deep trench in the seabed that forms where one *plate* pushes underneath another.

**official language** The language of a country that is spoken at work, at school and in government. The official language may be different from the language spoken in homes or with friends, and is not always the language spoken by the majority of the population.

**omnivore** An animal that eats both meat and plants. Omnivore means "everything-eater".

**orbit** The path of an object as it travels around, or orbits, another.

**ore** Rock containing metal that can be extracted.

**organic farming** A type of farming that doesn't use artificial chemicals and methods.

**organic food** Food produced by organic farming that contains no artificial chemicals.

**organism** A living thing, such as a plant, animal or *bacterium*.

**outback** The remote bush country of Australia.

**outcrop** An area of land where part of a rock formation reaches the surface.

**oxbow lake** A curved lake left behind when a river *meander* gets cut off from the rest of the river.

**ozone** A type of oxygen in which each *molecule* contains three oxygen *atoms* instead of two.

**ozone layer** A layer of *ozone* in the Earth's *atmosphere*, from 20 to 50km (12 to 30 miles) above the Earth's surface, which protects the Earth from the *Sun's* rays. The ozone layer may be being damaged by *chlorofluorocarbons*, or *CFCs*.

**Pangaea** The name scientists give to a huge continent that they think once existed on Earth. It gradually broke up to form the *continents* we have today.

**passport** An official document issued by the government of a country to a person who belongs to that country. A passport can allow travel to foreign countries, act as an identity card and give its owner the right to re-enter his or her *native* country.

**pastoral farming** A type of farming that involves raising and breeding animals.

**patriarchy** A system in which men are the most powerful members of families and of society.

**peninsula** A long piece of land that sticks out into the sea.

**permafrost** A layer of the ground that is permanently frozen.

**photosynthesis** A chemical process in plants, which converts sunlight into food.

**pidgin** A language made up of elements of two or more languages to help groups who speak different languages communicate.

**pilgrimage** A journey to a sacred place.

**planet** A celestial body that *orbits* a *star*. For example, Earth and Mars are planets which orbit the *Sun*.

**plate** One of the large pieces of *lithosphere* that make up the Earth's surface layer.

**plate tectonics** The theory that *plates* gradually move around and rub against each other.

**poles** The *North Pole* and the *South Pole*, the coldest points of the Earth and those that are farthest away from the *Equator*.

**pollution** Waste or dirt, such as exhaust from cars, that builds up faster than it can be broken down.

**population** The number of people living in a particular place.

**porous** Able to soak up water. Porous rock can soak up water like a sponge and store it underground.

**port** A town or city where ships can load and unload.

**precipitation** Rain, snow, hail or any other water falling from the sky.

**precision farming** A type of farming that uses the latest science and technology to grow crops more efficiently.

**primary industry** An industry that takes raw materials from the Earth. Mining and fishing are primary industries.

**Prime Meridian Line** An imaginary line that runs from north to south through Greenwich, England, at zero *degrees* of *longitude*. The time along the Prime Meridian Line is called Greenwich Mean Time.

**projection** A representation of the Earth's surface on a flat map.

**quaternary industry** An industry, such as accountancy, in which information is bought and sold.

**radar** A system that detects objects such as clouds by sending out radio waves and collecting the signals that bounce back. Radar stands for **RA**dio **D**etecting **A**nd **R**anging.

**radiation** Energy, such as light, heat or *radioactive* particles, that radiates (flows outward) from an energy source. For example, the *Sun* radiates light and heat.

**radioactive** A substance that gives out *radiation*. Radioactive substances, such as uranium, give off particles which can be harmful.

**refugee** A person who has fled from their country to escape some danger or problem.

**remote sensing** Recording information from a long distance away; for example, measuring sea temperatures from a *satellite*.

**reservation** An area of public land set aside for a special purpose. For example, in North America European settlers forced Native Americans to live on reservations.

**rift valley** A valley formed on land where two *plates* of the Earth's *crust* pull away from each other.

**Ring of Fire** A group of volcanoes and *faults* that forms a huge ring in the Pacific Ocean.

**satellite** An object that *orbits* a *planet*. Many satellites are built to do particular jobs, such as monitoring the weather.

**scale** The size of a map in relation to the area it represents. If a map's scale is 1:100, 1cm on the map represents 100cm of the area shown.

**secondary industry** An industry, such as building or making cloth in a factory, that makes things out of raw materials.

**sedimentary rock** Rock made up of particles of sand, mud and other *debris* that have settled on the seabed and been squashed down to form hard rock.

**selective breeding** Developing plants and animals by choosing those with good qualities for farming.

**service industry** An industry, such as banking or waitressing, that involves people doing or supplying something for other people. See also **tertiary industry**.

**settlement** A collection of homes forming a community.

**sewage** Waste and dirty water from sinks and bathrooms.

**shaman** A religious leader who is believed to have magical powers.

**shanty town** A makeshift town on the outskirts of a city where people build their own homes out of waste materials.

**shifting agriculture** A system of farming in which people clear a small area of forest to use as farmland. After a few years, they move on to another area.

**site** The place where a *settlement* has been built.

**situation** A *settlement's* position in the surrounding area, such as in a gap in a range of hills.

**smog** A mixture of smoke and fog. Also a general word for *pollution*.

**Solar System** The *Sun* and the *planets, satellites* and other objects that *orbit* it.

**solar year** The amount of time it takes the Earth to *orbit* the *Sun* once. A solar year is 365.26 days.

**sonar** A method of bouncing sounds off objects and measuring the results in order to make maps. Sonar is used to map the seabed.

**southern hemisphere** The half of the Earth that lies south of the *Equator*.

**South Pole** The most southern point on the Earth, and one end of the *axis* the Earth spins around.

**species** (plural: **species**) A type of plant, animal or other living thing.

**stalactite** A column of stone hanging down inside a cave, made by water dripping from the roof and depositing dissolved minerals.

**stalagmite** A tower of stone rising from the ground in a cave, made by water dripping onto the floor and depositing dissolved minerals.

**star** A huge ball of burning gas in space. The *Sun*, in the middle of our *Solar System*, is a star.

**state** An area of land that has its own government, laws and money. It can also mean one of a number of regional governments forming a federation under a central government, as in the U.S.A.

**stoma** (plural: **stomata**) One of the tiny holes in the leaves of plants. A stoma allows gases and water in and out. See also **transpiration**.

**stratum** (plural: **strata**) A layer of rock.

**subduction zone** An area of the seabed where one *plate* of the Earth's *lithosphere* plunges beneath another, forming a deep trench.

**submersible** A small submarine used by scientists to explore the oceans and the seabed.

**Sun** The medium-sized *star* that lies in the middle of our *Solar System*.

**temperate** A type of *climate* that is mild and damp.

**terrace** One of a series of large steps dug into hillsides to hold soil and water in place for farming.

**tertiary industry** An industry, such as teaching or banking, that provides services for others.

**thermal spring** A flow of water heated by underground rocks that emerges on the Earth's surface. Also known as a hot spring.

**tidal wave** A type of very large wave. *Tsunamis* are not tidal waves, as they are caused by underwater volcanoes or earthquakes and have nothing to do with tides.

**tide** The daily rise and fall of the sea, caused by the Moon's *gravity*.

**time zone** A region where the same standard time is used.

**topsoil** The rich, uppermost layer of soil. It contains *humus* and *organisms* that make it *fertile*.

**transpiration** A process where water that has been sucked in through a plant's roots travels up to the leaves, and transpires, or evaporates, through the *stomata*.

**treeline** The height up a mountain above which there are no more trees (because it is too cold and windy for them to survive).

**tributary** A river that flows into a bigger river, instead of into the sea.

**tropics** The warm, wet areas on either side of the *Equator,* between the Tropic of Cancer and the Tropic of Capricorn.

**tsunami** A giant wave made by an earthquake, landslide or volcanic activity on the seabed causing the water to make waves.

**tundra** A type of land, found in the Arctic, where a layer of the ground is permanently frozen.

**turbine** A machine that converts turning power (such as the spinning of a waterwheel) into electricity.

**ultraviolet (UV)** A type of invisible *radiation* from the Sun which can cause skin damage.

**understorey** The level of a rainforest where small trees and plants grow, between the *canopy* and the forest floor.

**urbanization** An increase in the number of people living in towns and cities rather than in the countryside.

**visa** A stamp on a *passport* from the government of a country which shows that the owner is allowed to travel through that country for a fixed period of time.

**water table** The top level of *groundwater* that is stored in underground rock.

**yield** The amount of food or other produce that is grown on a particular piece of land.

# MAP INDEX

This is an index of the places and features named on the maps. Each entry consists of the following parts: the name (given in bold type), the country or region within which it is located (given in italics), the page on which the name can be found (given in bold type), and the grid reference (also given in bold type). For some names, there is also a description explaining what kind of place it is – for example a country, internal administrative area (state or province), national capital or internal capital. To find a place on a map, first find the map indicated by the page reference. Then use the grid reference to find the square containing the name or town symbol. See page 251 for help with using the grid.

## a

**Abaco**, *The Bahamas*, **271 L5**
**Abadan**, *Iran*, **303 E5**
**Abakan**, *Russia*, **304 E3**
**Abaya, Lake**, *Ethiopia*, **327 G2**
**Abeche**, *Chad*, **322 F6**
**Abeokuta**, *Nigeria*, **325 F7**
**Aberdeen**, *United Kingdom*, **314 D2**
**Aberystwyth**, *United Kingdom*, **314 C3**
**Abha**, *Saudi Arabia*, **303 D8**
**Abidjan**, *Ivory Coast*, **325 E7**
**Abilene**, *U.S.A.*, **270 G4**
**Abomey**, *Benin*, **325 F7**
**Abu Dhabi**, *United Arab Emirates, national capital*, **303 F7**
**Abuja**, *Nigeria, national capital*, **325 G7**
**Abu Kamal**, *Syria*, **302 D5**
**Abu Simbel**, *Egypt*, **323 H4**
**Acapulco**, *Mexico*, **272 E4**
**Accra**, *Ghana, national capital*, **325 E7**
**Acklins Island**, *The Bahamas*, **271 L6**
**Aconcagua**, *Argentina*, **280 E6**
**Adana**, *Turkey*, **302 C4**
**Adapazari**, *Turkey*, **317 J3**
**Ad Dakhla**, *Western Sahara*, **324 B4**
**Ad Dammam**, *Saudi Arabia*, **303 F6**
**Addis Ababa**, *Ethiopia, national capital*, **327 G2**
**Adelaide**, *Australia, internal capital*, **288 G6**
**Aden**, *Yemen*, **303 E9**
**Aden, Gulf of**, *Africa/Asia*, **303 E9**
**Admiralty Islands**, *Papua New Guinea*, **295 L4**
**Adrar**, *Algeria*, **324 E3**
**Adriatic Sea**, *Europe*, **316 E3**
**Adzope**, *Ivory Coast*, **325 E7**
**Aegean Sea**, *Europe*, **317 H4**
**Afghanistan**, *Asia, country*, **300 A4**
**Africa**, **263**
**Agadez**, *Niger*, **322 C5**
**Agadir**, *Morocco*, **324 D2**
**Agra**, *India*, **300 D5**
**Agrigento**, *Italy*, **316 E4**
**Agua Prieta**, *Mexico*, **272 C1**
**Aguascalientes**, *Mexico*, **272 D3**
**Agulhas, Cape**, *South Africa*, **328 C6**
**Agulhas Negras, Mount**, *Brazil*, **280 K4**
**Ahaggar Mountains**, *Algeria*, **324 G4**
**Ahmadabad**, *India*, **301 C6**
**Ahvaz**, *Iran*, **303 E5**
**Aix-en-Provence**, *France*, **315 F6**
**Aizawl**, *India*, **301 G6**
**Ajaccio**, *France*, **315 G6**
**Ajdabiya**, *Libya*, **322 F2**
**Ajmer**, *India*, **300 C5**
**Akhisar**, *Turkey*, **317 H4**
**Akita**, *Japan*, **299 P3**
**Akjoujt**, *Mauritania*, **324 C5**
**Akola**, *India*, **301 D6**
**Aksaray**, *Turkey*, **317 K4**
**Aksu**, *China*, **300 E2**
**Alabama**, *U.S.A., internal admin. area*, **271 J4**
**Al Amarah**, *Iraq*, **303 E5**
**Aland Islands**, *Finland*, **312 F3**
**Alanya**, *Turkey*, **317 J4**
**Al Aqabah**, *Jordan*, **303 C6**
**Alaska**, *U.S.A., internal admin. area*, **268 D2**

**Alaska, Gulf of**, *North America*, **268 E3**
**Alaska Peninsula**, *U.S.A.*, **268 D3**
**Alaska Range**, *U.S.A.*, **268 D2**
**Alavus**, *Finland*, **312 G3**
**Al Ayn**, *United Arab Emirates*, **303 G7**
**Albacete**, *Spain*, **315 D7**
**Albania**, *Europe, country*, **317 F3**
**Albany**, *Australia*, **288 C7**
**Albany**, *Georgia, U.S.A.*, **271 K4**
**Albany**, *New York, U.S.A., internal capital*, **271 M2**
**Al Bayda**, *Libya*, **322 F2**
**Alberta**, *Canada, internal admin. area*, **268 H3**
**Albert, Lake**, *Africa*, **327 F3**
**Albino Point**, *Angola*, **328 B3**
**Alboran Island**, *Spain*, **315 D7**
**Alborg**, *Denmark*, **313 D4**
**Albuquerque**, *U.S.A.*, **270 E3**
**Aldabra Group**, *Seychelles*, **329 J1**
**Aleppo**, *Syria*, **302 C4**
**Alesund**, *Norway*, **312 C3**
**Aleutian Islands**, *U.S.A.*, **269 A3**
**Alexander Archipelago**, *Canada*, **268 F3**
**Alexander Bay**, *South Africa*, **328 C5**
**Alexandria**, *Egypt*, **323 G2**
**Algeciras**, *Spain*, **315 C7**
**Algeria**, *Africa, country*, **324 F3**
**Algiers**, *Algeria, national capital*, **324 F1**
**Al Hillah**, *Iraq*, **302 D5**
**Al Hoceima**, *Morocco*, **324 E1**
**Al Hudaydah**, *Yemen*, **303 D9**
**Ali Bayramli**, *Azerbaijan*, **302 E4**
**Alicante**, *Spain*, **315 D7**
**Alice Springs**, *Australia*, **288 F4**
**Aligarh**, *India*, **300 D5**
**Al Jawf**, *Libya*, **322 F4**
**Al Khums**, *Libya*, **322 D2**
**Al Kut**, *Iraq*, **303 E5**
**Allahabad**, *India*, **300 E5**
**Almaty**, *Kazakhstan*, **300 D2**
**Almeria**, *Spain*, **315 D7**
**Almetyevsk**, *Russia*, **311 G3**
**Almirante**, *Panama*, **273 H6**
**Al Mubarrez**, *Saudi Arabia*, **303 E6**
**Al Mukalla**, *Yemen*, **303 E9**
**Alor Setar**, *Malaysia*, **294 B2**
**Alps**, *Europe*, **316 D2**
**Al Qamishli**, *Syria*, **302 D4**
**Alta**, *Norway*, **312 G1**
**Altai Mountains**, *Asia*, **298 D1**
**Altamira**, *Brazil*, **279 H4**
**Altay**, *China*, **300 F1**
**Altay**, *Mongolia*, **298 E1**
**Altun Mountains**, *China*, **300 G3**
**Aluksne**, *Latvia*, **313 H4**
**Alytus**, *Lithuania*, **313 H5**
**Amadjuak Lake**, *Canada*, **269 M2**
**Amami**, *Japan*, **299 L5**
**Amarillo**, *U.S.A.*, **270 F3**
**Amazon**, *South America*, **278 H4**
**Amazon Delta**, *Brazil*, **279 J3**
**Ambanja**, *Madagascar*, **329 J2**
**Ambato**, *Ecuador*, **278 C4**
**Amber, Cape**, *Madagascar*, **329 J2**
**Ambilobe**, *Madagascar*, **329 J2**
**Ambon**, *Indonesia*, **295 G4**
**Ambositra**, *Madagascar*, **329 J4**

**American Samoa**, *Oceania, dependency*, **286 F6**
**America, United States of**, *North America, country*, **270 F3**
**Amiens**, *France*, **314 E4**
**Amman**, *Jordan, national capital*, **303 C5**
**Amravati**, *India*, **301 D6**
**Amritsar**, *India*, **300 C4**
**Amsterdam**, *Netherlands, national capital*, **314 F3**
**Am Timan**, *Chad*, **322 F6**
**Amu Darya**, *Asia*, **302 H4**
**Amundsen Gulf**, *Canada*, **268 G1**
**Amundsen Sea**, *Antarctica*, **333 Q3**
**Amur**, *Asia*, **305 G3**
**Anadyr**, *Russia*, **305 J2**
**Anadyr, Gulf of**, *Asia*, **305 K2**
**Analalava**, *Madagascar*, **329 J2**
**Anambas Islands**, *Indonesia*, **294 C3**
**Anchorage**, *U.S.A.*, **268 E2**
**Ancona**, *Italy*, **316 E3**
**Andaman Islands**, *India*, **301 G8**
**Andaman Sea**, *Asia*, **296 C5**
**Andara**, *Namibia*, **328 D3**
**Andes**, *South America*, **280 E5**
**Andorra**, *Europe, country*, **315 E6**
**Andorra la Vella**, *Andorra, national capital*, **315 E6**
**Andreanof Islands**, *U.S.A.*, **269 B3**
**Androka**, *Madagascar*, **329 H5**
**Andros**, *The Bahamas*, **271 L6**
**Aneto, Pico de**, *Spain*, **315 E6**
**Angel Falls**, *Venezuela*, **278 F2**
**Angers**, *France*, **314 D5**
**Angkor**, *Cambodia*, **296 D5**
**Angoche**, *Mozambique*, **329 G3**
**Angola**, *Africa, country*, **328 C2**
**Angra do Heroismo**, *Azores*, **324 K10**
**Angren**, *Uzbekistan*, **300 C2**
**Anguilla**, *North America*, **272 M4**
**Anjouan Island**, *Comoros*, **329 H2**
**Ankara**, *Turkey, national capital*, **317 K3**
**Annaba**, *Algeria*, **324 G1**
**An Najaf**, *Iraq*, **303 D5**
**Annapolis**, *U.S.A., internal capital*, **271 L3**
**An Nasiriyah**, *Iraq*, **303 E5**
**Anqing**, *China*, **299 J4**
**Anshan**, *China*, **299 K2**
**Antalaha**, *Madagascar*, **329 K2**
**Antalya**, *Turkey*, **317 J4**
**Antalya, Gulf of**, *Turkey*, **317 J4**
**Antananarivo**, *Madagascar, national capital*, **329 J3**
**Antarctica**, **333 B4**
**Antarctic Peninsula**, *Antarctica*, **333 T2**
**Anticosti Island**, *Canada*, **269 N4**
**Antigua and Barbuda**, *North America, country*, **272 M4**
**Antofagasta**, *Chile*, **280 D4**
**Antsalova**, *Madagascar*, **329 H3**
**Antsirabe**, *Madagascar*, **329 J3**
**Antsiranana**, *Madagascar*, **329 J2**
**Antwerp**, *Belgium*, **314 F4**
**Aomori**, *Japan*, **299 P2**
**Aoraki**, *New Zealand*, **289 P8**
**Apalachee Bay**, *U.S.A.*, **271 K5**
**Aparri**, *Philippines*, **297 H4**
**Apatity**, *Russia*, **312 K2**

**Apennines**, *Italy*, **316 E3**
**Apia**, *Samoa, national capital*, **286 F6**
**Appalachian Mountains**, *U.S.A.*, **271 K3**
**Aqsay**, *Kazakhstan*, **311 G3**
**Aqtau**, *Kazakhstan*, **302 F3**
**Aqtobe**, *Kazakhstan*, **311 H3**
**Arabian Desert**, *Africa*, **323 H3**
**Arabian Peninsula**, *Asia*, **303 E7**
**Arabian Sea**, *Asia*, **303 G8**
**Aracaju**, *Brazil*, **279 L6**
**Arad**, *Romania*, **317 G2**
**Araguaia**, *Brazil*, **279 H6**
**Araguaina**, *Brazil*, **279 J5**
**Arak**, *Iran*, **302 E5**
**Aral**, *Kazakhstan*, **302 H2**
**Aral Sea**, *Asia*, **302 G2**
**Arapiraca**, *Brazil*, **279 L5**
**Araraquara**, *Brazil*, **280 J4**
**Araure**, *Venezuela*, **278 E2**
**Arbil**, *Iraq*, **302 D4**
**Arctic Ocean**, **332 A4**
**Ardabil**, *Iran*, **302 E4**
**Arendal**, *Norway*, **312 D4**
**Arequipa**, *Peru*, **278 D7**
**Argentina**, *South America, country*, **281 E7**
**Argentino, Lake**, *Argentina*, **281 D10**
**Arhus**, *Denmark*, **313 D4**
**Arica**, *Chile*, **280 D3**
**Arica, Gulf of**, *South America*, **278 D7**
**Arizona**, *U.S.A., internal admin. area*, **270 D4**
**Arkansas**, *U.S.A.*, **271 G3**
**Arkansas**, *U.S.A., internal admin. area*, **271 H4**
**Arkhangelsk**, *Russia*, **304 C2**
**Armenia**, *Asia, country*, **302 D3**
**Armidale**, *Australia*, **289 K6**
**Arnhem**, *Netherlands*, **314 F4**
**Arnhem Land**, *Australia*, **288 F2**
**Arqalyq**, *Kazakhstan*, **302 J1**
**Ar Ramadi**, *Iraq*, **302 D5**
**Ar Raqqah**, *Syria*, **302 C4**
**Aruba**, *North America*, **273 K5**
**Aru Islands**, *Indonesia*, **295 J5**
**Arusha**, *Tanzania*, **327 G4**
**Arzamas**, *Russia*, **310 E2**
**Asahikawa**, *Japan*, **299 P2**
**Asansol**, *India*, **301 F6**
**Ashgabat**, *Turkmenistan, national capital*, **302 G4**
**Ashkhabad**, *Turkmenistan, national capital*, **302 G4**
**Asia**, **263**
**Asir**, *Saudi Arabia*, **303 D7**
**Asmara**, *Eritrea, national capital*, **323 J5**
**Assab**, *Eritrea*, **323 K6**
**As Sulaymaniyah**, *Iraq*, **302 E4**
**Assumption**, *Seychelles*, **329 J1**
**Astana**, *Kazakhstan, national capital*, **304 D3**
**Astove**, *Seychelles*, **329 J2**
**Astrakhan**, *Russia*, **311 F4**
**Asuncion**, *Paraguay, national capital*, **280 G5**
**Aswan**, *Egypt*, **323 H4**
**Aswan High Dam**, *Egypt*, **323 H4**
**Asyut**, *Egypt*, **323 H3**
**Atacama Desert**, *Chile*, **280 E3**

Minneapolis, *U.S.A.,* 271 H2
Minnesota, *U.S.A., internal admin. area,* 271 G1
Minorca, *Spain,* 315 E6
Minot, *U.S.A.,* 270 F1
Minsk, *Belarus, national capital,* 313 H5
Miri, *Malaysia,* 294 D3
Mirim Lake, *Brazil,* 280 H6
Miskolc, *Hungary,* 313 G6
Misool, *Indonesia,* 295 H4
Misratah, *Libya,* 322 E2
Mississippi, *U.S.A.,* 271 H4
Mississippi, *U.S.A., internal admin. area,* 271 H4
Mississippi Delta, *U.S.A.,* 271 J5
Missoula, *U.S.A.,* 270 D1
Missouri, *U.S.A.,* 270 G2
Missouri, *U.S.A., internal admin. area,* 271 H3
Mistassini, Lake, *Canada,* 269 M3
Mitwaba, *Democratic Republic of Congo,* 326 E5
Mkushi, *Zambia,* 328 E2
Mmabatho, *South Africa,* 328 E5
Moanda, *Gabon,* 326 B4
Mobile, *U.S.A.,* 271 J4
Mochudi, *Botswana,* 328 E4
Mocuba, *Mozambique,* 329 G3
Modena, *Italy,* 316 D2
Mogadishu, *Somalia, national capital,* 327 J3
Mogao Caves, *China,* 298 E2
Mohilla Island, *Comoros,* 329 H2
Mo i Rana, *Norway,* 312 E2
Mojave Desert, *U.S.A.,* 270 C4
Moldova, *Europe, country,* 317 J2
Moldoveanu, Mount, *Romania,* 310 C4
Molepolole, *Botswana,* 328 E4
Mollendo, *Peru,* 278 D7
Molokai, *U.S.A.,* 271 P7
Molopo, *Africa,* 328 D5
Molucca Sea, *Indonesia,* 295 F4
Mombasa, *Kenya,* 327 G4
Monaco, *Europe, country,* 315 F6
Monastir, *Tunisia,* 322 D1
Monchegorsk, *Russia,* 312 K2
Monclova, *Mexico,* 272 D2
Moncton, *Canada,* 269 N4
Mongo, *Chad,* 322 E6
Mongolia, *Asia, country,* 298 F1
Mongu, *Zambia,* 328 D3
Monrovia, *Liberia, national capital,* 325 C7
Montalvo, *Ecuador,* 278 C4
Montana, *U.S.A., internal admin. area,* 270 E1
Montauban, *France,* 315 E5
Montego Bay, *Jamaica,* 273 J4
Montenegro, Serbia and, *Europe, country,* 317 G2
Monterrey, *Mexico,* 272 D2
Montes Claros, *Brazil,* 280 K3
Montevideo, *Uruguay, national capital,* 280 G6
Montgomery, *U.S.A., internal capital,* 271 J4
Montpelier, *U.S.A., internal capital,* 271 M2
Montpellier, *France,* 315 E6
Montreal, *Canada,* 269 M4
Montserrat, *North America,* 272 M4
Monywa, *Burma,* 296 C3
Moose Jaw, *Canada,* 268 J3
Mopti, *Mali,* 325 E6
Moree, *Australia,* 289 J5
Morelia, *Mexico,* 272 D4
Morocco, *Africa, country,* 324 D2
Morogoro, *Tanzania,* 327 G5
Morombe, *Madagascar,* 329 H4
Moroni, *Comoros, national capital,* 329 H2
Morotai, *Indonesia,* 295 G3
Morpara, *Brazil,* 280 K2
Moscow, *Russia, national capital,* 310 D2
Moshi, *Tanzania,* 327 G4
Mosquitos, Gulf of, *North America,* 273 H5
Mossendjo, *Congo,* 326 B4
Mossoro, *Brazil,* 279 L5

Most, *Czech Republic,* 316 E1
Mostaganem, *Algeria,* 324 F1
Mostar, *Bosnia and Herzegovina,* 316 F3
Mosul, *Iraq,* 302 D4
Moulmein, *Burma,* 296 C4
Moundou, *Chad,* 326 C2
Mount Gambier, *Australia,* 288 H7
Mount Hagen, *Papua New Guinea,* 295 K5
Mount Isa, *Australia,* 288 G4
Mount Li, *China,* 298 G4
Moyale, *Ethiopia,* 327 G3
Moyobamba, *Peru,* 278 C5
Mozambique, *Africa, country,* 329 F3
Mozambique, *Mozambique,* 329 H2
Mozambique Channel, *Africa,* 329 G4
Mpika, *Zambia,* 328 F2
Mtwara, *Tanzania,* 327 H6
Mudanjiang, *China,* 299 L2
Mueda, *Mozambique,* 329 G2
Mufulira, *Zambia,* 328 E2
Multan, *Pakistan,* 300 C4
Mumbai, *India,* 301 C7
Mumbue, *Angola,* 328 C2
Munhango, *Angola,* 328 C2
Munich, *Germany,* 314 E4
Munster, *Germany,* 314 F4
Murcia, *Spain,* 315 D7
Murmansk, *Russia,* 312 K1
Murom, *Russia,* 310 E2
Murray, *Australia,* 288 G6
Murzuq, *Libya,* 322 D3
Muscat, *Oman, national capital,* 303 G7
Mutare, *Zimbabwe,* 329 F3
Mutoko, *Zimbabwe,* 328 F3
Mutsamudu, *Comoros,* 329 H2
Mutshatsha, *Democratic Republic of Congo,* 326 D6
Mwali, *Comoros,* 329 H2
Mwanza, *Tanzania,* 327 F4
Mwene-Ditu, *Democratic Republic of Congo,* 326 D5
Mweru, Lake, *Africa,* 328 E1
Mwinilunga, *Zambia,* 328 D2
Myanmar, *Asia, country,* 296 C3
Myitkyina, *Burma,* 296 C2
Mykolayiv, *Ukraine,* 310 C4
Mysore, *India,* 301 D8
Mzuzu, *Malawi,* 329 F2

## n

Naberezhnyye Chelny, *Russia,* 311 G2
Nabeul, *Tunisia,* 316 D4
Nacala, *Mozambique,* 329 H2
Nador, *Morocco,* 315 D8
Naga, *Philippines,* 297 H5
Nagasaki, *Japan,* 299 L4
Nagoya, *Japan,* 299 N3
Nagpur, *India,* 301 D6
Nain, *Canada,* 269 N3
Nairobi, *Kenya, national capital,* 327 G4
Najran, *Saudi Arabia,* 303 D8
Nakhodka, *Russia,* 299 M2
Nakhon Ratchasima, *Thailand,* 296 D5
Nakhon Sawan, *Thailand,* 296 D4
Nakhon Si Thammarat, *Thailand,* 296 D6
Nakuru, *Kenya,* 327 G4
Nalchik, *Russia,* 302 D3
Namangan, *Uzbekistan,* 300 C2
Namib Desert, *Africa,* 328 B3
Namibe, *Angola,* 328 B3
Namibia, *Africa, country,* 328 C4
Nam Lake, *China,* 300 G4
Nampo, *North Korea,* 299 L3
Nampula, *Mozambique,* 329 G3
Namsos, *Norway,* 312 D2
Namur, *Belgium,* 314 F4
Nanaimo, *Canada,* 268 G4
Nanchang, *China,* 299 J5
Nancy, *France,* 314 F4
Nanded, *India,* 301 D7
Nanjing, *China,* 299 J4
Nanning, *China,* 298 G6
Nanping, *China,* 299 J5
Nantes, *France,* 315 D5
Napier, *New Zealand,* 289 Q7

Naples, *Italy,* 316 E3
Narmada, *India,* 301 C6
Narva, *Estonia,* 312 J4
Narvik, *Norway,* 312 F1
Nashik, *India,* 301 C6
Nashville, *U.S.A., internal capital,* 271 J3
Nasi Lake, *Finland,* 312 G3
Nassau, *The Bahamas, national capital,* 271 L5
Nasser, Lake, *Egypt,* 323 H4
Natal, *Brazil,* 279 L5
Natitingou, *Benin,* 325 F6
Nauru, *Oceania, country,* 286 D5
Navapolatsk, *Belarus,* 313 J5
Navoiy, *Uzbekistan,* 300 B2
Nawabshah, *Pakistan,* 300 B5
Naxcivan, *Azerbaijan,* 302 E4
Nazca, *Peru,* 278 D6
Nazret, *Ethiopia,* 327 G2
Ndalatando, *Angola,* 328 B1
Ndele, *Central African Republic,* 326 D2
Ndjamena, *Chad, national capital,* 322 E6
Ndola, *Zambia,* 328 E2
Near Islands, *U.S.A.,* 269 A3
Nebraska, *U.S.A., internal admin. area,* 270 F2
Necochea, *Argentina,* 281 G7
Negombo, *Sri Lanka,* 301 D9
Negro, *Brazil,* 278 F4
Negro, Cape, *Peru,* 278 B5
Negros, *Philippines,* 297 H6
Neiva, *Colombia,* 278 C3
Nekemte, *Ethiopia,* 327 G2
Nellore, *India,* 301 D8
Nelson, *New Zealand,* 289 P8
Nelspruit, *South Africa,* 328 F5
Nema, *Mauritania,* 325 D5
Neman, *Europe,* 313 G5
Nepal, *Asia, country,* 300 E5
Netherlands, *Europe, country,* 314 F3
Netherlands Antilles, *North America, dependency,* 273 L5
Nettiling Lake, *Canada,* 269 M2
Neuquen, *Argentina,* 281 E7
Nevada, *U.S.A., internal admin. area,* 270 C3
Nevers, *France,* 315 E5
New Amsterdam, *Guyana,* 279 G2
Newark, *U.S.A.,* 271 M2
New Britain, *Papua New Guinea,* 295 M5
New Brunswick, *Canada, internal admin. area,* 269 N4
New Caledonia, *Oceania,* 289 M4
Newcastle, *Australia,* 289 K6
Newcastle upon Tyne, *United Kingdom,* 314 D3
New Delhi, *India, national capital,* 300 D5
Newfoundland, *Canada,* 269 P4
Newfoundland, *Canada, internal admin. area,* 269 N3
New Guinea, *Asia/Oceania,* 295 J4
New Hampshire, *U.S.A., internal admin. area,* 271 M2
New Ireland, *Papua New Guinea,* 295 M4
New Jersey, *U.S.A., internal admin. area,* 271 M3
New Mexico, *U.S.A., internal admin. area,* 270 E4
New Orleans, *U.S.A.,* 271 J5
New Plymouth, *New Zealand,* 289 P7
Newport, *United Kingdom,* 314 D4
New Siberia Islands, *Russia,* 305 H2
New South Wales, *Australia, internal admin. area,* 288 H6
New York, *U.S.A.,* 271 M2
New York, *U.S.A., internal admin. area,* 271 M2
New Zealand, *Australasia, country,* 289 Q8
Ngami, Lake, *Botswana,* 328 D4
Ngaoundere, *Cameroon,* 326 B2
Ngoma, *Zambia,* 328 E3
Nha Trang, *Vietnam,* 296 E5
Niagara Falls, *North America,* 269 M4
Niamey, *Niger, national capital,* 325 F6
Nias, *Indonesia,* 294 A3

Nicaragua, *North America, country,* 273 G5
Nicaragua, Lake, *Nicaragua,* 273 H5
Nice, *France,* 315 F6
Nicobar Islands, *India,* 301 G9
Nicosia, *Cyprus, national capital,* 317 K5
Nieuw Nickerie, *Surinam,* 279 G2
Niger, *Africa,* 325 G7
Niger, *Africa, country,* 322 D5
Niger Delta, *Nigeria,* 325 G8
Nigeria, *Africa, country,* 325 F7
Niigata, *Japan,* 299 N3
Nikopol, *Ukraine,* 310 C4
Niksic, *Yugoslavia,* 317 F3
Nile, *Africa,* 323 H3
Nile Delta, *Egypt,* 323 H2
Nimes, *France,* 315 F6
Ningbo, *China,* 299 K5
Niono, *Mali,* 325 D6
Nioro du Sahel, *Mali,* 325 D5
Nipigon, Lake, *Canada,* 269 L4
Nis, *Yugoslavia,* 317 G3
Nitra, *Slovakia,* 313 F6
Niue, *Oceania,* 286 G6
Nizhniy Novgorod, *Russia,* 310 E2
Nizhniy Tagil, *Russia,* 311 H2
Njazidja, *Comoros,* 329 H2
Njinjo, *Tanzania,* 327 G5
Nkongsamba, *Cameroon,* 326 A3
Nogales, *Mexico,* 272 C1
Nokaneng, *Botswana,* 328 D3
Norfolk Island, *Australia,* 289 N5
Norilsk, *Russia,* 304 F3
Norrkoping, *Sweden,* 312 F4
North America, 262
North Bay, *Canada,* 269 M4
North Cape, *New Zealand,* 289 P6
North Cape, *Norway,* 312 J1
North Carolina, *U.S.A., internal admin. area,* 271 K3
North Dakota, *U.S.A., internal admin. area,* 270 F1
Northern Ireland, *United Kingdom, internal admin. area,* 314 C3
Northern Mariana Islands, *Oceania,* 286 B3
Northern Territory, *Australia, internal admin. area,* 288 F3
North European Plain, *Russia,* 310 C2
North Frisian Islands, *Europe,* 314 F3
North Island, *New Zealand,* 289 Q7
North Korea, *Asia, country,* 299 L2
North Sea, *Europe,* 314 E2
North West Cape, *Australia,* 288 B4
Northwest Territories, *Canada, internal admin. area,* 268 G2
Norway, *Europe, country,* 312 D3
Norwegian Sea, *Europe,* 312 C2
Norwich, *United Kingdom,* 314 E3
Nosy Be, *Madagascar,* 329 J2
Nosy Boraha, *Madagascar,* 329 J3
Nottingham, *United Kingdom,* 314 D3
Nouadhibou, *Mauritania,* 324 B4
Nouakchott, *Mauritania, national capital,* 324 B5
Noumea, *New Caledonia,* 289 N4
Nova Iguacu, *Brazil,* 280 K4
Nova Mambone, *Mozambique,* 329 G4
Novara, *Italy,* 316 D2
Nova Scotia, *Canada, internal admin. area,* 269 N4
Novaya Zemlya, *Russia,* 304 C2
Novgorod, *Russia,* 312 J4
Novi Sad, *Yugoslavia,* 317 F2
Novo Mesto, *Slovenia,* 316 E2
Novocherkassk, *Russia,* 310 E4
Novorossiysk, *Russia,* 302 C3
Novosibirsk, *Russia,* 304 E3
Novyy Urengoy, *Russia,* 304 D2
Nubian Desert, *Africa,* 323 H4
Nueva Loja, *Ecuador,* 278 C3
Nukualofa, *Tonga, national capital,* 286 F7
Nukus, *Uzbekistan,* 302 G3
Nullarbor Plain, *Australia,* 288 E6
Nunavut, *Canada, internal admin. area,* 269 K2
Nungo, *Mozambique,* 329 G2
Nunivak Island, *U.S.A.,* 268 C3

San Sebastian, *Spain*, 315 D6
Santa Clara, *Cuba*, 273 H3
Santa Cruz, *Bolivia*, 280 F3
Santa Cruz, *Ecuador*, 278 N10
Santa Cruz Islands, *Solomon Islands*, 289 N2
Santa Elena, *Venezuela*, 278 H4
Santa Fe, *Argentina*, 280 F6
Santa Fe, *U.S.A., internal capital*, 270 E3
Santa Maria, *Brazil*, 280 H5
Santa Marta, *Colombia*, 278 D1
Santander, *Spain*, 315 D6
Santarem, *Brazil*, 279 H4
Santa Rosa, *Argentina*, 281 F7
Santiago, *Chile, national capital*, 280 D6
Santiago, *Dominican Republic*, 273 K4
Santiago, *Panama*, 273 H6
Santiago de Compostela, *Spain*, 315 B6
Santiago de Cuba, *Cuba*, 273 J3
Santiago del Estero, *Argentina*, 280 F5
Santo Antao, *Cape Verde*, 325 L11
Santo Domingo, *Dominican Republic, national capital*, 273 L4
Santo Domingo de los Colorados, *Ecuador*, 278 C4
San Valentin, Mount, *Chile*, 281 D9
Sanya, *China*, 298 G7
Sao Francisco, *Brazil*, 279 L5
Sao Jose do Rio Preto, *Brazil*, 280 J4
Sao Luis, *Brazil*, 279 K4
Sao Miguel, *Azores*, 324 K10
Sao Nicolau, *Cape Verde*, 325 M11
Sao Paulo, *Brazil*, 280 J4
Sao Roque, Cape, *Brazil*, 279 L4
Sao Tiago, *Cape Verde*, 325 M11
Sao Tome, *Sao Tome and Principe, national capital*, 325 G8
Sao Tome and Principe, *Africa, country*, 325 G8
Sapporo, *Japan*, 299 P2
Saqqara, *Egypt*, 323 H3
Sarajevo, *Bosnia and Herzegovina, national capital*, 317 F3
Saransk, *Russia*, 310 F3
Sarapul, *Russia*, 311 G2
Saratov, *Russia*, 311 F3
Saratov Reservoir, *Russia*, 311 F3
Sardinia, *Italy*, 316 D3
Sargodha, *Pakistan*, 300 C4
Sarh, *Chad*, 326 C2
Sarremaa, *Estonia*, 312 G4
Saskatchewan, *Canada, internal admin. area*, 268 J3
Saskatoon, *Canada*, 268 J3
Sassari, *Italy*, 316 D3
Satu Mare, *Romania*, 317 G2
Saudi Arabia, *Asia, country*, 303 E7
Sault Ste. Marie, *Canada*, 269 L4
Saurimo, *Angola*, 328 D1
Savannah, *U.S.A.*, 271 K4
Savannakhet, *Laos*, 296 D4
Sawu, *Indonesia*, 295 F6
Sawu Sea, *Indonesia*, 295 F5
Schwerin, *Germany*, 314 G3
Scotland, *United Kingdom, internal admin. area*, 314 C2
Seattle, *U.S.A.*, 270 B1
Seeheim, *Namibia*, 328 C5
Sefadu, *Sierra Leone*, 325 C7
Seg, Lake, *Russia*, 312 K3
Segou, *Mali*, 325 D6
Seine, *France*, 314 E4
Sekondi-Takoradi, *Ghana*, 325 E8
Selebi-Phikwe, *Botswana*, 328 E4
Selibabi, *Mauritania*, 325 C5
Selvas, *Brazil*, 278 E5
Semarang, *Indonesia*, 294 D5
Semenov, *Russia*, 310 E2
Semiozernoe, *Kazakhstan*, 311 J3
Sendai, *Japan*, 299 P3
Senegal, *Africa*, 325 C5
Senegal, *Africa, country*, 325 B6
Seoul, *South Korea, national capital*, 299 L3
Serang, *Indonesia*, 294 C5
Serbia and Montenegro, *Europe, country*, 317 G2

Seremban, *Malaysia*, 294 B3
Sergiyev Posad, *Russia*, 310 D2
Serov, *Russia*, 311 J2
Serowe, *Botswana*, 328 E4
Serpukhov, *Russia*, 310 D3
Serres, *Greece*, 317 G3
Sesheke, *Zambia*, 328 D3
Setif, *Algeria*, 324 G1
Setubal, *Portugal*, 315 B7
Sevastopol, *Ukraine*, 317 K2
Severn, *United Kingdom*, 314 D3
Severnaya Zemlya, *Russia*, 305 F2
Severomorsk, *Russia*, 312 K1
Sevettijarvi, *Finland*, 312 J1
Seville, *Spain*, 315 C7
Seward, *U.S.A.*, 268 E2
Seward Peninsula, *U.S.A.*, 268 C2
Seychelles, *Indian Ocean, country*, 329 J1
Seydhisfjordhur, *Iceland*, 312 Q2
Sfax, *Tunisia*, 322 D2
Shalqar, *Kazakhstan*, 302 G2
Shanghai, *China*, 299 K4
Shannon, *Ireland*, 314 C3
Shantou, *China*, 299 J6
Shaoguan, *China*, 299 H6
Sharjah, *United Arab Emirates*, 303 G6
Sharm el Sheikh, *Egypt*, 323 H3
Shasta, Mount, *U.S.A.*, 270 B2
Sheffield, *United Kingdom*, 314 D3
Shenyang, *China*, 299 K2
Shepetivka, *Ukraine*, 313 H6
Shetland Islands, *United Kingdom*, 314 D1
Shieli, *Kazakhstan*, 302 J3
Shihezi, *China*, 300 F2
Shijiazhuang, *China*, 299 H3
Shikoku, *Japan*, 299 M4
Shillong, *India*, 300 G5
Shiraz, *Iran*, 303 F6
Shishaldin Volcano, *U.S.A.*, 269 C3
Shiyan, *China*, 298 H4
Shizuoka, *Japan*, 299 N3
Shkoder, *Albania*, 317 F3
Shreveport, *U.S.A.*, 271 H4
Shumen, *Bulgaria*, 317 H3
Shymkent, *Kazakhstan*, 300 B2
Sialkot, *Pakistan*, 300 C4
Siauliai, *Lithuania*, 313 G5
Sibiti, *Congo*, 326 B4
Sibiu, *Romania*, 317 H2
Sibolga, *Indonesia*, 294 A3
Sibu, *Malaysia*, 294 D3
Sicily, *Italy*, 316 E4
Sicuani, *Peru*, 278 D6
Sidi-Bel-Abbes, *Algeria*, 324 E1
Sidon, *Lebanon*, 302 C5
Sidra, Gulf of, *Africa*, 322 E2
Sierra Leone, *Africa, country*, 325 C7
Sierra Morena, *Spain*, 315 C7
Sierra Nevada, *Spain*, 315 D7
Sierra Nevada, *U.S.A.*, 270 B3
Siglufjordhur, *Iceland*, 312 P2
Siguiri, *Guinea*, 325 D6
Sikasso, *Mali*, 325 D6
Sikhote Alin Range, *Russia*, 299 N1
Siling Lake, *China*, 300 F4
Simao, *China*, 298 F6
Simeulue, *Indonesia*, 294 A3
Simferopol, *Ukraine*, 317 K2
Simpson Desert, *Australia*, 288 G4
Sinai, *Egypt*, 323 H3
Sinai, Mount, *Egypt*, 323 H3
Sincelejo, *Colombia*, 278 C2
Sines, *Portugal*, 315 B7
Singapore, *Asia, country*, 294 B3
Singapore, *Singapore, national capital*, 294 B3
Sinnamary, *French Guiana*, 279 H2
Sinuiju, *North Korea*, 299 K2
Sioux City, *U.S.A.*, 271 G2
Sioux Falls, *U.S.A.*, 271 G2
Sirjan, *Iran*, 303 G6
Sittwe, *Burma*, 296 B3
Sivas, *Turkey*, 302 C4
Skagen, *Denmark*, 313 D4
Skagerrak, *Europe*, 313 C4

Skelleftea, *Sweden*, 312 G2
Skikda, *Algeria*, 324 G1
Skopje, *Macedonia, national capital*, 317 G3
Skyros, *Greece*, 317 H4
Slavonski Brod, *Croatia*, 316 F2
Sligo, *Ireland*, 314 B3
Sliven, *Bulgaria*, 317 H3
Slovakia, *Europe, country*, 313 F6
Slovenia, *Europe, country*, 316 E2
Slovyansk, *Ukraine*, 310 D4
Slupsk, *Poland*, 313 F5
Slutsk, *Belarus*, 313 H5
Smallwood Reservoir, *Canada*, 269 N3
Smola, *Norway*, 312 C3
Smolensk, *Russia*, 313 J5
Sobradinho Reservoir, *Brazil*, 279 K6
Sobral, *Brazil*, 279 K4
Sochi, *Russia*, 302 C3
Society Islands, *French Polynesia*, 287 J6
Socotra, *Yemen*, 303 F9
Sodankyla, *Finland*, 312 H2
Sodertalje, *Sweden*, 312 F4
Sofia, *Bulgaria, national capital*, 317 G3
Sohag, *Egypt*, 323 H3
Sokhumi, *Georgia*, 302 D3
Sokode, *Togo*, 325 F7
Sokoto, *Nigeria*, 325 G6
Solapur, *India*, 301 D7
Solikamsk, *Russia*, 311 H2
Solomon Islands, *Oceania, country*, 286 D5
Solomon Sea, *Papua New Guinea*, 295 M5
Solwezi, *Zambia*, 328 E2
Somalia, *Africa, country*, 327 J2
Somerset Island, *Canada*, 269 K1
Songea, *Tanzania*, 327 G6
Songo, *Mozambique*, 329 F3
Son La, *Vietnam*, 296 D3
Sorong, *Indonesia*, 295 H4
Soroti, *Uganda*, 327 F3
Soroya, *Norway*, 312 G1
Sotra, *Norway*, 312 C3
Souk Ahras, *Algeria*, 316 C4
Sousse, *Tunisia*, 322 D1
South Africa, *Africa, country*, 328 D6
Southampton, *United Kingdom*, 314 D4
Southampton Island, *Canada*, 269 L2
South Australia, *Australia, internal admin. area*, 288 F5
South Bend, *U.S.A.*, 271 J2
South Carolina, *U.S.A., internal admin. area*, 271 K4
South China Sea, *Asia*, 297 F5
South Dakota, *U.S.A., internal admin. area*, 270 F2
South East Cape, *Australia*, 288 J8
Southend-on-Sea, *United Kingdom*, 314 E4
Southern Ocean, 262
Southern Sierra Madre, *Mexico*, 272 D4
South Georgia, *Atlantic Ocean*, 281 L10
South Island, *New Zealand*, 289 N8
South Korea, *Asia, country*, 299 L3
South Orkney Islands, *Atlantic Ocean*, 281 J12
South Sandwich Islands, *Atlantic Ocean*, 281 N10
South Shetland Islands, *Atlantic Ocean*, 281 G12
South West Cape, *New Zealand*, 289 N9
Spain, *Europe, country*, 315 D7
Split, *Croatia*, 316 F3
Spokane, *U.S.A.*, 270 C1
Spratly Islands, *Asia*, 297 F5
Springfield, *Illinois, U.S.A., internal capital*, 271 J3
Springfield, *Massachusetts, U.S.A.*, 271 M2
Springfield, *Missouri, U.S.A.*, 271 H3
Springs, *South Africa*, 328 E5
Sri Jayewardenepura Kotte, *Sri Lanka, national capital*, 301 E9
Sri Lanka, *Asia, country*, 301 E9
Srinagar, *India*, 300 C4

Standerton, *South Africa*, 328 E5
Stanley, *Falkland Islands*, 281 G10
Stara Zagora, *Bulgaria*, 317 H3
Staryy Oskol, *Russia*, 310 D3
Stavanger, *Norway*, 312 C4
Stavropol, *Russia*, 302 D2
Steinkjer, *Norway*, 312 D2
Stellenbosch, *South Africa*, 328 C6
Sterlitamak, *Russia*, 311 H3
Stewart Island, *New Zealand*, 289 N9
Stockholm, *Sweden, national capital*, 312 F4
Stoeng Treng, *Cambodia*, 296 E5
Stoke-on-Trent, *United Kingdom*, 314 D3
Stora Lule Lake, *Sweden*, 312 F2
Storavan Lake, *Sweden*, 312 F2
Stor Lake, *Sweden*, 312 E3
Stornoway, *United Kingdom*, 314 C2
Stranraer, *United Kingdom*, 314 C3
Strasbourg, *France*, 314 F4
Sturt Stony Desert, *Australia*, 288 G5
Stuttgart, *Germany*, 314 G4
Subotica, *Yugoslavia*, 317 F2
Suceava, *Romania*, 317 H2
Sucre, *Bolivia, national capital*, 280 E3
Sudan, *Africa, country*, 323 G5
Sudbury, *Canada*, 269 L4
Suez, *Egypt*, 323 H3
Suez Canal, *Egypt*, 323 H2
Suhar, *Oman*, 303 G7
Sukkur, *Pakistan*, 300 B5
Sukses, *Namibia*, 328 C4
Sula, *Norway*, 312 C3
Sula Islands, *Indonesia*, 295 G4
Sullana, *Peru*, 278 B4
Sulu Archipelago, *Philippines*, 297 H6
Sulu Sea, *Asia*, 297 G6
Sumatra, *Indonesia*, 294 B3
Sumba, *Indonesia*, 295 E5
Sumbawa, *Indonesia*, 294 E5
Sumqayit, *Azerbaijan*, 302 E3
Sumy, *Ukraine*, 310 C3
Sunderland, *United Kingdom*, 314 D3
Sundsvall, *Sweden*, 312 F3
Superior, Lake, *U.S.A.*, 271 J1
Sur, *Oman*, 303 G7
Surabaya, *Indonesia*, 294 D5
Surakarta, *Indonesia*, 294 D5
Surat, *India*, 301 C6
Surgut, *Russia*, 304 D2
Surigao, *Philippines*, 297 J6
Surinam, *South America, country*, 279 G3
Surt, *Libya*, 322 E2
Sutherland Falls, *New Zealand*, 289 N8
Suva, *Fiji, national capital*, 289 Q3
Suwalki, *Poland*, 313 G5
Suwon, *South Korea*, 299 L3
Svalbard, *Norway*, 304 A2
Svolvaer, *Norway*, 312 E1
Svyetlahorsk, *Belarus*, 313 J5
Swakopmund, *Namibia*, 328 B4
Swan Islands, *Honduras*, 273 H4
Swansea, *United Kingdom*, 314 D4
Swaziland, *Africa, country*, 328 F5
Sweden, *Europe, country*, 312 E3
Swift Current, *Canada*, 268 J3
Swindon, *United Kingdom*, 314 D4
Switzerland, *Europe, country*, 316 C2
Sydney, *Australia, internal capital*, 289 K6
Sydney, *Canada*, 269 N4
Syktyvkar, *Russia*, 311 G1
Sylhet, *Bangladesh*, 300 G5
Syracuse, *Italy*, 316 E4
Syracuse, *U.S.A.*, 271 L2
Syr Darya, *Asia*, 302 H2
Syria, *Asia, country*, 302 C4
Syrian Desert, *Asia*, 303 C5
Syzran, *Russia*, 311 F3
Szczecin, *Poland*, 313 E5
Szeged, *Hungary*, 313 G7
Szekesfehervar, *Hungary*, 313 F7
Szombathely, *Hungary*, 313 F7

**t**

Tabora, *Tanzania*, 327 F5

Tabriz, *Iran*, 302 E4
Tabuk, *Saudi Arabia*, 303 C6
Tacloban, *Philippines*, 297 J5
Tacna, *Peru*, 278 D7
Tacoma, *U.S.A.*, 270 B1
Tacuarembo, *Uruguay*, 280 G6
Tademait Plateau, *Algeria*, 324 F3
Tadmur, *Syria*, 302 C5
Taegu, *South Korea*, 299 L3
Taejon, *South Korea*, 299 L3
Tagus, *Europe*, 315 B7
Tahat, Mount, *Algeria*, 324 G4
Tahiti, *French Polynesia*, 287 J6
Tahoua, *Niger*, 322 C6
Taian, *China*, 299 J3
Taichung, *Taiwan*, 299 K6
Tai Lake, *China*, 299 J4
Tainan, *Taiwan*, 299 K6
Taipei, *Taiwan, national capital*, 299 K5
Taiping, *Malaysia*, 294 B3
Taiwan, *Asia, country*, 299 K6
Taiwan Strait, *Asia*, 299 J6
Taiyuan, *China*, 298 H3
Taizz, *Yemen*, 303 D9
Tajikistan, *Asia, country*, 300 B3
Taj Mahal, *India*, 300 D5
Tajumulco, *Guatemala*, 272 F4
Taklimakan Desert, *China*, 300 E3
Talara, *Peru*, 278 B4
Talaud Islands, *Indonesia*, 295 G3
Talca, *Chile*, 281 D7
Taldyqorghan, *Kazakhstan*, 300 D1
Tallahassee, *U.S.A., internal capital*, 271 K4
Tallinn, *Estonia, national capital*, 312 H4
Taltal, *Chile*, 280 D5
Tamale, *Ghana*, 325 E7
Tamanrasset, *Algeria*, 324 G4
Tambacounda, *Senegal*, 325 C6
Tambov, *Russia*, 310 E3
Tampa, *U.S.A.*, 271 K5
Tampere, *Finland*, 312 G3
Tampico, *Mexico*, 272 E3
Tana, Lake, *Ethiopia*, 327 G1
Tandil, *Argentina*, 281 G7
Tanga, *Tanzania*, 327 G5
Tanganyika, Lake, *Africa*, 326 E5
Tangier, *Morocco*, 324 D1
Tangshan, *China*, 299 J3
Tanimbar Islands, *Indonesia*, 295 H5
Tanjungkarang-Telukbetung, *Indonesia*, 294 C5
Tanjungredeb, *Indonesia*, 294 E3
Tanta, *Egypt*, 323 H2
Tan-Tan, *Morocco*, 324 C3
Tanzania, *Africa, country*, 327 F5
Tapachula, *Mexico*, 272 F5
Tapajos, *Brazil*, 279 G5
Tarakan, *Indonesia*, 294 E3
Taranto, *Italy*, 316 F4
Taraz, *Kazakhstan*, 300 C2
Targu Mures, *Romania*, 317 H2
Tarija, *Bolivia*, 280 F4
Tarim Basin, *China*, 300 E3
Tarkwa, *Ghana*, 325 E7
Tarnow, *Poland*, 313 G6
Tarragona, *Spain*, 315 E6
Tartagal, *Argentina*, 280 F4
Tartu, *Estonia*, 312 H4
Tartus, *Syria*, 302 C5
Tashkent, *Uzbekistan, national capital*, 300 B2
Tasmania, *Australia, internal admin. area*, 289 J8
Tasman Sea, *Australasia*, 289 L7
Tataouine, *Tunisia*, 322 D2
Taunggyi, *Burma*, 296 C3
Taupo, Lake, *New Zealand*, 289 Q7
Taurus Mountains, *Turkey*, 317 J4
Tavoy, *Burma*, 296 C5
Tawau, *Malaysia*, 295 E3
Taytay, *Philippines*, 297 G5
Taza, *Morocco*, 324 E2
Tbilisi, *Georgia, national capital*, 302 D3
Tchibanga, *Gabon*, 326 B4
Tebessa, *Algeria*, 324 G1

Tegal, *Indonesia*, 294 C5
Tegucigalpa, *Honduras, national capital*, 273 G5
Tehran, *Iran, national capital*, 302 F4
Tehuacan, *Mexico*, 272 E4
Tehuantepec, Gulf of, *Mexico*, 272 E4
Tehuantepec, Isthmus of, *Mexico*, 272 E4
Tekirdag, *Turkey*, 317 H3
Tel Aviv-Yafo, *Israel*, 303 B5
Teller, *U.S.A.*, 268 C2
Temuco, *Chile*, 281 D7
Ten Degree Channel, *India*, 301 G9
Tenerife, *Canary Islands*, 324 B3
Tenkodogo, *Burkina Faso*, 325 E6
Tennessee, *U.S.A.*, 271 J3
Tennessee, *U.S.A., internal admin. area*, 271 J3
Teofilo Otoni, *Brazil*, 280 K3
Teotihuacan, *Mexico*, 272 E4
Terceira, *Azores*, 324 K10
Teresina, *Brazil*, 279 K4
Ternate, *Indonesia*, 295 G3
Terni, *Italy*, 316 E3
Ternopil, *Ukraine*, 313 H6
Terracotta Army, *China*, 298 G4
Terra Firma, *South Africa*, 328 D5
Teseney, *Eritrea*, 323 J5
Tete, *Mozambique*, 329 F3
Tetouan, *Morocco*, 324 D1
Tetovo, *Macedonia*, 317 G3
Texarkana, *U.S.A.*, 271 H4
Texas, *U.S.A., internal admin. area*, 270 G4
Thailand, *Asia, country*, 296 D4
Thailand, Gulf of, *Asia*, 296 D6
Thai Nguyen, *Vietnam*, 296 E3
Thames, *United Kingdom*, 314 D4
Thanh Hoa, *Vietnam*, 296 E4
Thar Desert, *Asia*, 300 B5
Thasos, *Greece*, 317 H3
Thaton, *Burma*, 296 C4
Thessaloniki, *Greece*, 317 G3
Thies, *Senegal*, 325 B6
Thika, *Kenya*, 327 G4
Thimphu, *Bhutan, national capital*, 300 F5
Thompson, *Canada*, 269 K3
Three Points, Cape, *Africa*, 325 E8
Thunder Bay, *Canada*, 269 L4
Tianjin, *China*, 299 J3
Tibesti Mountains, *Africa*, 322 E4
Tibet, *China*, 300 F4
Tibet, Plateau of, *China*, 300 F4
Tidjikja, *Mauritania*, 324 C5
Tien Shan, *Asia*, 300 D2
Tierra del Fuego, *South America*, 281 E10
Tighina, *Moldova*, 317 J2
Tigris, *Asia*, 303 E5
Tijuana, *Mexico*, 272 A1
Tikal, *Guatemala*, 272 G4
Tikhvin, *Russia*, 312 K4
Tillaberi, *Niger*, 325 F6
Timbuktu, *Mali*, 325 E5
Timisoara, *Romania*, 317 G2
Timor, *Asia*, 295 F5
Timor Sea, *Asia/Australasia*, 295 G6
Tindouf, *Algeria*, 324 D3
Tirana, *Albania, national capital*, 317 F3
Tiraspol, *Moldova*, 317 J2
Tiruchirappalli, *India*, 301 D8
Titicaca, Lake, *South America*, 278 E7
Tlemcen, *Algeria*, 324 E2
Toamasina, *Madagascar*, 329 J3
Tobago, *Trinidad and Tobago*, 272 M5
Toba, Lake, *Indonesia*, 294 A3
Tobol, *Russia*, 311 K2
Tobolsk, *Russia*, 311 K2
Tobyl, *Kazakhstan*, 311 J3
Tocantins, *Brazil*, 279 J4
Togo, *Africa, country*, 325 F7
Tokelau, *Oceania*, 286 F5
Tokyo, *Japan, national capital*, 299 N3
Tolanaro, *Madagascar*, 329 J5
Toledo, *Spain*, 315 D7
Toledo, *U.S.A.*, 271 K2
Toledo Bend Reservoir, *U.S.A.*, 271 H4

Toliara, *Madagascar*, 329 H4
Tolyatti, *Russia*, 311 F3
Tolybay, *Kazakhstan*, 311 J3
Tomakomai, *Japan*, 299 P2
Tombouctou, *Mali*, 325 E5
Tomsk, *Russia*, 304 E3
Tonga, *Oceania, country*, 286 F6
Tongliao, *China*, 299 K2
Tonkin, Gulf of, *Asia*, 296 E4
Tonle Sap, *Cambodia*, 296 D5
Toowoomba, *Australia*, 289 K5
Topeka, *U.S.A., internal capital*, 271 G3
Top, Lake, *Russia*, 312 K2
Topoli, *Kazakhstan*, 311 G4
Torghay, *Kazakhstan*, 311 J4
Tornio, *Finland*, 312 H2
Toronto, *Canada, internal capital*, 269 M4
Torrens, Lake, *Australia*, 288 G6
Torreon, *Mexico*, 272 D2
Torres Strait, *Australasia*, 288 H2
Tortuga Island, *Venezuela*, 278 E1
Toubkal, *Morocco*, 324 D2
Tougan, *Burkina Faso*, 325 E6
Touggourt, *Algeria*, 324 G2
Toulon, *France*, 315 F6
Toulouse, *France*, 315 E6
Tours, *France*, 314 E5
Townsville, *Australia*, 288 J3
Toyama, *Japan*, 299 N3
Tozeur, *Tunisia*, 322 C2
Trabzon, *Turkey*, 302 C3
Tralee, *Ireland*, 314 B3
Transantarctic Mountains, *Antarctica*, 333 S4
Transylvanian Alps, *Romania*, 317 G2
Trapani, *Italy*, 316 E4
Trento, *Italy*, 316 D2
Trenton, *U.S.A., internal capital*, 271 M2
Tres Arroyos, *Argentina*, 281 F7
Tres Marias Reservoir, *Brazil*, 280 J3
Tres Puntas, Cape, *Argentina*, 281 E9
Trieste, *Italy*, 316 E2
Trincomalee, *Sri Lanka*, 301 E9
Trinidad, *Bolivia*, 280 F2
Trinidad, *Trinidad and Tobago*, 272 M5
Trinidad and Tobago, *North America, country*, 272 M5
Tripoli, *Lebanon*, 302 C5
Tripoli, *Libya, national capital*, 322 D2
Trivandrum, *India*, 301 D9
Trnava, *Slovakia*, 313 F6
Trois-Rivieres, *Canada*, 269 M4
Tromso, *Norway*, 312 F1
Trondheim, *Norway*, 312 D3
Troyes, *France*, 314 F4
Trujillo, *Peru*, 278 C5
Tsau, *Botswana*, 328 D4
Tses, *Namibia*, 328 C5
Tshabong, *Botswana*, 328 D5
Tshane, *Botswana*, 328 D4
Tshikapa, *Democratic Republic of Congo*, 326 D5
Tshwane, *Botswana*, 328 D4
Tsimlyansk Reservoir, *Russia*, 310 E4
Tsiroanomandidy, *Madagascar*, 329 J3
Tsumeb, *Namibia*, 328 C3
Tuamotu Archipelago, *French Polynesia*, 287 K6
Tubmanburg, *Liberia*, 325 C7
Tubruq, *Libya*, 322 F2
Tubuai Islands, *French Polynesia*, 287 J7
Tucson, *U.S.A.*, 270 D4
Tucupita, *Venezuela*, 278 F2
Tucurui Reservoir, *Brazil*, 279 J4
Tugela Falls, *South Africa*, 328 E5
Tuguegarao, *Philippines*, 297 H4
Tula, *Russia*, 310 D3
Tulcea, *Romania*, 317 J2
Tulsa, *U.S.A.*, 271 G3
Tumaco, *Colombia*, 278 C3
Tumbes, *Peru*, 278 B4
Tunduma, *Tanzania*, 327 F5
Tunduru, *Tanzania*, 327 G6
Tunis, *Tunisia, national capital*, 322 D1
Tunisia, *Africa, country*, 322 C2
Tunja, *Colombia*, 278 D2

Tupelo, *U.S.A.*, 271 J4
Tupiza, *Bolivia*, 280 E4
Turbat, *Pakistan*, 303 H6
Turbo, *Colombia*, 278 C2
Turin, *Italy*, 316 C2
Turkana, Lake, *Africa*, 327 G3
Turkey, *Asia, country*, 302 C4
Turkistan, *Kazakhstan*, 300 B2
Turkmenabat, *Turkmenistan*, 302 H4
Turkmenbasy, *Turkmenistan*, 302 F3
Turkmenistan, *Asia, country*, 302 G4
Turks and Caicos Islands, *North America*, 273 K3
Turku, *Finland*, 312 G3
Turpan, *China*, 300 F2
Turpan Depression, *China*, 300 G2
Tuscaloosa, *U.S.A.*, 271 J4
Tuvalu, *Oceania, country*, 286 E5
Tuxtla Gutierrez, *Mexico*, 272 F4
Tuzla, *Bosnia and Herzegovina*, 317 F2
Tuz, Lake, *Turkey*, 317 K4
Tver, *Russia*, 310 D2
Twin Falls, *U.S.A.*, 270 D2
Tynda, *Russia*, 305 G3
Tyrrhenian Sea, *Europe*, 316 D3
Tyumen, *Russia*, 311 K2

## U

Ubangi, *Africa*, 326 C3
Uberaba, *Brazil*, 280 J3
Uberlandia, *Brazil*, 280 J3
Ubon Ratchathani, *Thailand*, 296 D4
Ucayali, *Peru*, 278 D5
Udaipur, *India*, 301 C6
Uddevalla, *Sweden*, 312 D4
Udon Thani, *Thailand*, 296 D4
Uele, *Democratic Republic of Congo*, 326 D3
Ufa, *Russia*, 311 H3
Uganda, *Africa, country*, 327 F3
Uitenhage, *South Africa*, 328 E6
Ujung Pandang, *Indonesia*, 295 E5
Ukhta, *Russia*, 304 C2
Ukraine, *Europe, country*, 310 C4
Ulan Bator, *Mongolia, national capital*, 298 G1
Ulanhot, *China*, 299 K1
Ulan Ude, *Russia*, 305 F3
Ulm, *Germany*, 314 G4
Uluru, *Australia*, 288 F5
Ulyanovsk, *Russia*, 311 F3
Uman, *Ukraine*, 313 J6
Ume, *Sweden*, 312 F2
Umea, *Sweden*, 312 G3
Umnak Island, *U.S.A.*, 269 C3
Umtata, *South Africa*, 328 E6
Unalaska Island, *U.S.A.*, 269 C3
Ungava Bay, *Canada*, 269 N3
Ungava Peninsula, *Canada*, 269 M2
Unimak Island, *U.S.A.*, 269 C3
United Arab Emirates, *Asia, country*, 303 F7
United Kingdom, *Europe, country*, 314 D3
United States of America, *North America, country*, 270 F3
Upington, *South Africa*, 328 D5
Uppsala, *Sweden*, 312 F4
Ural, *Asia*, 311 G4
Ural Mountains, *Russia*, 311 H2
Uray, *Russia*, 311 J1
Urganch, *Uzbekistan*, 300 A2
Urmia, *Iran*, 302 E4
Uruapan, *Mexico*, 272 D4
Urucui, *Brazil*, 279 K5
Uruguaiana, *Brazil*, 280 G5
Uruguay, *South America, country*, 280 G6
Urumqi, *China*, 300 F2
Usak, *Turkey*, 317 J4
Ushuaia, *Argentina*, 281 E10
Uskemen, *Kazakhstan*, 304 E3
Utah, *U.S.A., internal admin. area*, 270 D3
Utsjoki, *Finland*, 312 H1
Utsunomiya, *Japan*, 299 N3
Uy, *Asia*, 311 J3
Uyuni, *Bolivia*, 280 E4
Uzbekistan, *Asia, country*, 304 D3

# GENERAL INDEX

In this index, words that have a lot of page numbers may have a number in **bold** to show where to find the main explanation. The maps are listed in a separate index on pages 376–389.

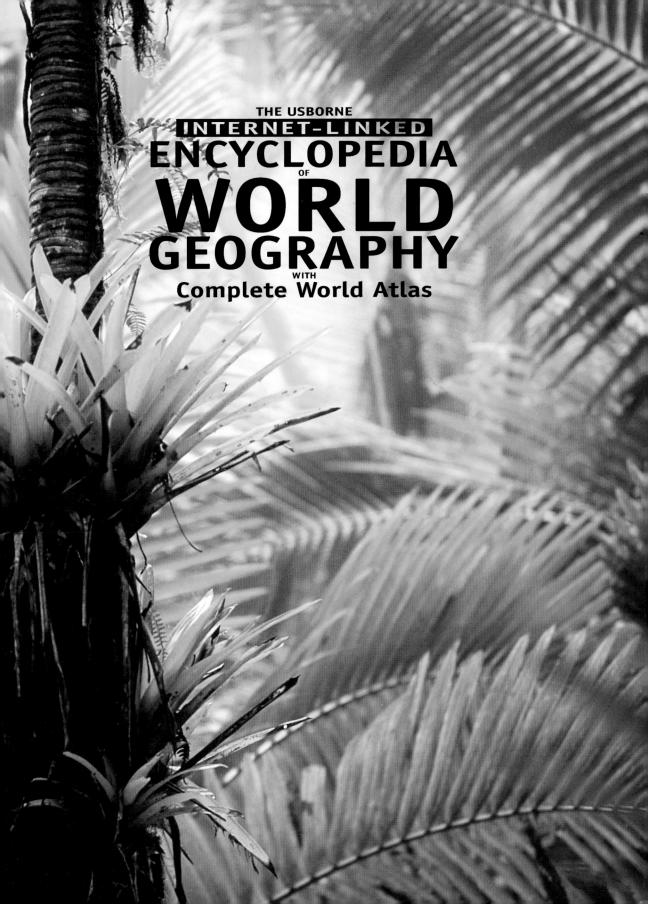

THE USBORNE
**INTERNET-LINKED**
ENCYCLOPEDIA
OF
WORLD
GEOGRAPHY
WITH
Complete World Atlas